THE ESCAPE LINE

THE ESCAPE LINE

HOW THE ORDINARY HEROES OF DUTCH-PARIS RESISTED THE NAZI OCCUPATION OF WESTERN EUROPE

MEGAN KOREMAN

OXFORD
UNIVERSITY PRESS

OXFORD
UNIVERSITY PRESS

Oxford University Press is a department of the University of Oxford.
It furthers the University's objective of excellence in research, scholarship,
and education by publishing worldwide. Oxford is a registered trade mark of
Oxford University Press in the UK and certain other countries.

Published in the United States of America by Oxford University Press
198 Madison Avenue, New York, NY 10016, United States of America.

Library of Congress Cataloging-in-Publication Data
is on file with the Library of Congress

978-0-19-066227-1

Frontispiece: Pyrenees, January 31, 1944. The *passeur* Bazerque (far left with beret),
Father L. Laureijssen (center with glasses and beret), H. Guyt, J. Klijzing, and
D. Goedhuis (group of three in front of the hut), and Allied aviators.
John Henry Weidner Papers, Hoover Institution Library &
Archives, Stanford University, box 74.

1 3 5 7 9 8 6 4 2

Printed by Sheridan Books, Inc.,
United States of America

For Case, Michael, William, and Henry

CONTENTS

———◦◦◦◦———

MAPS

ACKNOWLEDGMENTS

This book, like its subject, required many forms of assistance and support from many people in many places. I am grateful to them all, especially to those listed below.

Both the escape line and the book needed financing. My thanks to the Weidner Foundation and the Prins Bernhard Cultuurfonds for generously funding the research and part of the writing of the book. Half of the proceeds will go toward the Weidner Foundation's mission of encouraging others to act in the spirit of altruism that illuminated John Henry Weidner and his colleagues in Dutch-Paris. Particular thanks go to Kurt Ganter, who has believed in this book since before I ever heard of Dutch-Paris. I would also like to thank Elaine Bedel, Bill Ervin, Larry Geraty, Joe Matar, Steve Morgan, and Naomi Weidner for their support.

The Weidner Foundation wishes to recognize the generous contributions of the following: Charles Bartelings, Bert and Eliane Beach, Norman Beaupre, Elaine Bedel, Beit Chaim Chabad Center of Lexington, Roy Branson, Janet Holmes Carper, Dale Brown, Paul and Kathleen Caubo, Mr. and Mrs. J. H. Caubo, Jerry and Phalia Louder, Ramona Richli Clark, Glenn Coe, Henry Coil, Maarten and Wilhelmine Eliasar, William and Joan Ervin, Dr. and Mrs. Norman Farley, Kurt and Lani Ganter, Larry and Gillian Geraty, the Lowell and Harriet Glazer Family Foundation, Michael Goldware, Reynir Gudmundsson and Lourdes Morales-Gudmundsson,

Amy Harrison, Tomas Heyer, Hielke Hijmans, Willy Hijmans, Solomon and Rebecca Kaspin, Sylvan Katz, Daniel and Elissa Kido, Ed and Beverly Krick, Marcella Langhout, Maria Matar, Frank Mazzaglia, Jan Webb McQuistan, Leon M. Mordoh, Mr. and Mrs. Stan Morrison, Ali Sahabi, The Charles and Mildred Schnurmacher Foundation, Temple Beth Shalom, H. Eric Schockman, Mark E. Silverman, Rob and Brooke Smith, Mr. and Mrs. D. Townsend, Stanley and Clare Tozeski, Lilya and John Wagner, Myron F. Wehtje, Naomi Weidner, Tom and Audrey Williams, and Pieter Rudolph Zeeman.

Although resistance and writing are often solitary efforts, neither resisters nor authors can work completely on their own. Throughout this project I have relied on the unfailing support and enthusiasm of Janet Carper and Maarten Eliasar. I cannot thank them enough for their friendship, hospitality, and never-ending willingness to guide me through the intricacies of French and Dutch. Nor can I thank Hélène Lesger enough for her friendship and perseverance in representing this book.

Prof. dr. Willy Hijmans welcomed me warmly on many trips to the Netherlands and shared his memories of his experiences in Dutch-Paris with great generosity. My thanks to him and his family for their support of my research and this book.

I have benefited greatly from the generosity of David Delfosse, who has unstintingly shared his own painstaking research on the evasion of the crew of the *Sarah Jane*. I am also grateful for the collegial support of Bob Moore and Sierk Plantinga.

My thanks also to Robert F. Anderson, Charles Bartelings, Jan van Borssum Buisman, Joke Folmer, Willy Hijmans, Mary Lutz, Rudy Zeeman, and Anna Zurcher. It has been an honor to talk to you about the heroism of your youth.

For sharing their families' stories and photographs I am indebted to Michael Bottenheim, Mariette Bremell, Nicolas Bremell, André Caubo, Harry Caubo, Joseph Caubo, Maarten Eliasar, Peter Hartog, Paul Gans, Brigitte Giani, Ype Henry, Rita Goldberg, Herman Grishaver, Case Koreman, Marcella Langhout, Richard Lehmann and family, Daniel Lebouille, Marie-José Lebouille, Jan Naijé, Marianne Senf, Gaia Son, Alain Souloumiac, Dolly Starink, Dorine Starink, Leentje van der Harst, Micheline van Lint Nieuwkerk, Chris van Oosterzee, Bep and Arie van Vliet, Ben van Vliet, Kees van Vliet, and Fred Zurcher. My thanks also to all the readers of my blog, *How to Flee the Gestapo: Searching for the Dutch-Paris Escape Line* (www.dutchparisblog.com).

Like everyone in Dutch-Paris, I relied on the goodwill of men and women with access to information and other necessary goods. I am grateful to the staffs of all thirty-two archives that I consulted for my research. Some archivists, however, went far beyond professional efficiency to help me. They found interesting, even uncataloged documents for me; shepherded my requests for permission to see classified documents; allowed me to work beyond normal visiting hours; and shared their own desk space with me. In the Netherlands I would like to thank Hubert Berkhout and René van Heijningen at the Nederlands Instituut voor Oorlogsdocumentatie; Frans van Domburg at the Stichting '40–'45, and Raymund Schütz at the archives of the Nederlands Rode Kruis. I am indebted to Sierk Plantinga, now retired from the Nationaal Archief, for his unfailing assistance over several years. In Belgium I would like to thank Wim de Hertogh at the Protestantse Kerk, Dirk Martin at CEGES/SOMA (Centre for Historical Research and Documentation on War and Contemporary Society), Gert de Prins at the Directie-generaal Oorlogsslachtoffers, Filip Strubbe of the Belgian Rijksarchief, and Kees Veenstra of the Nederlandsche Vereeniging. In France I wish to thank Anne-Sophie Cras of the Centre d'archives diplomatiques à Nantes; Guido Delameillieure at the Archives historiques de l'Adventisme en Europe, section Collonges-sous-Salève; Chantal Jorro of the Centre de l'historie de la Résistance et de la Déportation, Lyon; and Chantal Pagès and the staff of the Archives départementales de la Haute-Garonne. I am especially grateful for the generous and creative assistance of Capitaine S. Longuet and the staff at the Bureau Résistance of the Service historique de la Défense à Vincennes and Pascal Hureau of the Division des Archives des Victimes des Conflits Contemporains, Service historique de la Défense à Caen. In Switzerland I could not have done my research without the personal assistance of Pierre Flückiger at the Archives d'Etat de Genève. In the United States I am indebted to Stan Tozeski of the Weidner Archives, which were in Massachusetts when I read them. I am also grateful for the extra effort provided by Danielle Scott Thomas and Rachel Bauer at the Hoover Library & Archives, which now houses Weidner's papers.

A number of people shared their thoughts on war and resistance with me. Some of them even read early drafts of the book. My thanks to Bruce Bolinger, H. R. Boudin, Jean-Yves Boulard, Frits Broeyer, Hanna

Diamond, Guido Erreygers, Robert Gildea, Susan Jotte, Sue Peters, Peter Romijn, Lynne Taylor, Rudi Vandoorslaer, Hans de Vries, and Tami Whited. For their constructive patience with early drafts I particularly wish to thank Janet and Tom Carper, Maarten Eliasar, Willy Hijmans, Hélène Lesger, Bob Moore, and Rudy Zeeman.

For their help with logistical and technical difficulties, my thanks to William Arink, Bernie Cantor, Tom Carper, Mike Piskie, and Els Smit-Wilmer.

I am grateful for the hospitality of Kurt and Lani Ganter, Scott Goodall, Charlene and Jim Griffin, Pax Gritter, Page Herrlinger and Paul Friedland, Karien and Geert Verduyn, Arie and Bep van Vliet, and the family of Jean and Anna Zurcher.

The Dutch edition would never have happened without the long-term support of Maarten Eliasar and Hélène Lesger. My thanks to them, to Sierk Plantinga, and to all the editorial team. My thanks also to Tim Bent and his colleagues at Oxford University Press for their work on the American edition.

For their unending patience with a project that seemed as if it would never end, and for tolerating my absences, I thank my family.

It goes without saying that any errors or misinterpretations in the book are mine alone.

THE ESCAPE LINE

Swiss customs house in the Genevois, 1943.

Introduction

The Choice

IN THE EARLY SUMMER OF 1942, two years into the German occupation of the Netherlands, Belgium, and northern France, a Dutch businessman named Jean Weidner received a letter at his textile shop in the unoccupied zone of France known as Vichy. It came from a Jewish business acquaintance who had fled the Netherlands rather than report for deportation "to the east." He explained that he and his wife, a renowned soprano, had made it through occupied territory, over the Dutch border, over the Belgian border, and over the Demarcation Line that divided France, only to be arrested by Vichy French police. A judge had given them the standard sentence handed out to foreigners caught near a border in southern France: one month in prison. They feared they would be sent to one of Vichy's notorious internment camps at the end of that month.[1]

Although he carried a Dutch passport, Weidner had grown up on the Franco-Swiss border and spoke French more fluently than Dutch. He had nothing to worry about from the French authorities as long as he did not draw attention to himself. His business was doing well. He had just married. To help his acquaintance he could take one of several courses of action, each more dangerous to himself. He could choose to do nothing and avoid trouble by ignoring the letter. Or he could offer legally sanctioned forms of assistance, such as sending money to the prison to pay for extra food. He could also pass the problem to the Dutch consulate in Lyon. In fact Weidner had done some volunteer work on behalf of refugees over the previous two years and knew that the consul could arrange for the couple to be placed in *résidence assignée* in a village rather than in an internment camp.[2] At that time assigned residence looked like a safe enough place for Dutch Jews.[3]

But Weidner and his new French wife, Elisabeth Cartier, were not the sort to compromise on matters of principle. The son of a Seventh-day Adventist minister, Weidner had been raised in a devout household with a clear vision of right and wrong and an absolute dedication to righteous living. On a more practical level, he knew how bad conditions actually were in Vichy's internment camps and that the Nazis and their collaborators had malicious intentions toward Jews. He also knew that neutral Switzerland would provide protection from the Germans but that the Swiss authorities had closed the borders.

Weidner and Cartier made a choice that might have seemed normal to them but seems astonishingly heroic in retrospect. They decided to smuggle Weidner's acquaintances into Switzerland. The Jewish couple would then be safe from the Nazis, but they themselves would no longer be safe

Elisabeth Cartier and Jean Weidner, 1942.

in France. By spiriting the fugitives away as soon as they were released from prison, by hiding them for a few days, and by arranging for them to cross the Franco-Swiss border illegally, Weidner and Cartier broke a number of French and Swiss laws.

In the context of the occupation and the Second World War, breaking such laws in order to rescue a Jewish couple from persecution turned Weidner and Cartier into outlaws. In fact by breaking what they felt were unjust laws not for their own gain but in order to protect others from persecution, they joined the resistance.

Resistance cannot be understood apart from its context of daily life under German occupation. Civilians everywhere struggled with short-ages, oppression, and fear, but the magnitude and details of each differed from one occupation zone to the next. They also changed over time with the progress of the war and the reaction of the occupation authorities to military developments. Every civilian had to work out some sort of per-sonal accommodation to living under occupation. Collaborators joined the occupiers and, at least at the beginning, enjoyed the privileges of power. The vast majority of civilians withdrew into the daily struggle of making ends meet and surviving. Resisters accommodated themselves to the occupation by opposing it. Like Weidner and Cartier they shifted from law-abiding citizens to lawbreakers.

Occupation, however, did not take the same form in every country or even in every region of a country. In May and June 1940 Hitler's Wehrmacht swept through western Europe in six weeks, leaving civilians in the Netherlands, Belgium, and France stunned. But Hitler had much more fundamentally dark aspirations than simply conquering Europe. He intended to refashion society according to the Nazi worldview. His Thousand Year Reich would abolish democracy in favor of a vaguely feudal system of leaders and followers. It would tolerate no rival ideolo-gies, such as communism or Christianity. As became clear over time, starting with the euthanasia programs practiced on German citizens in the mid-1930s, the Reich would favor those whom Nazi ideology deemed superior at the cost of those it branded inferior. Nazis based these catego-rizations on a pseudo-science of "race" that claimed that an individual's bloodline or genetics determined that person's rightful place in the world.[4] In their view, Germanic Aryans reigned supreme, followed by other so-called Germanic nations such as the Dutch. Then came other

Western Europe 1942

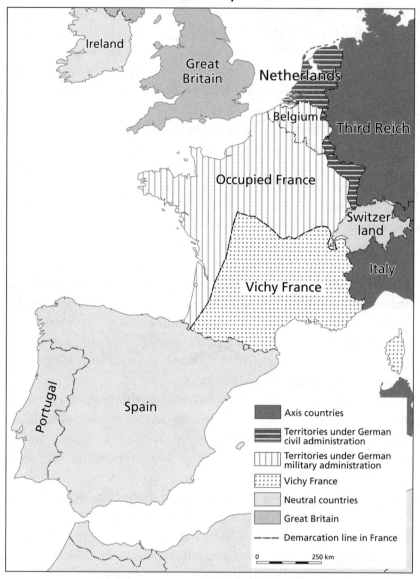

western European nations, such as the French. The Slavs of eastern Europe figured on this Nazi scheme as "subhuman." Jews occupied the lowest rung, both beneath everyone else and the greatest threat to Aryans. German occupation policy followed this Nazi ideology, treating each ethnic nation according to its place on the Nazi racial hierarchy.

The Dutch people, who played such an important role in the story this book tells, had their own particular experience of occupation. After the Wehrmacht invaded the Netherlands, Queen Wilhelmina and Prime Minister Pieter Gerbrandy escaped to exile in London, leaving behind bureaucrats with orders to keep the civil service functioning for the sake of the people.[5] Hitler installed a civilian occupation regime in the country. This sounded better than it turned out to be because it allowed zealots from the Nazi Party and the Nazi Party's police agencies, such as the Gestapo, to establish themselves in positions of power with very few checks on their activities.

At the beginning of the occupation, when the Nazis still assumed that the Dutch would be happy to join their vision of Aryan domination, the German authorities allotted the Dutch preferential treatment. They released Dutch prisoners of war, for instance, but imprisoned French POWs. In February 1941, however, they reacted brutally to the strike that the people of Amsterdam called to protest the mistreatment of Jews. Relations deteriorated steadily after that. The authorities closed Dutch universities. The German commander in the Netherlands recalled Dutch POWs for internment and labor in April 1943. At the end of the war the German occupation forces deliberately starved those Dutch civilians caught under their control during the deadly "Hunger Winter" of 1944–45.

In contrast, Hitler installed a military occupation regime in Belgium, where he had no reason to expect the people to welcome German troops.[6] Belgians had not forgotten the German occupation of their country in the First World War, during which they endured starvation, harsh punishments, and the forced deportation of tens of thousands of men as slave labor. Because the commanding officer of the occupation troops in Belgium during the Second World War was not himself a Nazi, party zealots had difficulty establishing themselves and their agencies in the country. They were present, of course, but not to the same degree or with the same power as in the Netherlands. In effect, the military occupation shielded the Belgian people from the worst excesses of Nazi rule.

The Germans still deported Jews from Belgium. They still rounded up young men from the streets of Brussels as slave labor for the Third Reich. The Belgian people still suffered from rationing, curfews, and other restrictions. But there was more food in Belgium than in the Netherlands.

And at least one Dutch resister who crossed back and forth between the countries felt freer and safer in Belgium than at home.[7]

France, farther south, was yet another matter. Technically the Wehrmacht did not defeat the French Army in June 1940 because the French government signed an armistice with Hitler before that could happen.[8] The Armistice divided France into five occupation zones. The northern departments along the Belgian border were placed under the control of the military occupation authorities in Brussels. Alsace was annexed to the Third Reich. The rest of the northern third of the country and the western seaboard along the Atlantic were occupied and placed under the control of a German *kommandant* in Paris. For the moment a small area along the Alps went to Germany's ally Italy. The southern part of the country remained unoccupied but also cut off from the rest of the country by a Demarcation Line as closely guarded as an international border.

The southern, unoccupied zone was also known as the "free zone" or, most commonly, "Vichy" because the French government had settled in the spa town of Vichy after fleeing from Paris ahead of the invading German Army. France had been a republic until that military crisis, when Parliament voted to confer full powers on Marshall Philippe Pétain, who turned the government into the Etat Français, or French State.

As the preserve of right-wing conservatives, the Vichy regime sympathized with Nazi social goals. As one example, they both encouraged women to leave the workplace in order to raise children. More tellingly in the context of the times, the Vichy regime repudiated the French Republic's welcoming attitude to immigrants, to the point of revoking the naturalized status of people who had earned their French citizenship more than ten years earlier.

From the perspective of most French civilians, however, Vichy's greatest failing was its attempt to maintain French sovereignty and to win a favorable position in Hitler's New Order. This led the regime to insist that French police do the Germans' dirty work, such as rounding up Jews for deportation. Similarly Vichy insisted on choosing the hostages the Germans would shoot, thereby implicating the French government in crimes against its own citizens. After the Germans occupied the southern zone in November 1942 and dismantled the Demarcation Line in March 1943, the Etat Français continued to administer the southern zone, promote its own agenda, and cooperate with the German occupation authorities until the Liberation in 1944.

No matter where they lived, all civilians in occupied Europe suffered from the fundamental restrictions imposed on daily life by pervasive shortages. Production of both food and manufactured goods fell below prewar levels and stayed there. Farmers had to contend with insufficient help, a lack of fertilizer, broken equipment that could not be repaired, and increased paperwork. Something as trivial as a shortage of baling twine could confound an entire hay harvest. In addition, coal, gasoline, and other natural resources were routinely diverted from civilian to military use.

Every government imposed rationing systems that shared out the common resources with more or less success. Civilians had to use ration coupons or tickets to buy most kinds of food, clothing, shoes, and fuel. People stretched their resources with things like clothing swaps and even converting gasoline engines in delivery vans and buses into wood-burning engines known as *gazogènes*.

These shortages had far-reaching implications for everyday life. Women and children spent long hours standing in line to buy basic necessities. Shortages of food undermined the general population's health. Shortages of clothing chipped away at morale as everyone started looking more ragged and people had to walk around in uncomfortable shoes with wooden soles. The gasoline shortage meant that only Germans, collaborators, and emergency services drove in cars. Everyone else walked, pedaled bicycles with wooden wheels, or crowded onto the trains and trams. Popular opinion—not unjustified—held that only the Germans and their collaborators were well-fed and well-dressed during the war.

The constant shortages led citizens into routine disobedience. When the official rationing systems failed, as they often did, people had no choice but to turn to the black market. The black market encompassed every shade of gray, from a farmwife selling her cousin extra eggs at prewar prices to organized criminal gangs charging extortionate rates. But any shade of gray counted as breaking the law, which meant that almost everyone broke the law on a regular basis. From there it was not such a big step to breaking the law against reading underground newspapers. Indeed the occupation led most civilians into complicated negotiations between the law, their conscience, and their needs. Even that strict pillar of rectitude, Jean Weidner's pastor father, engaged in hair-splitting. When a German soldier rang his doorbell in The Hague to confiscate bicycles, Weidner Senior told him that his wife's bicycle was on the first floor. Because the Germans were interested only in men's bicycles, the soldier left. If the soldier had been more precise in his language, though, and asked about men's bicycles, the minister would have felt obliged to tell him that his own bicycle was also in the house.⁹ It was still a great leap to active resistance, but maybe not so far to small acts that supported resistance, such as looking the other way.

The restrictions of wartime life extended far beyond the persistent lack of food, fuel, and goods into the less tangible realm of civil liberties. Occupation meant a sharp increase in policing and surveillance by a variety of German police agencies as well as by collaborationist units and the local police. In addition to the notorious Nazi secret police, the Gestapo, civilians could fall afoul of the regular German police commonly known as the Grüne polizei (green police) for their uniforms; the DSK (Devisenschutzkommando), who controlled the flow of currency and valuables; the SD (Sicherheitsdienst) or SS security service; or even military police authorities such as the Abwehr (military intelligence) or the Geheime Feldpolizei (GFP, secret military police), some of whom did not wear uniforms. At some point German custom agents and border troops reinforced the local guards on the borders. Paramilitary collaborators such as the *Milice* in France also wielded police powers, as did the regular local and national police forces.

In many places, particularly near borders, civilians required special passes to be more than a few miles from home. In fact the occupation authorities required civilian adults and teenagers to carry identification papers at all times. At minimum men and women needed basic identification cards issued by the local authority. The identification cards introduced in the Netherlands during the occupation were deliberately complex and difficult to forge. The Belgians, on the other hand, kept their identification card as simple and easy to forge as possible. In addition civilians needed to show their ration cards and, depending on the circumstances, marriage certificates, work certificates, and documents detailing why a man of military age was not in uniform. Police could demand these documents at any time and place, although they were less likely to accost a woman in a rural hamlet than a man in a big city.

Censorship of course restricted the circulation of news and information. Listening to the news on BBC radio from London or Swiss Radio constituted a criminal offense, one that Vichy prosecuted. Nevertheless many underground papers relayed the news from the BBC or Swiss Radio in order to counterbalance the obvious propaganda printed in official papers. In France civilians also had to watch what they said on the telephone and wrote in letters because of the censors.

The Nazis may have acted more circumspectly in the West than in the East, but they still behaved like the victorious conquerors they were. They pursued their enemies and exploited the occupied territories and their inhabitants to their own advantage and according to their own ideology. In the West the occupation authorities began persecuting Jews in subtle ways, such as gradually isolating them and depriving them of their livelihood. They did not massacre Jews there. Instead they "resettled them in the East," which meant sending them to extermination camps in order to kill them. The process of deporting Jews began in early 1942. By the middle of 1943 most Jews there had either been interned or deported or had found ways to escape or hide. German agencies and their collaborators continued to hunt for Jews until the end.

The exigencies of fighting the war, however, began to outweigh Nazi ideology in occupation policies and patterns of persecution. By mid-1943 the Third Reich was starting to crack under the strain of military events. Although the Wehrmacht enjoyed great success when Hitler invaded the Soviet Union in June 1941, the Eastern Front drained Germany of men and materiel. The military tide turned against the Wehrmacht in February 1943 with its catastrophic defeat at Stalingrad. By that time the United States had entered the war following the bombing of Pearl Harbor in December 1941 and had had time to establish air bases in England from which the Allies bombed German cities.

Because the Wehrmacht was engaged over vast territories and suffering staggering losses on the Eastern Front, almost all German men were in uniform rather than in their factories or on their farms. Refusing to mobilize German women for ideological reasons, the Nazis had been replacing their own workforce with foreign labor since the war began. Some of these workers were paid; some were no more than slaves kidnapped off the streets of their home villages; some were political prisoners; and some were POWs. Even so, there were not enough of them to keep the war machine going. In 1943 the occupation authorities demanded workers from the Netherlands, Belgium, and France. When not enough men volunteered for the jobs, they established forced labor drafts.

The occupation authorities introduced compulsory labor in the Third Reich for Belgians in October 1942. In the Netherlands they gave the previously protected group of university students the choice of signing a loyalty oath in spring 1943 or reporting for work in Germany with their age cohort. The Vichy authorities tried various plans until implementing a forced labor draft in February 1943. The general population in all three countries resented these measures and considered the men involved to be the victims of persecution. Some men reported for duty, but others went into hiding or fled to neutral lands. In southern France the forced labor draft, more than any other issue, turned opinion in favor of the Resistance.[10]

Resisters opposed the German occupation of their countries and Nazi ideology in a variety of ways, which can be usefully categorized as "military" or "civil."[11] As you would expect, military resistance engaged the enemy through violence by such means as sabotage and partisan warfare as well as gathering intelligence of use to the Allied armies. The actions of military resisters have always received more attention than those of civil resisters if only because they made a more noticeable impact. Everyone within miles knew if a train derailed or an ammunition dump exploded. More devastating, the Germans usually demanded the deaths of fifty civilians in retribution for the assassination of one German officer in France. The victims of such reprisals rarely had anything at all to do with the attack or even the resistance. At the Liberation it was the military resisters who joined the Allied armies and rounded up collaborators in their hometowns.

Civil resistance, on the other hand, used much quieter, nonviolent means to protect civil society from the inroads of Nazism. It rarely provoked reprisals. The printing and distributing of illegal newspapers, magazines, and books counts as civil resistance, as do illegal efforts to keep democracy going by, for example, taking a political party underground and preparing for a postwar future led by the Resistance. Resistance with a capital "r" refers to this politically organized movement that gained official status after the war. The resistance with a small "r" refers to the more widespread, spontaneous, and grass-roots efforts of civilians to oppose the Nazi occupation. You could resist without belonging to a Resistance network.

Resistance began with the occupation as small groups of people found ways to oppose the new status quo. The form of resistance depended on the location and skills of the man or woman who had the original idea.[12] Families who lived on the Dutch border, for example, helped British and French soldiers get across it so they could escape capture during the debacle of 1940. Educated individuals in Paris and other cities wrote newsletters by hand or typed several copies with carbon paper and distributed them. For the most part these grass-roots resistance organizations began as local efforts by people with some personal connection with each other, even if it was once or twice removed through a relative or coworker. The connection often involved membership in some sort of community, whether a village, a political party, a church, a school, a sports team, or a place of employment.

This trusted circle of like-minded conspirators did not necessarily have all the skills or goods they needed. They might not have the artistic ability to forge identity documents or a job in a police station that would tell them when to expect the next German patrol. That meant they would have to risk exposing their illegal activities to a stranger who did have access to what they needed. If they chose well, that stranger joined the group.[13]

Certain people with jobs at the intersection of the clandestine and official worlds, such as police officers and secretaries in town halls, were likely to be approached by more than one group and may even have started their own. They served as a nexus of resistance in their area, creating connections between groups that would otherwise have no contact.

Over time nationwide resistance networks and movements developed. Some, such as the French Libération-Sud, which later joined the Mouvements unis de la Résistance (United Movements of the Resistance), grew out of prewar political contacts and activities. Others, such as the Noyautage d'administrations publiques (Civil Service Network) relied upon the cooperation of professional colleagues. Such national networks expanded in two ways. They either started a branch in a new place themselves or merged with an already existing group. A small, local circle might join a national network out of a sense that they could do more united with others or because the network offered the money and expertise they needed.

In the French case, resistance developed in two places: in France itself and abroad. General Charles de Gaulle, who retreated to London when the Germans occupied France, established himself as the leader of the Free French. He sent representatives into occupied France to unite the various Resistance movements there under his authority in order to give legitimacy to his claims to represent the French among the Allies. Most, but not all, of the large French networks joined de Gaulle because they could appreciate the benefits of opposing the Germans with a united front. The *maquis*, or military partisan units, for example, had a better chance of getting weapons if they belonged to the official Forces Françaises de l'Interieur (FFI, French Forces of the Interior) under de Gaulle. The Resistance succeeded inasmuch as de Gaulle led the provisional government at the Liberation, but it never fully represented all resisters in France. The Dutch, on the other hand, came closest to having both a unified and national Resistance and resistance.[14]

The Allies also involved themselves in resistance where it could benefit the military campaign by causing trouble behind enemy lines or protecting Allied servicemen. Both the American Office of Strategic Services (OSS) and the British Special Operations Executive (SOE) parachuted agents into occupied Europe. Some were sent to train military resisters and equip them to support the regular armies. Some were sent to gather military intelligence. Others coordinated escape lines, such as the Burgundy and Pat O'Leary Lines, in order to get aviators and POWs out of occupied territory. All of them accomplished their missions by working with local resisters.

Whether as part of a small, local group or a nationwide network, and whether or not sponsored by the Allies or a government in exile, there were many ways to resist: militarily by sabotage and fighting; intellectually by printing reliable information and arguments against Nazism; economically by doing shoddy work or disrupting shipments; or by helping the persecuted. Every group, no matter its size, location, or task, needed three things: a secure form of communication, information, and money.

Obviously members of small groups could just talk to each other in person. But once a group grew beyond a single neighborhood and a handful of people, it needed couriers and postboxes. Couriers delivered messages and documents, sometimes traveling long distances by train or bicycle and often going into new places while carrying compromising papers. Despite the dangers, couriers tended to be young women because German soldiers and police paid less attention to women than to men and it was assumed that a young woman would at least have a chance of flirting her way out of a tight spot.

A postbox was a person who worked in a public place where members of a group could leave and pick up messages. The owner of a café made an excellent postbox because many people went in and out of a café from early in the morning until late at night. No one would think it strange if the owner spoke to a customer or if the customer came in every day or even more than once a day.

Resisters also needed information. Every civilian was safer if he or she knew the whereabouts of local police units. Resisters also had a vocational interest in all sorts of administrative details that shaped daily life. The men and women working in escape lines, for example, had to keep abreast of the latest regulations regarding travel in border zones and identity documents as well as train schedules and the location and safety of friendly inns and restaurants. They relied on their own observations, their contacts in the wider community, and colleagues in the police force and civil service for such information.

Resistance groups of every size also needed money in order to buy things like food and newsprint on the black market, to pay for everyday expenses such as train tickets, and for bribes. Money came from a variety of sources, including the resisters' own savings, donations, loans, and, on occasion, armed robbery of post office banks. By 1944 many national networks had their own finance branch with the backing of bankers, industrialists, the British or Americans, or a government in exile.

Once a man or woman made the decision to resist and found an opportunity to act, however, he or she still had to consider family obligations. It was possible, and in many ways preferable, to remain in one's ordinary life while resisting. If resisters stayed in their home and job, they had legitimate identification papers and ration coupons. Resisters just needed a way to camouflage the resistance activities among their usual occupations. Of course some people needed their job in order to resist. A woman who worked in the registry office at the town hall and made false documents for her clandestine group while making legitimate documents for the public, made a much greater contribution by going to work every day than if she went into hiding. A banker who allowed resisters to set up false accounts in his bank made a bigger contribution by staying on the job than he would have in a hiding place; it would also be safer for his family if he did not suddenly disappear, leaving them to answer awkward questions.

Sometimes, however, a resister did need to disappear before the police arrived. It was possible for an entire family to move to a new town under a new name, but in most cases resisters went underground on their own. It meant either hiding, which implied an end to resistance activity, or leaving behind one's own identity, family, friends, and neighborhood to live under a false name as a stranger somewhere else. Resisters who lived underground moved constantly and switched their identification documents regularly.

They could not earn a living, so they had to get by on what they took with them or got from their colleagues. At the same time the cost of everything rose because they had to rely on restaurants and hotels, sometimes without the correct ration coupons, which meant paying black market prices.

Some resisters, particularly couriers and guides, lived between these two worlds. They kept their true identity when at home but used a false identity when traveling to deliver messages or escort fugitives. But they had to have a good excuse for their absences or their neighbors would start asking questions. And questions led to the sort of trouble that might put one in a torture chamber.

The German occupation authorities in western Europe used terror to discourage resistance by cultivating confusion and dread among the population.[15] Rather than spelling out what constituted an infraction and what the penalties would be, they preferred to let potential malcontents draw their own conclusions from exemplary actions, such as the execution of hostages.

The authorities made an announcement when they imprisoned local dignitaries as hostages and when French citizens were deported for listening to foreign radio broadcasts. They made it clear in the Netherlands that a father might well be taken for forced labor if his son did not report for work in Germany on the appointed day. Large, prominently placed posters announced the execution of civilians for acts of resistance, which could range from killing a German soldier to distributing an illegal newssheet. The official punishment for helping Allied airmen was the execution of all men in the helper's extended family and the deportation of all women, though the authorities did not always carry out this threat to its fullest extent. They did not specify what the punishment was for helping Jews in France.[16]

Civilians could not predict what would happen after someone was arrested. Some prisoners could receive visitors and care packages and were given trials. Others fell under the infamous Nacht und Nebel (Night and Fog) decree that cut them off from any communication whatsoever with the outside world or even other prisoners. For their families and friends it was as if they had disappeared into the fog of night. The public did not know what the authorities would do in any particular situation on any particular day.

Given the difficulty of everyday life under German occupation, it is no surprise that before the Allies landed on the Normandy beaches in June 1944, only a minority of at most 10 percent of the population in western

Europe took a stand on one side or the other as a collaborator or a resister. According to someone who had reason to know, only one out of every fifty patriotic Dutch expatriates in France had the courage to risk his or her life.[17] Resisters, however, acted according to their hopes and despite their fears.

All resisters, whether they started a group or were recruited because of their job, volunteered for the dangers and anxiety inherent in opposing the status quo. They did so as an extreme response to Hitler's Third Reich and the German occupation. But they did not all frame the problem in the same way. Military resisters, obviously, prioritized the war and engaged it on the home front with weapons in hand. Intellectual resisters wielded the pen to win the minds of their compatriots. Others defied Nazism at its most fundamental level by protecting its victims.

As an ideology that thrived on hate and exclusion, Nazism generated a constant succession of victims. The Nazis thought that they, and by extension the German nation, were surrounded by enemies, including Jews, Sinti and Roma, communists and other left-wing political activists, Jehovah's Witnesses, and, after the war started, resisters and Allied servicemen. It did not really matter to the Nazis that some of these categories, such as Allied servicemen, posed a much more concrete threat to them than others, such as Jehovah's Witnesses. Hitler set up the first concentration camp to punish his political enemies as soon as he took power in 1933 and pursued every person of any age that he branded an enemy until the collapse of the Third Reich in 1945.

Not surprisingly, from the beginning the Nazi seizure of power triggered a flood of refugees as Leftists and Jews went west to get away from them. Jews from Central Europe looked for safety in the Netherlands, Belgium, and France in such numbers that diplomats met to address the refugee crisis.[18] But the situation was about to deteriorate exponentially. Some 465,000 Spanish Republican refugees poured into France when Franco won the Spanish Civil War in 1939. Then, in the summer of 1940, eight to ten million men, women, and children clogged the roads of western Europe in their haste to get away from the advancing German Army. The refugees overwhelmed the towns and cities of southern France, where they were caught between the Germans to the north and west, the Alps to the east, and the Mediterranean Sea and Pyrenees Mountains to the south. The experience was so traumatic that it is remembered by a biblical name: L'Exode (the Exodus).[19]

A few months later, in the fall of 1940, the German occupation authorities allowed Dutch, Belgian, Luxembourgian, and French citizens to return to their homes in occupied territory as long as they were not Jewish. Jews stayed in southern France with the political exiles, who had good reason to believe that the Nazis would arrest them if they could.[20] The xenophobic Vichy regime responded to these foreign refugees, not all of whom were Jews, by expanding the entirely inadequate internment camps that the French Republic had slapped together to house the Spanish Republican refugees who arrived in 1939. However, in the case of Dutch, Luxembourgian, and Belgian nationals who could prove a certain level of financial independence, the Vichy authorities allowed Jews to reside in assigned villages rather than internment camps. This attempt to control refugees and, indeed, foreigners, with police surveillance only partially succeeded. From that point on, refugees who evaded arrest by German or French police went underground as fugitives.

The types of people who moved about illegally in occupied territory changed with the circumstances of the military war and Nazi occupation policies. The war's first fugitives were British and other Allied soldiers who evaded capture during the rapid German victories in the spring of 1940, quickly followed by French POWs making their own way home from POW camps without permission. By 1941 Dutch and Belgian workers assigned to jobs at German installations or worksites in France started walking away from untenable conditions in hopes of returning home. In 1942 Jewish families faced with deportation chose to go into hiding or flee to the promised safety of unoccupied territory. The number of fugitives swelled in 1943, when the German occupation authorities insisted on forced labor drafts. Rather than work in the Third Reich, young men from the Netherlands, Belgium, and France went into hiding or tried to get to England to fight with the Allies. Aviators who bailed out of their crippled bombers and fighters joined them in the illegal trek toward England. The number of these servicemen evaders, so called because they were evading capture, increased dramatically in 1943, when the U.S. Army Air Force (USAAF) and the Royal Air Force (RAF) started coordinated round-the-clock bombing of Germany. In addition to these groups, a constant stream of resisters who had been "burned" at home traveled illegally to other cities and countries to escape arrest.

At least in theory fugitives could survive the occupation if they found a hiding place and sources of support. Some fugitives, however, needed or wanted to get out of their home country or even occupied territory alto-gether. Many Jews looked to neutral Switzerland as a safe haven. Neutral Spain could also be reached by land, but was far less appealing. In the first place, General Franco clearly favored his fellow fascists in Germany and Italy and, indeed, owed his position to their military support. In the second place, Spain had not recovered economically from its three-year civil war.

Such considerations carried less weight for other fugitives, such as men belonging to the Allied armies or intending to join them, or individuals with information or skills needed by governments in exile in London. They were not looking for a place to hide but a way to get out of continen-tal Europe altogether. Some of these fugitives braved the English Channel and the North Sea, but most made their way over land to Spain and then to Portugal or Gibraltar, from whence they could leave for Allied bases in England or North Africa. The 1,700 Dutch men and handful of women who successfully reached England and the unknown number of their compatriots who were captured along the way are called *Engelandvaarders*.[21]

In some extraordinary cases the fugitives had enough personal resources and good luck to make their own way out of occupied territory. But most people needed help. Whether they were Jewish children or Allied airmen, refugee fugitives needed false documents, a way to get food and clothing without ration cards, hiding places, and guidance to cross forbidden fron-tier zones and international borders. The men and women who supported such refugee fugitives in hiding or aided their escape from enemy territory formed a distinct branch of resistance, sometimes called humanitarian re-sistance or rescue. Those who assisted Jews are usually called "rescuers," while those who assisted Allied servicemen are known as "helpers."

In many ways this was the least organized branch of resistance. Help was offered in many shapes and configurations. Some rescuers worked alone without belonging to any resistance organization by hiding an individual or family in their own home or on their farm. Agreeing to hide someone meant agreeing to an indefinite period of being afraid of neighbors and strangers, of finding food without enough ration coupons, and of sharing your home with strangers. It meant putting yourself and your family at risk.

There were also entire villages, such as Chambon-sur-Lignon in France, where the people worked together to save Jews.[22] Some rescuers formed illegal organizations specifically to hide Jews. Dutch university students in the Utrechtse Kindercomité (Utrecht Children's Committee) spirited Jewish children to hiding places during the massive deportations of Jews from the Netherlands in 1942. In Brussels the underground Comité de défense des Juifs (CDJ, Committee for the Defense of Jews) hid and defended Jews during the occupation.

As the pattern of persecution shifted during the occupation, resistance groups took on the challenge of hiding labor evaders and other fugitives, some of whom might have been Jewish. The Dutch Landelijke Organisatie (National Organization) ran a national network of hiding places and support for Dutch *onderduikers* who "dove under" to hide from German police and labor authorities. The most extensive French networks had similar sections to look after their members who had gone into hiding or the families of those who had been arrested.

For those who did not want to hide, other helpers escorted them across and out of occupied territory. Some such circles of helpers operated in a particular place along a border where the helpers themselves lived or worked. As local residents, they might own property that abutted or even straddled an international border. Arthur and Jeanne Lavergnat, who occasionally worked with Jean Weidner and Elisabeth Cartier to smuggle people into Switzerland, had a front door in France and a back garden in Switzerland. The helpers in such local escape lines knew the paths through the woods that circumvented the official border posts. They could observe the patterns of official patrols while going about their everyday lives. Such groups stayed in place to usher people over the border and sometimes back again. The Smit–van der Heijden group near Hilvarenbeek and the Groep Vrij in Maastricht, for example, specialized in crossing the Dutch-Belgian border. Fugitives came to them on the Dutch side. They took the fugitives over the border and passed them on to other helpers belonging to other groups on the Belgian side.

Other escape lines guided fugitives long distances, across an entire country or, more rarely, more than one country. The most well-known of these had Allied backing. The Americans and British parachuted agents into occupied territory to create escape lines such as the Shelbourne Line specifically to extract Allied aviators. The famously successful Comet Line was organized and run by Belgians with financial backing from the British and brought 688 Allied servicemen and 68 civilians to Spain.[23] Like the Comet Line, most specialized in helping a particular type of fugitive. Some lines run by Jewish resisters, for example, focused on taking Jews out of occupied territory.[24]

An escape line required many more members than other forms of resistance in order to provide the necessary money, communications, and supplies, including safe houses, food, false documents, and clothing for disguises. Everything had to be paid for in cash in the local currency. The helpers were strung out over great distances in a chain of safe houses. Couriers and guides traveled back and forth to escort fugitives, who needed a new set of false documents for every occupation zone they traveled through. Every journey exposed both helpers and fugitives to document inspections and police cordons at train stations and frontier posts as well as on public transportation. In addition German police, especially the Abwehr, took a particular interest in escape lines that helped aviators and other men trying to join or rejoin the Allies. They had great success infiltrating and rounding up such networks.

It is difficult to estimate how many men and women offered help to fugitives under the occupation because many worked alone and many died in the concentration camps before they could tell their stories. Information about many escape lines can be found only as mentions in the memoirs of those individuals they helped who survived the war and published a book about it.

Just after the war British officers identified 100,000 helpers of Allied servicemen in all of Europe.[25] The historian Emilienne Eychenne estimates that 0.14 percent of the population of the department of Haute-Garonne and 0.12 percent of the population of the city of Toulouse were involved in taking fugitives over the Pyrenees illegally.[26] By 2016 Yad Vashem, the Holocaust Remembrance Center in Jerusalem, had recognized 26,120 Righteous among the Nations who rescued Jews during the war, a conservative number. These numbers, however, merely suggest how many men and women engaged in rescue work. In at least one case Yad Vashem chose to honor a single man as the representative of the three hundred men and women in his escape line. Some people could appear on both lists, and some people who belong on one or the other surely do not appear on either. Neither list includes helpers of French POWs or resisters, unless they also helped aviators or Jews. Yet even adding the two lists together and doubling or tripling the number gives an estimated number of helpers in Europe at less than 1 percent of the 1940 European population of 416 million.

Membership numbers are not the only unknown facts about escape lines and other resistance networks. Since the end of the war the Resistance has been the stuff of legend, politics, and movies, but not, really, of history. History relies on documents for evidence, of which, until recently, there were very few available about resistance. After all, common sense dictated that resisters would not leave a paper trail. But the war and its heroes played too large a role in postwar politics and popular memory to be forgotten.[27] Postwar governments that based their legitimacy on representing the Resistance established institutes to write the history of the national Resistance. In France it was the Comité d'histoire du deuxième guerre mondiale (Committee for the History of the Second World War), and in the Netherlands it was the Rijksinstituut voor Oorlogsdocumentatie (Royal Institute for War Documentation). These institutes and others gathered information and interviews and issued books and articles about the history of the war in their respective nations. Other historians had to rely on the memoirs of resisters, which tended to be written by men and women with elite backgrounds and leadership positions, some of whom had contemporary agendas in mind when they wrote. Alternatively historians could interview resisters decades after the events to create an oral history.

In the early 1990s a scholar needed special permission, called a dérogation, to see any document in the French archives that concerned the period from 1939 to 1945. The scholar had to apply for a dérogation for each document by its catalog number and wait for departmental and national police and cultural authorities to approve the request. Not all of the documents from the war had been cataloged, and some of the catalogs for wartime materials that did exist were kept under lock and key in the archivists' offices. If a scholar could not get a catalog number for a document, he or she could not even request to see it. To a certain degree this followed standard privacy protocols that restricted access to archives until fifty or sixty years after their creation. It was not especially difficult to get permission to see mundane files about, say, the potato crop during the war, if only because those catalogs were shelved in the open with all the others. But it was difficult to get permission to see files about resistance and other delicate subjects such as collaborators and the purge of collaborators.

All of this changed dramatically in the late 1990s and early 2000s. The French Parliament passed a new archival law that opened most of the wartime documents to the public. Of course some documents, such as court cases, still require a dérogation. Other governments also opened or declassified their wartime, resistance-related archives.[28] As it turns out, common sense was wrong. Resisters did leave a paper trail; even before the war ended a variety of agencies started compiling dossiers on them.

Every agency had its own mission that framed the information in its files. At the time no one needed to know why a man or woman resisted; the reason was self-evident and the question was irrelevant to the bureaucratic task at hand. They asked what, where, when, how, and with whom. The Dutch Red Cross, for example, set itself the herculean task of reconstructing what happened to the Dutch population during the catastrophe of the war. So they asked resisters who returned from the concentration camps when they had been arrested and who else had been arrested with them; whom they had seen in the camps, and whom they had seen die there.

The government agencies in charge of resistance veterans' affairs in each country wanted proof that an individual had served in the resistance and that the arrest or injury for which he or she requested compensation resulted from resistance activity. These files range from single letters in which a recognized Resistance leader attests that so-and-so belonged to his or her Resistance organization to heavy folders stuffed with letters, depositions, and police reports about what the individual in question did or did not do during the occupation. They are nonetheless incomplete because some men and women never applied for official recognition. Some died during the war. Others felt they had simply done their duty and neither wanted nor deserved anything for it. In some families the husband and father represented the entire family. All such files remained in the offices of the administrators in charge of veterans' or victims' affairs until the majority of their clients died. They have only recently been moved to public archives, and some are still in the process of being cataloged.

Such agencies concerned themselves with men and women from every branch of resistance, but escape lines left additional traces both during and after the war. For those who took refuge in Switzerland, the Swiss authorities kept files on every refugee who entered the country during the war. These are not entirely reliable, however, because guides told refugees to tell the Swiss border guards they had not had any help crossing the border. But the files do contain accurate dates and places. For Engelandvaarders, the Dutch government in exile in London interviewed every man or woman who arrived from occupied territory to determine their story before and during their escape. The U.S. and British military authorities also questioned all Allied servicemen who returned to England about the technical details of their last mission and what happened to them in occupied territory. They used these "escape and evasion reports" to prepare escape aids and lessons for other aviators. At the Liberation, officers created thousands of "helper files" to determine who had helped Allied airmen in order to award honors and, when necessary, practical assistance in the form of food, medicine, money, and the like.

The official historical institutes also created archives that are full of interviews, reports, and documents. Many are now available at the original institute's successor or in the national archives. In addition to such specialized archives historians can consult the usual sources of court cases, police reports, and administrative reports. All of these sources add up to a much more detailed picture of the everyday operation of resistance than historians thought possible even ten years ago.

Nonetheless one gaping hole remains in the sources: the German side of the story. German police notoriously burned boxes and boxes of files before they retreated from France, Belgium, and the Netherlands. There are in fact a few singed papers in the archives today that civilians retrieved from these Gestapo bonfires, but the vast majority of documents were lost. Without them it is impossible to know what the German officers in charge of suppressing resistance knew, when they knew it, or why they did what they did. It is even difficult to determine which German police units participated in any particular raid because the civilian victims did not know who was arresting them unless the men wore distinctive uniforms. As late as July 1946, French police were still trying to figure out who arrested and shot a French inspector who lived on the Swiss border, leading to his death in a concentration camp. All the witnesses could say was that the men who took away the inspector were wearing plain clothes and spoke with German accents.[29]

Families have contributed memoirs, diaries, photographs, and memorabilia, such as false identity documents, to museums and archives. One of the largest private collections of resistance-related materials belonged to Jean Weidner, the man who received the letter from the French prison at his textile shop in 1942. Within weeks after Weidner and Cartier smuggled the letter's author and his wife into Switzerland they had enlisted enough friends and acquaintances to take hundreds of refugees from Lyon over the Swiss border to Geneva. More and more people asked them for help until, just over a year later, in September 1943, Weidner committed himself to expanding their escape line north to the Netherlands and south to Spain. He did so by joining forces with other rescuers already at work in Brussels, Paris, Toulouse, and the Pyrenees. Together they formed the only resistance network to span the Netherlands, Belgium, and France. By the end of the occupation Weidner and his more than three hundred colleagues were hiding Jews in France and Belgium; taking Jews, Engelandvaarders, Allied airmen, and other fugitives to Switzerland and Spain; and serving as a clandestine courier service for other resisters, churches, aid organizations, and families separated by war.

But they did not have a name for their network until one evening in Paris in January 1944, when an Allied aviator asked who was helping him. Thinking on his feet, the helper said, "Dutch-Paris" because he and most of the group's leaders were Dutch and they were going through Paris. When the aviator got to London he told the officers there that he and his companions had escaped thanks to Dutch-Paris. Weidner accepted the name as a fait accompli at the Liberation because now that they had come into the open, the group needed a name to fill out paperwork and answer questions.

After France was liberated but before Germany surrendered, in November 1944, Weidner took command of a temporary Dutch intelligence unit based in Paris with orders to find Dutch collaborators in France and Belgium. That position, his new rank of captain in the Dutch Army, and his reputation as the leader of an extraordinary resistance line, gave Weidner the authority and clout to investigate what happened in Dutch-Paris. He and his lieutenants persuaded many of their Dutch-Paris colleagues to write reports about their activities in the line. They also participated in French and Dutch police investigations into the cause of arrests in the line and cooperated closely with American and British officers researching wartime help to aviators.

Unusually Weidner was able to have Dutch-Paris recognized as an official Resistance organization in France, Belgium, and the Netherlands. That official recognition gave his colleagues the status and benefits of resisters and gave Weidner himself the responsibilities of chef du réseau (network chief) in perpetuity. Weidner kept carbon copies of all his correspondence and brought it with him when he immigrated to California in the 1950s; he was still writing attestations of the resistance activities of some of his colleagues thirty years later. This is the first book to reconstruct the story of Jean Weidner and the Dutch-Paris escape line using Weidner's personal papers and documents in thirty-two archives in the Netherlands, Belgium, France, Switzerland, Germany, the United Kingdom, and the United States.

Weidner's papers give a uniquely detailed picture of a large underground organization in operation. For instance, because Weidner wrote reports on his biweekly trips across western Europe and kept them in Switzerland during the occupation, the historian can reconstruct his clandestine movements from October 1943 to June 1944. Certain things, however, cannot be recovered. Except for Allied aviators, Weidner and his colleagues did not keep lists of the thousands of people they helped. They did not need such lists because they wanted only to help whoever needed help at that moment. Besides, if any such list had fallen into German or collaborationist hands, both the helpers and those they were helping would have risked arrest and worse.

The roster of men and women in the line must also be considered incomplete because some of them died in concentration camps. Because they did not return after the war, these men and women could not name their associates who had worked exclusively with them for safety's sake. Furthermore at least two members of Dutch-Paris burned their papers during the war when they heard of a colleague's arrest. German police captured other documents when they raided a safe house and a resister's home. Without the German police reports, however, it is impossible to know what those documents contained. Yet even without lists of the civilians they helped or the German documents regarding the arrests that decimated the line, the available sources make it possible to reconstruct the membership and activities of Dutch-Paris to an unexpected degree.

During the occupation, Dutch-Paris functioned as a vast, clandestine welfare agency and courier service that supported 1,500 refugees in hiding and took another 1,500 to safety in Switzerland and Spain. The line ran through western Europe like a river of goodwill, carrying fugitives and messages out of occupied territory. Fed by the small streams of local resistance groups in the Netherlands and southern and eastern Belgium, the line's river began in Brussels. From there it flowed south to Paris, where it gathered more fugitives and messages from French resistance groups. In Paris the river forked southeast, toward Switzerland, and south to Spain.

The Swiss branch flowed through Lyon, Annecy, and Collonges-sous-Salève on its way to Geneva. The Spanish branch went straight south to Toulouse, where the river fanned out to cross the Pyrenees in the Haute-Garonne and the Ariège, mostly in the Luchonnais and Commingeoise valleys. A small tributary flowed from Geneva to Lyon and then to Toulouse and over the mountains into Spain.

The 330 men and women of Dutch-Paris routinely crossed four international borders and seven occupation zones, spoke three languages, and dealt in cash in four currencies. Indeed from their perspective they reconfigured the map of western Europe from a collection of nation-states into a simple dichotomy of occupied and unoccupied territory. Some had served in the First World War or even the battles of 1940, but with one, possibly two exceptions, none had any training in clandestine activity.

Young, unmarried men and women, many of them university students, did much of the footwork in Dutch-Paris. But the line could not have functioned without the contributions of older men and women who had jobs with access to food, documents, information, and other important items. Some owned shops; others ran government offices, banks, or companies; some farmed their own land. These were respectable citizens with homes and savings they were willing to share with strangers. Brought up to tell the truth and to obey authority, they now forged documents, falsified their identity, and regularly broke dozens of laws.

Except for their illegal work, the hundreds of men and women who belonged to Dutch-Paris had little in common. They came from the Netherlands, Belgium, France, Switzerland, even Romania and Canada. They spoke Dutch or French and sometimes English. They were Protestants, Catholics, Jews, and atheists. Political parties meant nothing to them. Right or Left, if a man or woman volunteered to make a contribution to the "goede zaak" (good fight), he or she was welcome. The one thing that all the members of Dutch-Paris had in common was a firm belief in the dignity of every human being and the courage to act on it.

This is the story of how the unarmed students, housewives, civil servants, businessmen, bankers, and ministers in the Dutch-Paris escape line banded together to fight the Nazis by protecting their victims, and the price these otherwise ordinary heroes paid for their resistance.

Gare d'Annecy, Annecy, France, 1950.

I

Escape to Switzerland

THE SPRINGS OF RESISTANCE that merged into the river of Dutch-Paris bubbled up at different times and places when individual men and women chose to help a fugitive. But the story of how these particular resisters found each other across eight hundred miles of occupied territory to create a successful escape line began in Lyon in the summer of 1942, when Jean Weidner opened a letter from a French prison. Every resistance network needed a leader to link the disparate circles together and oversee its operations.[1] Circumstances and the force of his conviction made Weidner the leader of Dutch-Paris.

Weidner was born in Brussels in 1912, the son of a Seventh-day Adventist pastor. His Dutch parents remained at their church posting in Belgium throughout the German occupation of that country during the First World War. Only after the war did Weidner Senior accept a new position, this time near Geneva, where it was hoped the young family could regain their health after the food shortages and other deprivations of the occupation. In 1925 they moved again, this time just over the French border to an Adventist seminary above the village of Collonges-sous-Salève, where Weidner's father taught Greek and Latin. Weidner himself spent most of his youthful leisure time in the mountains around the village, from where you can see Geneva on a clear day. For eight summers, starting in 1925, the young man peddled religious tracts in France and Belgium, gaining the fluency in traveling and meeting strangers that he would use so brilliantly during the war. Although devout, Weidner did not follow his father and grandfather into the ministry but went into business instead.[2]

When the Wehrmacht swept through western Europe in spring 1940, Weidner's parents and his younger sister were living in The Hague, and he and his sister Gabrielle lived in Paris. The war would separate the family

The seminary of the Seventh-day Adventists in Collonges-sous-Salève.

for the next five years. Like millions of others, Jean and Gabrielle fled south ahead of the German Army. After the French signed an armistice that enabled most refugees to go home, Gabrielle returned to her secretarial job at the Adventist church in Paris. Weidner, however, tried to take a ship to England to volunteer with the Allies. Unable to find passage, he and a childhood friend settled in Lyon, the biggest city in the unoccupied zone. It would later become known as the capital of the Resistance, but in the early years of the war it was better known as a collecting point for refugees. Sitting in the foothills of the Alps at the confluence of two rivers, the Rhone and the Saône, Lyon offered good train connections and other urban services as well as desirable proximity to neutral Switzerland.[3]

Weidner and his friend went into business together importing textiles from Switzerland. They both belonged to the semiofficial Christian organization dedicated to helping refugees, Amitié Chrétienne (Christian Fellowship), but their paths diverged in the resistance.[4] Weidner's partner joined a French intelligence network.[5] Sometime before May 1942, Weidner sheltered a Frenchman on his way to join de Gaulle in London, possibly for that intelligence network. But his real interest lay in helping the persecuted. He began by assisting Dutch refugees in southern France through the consulate in Lyon. He asked his French acquaintances to sponsor refugees and sent warm clothes and food to individuals in internment camps.[6]

In January 1942 Weidner married Elisabeth Cartier. The couple had met several years earlier when Cartier took classes at the Adventist seminary in Collonges-sous-Salève, although she was not, at that time, an Adventist. Cartier's father had been killed on the Western Front a couple of months before her birth in early 1915, after which her mother raised her near her own family in the Genevois. In January 1939, then twenty-four, Cartier took a secretarial job at the French consulate in Geneva, giving her an important entrée into French and Swiss officialdom. As women were expected to do at the time, she quit her job after their marriage, although she did not give up her connections in Geneva. When Weidner was not traveling on business, she lived with him in his hotel in Lyon. When he was traveling, she stayed with her mother outside of Geneva in Carouge, Switzerland.[7]

Shortly after their marriage a new wave of refugees flooded into Lyon in response to the start of mass deportations of Jews from western Europe to the extermination camps.[8] The first convoy to leave France for Auschwitz departed in March. On July 16–17, 1942, French police participated in a massive roundup of foreign Jews in Paris, including women and children, which is known as the Vel d'Hiv, after the sports arena in which they were gathered (the Velodrome d'Hiver). French police also arrested and interned foreign Jews in the Vichy zone that summer. The occupation authorities started deporting Jews from the Netherlands and Belgium in July, followed by mass arrests, internment, and more deportations.[9] Jews who understood that the deportation trains were taking people to their deaths and had the resources to flee made their illegal way to southern France in hopes of escaping. In the summer of 1942, as many as one hundred new arrivals sought assistance at the Dutch consulate in Lyon every day.

The consul, a Frenchman named Maurice Jacquet, had inherited the position from a colleague at the offices of the Dutch life insurance company De Utrecht Vie only a few months earlier, in January 1942. Although neither he nor his secretary spoke Dutch, they both devoted themselves wholeheartedly to the extra work required to help the Dutch refugees who overwhelmed the insurance office that summer. Jacquet established a separate welfare office a short walk away and hired a number of refugees to act as

Maurice Jacquet, 1947.

Lyon

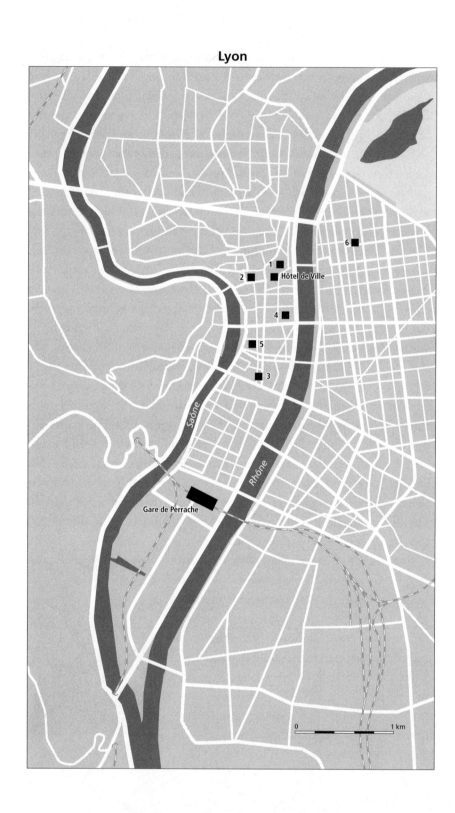

Saône

Rhône

1
2
Hôtel de Ville
4
5
3
6

Gare de Perrache

0   1 km

translators and to handle the paperwork of supplying the refugees with ration cards, identity documents, and legal residences.[10] At that time the Vichy authorities were willing to tolerate the presence of Dutch Jews under certain conditions, mainly that they not put any burden on the public purse.

Jacquet also cultivated a "réseau de complicités" (network of complicity) at the prefecture du Rhône that functioned as the administrative center for the region of Lyon, including the department of Haute-Savoie on the Swiss border. These contacts, who were concentrated in the service des étrangers (department for foreigners), helped Jacquet by arranging for the release of Dutch nationals after roundups or issuing passes for Jacquet or his assistants to visit French prisons.[11] His network included a police intendant, a clerk at the civil court, a government commissioner at the military tribunal, and the head of the service des étrangers at the prefecture of the Rhône.[12] Indeed, Jacquet's connections extended beyond the city. At least one French official working on the Demarcation Line between the occupied and unoccupied zones told Dutch refugees who had been caught crossing that border illegally to ask the Dutch consulate in Lyon for help.[13]

Over the course of the summer, however, southern France proved to be a dangerous place for non-French Jews. In August 1942, Vichy authorities began transferring Jews from its internment camps in the south to transit camps in the occupied zone. When Vichy police rounded up foreign Jews, including Dutchmen and Belgians, on the streets of Marseille and Lyon in July and August, many set their hopes on neutral Switzerland. In ordinary circumstances someone who wanted to travel from Lyon to Switzerland would take the train, crossing the border at Annemasse and arriving in Geneva the same day. But no Jew could simply board a train to Switzerland in 1942 and expect to arrive.

The Franco-Swiss border does not cross through mountains in the region of Geneva, called the Genevois. Instead it runs through a stream

LYON

Gare de Perrache – train station used by Dutch-Paris
1 13 rue du Griffon – Weidner's shop
2 5 rue Ste Catherine – The Weidners' hotel in Lyon
3 104 rue Hôtel de Ville (now rue Président Édouard Hérriot) – Dutch consulate
4 20 rue de la Bourse – *Bureau d'assistance néerlandais* – Office for assistance to Dutch refugees (located inside the Palais du Commerce)
5 11 rue de la Monnaie – Pillot's apartment
6 11 rue Crillon – home of Paul and Marthe Meyer

on flat land or through Lake Geneva. According to an international set-
tlement concluded in Napoleonic times, Geneva belongs to Switzerland,
but a thin ribbon of its valley and the mountains to the south belong to
the department of Haute-Savoie in France. Practical considerations separated the political border from the customs border, which lay four or so
miles inside France at a stop in the road called Le Chable, about ten minutes east of the village of Les Cruseilles. This allowed the farmers of the
Genevois, many of whom had houses in France and fields in Switzerland,
to sell their produce in Geneva rather than across the mountains in the
French town of Annecy or even Lyon.

When the war started in 1939, the Swiss closed the political border and
installed barbed wire.[14] In January 1941 they created a *zone militaire* a half-
mile deep along the border near Geneva. To pass through it individuals
needed an authorization signed by the commander of the border guards in
Geneva. On the French side, police, gendarmerie, and douaniers (customs
officers) stood guard. By day the gendarmes manned fixed posts and sent out
one-man patrols. At night they sent two men on patrol. Local people continued to move back and forth across the border to farm their fields, attend
high school or university classes in Geneva, or visit their relatives who lived
on the other side. Indeed there was so much regular traffic that a tram ran
between Geneva and the French border. But even local people were expected
to go through the formalities at official border posts once the war began.

In 1942 Swiss authorities reacted with alarm to the flood of Jews fleeing
the Nazis. On August 4 the Swiss closed the border to all "racial refugees,"
forcing any who had entered illegally to go back over the border into
France. This did not, however, stop the illegal crossings. Because Swiss
public opinion did not wholly support the ban on Jewish refugees, federal authorities secretly modified the refugee policy at the end of the
month and allowed local guards some discretion in its application.[15] The
Swiss continued to modify their refugee policy without making it public.
It was always difficult to predict whether or not Swiss guards would *refouler* (turn back or deport) refugees on any given day.[16]

Following the roundups of non-French Jews in Lyon on August 28,
Swiss customs agents demanded reinforcements because of a surge of clandestine border crossers. The Armée Territoriale de Genève installed an
eight-foot-high barbed-wire barricade along the border in the Genevois.[17]
These measures appeared to have some effect. The Swiss arrested eighty-
eight "racial refugees" in the Genevois on October 2, 1942, but only four

such refugees eighteen days later.[18] The drop in arrests, however, may have had more to do with French policing than with Swiss barricades.

Vichy French authorities were no more pleased than their neighbor by the thousands of Jews moving through the department of Haute-Savoie toward Switzerland.[19] They designated Haute-Savoie a *zone reservée* (reserved zone) that required authorization and passes to be in or travel through the area. Special police circulated on the trains and buses in the department, arresting at least ten Jews in each train during the course of that fall.[20]

If caught in the Haute-Savoie without the proper passes, a refugee automatically received a one-month prison sentence. The refugee served this sentence in the old prison, located on a peninsula between two rivers in Annecy that was reopened but not renovated during the war. If the refugee had successfully crossed the border but been *refoulé* by the Swiss, a standard fine of 1,200 French francs was added to the one-month prison term. This represented a significant sum at a time when the average wage for an industrial worker in Paris was 12.27 French francs per hour.[21] As of August 1942 Jews caught in the Haute-Savoie were sent to the internment camp of Rivesaltes outside of Perpignan after serving their prison term rather than being released to the less stringent surveillance of a "welcome center" or to a *résidence assignée* (assigned residence), as they had been earlier.

So when Weidner received the letter from his Dutch acquaintance asking for help because the French had caught him and his wife at the Demarcation Line, Weidner faced a moral dilemma. He had good reason to think that his Jewish acquaintances would not be safe in Vichy France. He also had reason to think they would be safe in Switzerland and that he could find a way to take them there. But doing so would involve breaking the law in two countries.

Weidner had been taught to obey the law. But he had also been raised to stand up for his principles. When he was a child in Switzerland, his pastor father would not allow him to attend school on Saturdays because Adventists observe the Sabbath on that day. Given the choice to send his son to school or spend the day in jail himself, Weidner's father chose to spend Saturdays behind bars.

In 1942 Weidner and Cartier chose their principles over the law. They smuggled the Jewish couple into Switzerland and within weeks were operating an escape line between Lyon and Geneva.

The couple had a number of qualifications for creating a workable escape line over the Franco-Swiss border. Although Weidner carried a

Dutch passport, people frequently mistook him for a Frenchman. He spoke French as his first language and went by the French form of his name, Jean, rather than the Dutch, Johann. Having lived most of his life in France, Weidner negotiated the French transportation system and bureaucracy like a native. He also had perfectly legitimate passes to travel between France and Switzerland on business. Vichy's xenophobia gave Weidner yet another advantage: the French police were looking for criminal foreigners; they were not suspicious of men who dressed in a suit and tie and spoke educated French. Weidner talked his way out of trouble more than once.

Weidner could also pass as a native in Switzerland—as long as he stayed in the French-speaking canton of Geneva. He knew the city well from growing up in the region and from his business. The fact that Cartier's mother lived just outside Geneva in the border village of Carouge gave them both a ready reason to be in Switzerland and a discreet base there.

Furthermore both Weidner and Cartier could do their illegal work within the bounds of their legitimate lives. Weidner, for example, kept to his habitual sales routes between Lyon, Annecy, and the Swiss border while traveling on his resistance business. Police and rail authorities were used to seeing him in those places and unlikely to question him. If they did, he could produce legitimate passes and legitimate reasons to be there.

Smuggling refugees into Switzerland from Lyon posed three main challenges. First, they needed to find a way to get foreigners—men, women, and children of all ages and backgrounds— through the Haute-Savoie. Second, they needed a way to get them over the border. And third, they needed to ensure that the fugitives they did manage to smuggle into Switzerland would be allowed to stay there rather than being turned back. Weidner and Cartier used the framework of their personal and professional lives to handle each of these problems.

They already had working relationships with men and women who

Elisabeth Cartier, 1942.

would join them in helping refugees illegally. Weidner, for example, had taken part in the discussions among members of Amitié Chrétienne from its earliest days, which gave him information and valuable contacts. He had also volunteered at the Dutch consulate, where Jacquet had access to information about Vichy policies, could issue identity documents and other papers, and knew of refugees who might want to make the journey to Switzerland.

Raymonde Pillot, 1942.

Weidner also had a young secretary, Raymonde Pillot, who was eager to do something against the Germans. Pillot grew up in Lyon with the memory of two older brothers killed on the Western Front during the First World War. Her third brother died as a soldier during the campaign of 1939–40. It was a mercy, she later thought, that her mother did not live to see German tanks on the streets of Lyon in 1940.

Pillot met Weidner and Cartier at the Adventist church in Lyon early in the occupation. She worked as his secretary in the textile business for several months before Weidner asked her to type illegal pamphlets, presumably as part of his early resistance activities around Amitié Chrétienne. She wanted to do much more than type, however, and in the end traveled so much as a courier that Cartier made her a present of rubber-soled shoes from Switzerland so that she could walk quietly when she was on the streets after curfew. By that time all the rubber in France was diverted to the war effort and civilians had to make do with wooden soles.[22]

Within Lyon itself Pillot did not have far to walk. She and her father lived in an apartment at 11 rue de la Monnaie in the old Presqu'Ile neighborhood, between the Saône and Rhône rivers, not far from the vast parade ground of the Place Bellecour. It would have taken Pillot only a few minutes to walk to Jacquet's offices at 104 rue Hotel de Ville (now rue du Président E. Herriot) and not much farther to the Dutch welfare office (office néerlandaise) at the Palais du Commerce. Weidner's shop at 13 rue Griffon, where Pillot ostensibly worked, lay several blocks farther north, close to city hall, the Weidners' hotel on the rue Sainte-Catherine, and the Amitié Chrétienne offices on the rue de Constantine. It was a longer walk in the opposite direction to the train station, the gare de Perrache,

Franco-Swiss Border in the Genevois

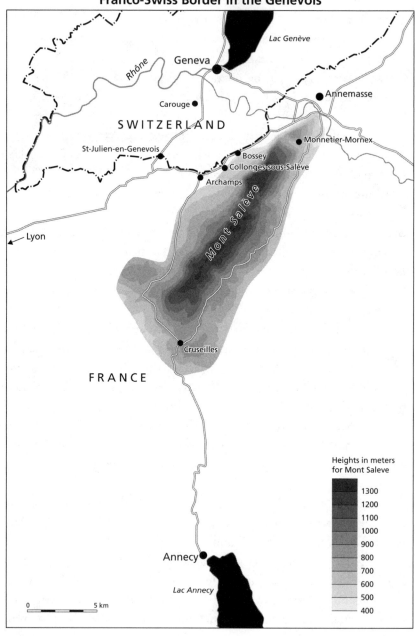

from which most passenger trains left during the war. She could walk to and from it in the shadows of narrow streets without having to cross any bridges, which were often guarded. The Pillots, father and daughter, opened their conveniently located home to Raymonde's resistance colleagues for clandestine meetings.

In August 1942 Weidner and Cartier addressed the problem of how to cross the *zone reservée* between Lyon and Geneva by establishing a base in Annecy, the capital of Haute-Savoie. Nestled on the shore of a deep Alpine lake under the watch of a medieval castle, Annecy's old quarter is graced by cobbled streets and deep sidewalks beneath arched roofs. Weidner knew it well enough before 1942 that he could call upon established relationships with other resisters and civil servants there.[23]

Because they themselves did not live in Annecy, Weidner and Cartier relied on the help of a woman whom everyone always referred to respectfully as Mademoiselle Meunier. A middle-aged woman who had never married and now cared for her elderly aunt, Marie Meunier sold souvenirs and haberdashery in her small shop, Au Mimosa, at 15 rue de la Poste, near Annecy's train station. Over the course of the war, Meunier sheltered 150 to 200 Dutch fugitives and several Allied aviators, despite living across the street from a collaborator.[24] She was also involved with the local resistance by, for example, providing warm clothing for the *maquis* hiding in the mountains surrounding the town.

Meunier could organize passage through town and shelter fugitives, but the escape line also needed friends in the prefecture. As the governmental and administrative center for the department, the prefecture was the source of vital information about Vichy's policies and their enforcement and of the official documents needed to live or move about in the reserved zone. Weidner had been cultivating useful connections there since at least March 1941. By 1943 he had several contacts among the civil servants working in Annecy's prefecture who were willing to issue false documents and even hide fugitives and disburse money to those in hiding.[25]

Those contacts undoubtedly smoothed the bureaucratic way for him to open a shop selling silk

Marie Meunier, 1939.

goods in Annecy during the summer of 1942. Overlooking the lake at 9 quai Eustache Chappuis, La Maison du Coupon was only an eight-minute walk from the train station and could be approached by several routes. Ostensibly purchased as a business for Cartier to run, the shop gave the couple the legal right to circulate anywhere in the Haute-Savoie, including along the border. It also gave them a convenient place to hide refugees along the route to Switzerland and to rest between trips themselves.[26] The fact that Weidner owned shops in both Lyon and Annecy also gave Pillot a legitimate reason to make regular trips between the two towns, even if she did so far more often than the textile trade demanded.

Annecy made a good stopping point between Lyon and the Swiss border because a number of trains circulated between the two towns every day. They were crowded enough to camouflage fugitives. Trains also circulated between Annecy and Geneva, but these were under strict surveillance by Vichy's special police. As locals, Weidner and Cartier knew that those policemen paid far less attention to the buses running between Annecy and the villages on the French side of the border, including Weidner's home village of Collonges-sous-Salève.

In Collonges, Weidner made contact with other resisters and called on his connections from his youth. He occasionally worked with the village's Catholic priest to smuggle Jews over the border.[27] One of his many false identification documents, made out in the name of "Paul Rey," came from Collonges's town hall.[28] More important, Weidner and Cartier recruited some of their coreligionists at the small Adventist seminary where Weidner's father had taught, up the mountain from the main village and its busy rectory.

Those Adventists who helped fugitives escape into Switzerland not only broke French law but parted from official SDA church policy, which counseled Adventists not to get involved in resistance activities. A small circle of teachers and students nevertheless helped shelter and guide refugee fugitives. Among others, Roger Fasnacht, a Swiss man in his early twenties who was the school's administrator, cached money and even couriers' bicycles at his home. He also guided fugitives over the border. Jean Zurcher, a young Swiss teacher, also served as both a courier and a guide. His wife, Anna Zurcher, who worked as Fasnacht's secretary, hid refugees in their attic. Similarly the Canadian-born wife of the school's director, Amy Mae Charpiot, hid refugees in her home and guided them to the border.[29]

Some of Jean Weidner's false identity cards, 1942–44.

Like others in the group, these helpers used their everyday activities to camouflage their resistance. Jean Zurcher, for example, rode his bicycle to and from Geneva for graduate classes at the university. Similarly Jacques Tièche lived with his parents at the seminary and attended high school in Geneva.[30] Both carried illegal documents back and forth. They rarely had any difficulty, although Zurcher had a close call in late 1943.

One day while he was waiting in line at the Swiss border post at Croix de Rozon, opposite Collonges, a customs agent asked Zurcher sotto voce, "You don't have anything?" He opened his jacket to show him a thick packet of envelopes. The official murmured, "Poor man," and gestured at the

Left, Jean and Anna Zurcher, 1941; *right,* Roger Fasnacht, 1941.

Left, Maurice Mathy, 1941; *right,* Maurice Tièche (father of Jacques Tièche), 1941.

uniformed Germans who were searching everyone as they stepped across the border. Zurcher got the point and slipped out of the customs building, walking a short distance back into Switzerland, where he disposed of the incriminating papers in a mailbox.[31] Whether the customs agent knew of Zurcher's illegal activities or just guessed, the incident demonstrates how resisters relied on the goodwill and even collusion of the general public to survive.

On occasion Cartier too carried false documents, underground newspapers, and money between Geneva and Annecy or Lyon. On such trips she preferred to cross the border illegally near the railway bridge at Archamps. Like Zurcher and other guides, she hid from motorized patrols under the bridge on the highway that parallels the French side of the border, then ran across to Switzerland.[32] Cartier could have gone through any of the official border posts because she had a permanent visa to travel legally between the two countries from her job at the French consulate in Geneva. She must have decided that she was more likely to be searched at an official crossing than caught running across the fields. Or perhaps it was quicker than waiting in the lines to go through document inspection and customs.

Having solved the problem of getting fugitives through the Haute-Savoie, Weidner and Cartier faced the challenge of how to get them across the border itself. Weidner's earliest attempts proved to be unnecessarily dramatic. In July 1942 he took the first couple he helped—the acquaintances who had written from the French prison—down the cliff face of the Salève, the flat-topped promontory to the south of Geneva, using the metal rings inserted in the rock for mountain climbers. They hid in a rabbit hutch for two nights and then ran across the border. The couple arrived in Geneva in need of hospitalization for exposure and exhaustion but eternally grateful to Weidner for saving them.[33]

Around the same time a Dutch Christian and his French wife who had been helping German deserters in northern France and fled to Lyon asked Consul Jacquet for help because the Gestapo had found their trail. The first thing Weidner did was verify their identities to make sure they were not German agents provocateurs. Then the three of them took a taxi to the highway that runs along the border near Collonges. When they reached a curve, Weidner told the driver to slow down and the couple to roll out of the moving vehicle and run toward Switzerland.[34]

Obviously families with elderly parents or young children could not undertake such physically demanding crossings. The group at the seminary and Weidner worked out a system in which refugees would take the bus from Annecy but get off at the stop before Collonges to avoid a notorious police checkpoint in the village. From the bus stop they would walk uphill to the seminary. The refugees would spend the rest of the day at the Charpiot home, in the Zurcher attic, in the Fasnacht home, or in one of two unused rooms in a campus building. At nightfall the refugees would follow a guide into Switzerland. To get there they first needed to walk back downhill. From the seminary they could go almost straight down to Collonges or veer to the left toward Archamps or to the right toward Bossey, all three of which villages lie along the border. Zurcher took the Route de la Croisette, which runs along the Salève below the school farm.[35] If Charpiot were guiding refugees, she would take them along a goat path past La Combes, walking some way ahead of the fugitives and wearing a scarf. If she saw any

The railway bridge by Archamps, 1943.

police or border guards, she would signal the alarm by taking off her scarf. When she put the scarf back on, it was safe to continue.[36]

In part because they were Swiss, Fasnacht and Zurcher often guided refugees over the border. They used several crossing places, the most frequent starting under the railway bridge at Archamps that stands parallel to the two-lane highway that runs along the border. Refugees crossed the road there, scrambled through the barbed wire, ran through a lightly wooded field, crossed a stream that is deep enough to get an adult's legs wet but not likely to drown anyone, and then ran uphill through grapevines. Only after getting through the unofficial no man's land between the barbed wire and the crest of the hill were they safely in Switzerland.

The barbed-wire barricades changed over the course of the war, but in 1942 they were generally single strings of wire arranged like a fence. They scratched skin and tore clothing but were not dense enough to stop a person. The guides usually held up the wire for the fugitives to pass underneath. If Swiss guards turned the refugees back over the border and their French counterparts did not arrest them, Anna Zurcher would feed and shelter them until her husband and Weidner organized another attempt.[37]

Weidner, however, did not rely on one route or group to smuggle refugees over the border. If none of their local contacts was available, Weidner seized the opportunity of the moment. On at least one occasion he paid a professional *passeur*, or guide who passed people over borders illegally. Other rescue groups also had to pay *passeurs* when their own volunteers were busy, sick, or known to the police.[38]

Such professionals expected to be paid for risking being shot or imprisoned. In the Haute-Savoie they tended to be local farmers working with taxi drivers based in towns where refugees might be looking for a way into Switzerland. Reputable *passeurs* like these generally charged 3,000 to 5,000 French francs per person, about half of what a successful small businessman like Weidner could earn in a month.[39] Others were no better than swindlers (*escrocs*), abandoning their clients to the police after taking their money. Such *passeurs* charged up to 20,000 French francs per person, which was enough to make even French gendarmes feel sorry for Jewish refugees.[40] Both the French and the Swiss authorities punished professional *passeurs* harshly, "seeing them as nothing other than traffickers of men with no scruples about getting rich on others' misfortunes."[41]

Weidner and Cartier's third challenge, ensuring that refugees would be allowed to remain in Switzerland, posed much greater difficulties than the other two. Once over the border, refugees needed to return to strict legality in order to stay there. The Dutch embassy supported Dutch refugees financially and diplomatically, but only those with the legal right to be in Switzerland. And only Swiss officials could issue the coveted legitimate refugee permits and entrance visas.

Weidner and Cartier were never quite certain of the details of Swiss refugee policy, which changed without notice. Rather than manufacture their clients' false documents to fit Swiss requirements for age and family status, they made sure that everyone they helped had permission to stay in Switzerland before they arrived.[42]

Cartier made a useful friend in Corporal Ferdinand Demierre, a controversial figure known for his champion marksmanship. Demierre wielded much greater power than his rank would suggest because he ran the cantonal border protection office that granted or refused admittance to refugees.[43] Indeed he appeared to the Dutch military attaché in Bern to run the entire Geneva police force. He also had a reputation for being influenced by money and favoring Dutch applicants.[44] Starting in early summer 1942, Cartier sent many refugees to him for residency permits once they arrived in Geneva.

She did not, however, rely solely on Demierre. A few fugitives whom she and her colleagues helped figured on the list of *non-refoulables*, who would not be turned away at the border. This list represented a compromise between Swiss policy and public opinion worked out in early October 1942 by the Swiss authorities and a French pastor who represented the Protestant Federation of France. A few Dutch names, mainly of Christians seeking political asylum, made it on the list at the request of the Dutch embassy in Bern and of the Dutch secretary general of the World Council of Churches in Formation, Willem Visser 't Hooft.[45]

In most other cases Cartier persuaded an unidentified Swiss man and an unnamed Swiss woman to issue the necessary authorizations before the fugitives approached the border. In deference to the heavy penalties imposed on Swiss citizens convicted of compromising the nation's neutrality by participating in any resistance to the Nazis, Cartier never disclosed their identities, even after the war.[46] After she recruited these Swiss helpers sometime in the winter of 1942–43, Weidner's group no longer needed to worry about their fugitives being turned back into occupied territory.

The security of knowing that fugitives would be welcome in Switzerland added time to an escape because a refugee had to wait for his or her particulars to be taken to Switzerland, the paperwork processed, and the necessary documents smuggled back into France. Sometimes refugees spent that time in a French prison; sometimes they hid in Lyon or Annecy.

In addition, every journey incurred expenses for train tickets, black market food, false documents, and occasionally *passeurs*. In 1942 those refugees who could pay their own way did so. But Weidner never turned anyone away for lack of funds. He charged affluent refugees a little extra to subsidize the less wealthy, and when necessary he used his own money.[47] He may also have received some money from the consulate in Lyon.

Weidner did not keep records of the people he and his resistance colleagues smuggled into Switzerland because it would have been both dangerous and unnecessary in the context of the time. But the number lies close to one thousand. How did these fugitives find him? Some, as we've seen, were personal acquaintances who asked Weidner for help, just as some Dutch refugees already in Switzerland asked Cartier to help family members still in France or even the Netherlands. Most fugitives, however, found Weidner through referral. He had gained a reputation among charitable circles in the Haute-Savoie and Lyon as a man who spoke Dutch and had a way into Switzerland.[48]

In Lyon, Jacquet recommended individuals to him as likely candidates for the crossing. Neither Jacquet nor Weidner investigated claims of Dutch citizenship too carefully. They helped people who were not themselves Dutch but whose children had been born in the Netherlands, as well as refugees who had traveled through the Netherlands on their long journey from eastern Europe. After the war a Jewish man remembered that on a dark day in Vichy France he had felt obliged to tell Weidner, "Ik ben geen Nederlander" (I am not Dutch). Weidner had replied, "Ik ken geen Nederlanders. Ik ken alleen mensen" (I don't see Dutchmen. I see only human beings).[49]

Nonetheless the majority of the people they helped were Dutch if only because, for bureaucratic reasons, the person in need had to claim to be Dutch for the Dutch consulate to find him or her.[50] Furthermore refugees often heard about potential helpers, and helpers often heard about people in need, by word of mouth. The rumor of Weidner's ability to help circulated in Dutch and French, meaning that people heard about him as a helper of Dutch men and women.[51]

In fact Weidner's ability to get people into Switzerland became somewhat of an open secret. When Maurits and Helena Stoppelman and their daughter, Hélène, were arrested in October 1942 on a train in Haute-Savoie for not having the proper travel documents, they were sent to the prison in Annecy. After they served the standard one-month sentence, a French captain released the family at dawn with a recommendation to ask the bishop for assistance. He sent them to a local family, who told them there was a Dutchman in town who took people to Switzerland. They went to see Weidner that very day. Unusually the Stoppelman family chose to stay in Annecy to help Weidner with the shop and other refugees. They did not leave for Switzerland until they heard that the French authorities had renewed their interest in them.[52]

In other cases Weidner himself found the refugees in need of help, such as the Dutch businessman Nico Gazan and his wife, Mary Stibbe. As Gazan later told Swiss gendarmes, they left their home in Belgium because the German authorities considered him to be Jewish according to the Nuremburg Laws, although he did not identify himself as such.[53] When they and their three traveling companions reached Lyon, they hired a professional *passeur* to get them to Switzerland at the steep price of 15,000 French francs per person. Surprisingly they were able to send their baggage on ahead to Geneva through Cook's travel agency in Lyon.

All went well on their journey through Haute-Savoie and over the border until a Swiss gendarme and his dog apprehended the group on Swiss soil before dawn on July 9, 1942. He marched them back to the border, where another gendarme gave them each a cigarette. After making sure no French policemen were in sight, the Swiss guards turned the refugees back over the border. A few hours later French gendarmes arrested them at a hotel in Collonges because one of their *passeurs* had lodged a complaint against the other *passeur* for stealing his cut of the fee.[54]

The fugitives received the standard penalty for being near the border plus a 1,200-franc fine for successfully crossing it. Gazan whiled away his month in the dank prison of Annecy playing bridge with murderers and gold smugglers and discussing the deportations to Poland with other Jewish refugees. He also had an unexpected visit from Weidner and Cartier, who brought food.

Returning to Lyon after their release, the Gazans found Weidner in an uncharacteristically pessimistic mood; he had heard, quite accurately, that Vichy would no longer allow Jews from the Netherlands, Belgium, and Luxembourg to stay in *résidence assignée*. Instead they would be treated like Jewish refugees from the East, meaning they would be interned and deported. Fortunately Weidner's sources also led him to a loophole in the law regarding travel in the reserved zone along the Swiss border. Foreigners were still allowed to visit spas in the Haute-Savoie as long as they were not identified as Jews. The Dutch consulate therefore issued Gazan a new identification document stating that he was Catholic, and a French police commissioner issued him a safe conduct to travel in Haute-Savoie for reasons of health.[55]

The Gazans left Lyon for Annecy on September 6, 1942. Following Weidner's instructions, they avoided the surveillance at the train station there by going to get a glass of water while all the other passengers exited the platform. They spent the night hiding in an unidentified upstairs room. On a bus to the border the next day, Mary feigned an indisposition that forced them to get off before reaching their stated destination. Half an hour later they arrived on foot at Cartier's uncle's farm.[56]

That evening, around twilight, Weidner appeared in a taxi already full with other passengers. The Gazans squeezed in. Before long they arrived at the customs "post of Chable, entrance to the free zone. The *douaniers* stopped our car and demanded the papers…[*sic*] of the car."[57] The taxi's documents being in order, the people continued their journey without having to show any of their own papers.

After dropping off the other passengers in the village of Collonges, Weidner and the Gazans got out at the seminary above the village. They then walked back down the mountain to the border. Weidner introduced them to a *passeur*, who must have been a local man whom Weidner trusted but was not one of the volunteers in the group. Weidner paid him with money Gazan had given him. The *passeur* made Gazan memorize a hand-sketched map by the light of a flashlight, then took them through the barbed wire under a bridge and over the road by Bossey-Veryrier. Although the *passeur* had Gazan repeat the directions before he left, the couple became disoriented in the fog and worried that they had stumbled back into France until they saw the lights of a café. After making sure they were in Switzerland and warming up inside, they zigzagged their way to the number 12 tram line. Early on the morning of September 9 they knocked on Cartier's mother's door. She welcomed them with tea and a makeshift bed.

After reporting to the Dutch consulate in Geneva that afternoon, they were advised to submit to Swiss formalities. The Gazans were just two of the fourteen Dutch and Jewish civilian refugees who were reported having entered Switzerland illegally during the week of September 8, 1942. Two of their original companions also arrived that week, while the third waited in Lyon for his parents.[58] At their obligatory interview with Corporal Demierre, he explained that he "gave first priority to Dutchmen." He gave the Gazans temporary residence permits and made an open-ended reservation for them at the Hotel International et Terminus, which still stands a few blocks from the train station in Geneva. They were safe.

The following month proved to be difficult for Weidner and his colleagues because of intensified repression by French authorities. Weidner considered the French police in the Haute-Savoie, especially the douaniers, to be "extremely hard on refugees" before November 1942.[59] Their attitude came from the top. For example, the prefect of Haute-Savoie forbade taxis to carry foreign passengers, whether or not they were Jews, without police authorization. He also complained that Consul Jacquet was issuing certificates of Dutch nationality to foreign Jews "who are trying to establish their identity," which was quite true.[60]

This hardening of the official French attitude in October made the work of rescue even more dangerous for both refugees and helpers, as seen in the story of Simon and André Eliasar. A young Jewish man, André had made an earlier, failed attempt to leave occupied territory. The second time he left, he traveled with his father. They made their own, difficult way from their home in The Hague to Lyon, but moved to a mountain hotel after the roundups of foreign Jews in Lyon in August.[61] When the village constabulary warned them that a denunciation by a traitor obliged the police to come back the next morning to arrest them, the Eliasars returned to Lyon. A Dutch volunteer at the consulate sent them to Weidner, who agreed to help.

Weidner arranged for an Alsatian student at the seminary in Collonges to escort the Eliasars from Annecy to Switzerland. Unfortunately the douaniers at the customs barrier at Le Chable arrested all three of them in what Weidner termed an "excess of zeal."[62] Unlike other protégés of Weidner's, the Eliasars did not walk out of Annecy's prison after completing their one-month sentence on November 3. Instead they were escorted under guard to the horrendous internment camp at Rivesaltes in accordance with French law. Whatever strings Weidner and his colleagues usually pulled to make it possible for Dutch prisoners to disappear when they left the prison did not work that day.

Weidner himself had been apprehended on October 14 by French gendarmes at Les Cruseilles, halfway between Annecy and the border. Determined to make him confess that he had been passing refugees into Switzerland, they beat him with rifle butts brutally enough that he underwent surgery in the early 1950s to repair the damage to his brain.[63] Weidner spent two days in chains before the gendarmes gave up and released him for lack of evidence. In a letter to a Dutch friend in France, Cartier explained that her husband had been able to withstand the two days of mistreatment because on that particular day he had not been busy with his usual illegal activities. In fact on that day he had been in Switzerland to visit his wife and fetch potatoes, allowing him to maintain that he had not passed anyone to Switzerland.[64]

In the few short months from June or July 1942, when he received the letter from his acquaintance in prison, to that October, when he himself was beaten in a French prison, Weidner tipped completely into the civil disobedience of resistance. He and Cartier had mobilized their connections and relationships into a fully functioning escape line from Lyon through Annecy to Geneva. They could provide false documents for Lyon and the reserved zone of Haute-Savoie as well as legitimate refugee permits for Switzerland. They could move fugitives of all ages safely through the trains and buses and over the border and provide hiding

Simon and André Eliasar, Scheveningen, 1942.

places whenever necessary. They had helpers among civil servants in the prefectures and on the border and among the local residents along the way. They had not perfected their security measures, but these were good enough that the French police could not prove any wrongdoing on Weidner's part despite their suspicions.

The war, however, was about to intrude on the Haute-Savoie and change the circumstances of rescue there. The Allies invaded French North Africa on November 8, 1942, which gave the Germans an excuse to invade the Vichy zone on November 11. At the same time, their Italian allies expanded their occupation zone north and west to include the departments of Haute-Savoie and Savoie. Although Vichy maintained administrative jurisdiction in southern France, German police and soldiers now operated openly in Lyon. The Italian Army occupied Annecy and patrolled the French side of the Swiss border. The German presence made resistance work more dangerous in Lyon, but the Italian occupation opened up new possibilities for rescue in Haute-Savoie.

Gare de Lyon-Perrache, Lyon, France, 1938.

2

The Beginnings of Dutch-Paris

THE GERMAN INVASION OF THE VICHY ZONE on November 11, 1942, and subsequent expansion of the Italian occupation zone radically altered the geography of persecution and rescue in France because the Italian authorities protected Jews. They considered any attempts by French or German officials to identify or remove Jews from their zone as an attack on their own authority and refused to hand over anyone.[1] However, the Italians' willingness to protect refugees from deportation did not extend to letting them walk into Switzerland. Sometimes Italian guards in Haute-Savoie turned a blind eye to clandestine border crossers; sometimes they opened fire.[2]

Nonetheless word soon spread that Jews did not necessarily have to get to Switzerland with all the anxiety about being accepted as a refugee there in order to be safe from deportation. Refugees flooded into the Italian zone from other parts of France. Dutch Jews who had been hiding in Vichy now joined those arriving from the north in asking Weidner and his colleagues for help.[3] For those who wanted to stay in the Italian zone, they arranged residency permits through the office of the official French Jewish organization, the Union générale des Israélites de France, in Chambéry (Savoie).[4] The paperwork was handled by a Dutch civil servant named Peter Naeff, who had had considerable practice hiding refugees when he worked at the Dutch consulate in Perpignan before moving to Lyon in early 1943. Indeed in May 1943 Weidner attributed any rescues still happening in the Lyon region to Naeff's work.[5]

Among others, Simon Eliasar, who had been arrested in Haute-Savoie in October 1942, benefited from Italian protection. After serving a one-month prison term in Annecy, Eliasar and his son André were transferred to the French internment camp at Rivesaltes. Conditions there appalled even the Germans, who closed the camp down. The Eliasars were taken to another French camp, Gurs, which lay in the foothills of the Pyrenees, closer to Toulouse. As a result of considerable paperwork, Simon was released from Gurs on May 31, 1943, with permission to live under police surveillance in the village of Landry (Savoie).[6] André, however, had been sent with other young men in the camp to work on the Atlantic defenses as forced labor. He engineered his own escape and arrival in the Italian zone in June 1943 but chose not to stay with his father. Instead Weidner and Elisabeth Cartier arranged for him to cross into Switzerland. He claimed political rather than racial asylum on the grounds that the German police were looking for him because he was AWOL from his forced labor posting.[7] Having political reasons greatly increased his odds of being granted refugee status by the Swiss.

The change in the geography of persecution meant that Weidner and his colleagues started extending their assistance far beyond the Swiss border in order to help refugees hiding in Vichy to relocate to the Italian zone. The open presence of German police and troops in southern France and of Italian troops along the Swiss border complicated illegal journeys as well as making them more dangerous for both guides and fugitives. Italian troops captured one of Weidner's helpers from the Adventist seminary, wounding him in the eye before he escaped.[8] Before November 1942 it had been possible to tell a French-speaking refugee to make his or her own way to a meeting point. Now all refugees needed guides for their entire trip. Weidner and Cartier needed more helpers and more hiding places.[9]

Around this time a refugee named Edmond Chait accepted Weidner's invitation to join the escape line. Like Weidner, Chait was born in Belgium

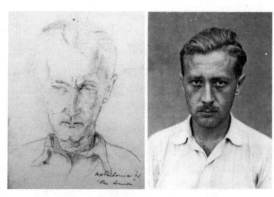

Left, Simon Eliasar, Gurs, 1943; *right*, André Eliasar, Switzerland, 1943.

in 1912. During the First World War his parents passed him through the barbed wire
along the Belgian-Dutch border to live with
his grandparents in the Netherlands, where
food was less scarce. During the Second World
War, Chait worked in the clandestine
Comité de Défense des Juifs in Antwerp. In
1942 he and his brother escaped to Lyon,
where they lived on Dutch papers supplied
by an uncle. French police arrested Chait as a
foreign Jew at a document inspection in July
or August that year. Because Chait had Dutch

Edmond Chait, 1943.

papers, Consul Jacquet was able to arrange his release from the prison of
St-Paul a few months later in November, just days before the Germans
officially arrived in the city.[10]

Chait volunteered as a translator at the consulate, but before long he
was helping Weidner arrange passage to Switzerland by delivering false
documents and escorting refugees to Annecy.[11] Weidner would come to
rely on him completely. Their resistance colleagues loved him for his sense
of humor and his uncanny ability to find good food anywhere. Those he
helped respected him for his absolutely professional demeanor when on
the job. U.S. military officials who interviewed him after the Liberation
described him as "refreshingly modest."[12]

Most people who joined the escape line at this time lived and worked
between Lyon and Geneva. The German invasion of southern France made
it somewhat easier to recruit local helpers, especially among French officials. Before November 1942 a French citizen who resisted rebelled against a
legally constituted, if morally compromised, French government. After that
date resistance had the more obviously patriotic cast of striking against
the foreign enemy.[13] On the other hand, with German police established
throughout the country, resistance became even more dangerous than it
had been before. It remained a minority activity.

Weidner and Cartier recruited new helpers from among their resistance, professional, and social circles. By late 1942 both of them had
contacts with other resistance groups working along the border.
Weidner knew other rescuers, and Cartier knew individuals involved
in intelligence work, presumably through her connections at the
French consulate in Geneva. With its location in a neutral country and

close to the French border, Geneva drew spies as well as refugees during the war. It made a good base for gathering intelligence from occupied territory.

For example, a captain at the French consulate in Geneva intro-duced Cartier to one of his illegal couriers in February 1943. That man simply added her documents to those he was already smuggling for a French intelligence network.[14] Cartier met Arthur Charroin in similar circumstances. As a French police inspector in the customs office of the subprefecture of St-Julien, which lies on the French side of the border, Charroin traveled regularly between Geneva, Annecy, and St-Julien on official business. He used those trips to carry unofficial documents for Allied intelligence networks and French resistance groups as well as to usher people over the border discreetly. When Cartier introduced Weidner to him in November 1942, Charroin agreed to pass docu-ments to one of their contacts among the Swiss customs officers and to facilitate illegal crossings by Weidner and other Dutchmen. Even though they had two elementary school–age daughters who would be orphaned if they were arrested, his wife, Alice, worked alongside her husband as a courier.[15]

By that time Weidner and Cartier were becoming well-known among French resisters for having a reliable route out of occupied territory and being willing to use it to assist other groups when they had people or docu-ments they needed to get in or out of Switzerland. As just one example, Weidner arranged a trip to Switzerland for François de Menthon, a leader of the national French resistance movement Combat who became minister of justice in de Gaulle's provisional government in 1944.[16] Later, when he was preparing to take de Menthon's family from their home near Annecy to Geneva, Weidner worked with a high-ranking police officer who was also in the resistance. After that Weidner could rely on timely warnings of police movements in the department, which saved him and several fugitives from arrest.[17]

As important as such connections among other resisters were for their own escape line, Weidner and Cartier recruited most of their helpers from among their professional and social circles. In June 1943, for example, a French customs collector working in St-Julien and living near the Adventist seminary joined their network.[18] To shelter refugees, they enlisted the proprietors of hotels and cafés in Annecy, as well as a pharmacy and a hotel in Les Cruseilles, halfway between the city and the border.[19] Similarly their partner in Annecy, Mademoiselle Meunier, recruited her friend, a Madame Voisin, to take people and documents to the Swiss border.[20]

In rare cases Weidner relied on his intuitive judgment to recruit a helper when an opportunity arose. It was risky, but in the end he had to rely on that same intuition when recruiting anyone, whether he had known them for years or been recently introduced. His instinct was good enough to steer him away from the agents provocateurs who fooled other Dutch resisters in Paris.

He found a new guide this way in February 1943 when he was eating dinner at a restaurant near Les Cruseilles, where he had been arrested four months earlier. The owner introduced Weidner to a distant cousin who was hiding from the compulsory French labor draft (Service du Travail Obligatoire, STO). By refusing to work in the Third Reich, nineteen-year-old Ernest Bouchet had already put himself outside the law. Weidner offered him what he eventually offered all his full-time agents: a modest stipend and reimbursement of expenses, such as train tickets. By accepting the job as a guide, Bouchet chose to resist rather than hide.

As a guide Bouchet would fetch refugees from Meunier's or Weidner's shop or some other hiding place in Haute-Savoie and take them by bus and by foot to the Café des Lilas in the small village of Les Mouilles outside St-Julien. He'd return at nightfall with a couple of friends to escort the refugees to the border. One of them would carry some of the heavy suitcases that every refugee seemed to have fifty yards or so ahead of the rest of the group. That way any unexpected patrols that came along would surprise a lone Frenchman who could engage them long enough to give the others time to hide. Once at the border the helpers would lift up the barbed wire so the adults could crawl under it, shove the suitcases after them, and pass the children through to the adults. Bouchet disliked this part the most because the little ones usually cried, which made his own return to France more dangerous by alerting any nearby border guards.[21]

Demand for help from the escape line never slowed because the German presence in the southern zone emboldened the Vichy regime's anti-Semitism. Even before November 1942 Vichy had intensified its persecution by limiting the movement and tagging the identification documents and ration cards of Jews.[22] After it the Etat Français allowed the deportation of foreign Jews from internment camps in southern France. In February and March 1943 the convoys from Vichy France included Dutch Jews.

Dutch refugees lost their previously favored status in Vichy France in November 1942 when the Dutch government in exile stopped sending money to support Dutch nationals to its consuls in southern France for fear that it would land in enemy hands. In response, the French authorities went so far as to imprison the Dutch consul-general despite his diplomatic immunity.[23] This diplomatic argument had serious practical consequences for Dutch expatriates and refugees living in France, none of whom could access their bank accounts in the Netherlands. In January 1943 the hand-ful of Dutch officials still working in Vichy's office for foreign residents and at the few consulates that remained open ran out of money to distrib-ute. Dutch pensioners could no longer pay their rent or their grocery bills. More seriously, Dutch Jews living in *résidence assignée* could no longer meet the monthly financial requirements and risked being sent to internment camps, from whence they were increasingly likely to be deported.

Because the diplomatic situation blocked the official channels for distributing assistance, Weidner, Jacquet, Naeff, and a few other Dutch expatriates in Lyon created a nonpolitical committee in the hope that the French and Germans would allow them to distribute money to Dutch nationals in the Vichy zone.[24] Weidner and Naeff used their own money to pay the allotments, totaling 350,000 French francs in February 1943, but they could not continue to do so indefinitely.[25] They were a small business-man and a civil servant, not millionaires. The committee delegated Weidner to go to Bern to ask the Dutch ambassador, J. J. B. Bosch van Rosenthal, who was loyal to the government in exile in London, for the necessary funds.

Weidner wrote to Cartier at her mother's home outside Geneva, who talked to Nico Gazan. Eager to help the couple who had brought him food in Annecy's prison and arranged his safe haven in Switzerland, Gazan made an appointment for Weidner to speak to the ambassador three weeks later. Weidner arrived in Switzerland several days ahead of time without going through the formalities at the border.

On March 23, 1943, he took the train from Geneva to Bern to speak to the ambassador. That evening Gazan ran into a discouraged Weidner at the station buffet. Bosch van Rosenthal had been sympathetic but had not agreed to do anything more than send a report to London. On the train back to Geneva, Gazan offered to introduce Weidner to an influential Dutch expatriate named Willem Visser 't Hooft. Gazan had met the pastor at a wedding and recently taken a job assembling care packages for POWs at the World Council of Churches in Formation (WCC), of which Visser 't Hooft was secretary general.

The next morning, Weidner and Cartier met with Visser 't Hooft, who had toured Vichy internment camps earlier in the war. The pastor did more than sympathize. He helped them come up with a plan to raise funds in Switzerland and handed Weidner a letter that authorized a Protestant pastor in France to release 100,000 French francs to him to distribute to Dutch refugees.[26] It was not enough to cover the pensions of Dutch expatriates, but it helped refugees, who could get by on 2,000 or so French francs per month.

The plan involved recruiting prominent Dutch expatriates in Switzerland to a new Comité Oecuménique pour les Réfugiés (Ecumenical Committee for Refugees). As the committee's secretary, Gazan typed out carbon copies of a circular in Dutch, French, and English in his hotel room. It pleaded for donations for the 1,200 Dutch Jewish refugees in France who, it explained, had been stripped of diplomatic help and were "in danger of slowly dying of starvation and misery."[27] Gazan mailed them to every potential donor whose address he could find. He also acted as a go-between for Weidner and the Dutch authorities, translating messages from Weidner's French to embassy Dutch whenever necessary. In addition to the circular that was aimed at wealthy, established residents of Switzerland, Weidner asked Dutch refugees there to contribute. He found the response disappointing.[28]

As welcome as any donations collected in Geneva were, whether they came from the WCC, the committee, or refugees, they posed a problem that Weidner and his colleagues would face over and over during the course of the war. The money raised in Switzerland was in Swiss francs, but the individuals who needed it could use only French, or later Belgian, francs to pay for anything they needed, from rent to medicine. The money had to be exchanged, but doing so legally involved paying taxes and drawing unwanted scrutiny. Of course a vibrant black market accommodated those needing discretion, but the rates were extortionate and the characters unsavory. And it would not solve the problem of moving large sums from one country to another on a regular basis. Not only did the German occupation authorities control currency exchanges and transfers through banks and other official channels, but a dedicated police force monitored the flow of cash and other valuables at the borders and in the big cities.[29]

Weidner and his colleagues, many of whom were businessmen or civil servants, devised several private methods of currency exchange and transfer.[30] One required the complicity of someone with bank accounts in more than one country. Because of his business, Weidner himself had accounts at banks in Paris, Lyon, and Geneva. In spring 1943 he and the Swiss committee came to such an agreement. Weidner distributed his own French francs to needy Dutch in France, who signed receipts on scraps of paper in exchange for the cash. After Weidner submitted the receipts in Switzerland, the committee reimbursed him by depositing Swiss francs into his account in Geneva. By late May Weidner had collected receipts for 295,000 French francs, and the committee had collected the equivalent of 200,000 French francs to reimburse him.[31] This could only be a short-term solution because the written receipts endangered whoever carried them and Weidner did not have limitless funds. He would eventually empty his own accounts.

This system worked equally well for moving money from the Netherlands to Belgium and from Belgium to France. In some cases families cooperated in such private transfers. For example, a Jewish refugee gave a certain sum in guilders to a man living in Maastricht. When the refugee arrived in Brussels, he contacted the man's son. The son gave him cash in Belgian francs equivalent to the sum deposited in his father's account in guilders at the official rate. This was far safer and financially advantageous for the refugee than exchanging the guilders on the black market would have been.[32]

Weidner's association with Visser 't Hooft at the WCC gave him access to a second method of exchanging and transferring currency: the channels used by French Protestants living in Switzerland to send money to rescuers in France. In one scenario Weidner took a letter of credit from the WCC in Geneva to a contact in Lyon, who cashed it for him.[33] But these borrowed channels were not foolproof. When Weidner knocked on the door of Visser 't Hooft's associate in Lyon in March 1943, the man had already distributed to other recipients the 100,000 French francs Visser 't Hooft had promised Weidner.[34] To avoid this and other misunderstandings, the pastor in charge of the Ecumenical Commission for Refugees of the WCC preferred to exchange Swiss francs collected on behalf of Dutch refugees at the official exchange rate, using his office's reserves of French francs. He would then send a courier over the Swiss border with a large packet of cash to deliver to Weidner at his home in Lyon.[35] Dutch expatriates in southern France also tried to raise loans to cover the allotments, but they made little progress without a written guarantee for the loan from the government in exile.[36]

Weidner continued to plead for government assistance as the only long-term solution. In a letter dated April 20, 1943, that he sent to the Dutch authorities via Gazan, he wrote that not one refugee had "received a single sou" through official channels and that if he and Naeff had done nothing the refugees would not have had enough to eat. He was particularly concerned about young Dutchmen like André Eliasar who had been taken out of Vichy's internment camps to do slave labor on the coastal defenses. "It is absolutely necessary to help these men without delay," he wrote. "We can raise funds, etc., but it will be quicker if we can do so in the form of loans with guaranteed repayment."[37] Under the name Henri Meunier, Weidner reiterated his pleas in May and June 1943 and February 1944.[38] In July 1943 he even sent a letter directly to the government in exile in London by the hand of François de Menthon, the French resistance leader whom he helped get into Switzerland.[39]

Part of the Dutch financial crisis in southern France resolved itself in April 1943, when the government in exile resumed sending money to support its citizens there via the Swedish embassy. This official money, however, could be distributed only through Vichy's bureau in charge of foreigners, which would not pay out any to Jews. For Dutch Jews or anyone else who did not want to make himself or herself known to the French authorities, the government in exile authorized the ambassador in Bern to borrow the considerable sum of 200,000 Swiss francs, or the equivalent of 11 million French francs at the official exchange rate. In August 1943 he contracted a standard, legal loan for half the amount at 3.5 percent interest from Crédit Suisse with the help of a Dutch expatriate whom Visser 't Hooft had first approached about the matter at a wedding.[40] All that money was spent on rescuing fugitives in France and Belgium in just six months.

However they raised the money, Weidner and his colleagues still had to distribute it to fugitives hidden throughout southern France and to men and women in internment camps or work units who had no legal right to receive it. For those in hiding Weidner and his colleagues developed a system of disbursal built on the official Dutch apparatus used before November 1942. Some of the money went to the few trustworthy consuls still working in southern France, such as Jacquet, who delivered it to refugees in hiding. Other fugitives received their allotments directly from Raymonde Pillot, Ernest Bouchet, or other couriers.

In order to get cash to prisoners, Weidner gave names and money to those humanitarian organizations sanctioned by Vichy to enter the camps and prisons, such as the Red Cross, the Quakers, and CIMADE. Weidner also asked these aid workers to identify any Dutch nationals under their care. When possible he used some of the money to send prisoners packages with food and clothing or to arrange their release from those noxious places.[41] In effect Weidner created what Visser 't Hooft later described as "a one-man relief agency" for Dutch refugees.[42]

Although most of the people whom Weidner and his colleagues helped in 1942 and early 1943 were Jews, another category of Dutchman on the lam in southern France increasingly drew on Weidner's resources and talents. These were the Engelandvaarders, so called because they left the occupied Netherlands to join Queen Wilhelmina in England. Some meant to join the Allied armies to fight, others to lend their expertise to the Dutch government in exile. Some tried their luck at crossing the North Sea, while others made their way with or without the help of escape lines via neutral Sweden or Spain. Some Engelandvaarders reported to the Dutch authorities in Switzerland without realizing they could not get to England directly from there. Others headed for Spain because the British held the fortress at Gibraltar on the southern tip of the Iberian Peninsula, and on the Atlantic Coast the Portuguese allowed ships to leave for England. Of course they gambled that Franco's regime would allow them to traverse nominally neutral Spain. Some Engelandvaarders spent many miserable months in Spanish internment camps; others passed through the country with little bother at all.[43]

The number of Engelandvaarders in France increased in the spring of 1943 in reaction to German attempts to squeeze more labor out of the Dutch. On March 13 the occupation authorities there introduced a loyalty oath for Dutch university students. The 85 percent who refused to sign lost their exemptions from labor conscription, which the Germans had imposed a year earlier. The next month the German authorities announced plans to intern Dutch soldiers.[44] All these students and soldiers now faced the same choice: unless they had jobs with official exemptions from forced labor, they could work (or fight) for the Germans, probably in Germany itself; surrender themselves as POWs; go into hiding; or leave the Netherlands. Of the estimated 1,700 Engelandvaarders, around 200 crossed France with the assistance of Weidner and his network.

Engelandvaarders came to Weidner's attention in the same ways that Jewish refugees did: they knew him personally; the consulate in Lyon referred them; or they were brought to his attention by his contacts in France. One young Dutchman, for example, knocked on Weidner's door because he was engaged to Weidner's younger sister, Annette, who was living with their parents in The Hague. Lykele Faber had made his own way to Paris, where he introduced himself to his (surprised) future sister-in-law, Gabrielle Weidner. She arranged for him to travel on from Paris to Annecy to join her brother. Faber helped Weidner with the escape line in and around Annecy for a couple of months before leaving for Spain in October 1943. After reaching England in December, he trained as a Dutch secret agent, twice parachuting behind enemy lines.[45] Faber survived the war, but the couple did not marry.

In most cases in 1942, however, Engelandvaarders found Weidner because French men and women asked him to take them off their hands. These Dutchmen had made their way to Switzerland, where they came under the control of General A. G. van Tricht, who had spent his career in the Netherlands East Indies and retired in 1938. He came out of retirement to serve the queen's government in exile as military attaché at the Dutch embassy in Bern. In addition to acting as a liaison, particularly with his American and British counterparts, Van Tricht bore official responsibility for all Dutch refugees in Switzerland. He combined this role with his military duties by making it possible for Dutchmen in Switzerland to join the Dutch forces in England. Before July 1942 he did this by selecting men with previous military training from among the refugees and infiltrating them in the so-called sealed trains. These trains took Jewish passengers from Switzerland to Spain without allowing anyone to get on or off in France. When the Swiss ended this arrangement under pressure from the Germans, Van Tricht had no alternative route.[46]

He assigned J. G. van Niftrik to find one. A Dutch reserve officer who had run a successful escape line over the Dutch-Belgian border earlier in the war, Van Niftrik made some extremely useful friendships in the Swiss intelligence services and proved to have a knack for hiding microfilm in everyday objects. Lacking personal knowledge of France, he interviewed refugees who arrived in Switzerland until he had pieced together a string of addresses where they had found help. He then sent small parties of Engelandvaarders to those places on the assumption that help would be forthcoming.[47] Unexpectedly faced with young Dutchmen, some of whom did not speak French, blend in, or have acceptable false documents, the helpers at these addresses usually called Weidner.

Before December 1942 Weidner found ways to get these men to the Dutch consuls in Perpignan and Toulouse, who were sending fugitives over the mountains into Spain.[48] The consuls' arrests in early 1943, however, closed the route from Perpignan. Weidner shifted his attention to Toulouse, where the acting consul had found a route over the Pyrenees. Nonetheless these Engelandvaarders were causing enough trouble for his contacts in Haute-Savoie that they figured high on Weidner's agenda when he made a second visit to Bern in August 1943.

In June Weidner requested another interview with the ambassador on behalf of the expatriate committee in Lyon, but it took several weeks for the embassy to arrange the necessary permissions with the Swiss. Weidner's usual source for such things could not help him at that time.[49] The Swiss authorities would not issue him a standard two-week visa without a valid return visa to France, which Weidner could not even apply for without compromising his illegal work by alerting the French gendarmerie to his conversations with the Dutch embassy. But the Swiss did agree to allow Weidner into the country if notified when and where he would cross the border. The embassy accordingly informed the Dutch consulate in Geneva to tell Cartier to tell her husband to let them know when he would arrive or, if time were short, to give that information to the Swiss consul in Annemasse, France. The consul there was on good enough terms with Weidner, or perhaps Cartier, that he carried documents across the border for them on his commute to and from his home in Geneva.[50]

Weidner crossed the Swiss border near St-Julien in the late afternoon of a day in early August. Ten minutes later he turned himself in to a Swiss gendarme. The gendarme found Weidner's name on the list of people who should not be *refouler* with instructions to telephone a certain lieutenant in Bern immediately.

After making the call, the gendarme went through the usual procedures for illegal entrants into the country. In answer to the questionnaire, Weidner claimed that he had come to Switzerland solely on "Dutch affairs" and to visit his wife and mother-in-law. The gendarme confiscated all of Weidner's valuables, including a pocketful of international change in pounds Sterling, U.S. and Canadian dollars, and French and Swiss francs. The cash was deposited in his name at the *Schweizerische Volksbank*, and a receipt for the total (minus 6 Swiss francs in fees) was duly forwarded to his mother-in-law's address.[51] It took more than one letter to get it back.

Like the refugees he and Cartier smuggled into the country, Weidner was sent to a reception center. But unlike those refugees, he was put under the authority of Lieutenant Paul Frossard de Saugy of the Geneva bureau of the Swiss Service des renseignements (SR, intelligence service).[52]

Weidner spent the week after being released from the reception center talking to the ambassador and Visser 't Hooft about Dutch refugees in France. He also spoke to Van Niftrik about the inadequate preparation of the Engelandvaarders he was sending into France. They agreed that Van Niftrik would equip the men in Switzerland and that Van Tricht would pay for the trips between Switzerland and Spain, but that Weidner would take responsibility for the men's passages across France and over the Pyrenees into Spain. The Swiss SR saw Weidner safely back under the barbed wire into France two weeks after his arrival.[53] From then on Weidner considered himself a member of the Swiss SR and had no trouble at the border, whether he wanted to come or go, openly or covertly.

Weidner had good cause to move cautiously when he returned to France, where the police clearly suspected his activities. Indeed Weidner had been held in chains and beaten with rifle butts by French gendarmes in October 1942. And he had had other encounters with the police since then. In April 1943 French gendarmes questioned him at his shop in Lyon because his name had been found in papers left behind by a young Dutch woman who had disappeared from the internment camp at Chateauneuf-les-Bains. Weidner convinced the officers that he had nothing to do with her disappearance, though he had in fact organized it.[54]

Not long afterward German police questioned both Weidner and Jacquet about another missing Dutch Jew. The Germans claimed that the refugee had given them Weidner's name. Again Weidner feigned innocence. Afterward he wrote an angry letter to the refugee, who was by then safely in Switzerland. Weidner reminded the man that without his and his colleagues' help he and his wife would be on a train to "die in Poland." He berated the refugee for "selfishness," for caring only about himself and not for those coming after him, and for writing down his, Weidner's, name and thus endangering the entire network. Worst of all, the refugee had not thanked the Swiss woman who had arranged his residency permit, despite being asked to do so. This Swiss helper had grown tired of taking risks for ungrateful strangers. After the war Weidner withdrew some of his accusations on the grounds that the Germans probably lied when they said the refugee gave them his name. But at the time, when he and his colleagues lived with constant danger in order to help strangers such as that refugee, his anger and frustration were very real.[55]

The Germans were not the only authorities taking notice of Weidner. The French Renseignements généraux (political police) had questioned him in Lyon a year earlier, in August 1942. They were investigating an anonymous letter of denunciation about his wife, accusing her of traveling to Switzerland at will on a passport issued by the consulate in Geneva when she should have been under the control of the police in Lyon because that was her husband's legal residence. The letter may have been motivated by someone envying Cartier's access to Swiss luxuries such as chocolate and coffee rather than any knowledge of her resistance work. But it interested the French authorities enough to order an investigation and therefore put the escape line at risk.[56]

The investigating officer, a young man only recently qualified for the job, gave the couple a glowing recommendation. The fact that her father had been killed in action during the First World War counted heavily in Cartier's favor. Weidner himself impressed the officer with his good job that brought in 8,000 to 10,000 French francs per month. The investigator explained the couple's lack of a permanent residence as the result of Weidner's business travel and noted that Weidner intended to move out of the hotel and establish a permanent home for his wife. Until then she spent most of her time with her mother in Geneva. Her superiors at the consulate there spoke well of her. The Renseignements généraux report concluded that Cartier was "very patriotic, she had worked a great deal for French POWs and there is no cause to consider her suspect."[57] Even though this particular incident was settled in their favor, neither Weidner nor Cartier could be certain that the anonymous letter writer would not try again with a different French police unit or with the Germans. Nor could they be sure of such a sympathetic investigating officer in the future.

French and German police had also been showing a disturbing interest in some of Weidner's colleagues. In June 1943 Weidner wrote that things in Lyon were "very hard" and that two guides (identities unknown) had been arrested. That summer the Gestapo came to the Dutch consulate, asking for Chait by both his brother's name and his own nom de guerre of the moment, Moreau.[58] Around that time Weidner's contact in the police in Annecy warned Weidner that he was *brûlé* in the region, meaning his cover was blown, because of the imprudence of a *passeur*.[59]

The brushes with the police involving Weidner's network reached a climax on September 6, 1943, when German police arrested Jacquet in Lyon as well as the secretary-general of the consular corps there. Both men underwent "serious questioning" regarding the disappearance of Dutch Jews but were not mishandled. The Spanish consul secured their release after five days.

As Jacquet remembered it, "These gentlemen of the Gestapo made me understand that if I wish to avoid further trouble, it would be preferable if I do not involve myself in the future with Dutch affairs, but, nevertheless, they made me promise not to abandon my welfare activities or the distribution of aid."[60] Presumably the Gestapo meant he should continue to help non-Jewish Dutch nationals with bureaucratic paperwork and money so they did not cause any difficulties for the occupation authorities, but that he should have nothing to do with Dutch resisters or Jews. This changed Jacquet's official title from consul to social assistant, but it did not dissuade him from using any and all means to help refugees.[61] It did make the insurance office that housed the consulate too dangerous for members of the organization, however. Pillot did not return there after Jacquet's arrest for fear that it was being watched or used as a trap. Indeed the Gestapo reappeared there at random intervals throughout the rest of the occupation.[62]

On the day they arrested Jacquet, the Germans also looked for Weidner and Naeff at their official addresses. Naeff very sensibly decided that this signaled the end of his own resistance work in France. He first fled to the home of an expatriate resister near the Spanish border, but then decided to go to Switzerland for health reasons.[63] Weidner himself stayed in the Alps to respond to the crisis caused by the Italian capitulation, which took place that same week, on September 8. German troops henceforth took control of what had been the Italian zone of occupation, putting every Jew whom Weidner and his colleagues had hidden in Haute-Savoie and Savoie in immediate danger of deportation. They needed to be warned, advised, and perhaps moved.

Eleven days after Jacquet's arrest, on September 17, a French customs agent in St-Julien-en-Genevois smuggled both Naeff and Weidner over the border into Switzerland in broad daylight a mere thirty feet from German soldiers. He did it in stages, taking one man at a time along the small path behind the customs buildings with a two-hour break between them. He took their personal baggage into Switzerland the next day.[64] Naeff described himself to the Swiss authorities as a fugitive who was wanted by the German police and in bad health. He spent the rest of the war working in the embassy's refugee office.[65]

Weidner now faced a choice for both himself and the escape line: he could remain safely in Switzerland with Cartier, who had left France for the duration of the war after Jacquet's arrest. Or he could return to France, which was now wholly occupied by the Germans, and live as a wanted man. He would have to abandon his life as Jean Weidner, respectable business owner, and go completely underground. A clandestine life required constant changes of alias, a series of false documents, and no fixed abode. It would be a life permeated by fear. Weidner spent two weeks in Switzerland, talking to Ambassador Bosch van Rosenthal, General van Tricht, and Visser 't Hooft.

Then he went back to France.

When he returned, he did so as the Dutch embassy's unofficial man in France and Belgium. He and his colleagues now had a threefold mission: assist Dutch refugees in need in occupied territory, escort Engelandvaarders to Spain, and carry microfilm between the Netherlands, Switzerland, and Spain.

Weidner's new, if unacknowledged, role as a sort of Dutch ambassador at large in occupied France and Belgium consisted mainly in distributing cash to Dutch men and women in hiding and bringing those in danger to Switzerland. Except for scale, neither of these differed greatly from what he and his colleagues had already been doing. Occasionally, however, Weidner did speak for the Dutch authorities in Switzerland. In late 1943, for example, Bosch van Rosenthal sent Weidner to the town of

Vichy to hold secret negotiations with French officials regarding the distribution of monetary aid to Dutch citizens in France. While he was there he also delivered a large sum of cash to the last ranking Dutch civil servant working in the Etat Français's bureaucracy.[66]

Weidner and his colleagues also continued to arrange the journeys of small groups of Engelandvaarders from Switzerland to Spain and to take refugees from across France to Switzerland. On occasion they escorted particular individuals at the request of the government in exile, but for the most part they continued to pick up fugitives where they found them. What changed was the distances they traveled. After September 1943 they extended the escape line all the way through northern France and Belgium into the Netherlands. And in early 1944 they started taking downed Allied aviators to Spain.

The third component of the mission—the intelligence work of ferrying microfilm—was the newest for the group. Of course couriers, especially Edmond Chait, had carried any number of papers before, but that had mostly been on an ad hoc basis of doing a favor for a friend. Adding another letter or envelope of cash to a journey that a courier was already making did not greatly increase his or her risks. Visser 't Hooft, however, asked them to set up a regular courier route for an intelligence network involving the Dutch Resistance and the Dutch government in exile and called the Zwitserse Weg, or Swiss Way.

As the secretary-general of the WCC based in Geneva, the pastor had been able to travel to London in early 1942. Struck by how truly cut off the London Dutch were from events and opinions in the occupied Netherlands, Visser 't Hooft had offered to act as a conduit of information between the government in exile and the Dutch people. He and resisters in the Netherlands created an ingenious system of hiding microfilm in the spines of esoteric academic books and mailing them to and from Sweden by regular post.[67] The process of making microfilms by photographing documents and peeling layers off the negatives was little known at the time but necessary to reduce the size. The resisters in the Netherlands sent reports on all aspects of civilian life, such as public opinion, public health, maintenance of the dikes and other vital infrastructure, activities of the occupation authorities, and copies of underground newspapers. The postal route, however, proved slow. Visser 't Hooft wanted Weidner to organize a faster and more flexible delivery service.

For security reasons Weidner kept the Swiss Way secret from almost all his colleagues, picking only a handful of couriers to carry the microfilm. Visser 't Hooft's associates in Geneva hid the film in fountain pens, hairbrushes, flashlights, and the like. They also coordinated the biweekly rendezvous in Belgium with their colleagues in Amsterdam and told Weidner the passwords of the week. At the military attaché's office, Van Niftrik made up false documents for the Swiss Way couriers that identified the men as employees of the Belgian Chamber of Commerce. Weidner, however, did not waste a journey across two borders on a single task. He or another courier combined the biweekly trip to exchange microfilm for the Swiss Way with other concerns, such as delivering money, making arrangements with colleagues, or escorting fugitives. The courier simply disappeared for a half day to make the microfilm exchange without telling anyone else about it.

As a condition of accepting these three missions, Weidner demanded complete autonomy in occupied territory. He felt deeply responsible for the safety of everyone in his network and did not think that anyone in Switzerland could appreciate the circumstances in occupied territory well enough to make decisions that might risk his people's safety. The ambassador, the military attaché, and Visser 't Hooft agreed. They would ask Weidner to deliver a microfilm on a specific date, talk to a certain person, or escort particular people of interest to the government in exile from the Netherlands to Spain, but Weidner alone would decide how any of those tasks would be accomplished and by whom. They also gave Weidner the autonomy to help refugees as he saw fit without putting any restrictions on who could or could not benefit from Dutch money. The funds for helping refugees came from the ambassador, Visser 't Hooft, and the expatriate committee in Switzerland. Van Tricht paid for the passages of Engelandvaarders, certain individuals on the run from the Gestapo, and aviators. Reimbursement for the travel expenses of Weidner and his full-time agents came from both Visser 't Hooft and Van Tricht. That usually covered hotel rooms, train tickets, and food, although it could also be used for false documents, disguises, and bribes.[68]

Before Weidner could accomplish any of these tasks, however, he needed to expand his network beyond Lyon and the Haute-Savoie to include the length of France and Belgium, from the Dutch border to the Swiss and Spanish borders. He knew the challenges from the start. A route as ambitious as this one would have to operate in two languages, five currencies, and five permutations of false documents. It would have to find illegal paths across four borders. It would require up-to-date information about the current policies and practices of repression in six distinct occupation zones, not to mention knowledge about which police forces were operating where. Weidner, Cartier, and Chait would need the help of not just a few trusted associates, but of hundreds of like-minded men and women.

Gare du Nord, Brussels, 1950.

3

Extending the Line through Brussels

IF WEIDNER AND HIS COLLEAGUES WERE GOING TO ESCORT fugitives from the Netherlands to Spain and relay microfilm from Geneva to Amsterdam, they were obviously going to have to extend their activities far outside of the Vichy zone and enlist many more helpers. Two facts of civilian life during the occupation determined the route for the extended network.

First, ordinary citizens traveled by public transport, by bicycle, or on foot. Private automobiles and the gasoline to run them were reserved for the Germans, their collaborators, and necessary services, such as those performed by doctors and clergy. Anyone who wanted to avoid notice took the train. Couriers like Weidner and his colleagues and those they helped went where the trains went, missed appointments if the trains were delayed, and risked injury from aerial bombardment or sabotage, just like all the other passengers.[1]

The railways had been built as national systems using the capital cities as hubs. That meant that anyone coming south from the Netherlands had to go through Brussels to get to Paris. The trains crossed the border at Feignes, where passengers disembarked once again to go through passport inspection and customs before reclaiming their seats on the same train. In Paris trains from Brussels arrived at one train station, the gare du Nord, but trains to Lyon and trains to Toulouse departed from the gare de Lyon and the gare d'Austerlitz, respectively. Passengers had to make their own way from one station to the next by Métro, bus, or taxi or on foot. Fugitives who were unfamiliar with the city ran a real risk of getting lost and of drawing the attention of police in the train stations and on the streets.

In addition civilians in France required different documents than civilians in Belgium or the Netherlands. Unless fugitives had travel papers authorizing them to travel a long distance, they needed a different set of false documents in France than the set they used in Belgium. The extended escape line was going to need colleagues in both Brussels and Paris to guide fugitives between train stations, shelter them overnight when necessary, and provide locally valid documents.

Second, the occupation authorities and the Vichy regime censored civilian mail, telegrams, and telephone calls. The only way to be certain that a message had been delivered and that it had not been intercepted en route was to deliver it by hand. Arrangements for something as complicated as an escape across western Europe needed to be made in person by someone with the authority to agree to a plan and carry it out along the entire route. For example, Weidner might meet a colleague from the Netherlands at a café in Brussels, listen to his colleague's proposals for individuals to take to Spain, discuss the arrangements, and set their next rendezvous. Decisions were made on the spot and carried out as agreed.[2] Weidner himself had such authority, of course, and so did the refugee turned courier Edmond Chait. But if they were to cover all of western Europe, they needed another courier who could travel easily in both France and Belgium and act as the line's leader when circumstances called for it.

In October 1943 a refugee whom Weidner had helped get into Switzerland introduced him to another refugee, Jacques Rens, who wanted to join his brother in England. Weidner promised to get Rens to Spain, but a few days later he asked Rens to join the line instead. Given the dangers inherent in the job, Weidner gave him a week to consider. Rens decided that he would rather fight with the resistance than with the Allies and accepted.[3]

Jacques Rens, 1943.

Born the son of a Jewish father and a Catholic mother, Rens went to both French-speaking and Dutch-speaking schools while growing up in Belgium. After a stint on the sea and a period in the diamond business, he started importing and exporting textiles. When the war began he tried to enlist in the Dutch Army but ended up in the French Foreign

Legion with thousands of other non-French volunteers. Demobilized in December 1940 according to the terms of the French Armistice with the Third Reich, Rens returned to the textile industry in Belgium. He and his parents fled to Switzerland after his father was briefly detained as a Jew.

From October 1943 to the Liberation of southern Holland in September 1944, Weidner, Chait, and Rens led the escape line, welfare service, and courier route known as Dutch-Paris. All three men were in their early thirties and spoke both Dutch and French. They were all small businessmen. One was a devout Seventh-day Adventist; one was raised in the Jewish tradition; and one grew up in a household with both Jewish and Catholic influences. Rens and Chait deferred to Weidner as the "chief" (*chef*), but they made any necessary decisions for the line on their own authority when he was not there, and their colleagues deferred to their leadership. Chait remained in occupied territory until summer 1944, but Weidner and Rens crossed back and forth into Switzerland. Weidner's trips in occupied territory generally lasted two weeks. His wife represented Dutch-Paris in Geneva when he was not there and continued to arrange passages into Switzerland.

The three leaders circulated along their own routes and safe houses, separate from the lodgings or meeting places of other members of Dutch-Paris.[4] They appeared in Brussels, Lyon, Annecy, Paris, and Toulouse when and where they had agreed to meet the last time they had talked to their colleagues. If someone needed them between those times, he or she could leave a message at a designated place, such as a café where the owner had agreed to act as a "postbox." Chait also received mail poste restante at the gare St Lazare in Paris under the name Mr. Van den Hove.[5] Because he gave his return address as the nonexistent town of Bending he did not have to worry about endangering any unknown legitimate Van den Hove.

Weidner and Rens traveled on the main-line trains, but Chait, who carried more incriminating documents that might lead police to people in hiding, favored the more local, less heavily monitored trains and tramways. He also had his own crossing over the Franco-Belgian border, at the village of Quiévrain, where a narrow river divides the two countries. He would go to the "usual café," as he put it, to contact the people who had helped him when he first escaped to France, in 1942.[6] When the coast was clear, he would cross the river by sidling along the outside of a pedestrian bridge that had been filled with barbed wire. The distance was not long, but it would have been easy to grab a barb by mistake and fall into the water

Chait demonstrates how he crossed the Franco-Belgian border, 1967.

below or to be trapped in plain sight if the barbs got tangled in clothing.[7] These elaborate security precautions caused problems when their colleagues lost track of them, but such inconveniences paled in comparison to what could happen if Weidner and his lieutenants were caught. If no one knew where they were, no one could be tortured into betraying them. If they were not caught, they could not be tortured into betraying everyone else.

While in Geneva Weidner typed out reports on his and his colleagues' activities in France and Belgium as well as expense accounts that covered monies spent on behalf of Engelandvaarders and refugees as well as those used by helpers. He dared to write down such information only because he was in Switzerland. But even there Weidner worried about spies and used code names for people and places. Many of them relied on polyglot puns most easily appreciated by speakers of Dutch and French. For instance, in the reports the Dutch diplomat Laatsman, which sounds like "last man" in Dutch as well as English, became "Dernierhom," which means "last man" in French. Another Dutch diplomat, Bas Bakker, became "Boulanger" because *bakker* and *boulanger* both mean "baker." Some of the codes relied on similar sounds, such as "Van Gellicum" becoming "gelatin." Thys van Roggen became "Glace" because the Dutch name "Thys" sounds like the Dutch word *ijs* (ice), which is translated as glace in French. Other code names relied on insider knowledge. Weidner always called Lyon "monburo" ("my office" in French) in reference to his business. He referred to Annecy as "Mimosa," invoking the name of Meunier's shop. Sometimes he simply referred to people by their noms de guerre or first names.[8]

Weidner left on his first expedition to expand his network northward at 1:00 p.m. on Wednesday, October 13, 1943. Lieutenant Paul de Saugy of the Swiss intelligence services ushered him over the border in broad daylight. Weidner then took the bus from St-Julien-en-Genevois to Annecy, where he had four hours to check in with his colleagues before catching the night train to Paris. Unexpectedly neither French nor German officials asked to see his papers during the twelve-hour trip.

Once in Paris Weidner had just enough time to walk from the gare de Lyon to the gare du Nord to catch the 8:00 a.m. train to Brussels. He passed without difficulty through both a French customs inspection and a German document inspection at the Franco-Belgian border. He carried false documents made out in the name of "Louis Segers" that had been arranged by Van Niftrik and purportedly issued by the Belgian Chamber of Commerce.[9] This false persona overlapped almost completely with Weidner's true identity as a traveling salesman. He knew from experience how to act and which trains to take. Legitimate businessmen, for example, reserved a place in a

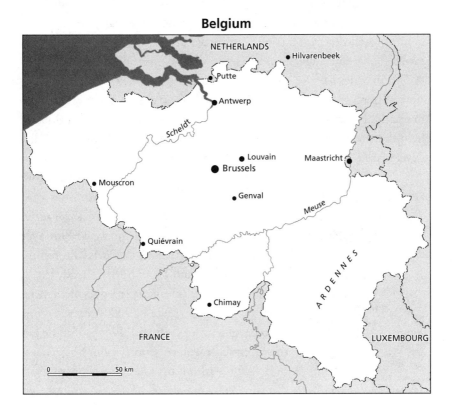

Belgium

sleeper car. They did not sit up all night in third class, and neither did "Louis Segers." He arrived in Brussels twenty-six hours after leaving Switzerland in what counted by wartime standards as an easy trip.

Weidner started his search for new colleagues in Brussels for practical reasons. In the first place, the city was close to the Netherlands without being in the Netherlands. Dutch-Paris couriers considered the Dutch-Belgian border to be one of the two most dangerous to slip through, rivaled only by the mountainous Spanish border.[10] Getting across it required local knowledge and excellent Dutch. Weidner himself never crossed it during the war because of his heavy French accent. Visser 't Hooft's contacts in Amsterdam, however, had a courier with experience on the Belgian border who could take Swiss Way microfilm to Brussels. Getting to Brussels from southern France to meet him for an exchange posed comparatively minor difficulties.

In the second place, both Visser 't Hooft and Weidner already had connections among resisters in Brussels.[11] Most usefully, Weidner had done a favor for a like-minded expatriate there named Benno Nijkerk.[12] Nijkerk had moved his metallurgy business from the Netherlands to Belgium in 1940 but spent most of his time helping Jews, particularly children left behind when their parents were deported. In May 1943 he journeyed to Switzerland in his capacity as treasurer of the Comité de Défense des Juifs (CDJ) in order to raise money among international Jewish aid organizations. After Swiss authorities turned him back at the border, Nijkerk went in search of a certain "Henri Meunier" in Lyon because a rumor in Brussels held that he helped Dutch Jews get into Switzerland. He may have discovered that "Meunier" was one of Weidner's many aliases through Chait,

who had worked for the CDJ in Antwerp before leaving for France a year earlier. Weidner gave Nijkerk letters of introduction to the Dutch community in Geneva and smuggled him over the Swiss border. This time the Swiss did not realize he was there until after he had already left.[13]

Nijkerk's success in eliciting pledges of financial support from international aid organizations posed problems of its own.[14] How could he get the promised regular subsidies from Switzerland to Belgium without the German occupation authorities knowing about it? Chait volunteered

Benno Nijkerk. 1942.

to serve as courier. Beginning in June 1943 he traveled between the Swiss border and Brussels twice a month, making over fifty such mail trips before the end of the occupation in September 1944. In addition to cash, he carried lists of children hidden in Belgium so their families would be able to find them after the war, lists of Jews who had been deported, general reports on the situation of Jews in Belgium, and the like. He also carried letters for individuals who were separated from family or friends by the war.[15]

When Weidner arrived in Brussels in October 1943, Nijkerk introduced his guest to other Dutch expatriates who had recently formed the Comité tot Steun voor Nederlandsche Oorlogschlachtoffers in België (Committee for the Support of Dutch War Victims in Belgium), simply called "the Comité" or sometimes the "organisatie Ten Kate," after its leader. Dutch expatriates ran the Comité as a clandestine welfare organization for Dutch fugitives in Brussels, doing illegal work similar to what Weidner had been doing in southern France. Unlike Weidner, however, they had no association with official representatives of the Dutch government. Nor did they have legal options in the way that Weidner and his colleagues had used *résidence assignée* to settle refugees in Vichy France.

The Comité began in spring 1942, when Jewish fugitives knocked on the door of a Dutch businessman living in Brussels.[16] After organizing a small group to find hiding places, the businessman approached a Dutch pastor about combining forces to help Jews. The businessman had contacts in the Jewish community and resources from the Belgian resistance organization Front de l'Indépendance (FI) with which the CDJ was affiliated. The pastor, Dominee A.G. B. ten Kate, whom Jews asked for help because of his position, provided extensive contacts among the non-Jewish expatriate community. Ten Kate had led the Protestantse Kerk Brussel (Dutch Protestant Church in Brussels) since 1927 and had belonged to the Nederlandsche Vereeniging, a social club of affluent Dutch businessmen, since before the war.[17] To begin with, the Belgian FI provided funds through the CDJ to support Jews in hiding. After October 1942, however, the expatriates had to use their own resources to hide Dutch Jews.[18]

By that time the businessman had moved on to more active ways of defending Jews. Indeed he was arrested in July 1943 in connection with an armed attack on a deportation train. That same summer the nature of refugees asking for help changed when young Dutchmen on the run from forced

Dominee A. G. B. ten
Kate, 1939.

labor and the threat of internment as POWs
showed up in Brussels. In response Ten Kate and
some of the other Dutch expatriates involved in
the rescue work created the Comité with the
stated goals of helping the young men while in
Belgium and sending them on to Switzerland or
Spain, providing financial help to those who
were not able to move on (mainly Jews), fetch-
ing people from the Netherlands, and main-
taining a courier service with the Netherlands
to bring letters, clothes, money, and the like.

Its members organized the Comité like a business, with a board of di-
rectors and two sections. The board operated much like that of any non-
profit organization, except, of course, that everything they were doing was
illegal. The board members brought useful connections and/or funds to
the organization and met every two weeks to audit its activities and review
the accounts submitted by the men in charge of daily operations.

That daily work fell into two categories: *sociaalwerk*, meaning the
support of Jews in hiding, and *transportwerk*, moving fugitives through
Brussels to Spain or Switzerland. Fugitives in hiding and those in transit
needed the same types of assistance – false documents, shelter, and money
– but the details of effective help differed for each.

Identity documents played a critical role in the lives of all civilians during
the occupation and caused constant anxiety for fugitives as they negotiated the endless inspections in occupied cities. The type and quality of a
person's false documents could literally make the difference between life
and death. If a Jew chose to hide in Belgium rather than risk the long
journey to Switzerland, he or she had no way of knowing when or even if
the Germans would lose the war. If Hitler won, a Jew would have to hide
for the rest of his or her life. It was much better to take on a false identity
that allowed one to move about the city and even get a job than to hide
inside for months or years. Such a false identity required a full panoply of
false documents: identity cards, ration cards, demobilization papers, work
papers, marriage certificates, and possibly more depending on the age and
gender of the holder.

The best documents were known as "true-false" because they used "true"
identities that were safely embedded in local population registers. They

either borrowed the name of a deceased person or used a name that some-one had added to the official registers. Such false identities held firm if German or local police telephoned the town hall that purportedly issued the documents in order to confirm their validity. Other reliable false documents claimed to be issued by a municipality where the records could not be verified because they had been destroyed by bombing or fire.

In late 1943 the Comité decided that the Front de l'Indépendance was charging them too much for false documents that they now had the re-sources to manufacture themselves.[19] For some documents, the public simply bought a blank official form in a shop and took it and a passport photo to their town hall to be filled out. In those cases the challenge for resisters lay in forging the necessary signatures and rubber stamps according to the latest directives. They also needed a civil servant to provide names from the registration lists or to plant false names in those registers to create "true-false" identities. The Comité had three known contacts in the town hall in Etterbeek (one of Brussels' nineteen municipalities). Most important, a police agent there named Antoine Devriendt provided false identity cards and false work papers as well as false passports to cross the Belgian-French border. He also warned them of impending raids and arranged for several members of the Comité to have telephone lines.[20]

Almost as urgently as false documents, Jews needed long-term housing where they could either stay out of sight or blend into the neighborhood. Weidner considered the task of finding hiding places to be "horribly dif-ficult" in both France and Belgium.[21] The Comité relied on a Belgian woman known simply as Madame Davignon, who began finding hiding places for the CDJ in 1941. Every single day, for three years, Davignon made the ten-mile trip from her home in Rixensart, southeast of the city, to one of several cafés in Brussels. There Ten Kate or another representa-tive of the CDJ or, later, the Comité would introduce her to new clients. Davignon prided herself on solving every case within forty-eight hours or taking the client to her own home to stay until she could find a suitable hiding place. If the client had what the Germans would think of as a "Jewish look," they traveled at night despite the curfew.

Davignon created her own local resistance network that specialized in sheltering and feeding Jews and evaders of the compulsory labor draft that was imposed in Belgium in October 1942. She had at least four safe houses in Brussels itself, where she met with her associates, cached foreign currency or documents, and temporarily hid Jews.[22] But she relied mostly on her neighbors in the villages of Rixensart and Genval. Her husband and son scoured the countryside for hiding places. Once she found lodging for a fugitive, Davignon made sure he or she was visited regularly with money and furnished with false documents. She also arranged for local merchants to supply them.[23]

Davignon chose people she knew well enough to trust. She also brought a small income into the area, distributed among landladies and merchants. By implicating so many of her neighbors, she built a community of silence that was stronger with each additional person who needed silence for safety. Each new person involved, however, also meant increased vulnerability for the community as a whole. It was fortunate for many people that the Waffen SS did no more than visit Davignon in August 1943 and did not take her away for serious interrogation.[24] She illustrates the primary importance of local, community-based groups within resistance networks, including the transnational network of Dutch-Paris.

Once they had established their clients in hiding, the Comité needed couriers to maintain regular contact with the refugees whom they supported in order to check on their well-being and to distribute each month's ration tickets and cash allotments for food, rent, and coal. Between September and December 1943 this amounted to two hundred people in Brussels plus five families in Antwerp and some single men hiding with Belgian partisans in the Ardennes.[25] Although some clients could come to cafés to pick up their own papers and money, others needed someone to bring it to them. Dutch-speaking fugitives might also have needed help getting off-the-record medical care in French-speaking Brussels.[26]

The fugitives helped by the *transportwerk* needed different sorts of shelter and documents. Most were Engelandvaarders who tended to be young men traveling alone or in small groups. They required shelter for only a few nights or a couple of weeks at the most. Such men could sleep at hotels or as acknowledged guests in private homes. Indeed many of the Engelandvaarders made their own way to the homes of family friends in Brussels before approaching the Comité for help.

Engelandvaarders did not need true-false identities because they were not trying to live in Belgium. But the papers they needed to travel across Belgium and into France were issued by the German occupation authorities. Forging German papers posed greater challenges because it was much harder to get the latest forms, and instructions for filling them out had to be extracted from the enemy's military office rather than from the local town hall. The members of the Comité, however, had many contacts in the clandestine worlds of the resistance and the black market. A mysterious Spaniard (or perhaps his name or pseudonym was "Spanjaard") provided examples of the official *Passierscheine* (travel permits), as well as examples and instructions for *Personalanweise* (identity cards), German stamps, German letterhead, and the like. A Belgian contact printed copies of these forms for the Comité, which they filled out themselves.[27]

With these German documents the Comité was able to camouflage some Engelandvaarders among legitimate contract workers.[28] A Dutchman could avoid working in the Third Reich if he voluntarily signed on with a company that worked for the Germans in western Europe before he was conscripted for labor. Such workers were sent wherever the German military needed them, such as the Atlantic Coast defenses or mines in France. Entitled to home leave and on limited contracts, these workers and their interpreters and supervisors moved between the Netherlands and the peripheries of France frequently and entirely legally. A contingent of young Dutch men being sent to fell timber in the Pyrenees, for example, provided effective cover for a young Engelandvaarder heading to the Spanish border in the Pyrenees.

The Comité, however, hesitated to send off its protégés without definite plans to get them over the mountains. Before October 1943 they paid for a few men to travel with a separate escape line run by a Polish officer turned *passeur*. But the Pole charged a prohibitive 12,000 French francs per Dutchman (less for Poles and Frenchmen).[29] They also passed Allied aviators to two Belgian escape lines, Comet and Service EVA. Members of the Comité did not rescue Allied aviators where they landed, but accepted them from other resisters in the Netherlands and Belgium who had picked them up after their planes crashed but had no way to get the airmen back to their bases in England. Neither the young men doing the daily footwork nor the older men managing the finances of the Comité found these arrangements with other escape lines satisfactory. They wanted to ensure their people's safety and control their expenses by having their own route to Spain.

Money posed as great a problem to Pastor ten Kate and his colleagues as it did to Weidner and his associates. They may have been volunteers, but everything they did cost money, often a lot of money. Many of the young people in Brussels were hiding from the Nazi racial laws or the German labor draft themselves and needed money to pay for train tickets, false documents, and meals. The fugitives they helped needed train tickets, false documents, shelter, and food; depending on circumstances they might also need clothing, medical care, coal, and petty cash. The Comité asked those who could pay for themselves to do so and paid for those who could not. For the most part the older generation in the group handled the financial aspects of rescue.

Like Weidner's group, the Dutch expatriates in the Comité benefited from donations made on behalf of Dutch refugees.[30] They also raised loans based in good part on the hope of victory. For example, Leopold Bosschart, the engineering director of the John Cockerill shipyard in Hoboken, Belgium, loaned the Comité the sizable sum of 100,000 Belgian francs on the understanding that if the Allies won the war the Dutch government in exile might pay him back.[31] That sum was enough to buy ration tickets for two hundred fugitives in hiding in August 1944. Unlike Weidner and his colleagues, the Comité also raised some money through the manufacture and sale of false documents.

Conditions in Belgium meant that the Comité became involved in their clients' finances in ways that Weidner had never needed to. In particular the Comité helped its protégés get their money out of the Netherlands and exchange it at the best possible rate. They were able to extract some cash and movable property that Jews had been forced to leave behind in the Netherlands by sending couriers to bring it to Belgium. They also enlisted the help of Dutch bankers in Belgium and the Netherlands who were willing to bend the rules to transfer money between the two countries.[32]

Dutch guilders, however, were of no use to people who had to pay cash for rent, food, and other necessities in Belgian francs. To complicate matters, the value of the guilder dropped rapidly, while the cost of goods rose at an inflationary rate in Belgium. In early 1942 the exchange rate was 1 guilder to 16.6 Belgian francs. By June 1943 a guilder was worth less than 10 francs.[33] It was costing Dutch expatriates and fugitives more and more to buy less and less, especially on the black market.

Brussels had a robust enough black market that certain currency traders would come to the house (or hiding place), providing the security of not going out on the streets for an exceptionally low exchange rate. The businessmen in the Comité tried to protect their clients from such dealings by exchanging their money for them. They kept their private rate as close to the most favorable legal rate as possible thanks to the willingness of some members to launder money through their businesses and the financial ingenuity of a Dutch insurance agent living in Brussels named Joseph Haenecour.

The father of seven, Haenecour had not forgiven the Germans, whom he referred to as the *schurkenvolk* (villainous folk), for the mistreatment of his Belgian grandmother and aunt during the First World War. He joined the Comité in September or October 1943 through a friend of a friend, but he had been engaged in clandestine finances since 1941. After he ran out of his own funds for private currency exchanges, Haenecour made contacts in the Brussels financial market who were willing to give him the advantageous rates. When those sources were exhausted, he found a Dutch cheese dealer with permission to trade on the Belgian Stock Exchange who exchanged guilders for him at the favorable official rate. This allowed the Comité to exchange money for its clients at a rate far better than anything offered on the black market and remarkably close to the official rate.[34] Now affluent clients could support themselves in hiding. This certainly helped the Comité's budget, but it did not provide any new funds for their illegal work.

When Nijkerk introduced Weidner to his colleagues in October 1943, the Comité's board consisted of Ten Kate, Nijkerk, and two expatriate businessmen, Edouard Regout and Cornelis van Schaardenburgh. The director of a mining company, Regout had lived in Belgium since 1925. His son, like the sons of many of the businessmen involved in the Comité, was old enough to become embroiled in the war. Regout expanded the Comité's contacts with the Belgian resistance beyond the left-wing FI through his connections with the Mouvement national royaliste (National Royalist Movement), a national network with conservative tendencies.[35] Van Schaardenburgh had long been involved in the Dutch colony in Brussels as a member of an expatriate charity and the same expatriate social club to which Ten Kate belonged.[36]

Two young men just starting out in business, Paul van Cleeff and Henri Vleeschdrager, were running the daily operations of both the *sociaalwerk* and the *transportwerk*. They had both fled the Netherlands

Henri Vleeschdrager, 1940s.

Hans Wisbrun, 1943.

with their families rather than report for deportation to the East, only to be captured by German police in Belgium or northern France. Vleeschdrager had broken out of a deportation train in October 1942 but been rearrested the following month in Lille. He met Van Cleeff and his family in a transit camp in Belgium. They were all deported together in December 1942, but the two young men jumped off the train when it slowed down in eastern Belgium. After escaping from the rail yard, they made their way to Brussels, to the home of an old school friend of Van Cleeff's father, Arie Nieulant-Pelkman. Van Cleeff's parents, brother, and sister all perished in Auschwitz.[37]

The escapees had come to the right place. Nieulant-Pelkman, his wife, G. L. van Ende, and their teenage daughter, Wies, had been helping Pastor ten Kate to hide Jewish refugees since May 1942.[38] Unable to get out of occupied territory, Van Cleeff and Vleeschdrager could either spend the rest of the war in hiding or join the resistance.[39] For young Jewish men like themselves, working in the resistance was a form of hiding in plain sight, moving about and defying the enemy by protecting the persecuted.

Van Cleeff recruited more helpers for the daily tasks of the Comité from among other Dutch refugees and Dutch university students. In the summer of 1943, for example, he met a young Dutch Jew who had already been hiding in Antwerp for a year. Despite the stiff leg that slowed him down and singled him out, Hans Wisbrun worked full-time for the Comité as a courier for as long as he retained his liberty.[40] A few of the Comité's Jewish clients who were hiding in Brussels also agreed to act as local couriers, visiting other Jews in hiding to deliver money and papers.[41]

That summer a mutual acquaintance introduced Van Cleeff to a charismatic Dutch student named David Verloop. Verloop and his childhood friend and fellow student, J. P. Bol, relocated to Brussels in June 1943, at a time when many men of their age and social standing had to go into hiding because they refused to sign the student loyalty oath and did not want to be interned as Dutch POWs. Ostensibly Verloop moved to Brussels to work on a doctorate in economics to complement his law degree, but he could not have spent much time in class. Because of his earlier work in the Utrechtse Kindercomité that rescued Jewish children, Verloop had a wide acquaintanceship among resistance-minded Dutch students. He offered his friends hospitality when they were in Brussels as well as arranging false Belgian documents for them.[42] Some of them passed through town as Engelandvaarders, but others joined the Comité. Bol also joined the Comité, but in the capacity of forger. Over the winter of 1943–44 he established a full-scale atelier in which he produced 1,100 to 1,200 false documents of various sorts for the use of the resisters themselves and the fugitives they helped.[43]

Another circle of Utrecht students came to the Comité through Pastor ten Kate, who was the uncle of one of them, a theology student named Chris ten Kate.[44] There were, indeed, many paths to the Comité, although they all lay through personal connections. A medical student at the University of Leiden named Willy Hijmans, for example, came to Brussels in the summer of 1943 after concluding that he could no longer find safe hiding places for Jews in the Netherlands.[45] On his first trip a businessman friend of a friend smuggled Hijmans across the border near Maastricht. Hijmans then went to Brussels, to the small apartment above a café rented by friends of his, stateless German Jews who had asked him to hide their money when they had fled the Netherlands. The family's sons introduced Hijmans to Van Cleeff as a person with the means to hide and support Jews in Belgium.[46] Van Cleeff agreed to take care of any fugitives Hijmans brought to Brussels, and Hijmans agreed to take messages back to the Netherlands. Hijmans could have arrived at the Comité through a more direct path. He and

David Verloop, 1940.

Chris ten Kate, 1943.

Verloop had worked together on the Kindercomité but did not realize for some time that they belonged to the same illegal organization in Belgium.

The elementary precautions of the clandestine life meant that men and women could easily work in the same network without knowing it. When Hijmans received a message to be at a rendezvous in Brussels to meet Weidner without enough notice to make his usual arrangements for crossing the border, he went in search of a university friend named Jan Nauta. After finding him playing field hockey, Hijmans told Nauta that he needed to get into Belgium. Without asking any questions or demanding an explanation, Nauta told him to take the train to Breda, a city in the southern part of the Netherlands; transfer to a bus to Bergen-op-Zoom, another nearby city; then take the local bus to the border village of Putte-Grens. From there he needed to walk back up the road a few hundred yards to a monastery and ask Brother Willem to show him the path across the border. Hijmans followed the instructions and arrived in Belgium in time for the meeting with Weidner. What the friends did not know until after the war was that they shared a contact in Brussels. Hijmans once passed an Engelandvaarder to a hotelkeeper in Brussels, who then passed the same man to Nauta to take to Paris.[47]

With the notable exception of the forger Bol, most students joined the Comité as couriers, either locally within Brussels or internationally between the Netherlands and Brussels and/or Brussels and Paris. The Utrecht student Piet Henry, for example, brought fugitives, correspondence, money, and documents from the Netherlands to Brussels on a regular basis.[48] Hijmans and Henry, who had met through the Kindercomité, sometimes worked together in Dutch-Paris to guide Engelandvaarders and Jews to Belgium. Hijmans collected the fugitives in the Netherlands, usually at a train station, and escorted them to the border town of Roosendaal. Henry then shepherded them across the border. Once in Belgium he took them on the steam tram to Antwerp, where it was easy enough to catch a train to Brussels. When in the Netherlands Henry used the (false) documents of a rationing inspector, and Hijmans used the (false) documents of an inspector from the coal department. Both disguises gave the young men exemptions from the German labor draft, permission to circulate near the border, and the right to have a bicycle.[49]

Students made good couriers because they were young and quick-witted. Social standing also gave them an advantage. Hijmans made a point of

Piet Henry, 1942.

wearing a jacket and tie on his five or six illegal trips across the border. The border guards and customs agents at the rural places where he crossed were looking for black market smugglers, whom they expected to be dressed like farmers or gangsters rather than like gentlemen. Hijmans put his false identity documents from whichever country he was not in at the moment into a pocket that he himself had sewn into the inside of his trousers, using skills he had learned as a boy scout. He did not want to give his mother any more cause to worry by asking her to do something so obviously related to illegal activity. When he crossed from south to north Hijmans also carried a pound of butter as an alibi. It was a good thing he did, because the one time he was stopped, he got away with nothing more than a 3-guilder fine for the illegal possession of butter. Hijmans was convinced that if the German border guard had understood his true errand, the guard would not have let him go.[50]

When Nijkerk introduced Weidner to Pastor ten Kate in October 1943, the Comité had a fully functioning network of helpers in Brussels and regular courier routes over the Dutch border. They also faced what they described as an "urgent" shortage of funds. The budget for that month showed that even with impressive receipts from the sale of false documents and private donations, the Comité could cover only three-quarters of the

Willy Hijmans's false papers and hidden pocket.

essential costs of supporting its clients with rent, food, and heat. Nevertheless they intended to double the allotments for current clients, take on new cases, and send young men to Spain so they could join the Allies in England, all of which would triple their costs.[51]

It did not take much discussion for the Comité as represented by Nijkerk and Pastor ten Kate to agree to join Weidner and his colleagues in the new network. After all, they were already doing the same illegal work in different locations. The Comité had a functioning resistance infrastructure in Brussels, contacts among Belgian resisters, and proven routes across the Belgian-Dutch frontier, all of which Weidner needed. In turn Weidner had two things the Comité needed: the ability to take fugitives to Spain and Switzerland and access to money. He offered to take their report on their work and finances to the ambassador and delivered it as soon as he returned to Switzerland a few days later.

As planned, Weidner returned to Brussels two weeks after his first visit. He could not, however, find Nijkerk because the Gestapo had picked up his trail. In this case Weidner had a password (*diesel train*) to contact Nijkerk's replacement as liaison for Dutch-Paris, Pastor ten Kate. But there were more than one missed appointment and lost microfilm in the early days of Dutch-Paris. Just the week before, Weidner and Nijkerk had each waited at a different address in Paris for a rendezvous that never happened. Some of the microfilms for the early Swiss Way exchanges were destroyed when a courier did not arrive at a particular time at a particular place, again because of simple misunderstandings. These confusions make Weidner and his colleagues sound like amateurs. But that is exactly what they were. Ten Kate was the pastor of a Protestant church, and Nijkerk and Weidner were businessmen. Their colleagues were secretaries, students, housewives, shopkeepers, and civil servants. They were principled people used to living open lives without any training in clandestine skills.

Weidner traveled to Brussels again in mid-November with the welcome news that Visser 't Hooft had allocated a sizable sum for the Comité, presumably from the same WCC funds that he had drawn on when Weidner needed money for refugees in Vichy earlier that year. Weidner and Pastor ten Kate worked out an elaborate arrangement for the transfer of this money from Swiss francs to Belgian francs. In Paris Weidner gave 100,000 French francs of his own money to a friend of his sister's named Catherine Okhuysen, who agreed to act as a private *bureau de change* for the Comité's protégés. Refugees on their way to Switzerland and Engelandvaarders on their way to Spain could give whatever amount they chose to Van Cleeff in Belgian francs before leaving Brussels. When they arrived in Paris they could withdraw the equivalent amount in French francs at close to the official rate from Okhuysen. The Comité would then use the Belgian francs left with Van Cleeff to support Dutch refugees remaining in Belgium. It took only a few weeks for the Comité to receive the specified amount in Belgian francs from fugitives and Okhuysen to disburse all the cash entrusted to her. At that point Visser 't Hooft reimbursed Weidner Swiss francs for the French francs he had given to Okhuysen.[52]

Unbeknownst to Weidner, German police arrested Van Cleeff at a meeting with a Belgian escape line on November 18, 1943. His colleagues thought that he would have been released if he had not had a "notebook with compromising notations" with him at the time of his arrest.[53] If he did, his notes must have been deeply encoded or partially destroyed because the German authorities charged him with being a

Catherine Okhuysen, 1945.

Jew in bad company rather than for the quite real transgressions against the occupation laws that he had committed.[54]

With Van Cleeff in prison, elementary prudence demanded that his colleagues change their addresses and their habits to protect themselves and their clients. That was relatively simple for the young men involved in the daily operations, such as Vleeschdrager and Verloop, who were themselves fugitives. But the expatriates who lived and worked in Brussels could not suddenly disappear from their homes and businesses without effectively declaring themselves to be resisters. If Pastor ten Kate left his church or Regout left his company, for example, the authorities would want to know why. The older expatriates in the Comité could do much more for the fugitives in terms of raising money, gathering information, and providing shelter and jobs if they remained at their own homes and jobs.

Most continued with their everyday lives, but they now had real cause to worry. The Gestapo was looking for Nijkerk. Unspecified German police were tapping Ten Kate's telephone line, although a friendly Belgian official warned the pastor early enough that no known harm came of it.[55] No one knew if these events and Van Cleeff's arrest were related. From the outside the German police looked monolithic and omnipresent. It would have been easy to assume the worst.

Van Schaardenburgh resigned from the board. The Dutch banker Jacques Verhagen, who was the administrative director of a bank, the Société Belge de Banque, took his place. Earlier in the occupation Verhagen had cashed large letters of credit issued by international Jewish organizations for Nijkerk, who was treasurer of the CDJ.[56] Like other middle-aged men involved in the Comité, Verhagen had a son who was old enough to be deported as forced labor, pressed into the Wehrmacht, or shot on some pretext. Like Ten Kate and Van Schaardenburgh, he belonged to the Nederlandsche Vereeniging.

The new board decided that the daily operations of the Comité should be reorganized to separate the *transportwerk* from the *sociaalwerk*. That way, if the Germans infiltrated one, they would not necessarily capture everyone involved in the other. They compartmentalized the two sections physically by renting a pension at 19 rue Franklin as a headquarters for the escape line. Beginning in December 1943 all transient fugitives stayed at the pension on their way through Brussels. The *sociaalwerk* continued to operate out of an apartment at 73 rue du Trône, which was closer to the center of the city than the pension.

A complete separation also required a strict division of personnel into one task or the other. Three men divided Van Cleeff's job as head of daily operations, which had grown increasingly complicated over the course of 1943 as the Comité struggled to meet the needs of Engelandvaarders as well as Jews. Van Cleeff's original partner who escaped from the deportation train with him, Vleeschdrager, took responsibility for the *sociaalwerk*. The charismatic Verloop took over the daily finances and "foreign affairs," meaning the couriers and passages to other countries. Despite his limp, Wisbrun acted as his assistant, often making the journey to and from Paris himself. Responsibility for false documents officially fell to Bol. The realities of clandestine life and the number of people available to do all the necessary work, however, meant that these divisions were clearer in theory than in practice. For instance, Vleeschdrager made weekly trips to Paris to meet with Dutch-Paris colleagues there as well as a few illegal trips to Utrecht and Amsterdam despite being in charge of the *sociaalwerk* in and around Brussels. He also helped Bol with false documents at the *transportwerk*'s headquarters.

The helpers of the Comité covered their tracks so well that after Van Cleeff's arrest Weidner had difficulties making contact when he returned to Brussels for the December 15 rendezvous. As he had done on his previous trip, Weidner went to the apartment of a Dutch widow, Petronella van Gellicum-Kamps, to pick up the Swiss Way microfilm. It was fortunate that he confused the apartment number because the widow's neighbor informed him that she had been arrested and that the Gestapo was lying in wait for anyone who rang her doorbell. In fact she had been arrested with Van Cleeff almost a month earlier. Verloop had sent a message to Paris, telling Weidner not to go to the widow's home, but it had gone astray.

When Ten Kate did not answer his bugged telephone, Weidner went to his house on the Heldenplein. He found the pastor somewhat anxious but determined and hopeful that Van Cleeff would be released.[57] Having made contact, Weidner introduced Jacques Rens as his new lieutenant with complete authority to speak for him in his absence. Rens had lived in Antwerp before fleeing to Switzerland so he knew Belgium well. In fact, on his trips there he slept at an undisclosed location in Antwerp rather than in Brussels.

Brussels

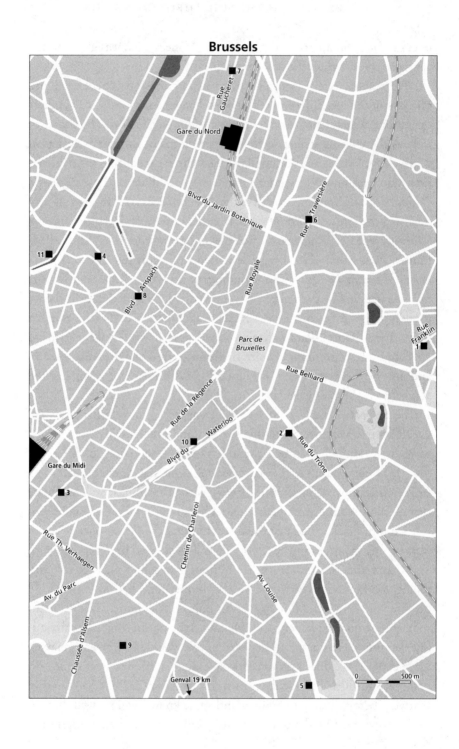

Weidner then turned his attention to two pressing problems: money and security. The Comité's October report had had the desired impact on the Dutch ambassador in Bern. Rens handed Verloop a stack of cash. For future contributions Ten Kate introduced Weidner to Verhagen, who agreed to set up an account for the Comité at his bank under a false name and to instruct his staff that three persons could make withdrawals from it without any questions. Verhagen also agreed to join Ten Kate on a sub-committee to determine how funds coming from Switzerland would be distributed among the Comité's charges.[58]

Having taken care of financial matters, Weidner turned his attention to lapses in security. In particular he objected that the student couriers were exposing the entire network to unnecessary risk by bringing whoever asked them for help from the Netherlands to Belgium without first vetting them. By this time intelligence officers in London had uncovered evidence of agents provocateurs at work among Dutch expatriates in Paris. There was no reason to think that German police were not using the same methods in Belgium and the Netherlands. Weidner and Verloop worked out a safer plan for selecting Engelandvaarder candidates, but they never implemented it because Dutch-Paris, despite all of their efforts, failed to establish a base north of the Dutch border.[59] The line continued to take fugitives from a number of possibly insecure sources.

BRUSSELS

Gare du Nord – Station for trains to and from the Netherlands
Gare du Midi – Station for trains to and from France
1 **rue Franklin 19** – Dutch-Paris safe house for the escape line
2 **rue du Trône 73** – Dutch-Paris safe house for the *sociaalwerk*
3 **Place des Héros 6** – home of Pastor Ten Kate
4 **Protestantse Kerk in Brussel** – Pastor Ten Kate's church
5 **Avenue Louise 453** – Headquarters of the Gestapo, where resisters were interrogated
6 **rue Travesière 8** – Headquarters of the *Geheime Feldpolizei*, where Allied airmen were interrogated
7 **Hotel Oud Antwerpen (rue Gaucheret 21)** – gathering place for Engelandvaarders and Allied airmen
8 **Café Hulstkamp (boulevard Anspach 74)** – meeting place and postbox for Dutch-Paris
9 **Prison of St. Gilles**
10 **Café du Tunnel (boulevard du Waterloo 55)** – meeting place for Mme Davignon
11 **Moussiaux's toy factory (quai du Hainaut 23)** – postbox for Dutch-Paris

Weidner also worried that too many people knew about the microfilm relay, which, once again, did not function smoothly. Weidner was supposed to meet a courier from Amsterdam at the popular Café Hulstkamp near the Bourse at 74 boulevard Anspach, run by a Dutch-born woman, another widow. The courier, however, was late, this time because he had been detained at the border.

Joseph "Jef" Lejeune passed his doctoral exams in criminology at the University of Louvain in 1942. Sometime in late 1942 or early 1943 the French caught him on the Swiss border and handed him over to the Germans. The memory of the subsequent interrogation still distressed him in the 1970s. He was, however, returned to the Netherlands instead of being imprisoned. Back home he joined a resistance group associated with the Swiss Way. His knowledge of the border region and his student identity card from a university near Brussels made him an obvious choice as courier to shuttle microfilm over the Dutch-Belgian border.[60]

Given recent events, Weidner and Ten Kate agreed that it would be safest to separate the Swiss Way intelligence line from both the *sociaalwerk* and the *transportwerk*. From then on, only a handful of men would handle the microfilm. Weidner, Rens, Chait, and later Paul Veerman would carry them between Switzerland and Belgium. Lejeune, A. L. A. Borst, and Nico van Dorp would ferry them between the Netherlands and Belgium. Swiss Way couriers would meet in the famous university town of Louvain rather than in the capital and without the knowledge or participation of anyone in the Comité.

It took several weeks to put this plan into effect. As of January 15, 1944, Weidner or Rens extended their biweekly trip to Brussels to include a side trip to Louvain, where they asked for Mr. Lejeune at 26 chaussée de Tirlemont. If he was not there, they were to go to the Café Vieil Heidelberg, place du Marché, and ask for Mr. Borst. Wherever they met, they employed a double password. For January 1944, for example, the courier from Switzerland would say "Jura," to which the courier from Amsterdam would reply, "Statue Jean-Jacques Rousseau."[61] This system functioned without a problem until the final chaotic weeks before the Liberation, when the trains no longer ran.

Weidner and his colleagues, however, carried microfilm and documents from a number of sources in addition to those passed along the Swiss Way. During the war many people collected intelligence on their own initiative, but few had the means to get it to the Allies. Although they themselves did not gather intelligence, the Comité received it from their contacts in the Netherlands and Belgium. Some of the students who routinely crossed the border for Dutch-Paris brought copies of underground papers from their hometowns with them to be passed on to London.[62] Other resisters passed them all sorts of documents, some military, some civilian, in the hope that they would forward them to the government in exile or the Allies. But there was just too much paper to smuggle across occupied territory. The Comité enlisted a photographer in Brussels who knew the secret of turning paper into microfilm and then gave the microfilm to Weidner, Rens, or Chait to take to the Dutch authorities in Switzerland. In urgent cases they sent a courier to Paris to hand the microfilm or document to Weidner there rather than wait for his regular biweekly visit.[63]

Weidner's partnership with the Comité extended the new network from Switzerland to the Netherlands. It increased aid to Dutch refugees in occupied territory by bringing government-in-exile funding to helpers in Belgium. It also established a regular courier route for the Swiss Way and opened a pathway for less officially organized sources of information to send intelligence to the Allies in London. But neither the courier service nor the escape line to Spain would function properly unless they had a base in Paris. Recruiting colleagues there proved to be far more challenging than anywhere else.

Gare du Nord, Paris, 1950.

4

Allies in Paris and Toulouse

As it had in Brussels, the railway system dictated that the expanded escape line go through Paris. It was possible to tack across France using short-distance local trains, as Edmond Chait sometimes did, but it required considerable time, local knowledge, and fluency in French. Foreigners had a better chance of passing unremarked on the crowded main-line trains. These went to Paris, but they did not go through it. Trains from the Netherlands and Belgium arrived at the gare du Nord. Trains to Lyon and Switzerland left from the gare de Lyon. Southbound trains to Toulouse left from the gare d'Austerlitz. A passenger traveling from Brussels to Toulouse got off the train in Paris at the gare du Nord and boarded another train at the gare d'Austerlitz, about an hour away by foot.

Weidner needed colleagues in Paris who could meet fugitives at the gare du Nord; take them through the city to a hiding place; organize food, lodging, and false documents for them; and then escort them through the city again to the station from which their next train would depart. Some left the same day, but most stayed in Paris for several days, if not weeks. Most fugitives also needed an escort to their next city, whether it be Lyon on the way to Switzerland or Toulouse on the way to Spain. Weidner could not know in advance how many fugitives his network would help in Paris, but it was unlikely that his personal contacts in the city would bring him enough helpers.

Weidner had not been to Paris since leaving it in a hurry before the German Army arrived in June 1940, but he had corresponded with rescuers there about helping Jews. That was not the sort of mail that could be sent across the Demarcation Line between occupied and unoccupied France without attracting the censors' attention. So most such letters and messages were carried by friends who traveled between the zones, such as the Adventist

Gabrielle Weidner, 1940.

pastor Oscar Meyer, brother to Weidner's colleague in Lyon, Pastor Paul Meyer.[1]

Of course Weidner's primary correspondent in Paris was his sister Gabrielle, who worked as a secretary at the Adventist church at 131 boulevard de l'Hôpital, a fifteen-minute walk south of the gare d'Austerlitz. Weidner sent her food and clothing from the southern zone as well as brotherly letters. On occasion the family news disguised plans for the escape of Jews from Paris to Switzerland. Gabrielle's primary role in these rescues was to convey information, although she did also run errands and stand in line to buy food for Jews interned at the transit camp in the suburb of Drancy.[2] She would continue to act as a postbox, receiving and distributing messages for Dutch-Paris and microfilm for the Swiss Way.

Gabrielle had her own small circle among rescuers in Paris to whom she introduced her brother. The most important of these was another child of Dutch expatriates, Catherine Okhuysen. Okhuysen's parents ran a farm about twenty-five miles south of Paris, but she worked as a secretary at the Dutch Chamber of Commerce in the city. In 1940 she was transferred within the Chamber to a charity established to help the thousands of Dutch refugees coming through Paris that spring in order to get away from the battle. Most went through Paris again in the fall on their way home.[3] She and another secretary at the Chamber of Commerce, Louise Roume, hid fugitives at Roume's apartment on the boulevard Montparnasse. Okhuysen's help to Dutch fugitives became so well known that her bosses started to worry the German authorities would close down their office because of it. Instead they fired her, although they claimed to have done so only on paper.[4] Indeed she helped so many people that the British officers who debriefed successful Engelandvaarders and evaders after they arrived in England concluded that every Dutch escape line that went through Paris went through her.[5] Fugitives and resisters alike knew her fondly as "Oky."

Gabrielle met Okhuysen in early 1943 through a Jewish family whom Okhuysen helped escape into the Vichy zone. After they arrived in

Switzerland, the family asked Weidner to retrieve money they had left in
Paris. He wrote to his sister, who went to talk to Okhuysen about the money.[6]
The young women became friends and colleagues. Okhuysen joined the
new line as soon as Weidner invited her. She began by disbursing French
francs to fugitives who had left Belgian francs with the Comité.

After she lost her job as a secretary, Okhuysen worked full time for
Dutch-Paris. In Paris she acted as a hostess to fugitives, particularly
Engelandvaarders. She also served the line as a courier. When necessary
she took messages across the country to Toulouse and returned to Paris
the same day, which involved a minimum of fourteen hours on trains. Her
friend Louise Roume also joined the line by opening her home to fugitives. Roume sent some refugees who arrived at her home through her own
contacts to Switzerland via Dutch-Paris.

On his first visit to Paris during the occupation, Weidner introduced
himself to another man with whom he had been arranging rescues through
the mail. Josephus "Jules" Mohr was the director of the KLM office there
but had little to do after the occupation authorities suspended air travel.
He took over as unofficial acting representative of the Dutch Red Cross in
northern France when the Germans removed his predecessor from the
position.[7] As such he could correspond with prisoners and meet Dutch
fugitives who came to the Red Cross offices at the Margarine Astra building on rue Miresmonil. Mohr opened his home to Weidner and assured
him that he would help with the *sociaalwerk* in Paris and the region.

Months earlier Weidner and Mohr had cooperated on a scheme to
rescue Dutch Jews using South American passports. While chatting with
a Swiss official Nico Gazan had discovered the opportunity of buying
these documents that would transform a European Jew into a protected
citizen of a neutral country. As a representative of the Red Cross, Mohr
identified likely candidates in the transit camp at Drancy. The military
attaché in Bern, General van Tricht, purchased the documents through a
Swiss lawyer, and Weidner sent them to Paris.[8] Mohr enlisted another expatriate, Brother Rufus Tourné, to smuggle the false documents into the
camp under the voluminous robes of his order.[9]

Born in 1901 in the Netherlands, Brother Rufus had been a tailor
before taking his religious vows. He had lived at the mother house of the
Congregation du Saint-Espirt on rue Lhomond near the Sorbonne since
1937. Because the congregation belonged to an international Catholic
order of priests and brothers and lived in central Paris, they received visitors

of all sorts and on both sides of the conflict. Some of their guests, such as German soldiers and foreign workers in good legal standing, had ration cards, but others, such as fugitives passed on from other religious houses and workers gone AWOL, did not. As the congregation's quartermaster, Brother Rufus could not feed everyone in the house using only what the rations allowed, so he relied on Dutch farmers who lived within reach of the light rail system for black market supplies. At times, he also relied on them to hide fugitives.[10]

Brother Rufus sheltered, fed, and equipped Engelandvaarders who knocked on his door, but he did not wait for fugitives to find him. He made the rounds of the jails, looking for Dutchmen who had been incarcerated because they were foreigners or were carrying illegal papers. Indeed there got to be so many desperate Dutchmen wandering around Paris in the fall of 1943 that he and a Dutch priest, Father L. J. A. Laureijssen, held office hours in the Café Belge on the rue St Quentin near the gare du Nord every day at 4:30 p.m. so their young compatriots could ask for help.[11]

Okhuysen, Mohr, and Brother Rufus had all worked with the official Dutch effort to assist Dutch refugees coming through Paris in 1940. Since then Mohr and Brother Rufus had colluded in at least one illegal scheme to help the persecuted. Weidner welcomed them into the new network, but he still needed more helpers. Because there was no expatriate group in Paris like the Comité, Weidner hoped to work through Dutch officials there, similar to the way he had worked with Dutch consuls in Vichy. His attempt to engage those men, however, met with suspicion because of a rumor that he had caused Jacquet's arrest in Lyon six weeks earlier. After Mohr cleared up the misunderstanding, the officials invited what seemed like everyone in the Dutch colony to a meeting to form what they called a government-sponsored resistance line. Appalled that anyone would advertise such a thing, Weidner wanted nothing further to do with those men.

But he had heard positive rumors about a minor diplomat at the Dutch consulate named Hermann Laatsman.[12] Laatsman had far too much clandestine experience to attend the meeting. His job at the consulate had put him

Herman Laatsman, 1939.

in a position to defy the occupation from its earliest days. Among other activities, he helped
Dutch workers evade untenable conditions at the
German submarine bases in western France and
was involved in an early escape line to Switzerland.[13]
Not surprisingly Laatsman had his own "network
of complicities" that included Frenchwomen
working at the police prefecture and at the rationing office as well as at least one Dutch farmer
living outside Paris.[14] He also had connections
with French resistance groups. When he could
not find hiding places for Jews, for example, he
passed them to a compatriot, Adolf Langhout, who had just completed his
Protestant theological training and who worked with French rescuers.[15]

Adolf Langhout, 1942.

Laatsman had already been living underground with his wife, Joseffa
Laatsman-Bekking, their young daughter, and his son from his first marriage for more than a year when Weidner arrived in Paris. Rather than
report to the train station when the German authorities ordered all Dutch
civil servants in Paris to return to the Netherlands in October 1942, the
family had taken a house under the mother's maiden name in St-Nom-la-
Bretèche, twenty miles outside the city. Laatsman was commuting into
Paris for his illegal work while German guards watched for him on the
Spanish border.[16]

Not surprisingly Laatsman heard the rumors about Weidner's escape
line in October 1943. Given what he knew of the family, Laatsman agreed
to meet with Weidner in person. Laatsman's father and the Weidners'
grandfather had served as pastors of the same Protestant church in Ghent.[17]
He had met Gabrielle at the Dutch consulate early in the war when she
was trying to send a letter to her parents and younger sister in The Hague.[18]
He had also been in indirect communication with Weidner earlier in the
occupation about escapes to Switzerland.

On November 3, 1943, Laatsman paid a visit to Gabrielle, who suggested
a stroll along the boulevard de l'Hôpital from the Adventist church to the
vast roundabout of the place d'Italie. Seeing young men plotting on every
corner, Laatsman noticed "a somewhat pale man coming toward [him],
dressed in black, bare headed, walking casually, studying [him] to estimate
who he was dealing with." Gabrielle whispered that it was her brother. Once

Paris

Sacré Coeur

7

Gare du Nord

Gare de l'Est

Rue la Fayette

Rue du Faubourg Poissonnière

vd Haussmann

Av. de la République

Livry-Gargan
19 km

16

Rue de Rivoli

Blvd Voltaire

10

t-Germain

Notre Dame

8

ardin du
xembourg

5
4 6

9

Gare de Lyon

Gare d'Austerlitz

Blvd de l'Hôpital

14

Key to map is on page 107

they were seated in a café, Weidner asked Laatsman to take responsibility for the Paris station of a government-approved escape line for Engeland-vaarders. Laatsman agreed to go to Switzerland with him to discuss the matter with the ambassador, who was the highest ranking diplomat loyal to the queen in Europe and thus his superior in the foreign service.[19]

Two weeks later Weidner, Rens, and Laatsman took the night train to Lyon. Weidner found nothing remarkable in the trip from Lyon to Switzerland and mentioned only that the unheated train left six hours late. The details made more of an impression on Laatsman, who was older but had not traveled as much during the occupation. While still in Paris he thought he recognized hundreds of other fugitives in the gare de Lyon, all trying to get out of the northern zone. He was nervous because his own false documents had not arrived in time, forcing him to use Weidner's, though the two did not resemble each other. To his amazement the inspectors on the train accepted the false identity card with Weidner's photo. In Lyon, Laatsman stayed overnight with the Swiss Adventist pastor Paul Meyer and his wife, Marthe. The couple often hosted Dutch-Paris couriers, stored messages and money for them, and prepared false documents for travel in the reserved zone of Haute-Savoie, using forms and stamps they hid in their home.[20]

When they arrived at the station in Annecy, an old man muttered something to Weidner as he shuffled past them, presumably telling them it was safe to proceed. Weidner and Laatsman then walked out of the station. They entered a shop by its front door, ate a light meal in a back room, left by the back door, and disappeared into an ambulance. Laatsman sat up front next to the driver while Weidner lay in the back on top of the microfilm he was carrying, feigning appendicitis. The guard at the customs post at Le Chable waved them through.[21]

Pastor Paul Meyer, 1935.

The Dutchmen left the ambulance at the hospital in St-Julien and sauntered through the border town until a bicyclist dropped a note at their feet. It was Inspector Arthur Charroin, on his way to see if the coast was clear. If he returned with his hat pulled to one side, it was safe to cross; otherwise they should wait until later. When Charroin pedaled past with his hat askew, they hurried to the barricade on the border, threw their jackets and bags over it, and dropped to the ground. Weidner held up the lowest rung of barbed wire while Laatsman crawled through the mud underneath it.

The Dutchmen ran through the five hundred yards of no man's land on the other side of the barbed wire, jumped over a stream, and dashed through a vineyard. The first Swiss guard they approached directed them to the next post, a bit farther away. Laatsman concluded (correctly) that Weidner must have belonged to the Swiss Intelligence Service because the second guard phoned for a car to take them to Geneva. Weidner explained that it was always best to inform the Swiss when he arrived, particularly if he brought with him someone unknown to them.

In Geneva, Weidner took Laatsman to meet Pastor Visser 't Hooft, who struck Laatsman as the "key figure in the Netherlands Resistance [sic]

PARIS

Gare d'Austerlitz – station for trains to and from Toulouse
Gare de Lyon – station for trains to and from Lyon and Switzerland
Gare du Nord – station for trains to and from Belgium and the Netherlands
  1 **23 rue du Laos** – Hiltermann's apartment
  2 **11 rue Jasmin** – Goetschel and Milleret's apartment building
  3 **67 avenue Victor Hugo** – Baron Brantsen's apartment
  4 **30 rue Lhomond** – *Congrégation du Saint Esprit* – Brother Rufus's home
  5 **24 rue Lhomond** – Physics laboratories of the *École normale supérieure*, hiding place for Allied aviators
  6 **33 rue Lhomond** – home of Émile and Julia Prilliez
  7 **189 rue Faubourg Poissonnière** – apartment building of the Caubo Family and Comiti
  8 **56 rue Monsieur le Prince** – Starink's hotel
  9 **159 boulevard Montparnasse** – Neyssel's apartment
 10 **9 rue du Trésor** – Larose-Reinaud's apartment
 11 **143 boulevard du Montparnasse** – Roume's apartment
 12 **12 square Gabriel Fauré** – Okhuysen's apartment
 13 **11 rue de Saussaies** – Gestapo headquarters
 14 **130 boulevard de l'Hôpital** – Seventh-day Adventist church and Gabrielle Weidner's home
 15 **44 rue Duranton** – bookshop that served as a postbox in spring 1944
 16 **Café l'Arc-en-ciel (19 rue des Fêtes)** – café where Suzy Kraay was arrested
 17 **33 rue du Miromesnil** – office of the Dutch Red Cross
 18 **109 Boulevard Malesherbes** – Dutch Chamber of Commerce and Refugee Office
Livry-Gargan – town where French resisters hid Allied airmen
Gazeran – farming community where several Dutch farmers lived
St-Nom-la-Bretèche – Laatsman's hiding place

abroad." The pastor arranged for him to stay at a hotel the Swiss police guarded to keep its guests' presence a secret. This protected Laatsman from being identified by German spies and the Swiss from being accused of violating their neutrality by assisting the Dutch and, by extension, the Allies. The Swiss, however, considered a visit to the Dutch embassy in Bern by a wanted resister such as Laatsman to be too flagrant a breach of their neutrality. Instead he met with the ambassador and the military attaché at the ambassador's home. The ambassador pledged the hefty sum of 10,000 Swiss francs to support needy Dutchmen in Paris and, presumably, northern France. Weidner paid 800 French francs for Laatsman's train ticket with sleeping berth. The ambassador offered the equivalent of 550,000 French francs, or enough for 687 trips from Paris to Lyon. Based on all he had seen, Laatsman concluded that Weidner's network had the secret and unofficial support of the government in exile.

Six days later Swiss officers courteously held up the barbed wire on the frontier for Weidner and Laatsman to crawl under. On the other side a Swiss woman who had crossed the border with them took Laatsman's arm without saying a word and walked with him some distance behind Weidner—creating an image of placid, local respectability. They followed Weidner into a house just minutes before a motorized German patrol zoomed past. There Alice Charroin, wife of the bicycling police inspector, cleaned the mud off their clothes and gave them a cup of warm coffee. The ersatz coffee alone would have been enough to tell Laatsman that he was back in occupied France.[22] He returned to Paris as the chief of the Paris station of the new network.

Laatsman's plans to recruit others to the network fell apart while he was still in Switzerland. Unbeknownst to him, the diplomats at the Paris embassy whom he intended to enlist were arrested while he was away. Those arrests scared other expatriates so much that they backed out of their earlier commitments to help. Laatsman did, however, still have three long-term colleagues who were at large and willing to help: Suzanne Hiltermann, Leo Marc Mincowski, and Jean-Michael Caubo.

Johannes Michael "Jean-Michael" Caubo, 1938.

A Dutch student at the Sorbonne who was fluent in several languages, Hiltermann met Laatsman at a Dutch gathering in late 1940. Considering him to be the most serious person there, she began helping him to get Dutch Jews to Switzerland.[23] She met Mincowski around the same time. The two worked closely together, using the same last name and the same address on their false identity cards. Indeed their colleagues in Dutch-Paris thought they were married or engaged. But Mincowski could not have been either; his wife and young daughter lived in Paris.[24] American aviators described him as six feet tall with black hair and the look of a "dope fiend," which may have implied that the stress of his very complicated double life haunted his expression.[25]

Like Hiltermann, Mincowski had a talent for languages. He had been born in Romania in 1913 but emigrated to France with his family before 1931. During the war he worked as a translator at the German embassy in Paris. After hours he gave Russian lessons to a German working in the economic section. No friend to the Nazis, the German diplomat passed embassy information to Mincowski and two Frenchmen at regular Friday-evening assignations in the Bois de Boulogne.[26] Mincowski passed the intelligence to Laatsman through Hiltermann, and probably also to the French resistance group to which he himself belonged.[27]

A month before Weidner arrived in Paris, in September 1943, French resisters from another group asked Hiltermann and Mincowski to find a way to get two American aviators back to England.[28] They accepted and enlisted several acquaintances to help feed and shelter those two Americans before they left for England by sea over the English Channel. Hiltermann and Mincowski never repeated that water route, but they did bring those same helpers with them into Dutch-Paris. To find boots and food for the airmen, Mincowski recruited another translator at the German embassy, the Swiss-born Jean Milleret. He in turn engaged French merchants for the supplies.[29] For lodging, Hiltermann asked Milleret's neighbor, Fernande Goetschel. The widow of a French military attaché, Goetschel spoke German and had lived in several European countries and Morocco before the war.[30] Hiltermann probably did not know it, but Goetschel had been hiding agents, documents, and weapons for the British Intelligence Service since April 1943.[31]

When Hiltermann needed new false documents in late 1943, Goetschel introduced her to a friend named Miguel Duchanel. Duchanel had been using his job at the town hall of Drancy to forge documents since 1941. He belonged to a small, local resistance group that was affiliated with the national, noncommunist but Left-leaning French resistance movement Libération Nord. Hiltermann later introduced Duchanel to Laatsman, who invited him to join Dutch-Paris as a forger. Duchanel accepted, giving Dutch-Paris access to false papers issued by the town hall of Drancy and to the resources of Duchanel's Parisian resistance circle. The most important of these was a café in a northern arrondissement where the owner allowed the group to meet and leave messages.[32]

Laatsman had another long-standing colleague in the Dutchman Jean-Michael Caubo. Caubo took good advantage of his position as the head purveyor and accountant for the Amsterdam-Paris express train Mitropa at the gare du Nord. He helped people evade checkpoints and used the company van and staff-only entrances for illegal deliveries.

Laatsman and Caubo had been engaged in illegal activity together for quite some time, and not only to assist refugees. They belonged to an unidentified intelligence line that sent messages hidden in pencils between Paris and Amsterdam every day on the morning and evening trains. Caubo watched the comings and goings on the trains to the Netherlands. His counterpart at Amsterdam Centraal station, a Mr. Van der Wildt, took charge of the exchange of political, economic, and military news.[33] Another of Laatsman's contacts, Baron Jacob K. J. Brantsen, undoubtedly also had a hand in that intelligence line. Brantsen joined the Dutch Intelligence Service during World War I and cultivated a large network of contacts in western Europe between the wars. He opened his home on the prestigious avenue Victor Hugo to Engelandvaarders and surely played a role in Dutch-Paris's intelligence work.[34]

After joining Weidner's new network, Caubo opened his home to the group as a meeting place and a depot for papers. He lived with his wife, twin sons, and daughter at 189 rue Faubourg Poissonnière, conveniently located only a short walk from the gare du Nord. When on a mission for Dutch-Paris, the teenage twins sometimes dressed alike and headed in different directions to confuse anyone who might be watching.[35] When Laatsman fell short of cash, Caubo loaned him enough to keep Dutch-Paris running in Paris until the promised money arrived from Switzerland.[36]

Jean-Michael Caubo, Marie Schenck, and their children,
Joseph, Henri, and Jeannine, 1943.

Caubo found another courier for Dutch-Paris among his neighbors at
189 rue Faubourg Poissonière, a young Corsican woman named Lucie
Comiti. When he and Laatsman paid her a visit in December 1943, Caubo
told Comiti that she could earn a lot of money working for the Germans
at the train station. She immediately responded, "I would rather hang
myself than work for those people." Laatsman exclaimed, "Voilà, that's
what we need." He explained that the network had begun as separate
groups in Lyon, Paris, and Brussels helping Jews hide or flee to Switzerland.
They had now linked together to create an escape line from the Netherlands to Switzerland and Spain. They would continue to help refugees but
would also be taking young men to Spain so they could join the Allies.
Comiti quit her job as a secretary to work full time for Dutch-Paris.[37]

In December 1943 Okhuysen introduced Weidner to two young
Dutchmen who were hiding a dozen or so Engelandvaarders in Paris.
They had been part of the escape line run by a Polish officer, but its route
to Spain had collapsed when the Pole and his Dutch lieutenant were arrested by the Germans a couple of weeks earlier. One of the two did not
want to work with Weidner, although he did accept money from him to
fund his own escape line.[38] The other, Albert Starink, joined Dutch-Paris

Albert Starink, 1943.

because he thought it was his best option to get the Engelandvaarders to Spain. A recently graduated engineer, Starink had a job with a construction firm in Paris that gave him legitimate papers to travel on business and a remarkably understanding employer.[39] Starink used the job as a cover when he traveled between Paris, Brussels, and the Netherlands as a courier.

Another young Dutch woman, Anna Neyssel, joined Dutch-Paris to help Starink and Okhuysen with Engelandvaarders. One of them described her to the Dutch authorities in London as taking care of Hollanders "like a mother."[40] Neyssel and Hiltermann had been at the Sorbonne together in 1940, but they did not know they worked in the same resistance organization until they met as prisoners at the women's concentration camp of Ravensbrück in 1944.[41]

The *sociaalwerk* in northern France consisted of delivering cash to Laatsman, Mohr, or pastors known to Visser 't Hooft to be distributed to the needy rather than doing the daily work of rescue, as Weidner's group and the Comité did in southern France and Belgium.[42] The *transportwerk*, however, required constant coordination because fugitives came from different places. Weidner accepted Engelandvaarders who were already in Paris. A number of Engelandvaarders showed up without warning at Starink's hotel in the Latin Quarter because the man who provided their false travel papers in Amsterdam gave them that address.[43] And, of course, the line brought fugitives of all sorts—refugees, Engelandvaarders, and later Allied aviators—from the Netherlands and Belgium to Paris on their way to Switzerland or Spain. Very few of them could transit through the city in one day. Even if they did not need new documents to travel in France, the train schedules did not always synchronize.

The guides from Brussels had to know when and where to pass their charges to the guides in Paris, and the people in Paris needed to know how many fugitives to expect. Because there were more fugitives than guides, Dutch-Paris worked on a convoy system. The Comité waited until they had a certain number of Engelandvaarders before taking anyone to Paris. The number varied but was usually four or more. The helpers in Paris then hid fugitives in the city until they had enough to take south toward Spain, often a dozen or more at a time.

Technically Laatsman was in charge of the group in Paris, but it never cohered. Starink, for one, did not accept Laatsman's authority and took orders only from Weidner. At best the Paris station of Dutch-Paris formed an uneasy alliance. They did what needed to be done, but some of the men simply did not get along with each other. As the line's leaders, Weidner, Chait, and Rens traveled to Paris constantly to divide responsibilities among their colleagues there and settle disputes. Verloop or one of the other young men from the Comité often came to the regular meetings to coordinate the passage of Engelandvaarders through Paris.

From the beginning Weidner and Laatsman worried that the number of fugitives moving through Paris and the size and sociability of the Dutch colony there increased the group's risks. They implemented a system in which Laatsman vetted all self-identified refugees and Engelandvaarders before they were given any help or introduced to anyone else in the group. The system prevented any German agents from infiltrating the line in Paris, but in a sense it was already too late. Agents provocateurs had found Laatsman's trail before he ever met Weidner.

In the summer of 1943 two paid informers, one Dutch and one Belgian, talked their way into a Dutch resistance group in Paris. Without realizing what he was doing, a young Dutchman introduced them around the Dutch colony as resisters. Another trusting expatriate gave one of the informers Laatsman's calling card and told him the names of the hotels that Laatsman used for refugees.[44] Of course no one in Paris knew this during the war. British officers pieced together the story by interviewing Engelandvaarders when they arrived in London during the occupation. They also found Laatsman's card among the belongings of the Belgian informer when they arrested him after the Liberation. Weidner, Laatsman, and everyone associated with them in Paris had good cause to worry about their safety.

Paris, however, served merely as a collecting point and way station. The goal for every fugitive on the line lay farther south, in Switzerland or Spain. To get to Switzerland from Paris, a refugee took a train to Lyon and then followed the route through Annecy and Collonges-sous-Salève that Weidner and Elisabeth Cartier had established more than a year earlier. To get to Spain a fugitive took the train to Toulouse and then went by local train and on foot through the mountains.

Three young women who served the line as full-time couriers— Okhuysen, Comiti, and Jacqueline Houry—usually escorted the convoys from Paris to Toulouse. Houry lived outside Paris, but Rens had recruited her through his contacts in Toulouse. Like the young women associated with Dutch-Paris in Toulouse, Houry was a Catholic university student. In Paris she worked primarily with Gabrielle Weidner and Okhuysen.[45] When necessary Hiltermann would join one or more of these women to escort fugitives to the Pyrenees, although she was not otherwise a courier. On occasion Rens or Chait joined a large convoy as its leader, especially if it included Allied aviators. The Spanish border posed a more formidable challenge than the Franco-Swiss border in the Genevois. Two thousand or so German customs officers, soldiers, and policemen enforced a twenty-mile-deep *zone interdite*, or forbidden zone, along the Spanish frontier and guarded the few roads into Spain. Their domination of the telephones, telegraphs, and roads and their near monopoly of motorized vehicles gave them the aura of being everywhere at once.[46] Fugitives and their guides could not walk around a guardhouse as they did on the Dutch border or slip under barbed wire in daylight hours as they did on the Swiss border. To get across the Spanish border they first had to travel into the foothills through the forbidden zone, which required special passes. Then they had to trek for miles through the mountains in the dark.

Weidner chose Toulouse as the line's base for the Pyrenees where convoys could gather and be supplied while waiting for favorable conditions to attempt the crossing into Spain. There were easier parts of the Pyrenees to walk through than the section of the Haute-Garonne south of Toulouse, where peaks reach as high as ten thousand feet and sudden snowstorms close the passes, even in July. Villages hug the mountainsides and river banks, and shepherd's huts dot the higher slopes, but only local men and women could hope to find their way across those mountains in the dark. It usually took three days and nights—if everything went well.

Nonetheless Toulouse had advantages. Regular trains ran there from both Paris and Lyon, and travelers did not need special passes in the city because it was not in the forbidden zone or the zone along the Atlantic Coast that the Germans had occupied in 1940. Most important, Weidner had already sent Engelandvaarders to Spain through two men in Toulouse. The first, Antonius Aarts, was a Dutch Jewish refugee who inherited the job of Dutch consul in Toulouse when the Germans arrested the actual consul in early 1943. The second, Gabriel Nahas, was a French medical student.

Weidner met Aarts in early 1943 when he delivered cash for Dutch refugees and prisoners in the region. The acting consul had found a notably efficient and reliable *filière*, or local escape line, from Toulouse to the Spanish villages of Lès and Canejan by befriending a refugee from the Spanish Civil War at the restaurant where they both ate dinner. That Spanish refugee had introduced the Dutch refugee to another Spanish refugee, an accountant named Audain "Antonio" Caparros-Muñoz, who had been an officer in the Spanish Republican Army but was now a *passeur*.

In the arrangement set up by Aarts and Caparros, Engelandvaarders lodged at an inn on the outskirts of Toulouse called the Panier Fleuri while the documents they would need in the *zone interdite* were forged by the brother-in-law of the *filière's* chief guide. A French widow named Marie Combes escorted the fugitives on the train to villages in the foothills, where they met their guides.[47] Weidner's friend and assistant in Geneva, Nico Gazan, crossed the Pyrenees by this route in only two days in September 1943, a notably easy crossing.[48]

Weidner met his second Toulousian contact for passages to Spain in June 1943 through his contacts among Christian resisters. A medical student at the University of Toulouse, Gabriel Nahas had been active in Catholic youth groups before the war. Nahas had a varied career in the Resistance, including serving as medical officer for a *maquis*, or partisan, unit in 1944. Before he joined the *maquis*, however, he acted as a broker between local *passeurs* who took people over the Pyrenees and escape lines that brought men to

Toulouse

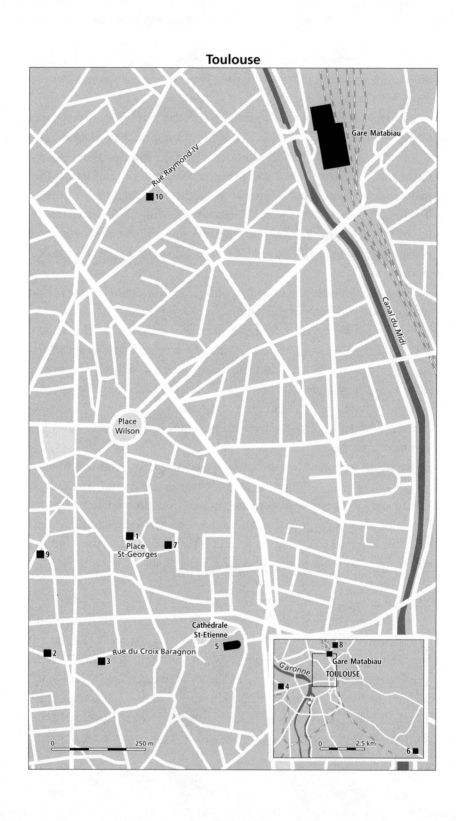

Gabriel Nahas, 1943.

Simone Calmels, 1943.

Toulouse.[49] Overall Nahas brokered passages on three routes, but he sent most Dutch-Paris evaders on one created by two Catholic university students.

The two young women tipped into resistance when male friends and relatives asked them for help getting into Spain so that they could join de Gaulle's Free French Army in North Africa. One of the students, Simone Calmels, did her illegal work without her physician father's knowledge and against his wishes. In June 1943 one of the men she helped introduced her to his cousin, a law student named Andrée Moulouguet. The women divided the work of getting their male friends to Spain. Moulouguet took care of the men in Toulouse. They recruited another law student, Anita Boucoiran, whose family also did not approve of her resistance work, to help in Toulouse.

Calmels fed and hid their fugitives in the market town of Saint-Girons in the foothills before passing them to a team of passeurs known to Engelandvaarders and Allied aviators as Palo and Mireille.[50] Pierre Treillet, or "Palo," worked for the French railways until

---

TOULOUSE

1 restaurant Chez Émile (place St-Georges)
2 rue de la Trinité – *Foyer Protestant* and dry cleaners used as meeting places and postboxes
3 restaurant À la Truffe du Quercy (17 rue Croix Baragnon)
4 "Villa du Crime" – hiding place for Allied aviators
5 Cathedral of St. Etienne – meeting place used by Nahas
6 Panier Fleuri – inn used by Engelandvaarders in 1942–1943
7 Milice prison from which Veerman, Weidner and Rens escaped
8 50 rue du Faubourg Bonnefoy, Father Aan de Stegge's parish
9 9 rue des Puits-Verts, Chait's safe house
10 20 rue Raymond IV – Calmel's home

he refused to supervise a train of French workers being sent to Germany in 1943. Instead he went underground as a *passeur*.[51] His partner, Henri Marot, known as "Mireille," worked as a bailiff until he was taken prisoner during the battles of 1940. He escaped from a POW camp and made his own way home, where he started guiding fugitives to Spain.[52] After the three students had organized their route from Toulouse to Spain via St. Girons and the *passeurs* Treillet and Marot, Moulouguet met Nahas at one of their safe houses. He proposed that they all work together, to which the three women agreed.[53]

When Weidner arrived in Toulouse on October 27, 1943, to make arrangements for Engelandvaarders coming from the north to join those coming from Switzerland on convoys over the Pyrenees, he found Dutch affairs there to be in dangerous confusion. The problem seemed to lie with Aarts, whom Weidner considered to be "always very willing but imprecise and disorderly." He had not distributed the welfare money Weidner had brought him earlier in the year. Worse, he disregarded the most elementary safety precautions. He added men to convoys without verifying their identity to make sure they were not agents provocateurs and gave out the names and addresses of other helpers to anyone who asked. Weidner worried that the route to Spain would be "ruined by his carelessness."[54] Because Nahas also needed help organizing convoys, Weidner asked a young Dutch woman, a would-be artist named Suzy Kraay, to assist them with Engelandvaarders in Toulouse.

A year earlier, in October 1942, Kraay had made her own way from Amsterdam to Paris, where the Laatsmans befriended her. She went to Lyon illegally on New Year's Day 1943 as a favor to the family, who wanted to know if Weidner could get them to Switzerland. The answer was yes, but the Laatsmans chose to stay in Paris. Kraay, however, remained in Lyon with false documents that Weidner provided and in lodging that he helped her find.[55] She made friends with a French woman her age who shared her artistic ambitions, named Josette Molland. After the suppression of the Demarcation Line in March 1943, the friends made two or three clandestine journeys to the Netherlands in order to make arrangements with Kraay's parents for the escape of Dutch Jews.[56] On one of those trips the young women delivered a package of cash to Weidner's parents in The Hague. The Weidners found Kraay to be thoroughly charming and enjoyed her day-long visit.[57]

During one of these trips to Amsterdam, Kraay and Molland went out to the café of the Hotel Americain on the Leidse Plein. There they ran into a young Dutchman whom Kraay had met in Paris the previous fall. Kraay's acquaintance introduced them to the man he was sitting with, a certain Van den Berg, who claimed to have access to an illegal radio transmitter and photographic negatives of the German defenses around the city. After the war Kraay described this Van den Berg as "a tall, thin man, bald (probably used to be a red head), gold glasses, large hawk nose, no moustache, hoarse voice." That same day, at the corner of Amstellaan and Amsteldijk, Van den Berg introduced her to his "courier," who went by the name Eugène. Kraay later described him as "a Frenchman, short, pale face, large horn rimmed glasses, pale blond hair with a bald spot, very striking, big, steel-blue eyes."

"Eugène" was no Frenchman. He was Richard Christmann, a ranking officer in the German military counterintelligence unit Abwehrstelle IIIF. Christmann had a great facility for languages and an easy manner. After the war a Dutch investigator described him as "worth his weight in gold" as a spy.[58] Van den Berg was really Hermanus Rouwendal, a Dutchman who was on Christmann's payroll as an informer and agent provocateur.

The women returned to Paris, where "Eugène" made himself useful providing travel documents and exchanging money for them. Of course this also made it easier for him to track them because he knew the names and numbers on their false documents. Back in the Netherlands, Rouwendal insinuated himself into the Kraays' scheme to smuggle a small group of Dutch Jews from Amsterdam to Lyon. He also tipped off the Sicherheitsdienst (German security service, separate from the Abwehr) to what he called the "hot-bed of Dutch resistance" at Kraay's usual hotel in Montmarte (Paris) in late May 1943, probably for a bounty.[59] A number of arrests followed.

Panicked by the arrests and against Weidner's advice, Kraay and Molland fled toward Spain. While they were still on the French side of the border, German police roused Kraay from her hotel bed but released her to the French authorities after a few hours' questioning. Weidner declined to vouch for Kraay in the French court in Pau when Molland sent him a telegram asking him to intervene. He obviously could not: to do so could have compromised the entire rescue effort. After serving the mandatory one month in prison handed out to foreigners caught too close to a French border, Kraay was transferred to Vichy's internment camp at Gurs.[60] She escaped from the camp in late October 1943 and returned to Lyon.

Somewhat surprisingly—given her arrest and increased visibility to the police—Weidner asked Kraay to work for Dutch-Paris in Toulouse. In hindsight it is easy to say that Weidner should have cut off all contact with Kraay when she reappeared in late 1943. But her arrest on the Spanish border followed the same pattern as the arrests of many Dutch fugitives on the Swiss border or the Demarcation Line, including the standard one month in prison and transfer to an internment camp. She must have given him a satisfactory explanation of her escape from Gurs.

Besides, Weidner had few, if any, other candidates for the job of organizing Dutch-Paris fugitives in Toulouse. He, Chait, and Rens were already fully occupied traveling between Annecy, Lyon, Paris, and Brussels. Raymonde Pillot in Lyon and Catherine Okhuysen in Paris were equally busy as couriers and still living in the open. Sending either of them to Toulouse would mean asking her to go underground before it was necessary. As an illegal foreigner and an escapee from an internment camp, however, Kraay would have to live underground wherever she went in France. Weidner also started the paperwork to establish a long-term refuge for Kraay near Annecy, but she chose to resist as part of Dutch-Paris instead.

After she arrived in Toulouse in early November, Kraay reported that it was only "thanks to the nonchalance of the French police" that more Dutchmen had not been arrested there. The biggest problem, in her opinion, was that all Engelandvaarders went to a single hotel, the Panier Fleuri, where they had nothing to do but talk. Furthermore the military attaché's office in Bern was not preparing them properly for their journey across France. The latest group to arrive from Switzerland had forgotten to look for a woman in a red scarf holding a newspaper at the gare Matabiau (Kraay herself). Others had balked at paying Nahas the fee of 5,000 French francs for the *passeur* that the military attaché had issued to them for that express purpose.[61] Nor could Aarts and Nahas be relied upon. The most recent group of Engelandvaarders had made three attempts to cross the high, snow-covered mountains with *passeurs* recommended by Aarts and Nahas, only to suffer injuries, arrests, and theft. They were all still in occupied territory.[62]

Rens left Switzerland a few days later to sort out the problems in Toulouse. By the next evening he had twenty-one Engelandvaarders to hide in the city.[63] He could only agree with the owners of the Panier Fleuri that having so many fugitives in one place endangered them all. He looked for alternate lodgings to spread them out, settled outstanding accounts with French helpers, and pressed the *passeurs* to take the Engelandvaarders to Spain.

Rens also consulted with an expatriate who had been helping Dutchmen get to Spain since 1940. The flamboyant Lil van Wijhe had retired with her late husband, a Dutch physician, to the village of Capendu, east of Toulouse between Carcassonne and Narbonne. According to family and Engelandvaarder legend, Van Wijhe had trained with the exotic dancer and executed German spy Mata Hari and worked for the British Intelligence Service in Amsterdam during the First World War.[64]

Whether or not she had any such training, Van Wijhe spent the Second World War working against the Germans. She recruited her first husband's teenage niece, Louise "Lulu" Balfet, at Christmas dinner in 1940. Balfet and her parents were refugees from Alsace who had settled nearby for the duration. The tall, blonde Lulu spent the occupation running errands for her aunt, which took her on occasion to talk to Simone Calmels.[65] Van Wijhe had also arranged her own route to Spain, which involved crossing the border in a freight train for an exorbitant fee. It was physically much easier than walking over the mountains but not guaranteed.[66] Three men whom Dutch-Paris sent on this route because of injuries in late November were captured when they were overheard talking to each other from their hiding places among the potatoes in a freight car.[67]

Both Kraay and several Engelandvaarders who successfully reached London asked the Dutch authorities to send money to Van Wijhe. German currency regulations blocked her own account in the Netherlands, and she was running out of belongings to pawn to underwrite her safe house and escape route.[68] On his first visit Rens took her enough cash to keep her household running for a month or more, but not enough for even a single passage on her freight train route. He found Van Wijhe to be a model of "helpfulness" with a "heart of gold." She agreed to host some of the exhausted and injured Engelandvaarders currently in Toulouse while they recuperated and to arrange their passage to Spain on her own train route.

Nine days after arriving in Toulouse, Rens dispatched fifteen Engeland-vaarders with the *passeurs* Treillet and Marot.[69] They included two Dutch secret agents, Pieter Dourlein and Ben Ubbink, who had been arrested as

Lil van Wijhe's villa in Capendu, 1912.

soon as they parachuted into the Netherlands in the intelligence catastrophe known as the Englandspiel. Months earlier German intelligence officers had captured wireless operators who had parachuted into occupied Holland and broken the Dutch and British codes. They arrested new agents as soon they arrived and fed false information back to London.[70] Dourlein and Ubbink had escaped from prison in the Netherlands and made their way to Annecy, where they came under Weidner's protection.

Coincidentally, on the same day that Weidner met the secret agents, angry French paramilitary collaborators belonging to the *Milice* were pouring into town to avenge the killing of one of their own by armed resisters. The situation was so tense that the old man who owned the small house where the secret agents were hiding in an upstairs room stood just inside the door with a hatchet, ready to defend them. Weidner and Chait conferred with the fugitives in the house: the two secret agents, a couple of Dutchmen, two Czechs, and an Englishman whom Weidner had brought from Switzerland. They chose to risk walking to the station and leaving by train. Chait escorted them as far as Lyon. Another courier, probably Pillot, took them to Toulouse.[71]

Within hours of arriving in Toulouse, Dourlein and Ubbink were hiking through the Pyrenees as part of an international convoy of close to thirty Dutchmen, other Europeans, and Allied servicemen. Snow, German patrols, and German searchlights that swept the mountainsides slowed them down. None of the Dutchmen had enough food with him. More than one of them, however, reported that one or two men in the convoy who did not speak Dutch carried cans of food which they ate without sharing. During one of their cold and cramped rests, Dourlein and Ubbink told their companions that the Germans were arresting Dutch agents as they parachuted into the Netherlands. No one believed them. The convoy made it to Spain on the fifth day, all of them exhausted, some of them with frostbite.[72]

Almost as soon as that convoy left, Rens realized that they had not taken enough food with them. Earlier groups of Engelandvaarders had come from Switzerland well stocked with high-energy foods, such as chocolate and condensed milk and even cognac. This was the first Dutch-Paris convoy to include men coming from the north without benefit of the provisions available in neutral Switzerland. In addition a few of the men, like Dourlein and Ubbink, had already been on the run for some time and passed through Toulouse too quickly to rest or resupply. After that, Dutch-Paris never sent a man over the Pyrenees without first buying three days' worth of food for him on the black market either in Paris or Toulouse.

It was clear that Dutch-Paris needed a permanent station chief in Toulouse to organize fugitives as they arrived, make sure they were properly equipped to cross the mountains, and deal with the *passeurs*. But who? The refugee turned consul Aarts had proven unreliable and was soon to go into hiding.[73] The medical student Nahas shocked Weidner by announcing that he was going to Switzerland on French and British business rather than for Dutch affairs. After that Nahas associated himself with the British-sponsored French escape line called "Françoise." He did, however, continue to broker *passeurs* for Dutch-Paris.[74] Indeed Weidner credited him with arranging 50 percent of the line's passages over the Pyrenees.[75] Kraay had been doing good work in Toulouse, but she insisted on going to Amsterdam after hearing that her father had been arrested three months earlier. She did not know, of course, that the informer Rouwendal had arranged her father's arrest after he accused him, rightly, of betraying a party of Jews.[76] Weidner told her that she would have to travel at her own risk and her own expense, but because she was a volunteer over whom he had no actual authority, he could do nothing more to discourage her.

Kraay did, however, agree to stay in Toulouse until they could replace her as the line's liaison there.[77]

For lack of anyone else, Rens and Chait shared the job in Toulouse in addition to their other tasks farther north. For couriers they relied on the enthusiastic group of women students—Calmels, Moulouguet, and Boucoiran—helped occasionally by Dutch-Paris couriers based in Paris. Weidner himself traveled to Toulouse so that he and Rens could deal directly with *passeurs* rather than rely on a middleman such as Nahas to make arrangements. They preferred to work with the Spaniard Caparros, the French team of Treillet and Marot, and another French *passeur*, named Jean-Louis Bazerque.

Better known by his mother's maiden name and his nom de guerre, "Charbonnier," Bazerque joined the regional Armée Sécrète after escaping from a POW camp.[78] A nationwide organization affiliated with de Gaulle's Free French, the Armée Sécrète engaged in the sort of military resistance that trained *maquis* groups in the hills, sabotaged trains, collected intelligence, and generally prepared to join the Allied armies in the hoped-for battle to liberate France. Its affiliation with the Armée Sécrète gave Bazerque's route an extensive intelligence network of forest wardens, shepherds, and other mountain dwellers; excellent relations with the local inhabitants; and well-armed guards.

These were reliable men, but Weidner concluded that the passage to Spain was "excessively expensive."[79] There were legitimate reasons for the high price. No matter who organized it, a clandestine journey through the Pyrenees involved many people, took several days, and ran considerable risks. *Passeurs* relied on a relay of helpers from one valley to the next. Those who escorted fugitives for the entire journey were gone from home too long to hold down a job. Furthermore, after their charges were safe in Spain, the guides had to go back into occupied France, sometimes along routes where the Germans had picked up the trail of the convoy and were searching for them.[80] Some passeurs provided food and lodging as well as guides and local knowledge. Caparros, for example, used part of the fees the fugitives paid to buy food and shelter for them during their two- or three-day treks and provided false work certificates for jobs within the *zone interdite* along the frontier to bolster their false identities.[81]

In March 1943 the local commander of the *Armée Sécrète* decided to regularize prices for clandestine passages in the region in order to stop the exploitation of fugitives. Thereafter he enforced a set price of 10,000 French francs per person for passages in his sector of the Haute-Garonne and Ariège.[82] This was a substantial sum from the perspective of a young working man at a time when a farm laborer in the mountainous department of Ariège south of Toulouse earned 500 French francs plus lodging and board per month, and a private in the French Army, who would have been demobilized and put on half-pay according to the terms of the Armistice, earned 425 French francs per month.[83] Even high school teachers earned only 3,000 francs per month, and retired captains received 4,000 francs. The editor of a national newspaper earned 5,000 francs per month.

It was not, however, a great deal of money from the perspective of the families living in the Pyrenees who had to rely on the black market to supplement their meager rations. In that region in 1943 it cost 80 French francs to purchase a bicycle tire with a ration coupon, which was almost as hard to get as the tire itself. It cost between 800 and 1,000 francs to buy the same tire on the black market. Sugar cost 10 francs per kilogram with a ration coupon, when it was available. On the black market a kilogram of sugar cost 200 francs in 1942, 300 francs in 1943, and 400 francs in May 1944. More tellingly for *passeurs* who walked miles through the mountains, a pair of leather-soled shoes (not boots) cost 4,000 French francs. They cost less with ration coupons, of course, but an adult received a ration coupon for a new pair of shoes only once every two years.[84]

Nevertheless Weidner did have reason to question the fees. Some *passeurs*, like Nahas, charged the Dutch a premium to subsidize the passages of men from their own countries.[85] They could do so because the Dutch, unlike the French, could not manage the Pyrenees on their own and because Weidner and his colleagues found the necessary cash through the Dutch, British, and American military attachés in Switzerland. Weidner and Rens could not bargain down the rate for Dutch-Paris fugitives, but they did establish better communications between the Dutch-Paris resisters in Toulouse and the *passeurs* in the Pyrenees.

Meanwhile Engelandvaarders continued to arrive at the gare Matabiau, sometimes without warning.[86] In December 1943 Rens and Chait sent a handful of them to Spain via Van Wijhe's freight train route. They also diverted two people to Switzerland for health reasons. Most of the Engelandvaarders, however, walked over the Pyrenees. On the 22nd Palo and Mireille left with a small convoy of three Frenchmen, two Italians, and seven Dutchmen whom Starink had gathered together in Paris. Two of the Engelandvaarders, the poet Lex Gans and Jack Bottenheim, had left the Netherlands with false SD papers in September and had dodged one disaster after another in France. They were joined by a Canadian flier, Hank Wardle, who had escaped to Switzerland from a POW camp and been sent to Toulouse by the Dutch military attaché as a courtesy to his British counterpart. The weather was bitter. Two days into the trek the Canadian commented, "Only complete idiots would exchange the friendly confinement of a German prisoner of war camp for the barbaric desolation of the Pyrenees in December."[87]

Lex Gans's Spanish identity papers, 1944.

Dutch-Paris lost its most reliable route over the Pyrenees on December 23 or 24, 1943, when Caparros's guide in Toulouse, Marie Combes, was arrested by German police at the gare Matabiau. How they knew that she and two fugitives, one of whom was Belgian, would be there is unknown, but they may have found her trail by interrogating Belgian resisters with whom she cooperated in Toulouse.[88] The same German roundup of Belgian resisters in the city affected Dutch-Paris again a week later. Gestapo agents raided the Panier Fleuri on December 31, arresting everyone there, including six men traveling with Dutch-Paris: two Engelandvaarders who joined Dutch-Paris in France, a Belgian and an Irishman sent from Switzerland, and a Dutchman and a Belgian introduced to the line by Nahas.

Unaware of these events, Rens and Weidner tried to telephone the inn to make reservations for two more Engelandvaarders in early January. When no one answered, they went there in person. Fortunately they arrived the day after the Gestapo withdrew. Rens settled their bill and crossed the Panier Fleuri off his list of safe houses. After talking to the innkeeper and other contacts, Weidner concluded that a Belgian agent provocateur had stayed at the Panier Fleuri just before the raid. Unfortunately he had certainly overheard the names of some Dutch-Paris helpers, such as "Jean" and "Suzy."[89]

It was time to expand Dutch-Paris's expatriate and resistance base in Toulouse. Weidner and Rens began by recruiting a man with a reputation for compassion and decisive action. Father John aan de Stegge had been caring for Dutch and Belgian immigrants in the diocese of Toulouse since the 1930s. During the war he helped anyone who asked, even intervening with the German authorities on behalf of prisoners.[90] Weidner and Rens visited him at his rectory on a Friday night when he was sick in bed. After introducing themselves as compatriots and trading observations about the weather, Weidner told him they were looking for safe houses for men on their way to Spain. He intended to keep the priest out of the usual flow of Dutch-Paris traffic so that only the leaders would call on him to deliver cash for refugees hiding in the area or for special occasions.

Worried that they might be Gestapo agents, Aan de Stegge asked his visitors if they thought he had nothing better to do in a parish of twelve thousand souls. For good measure he added that if a German fell out of an airplane he would give him as much help as an American or an Englishman, as long as what he wanted was spiritual aid. After a pause Weidner offered to have any message the priest chose read over the BBC in order to earn his trust. Always careful, Aan de Stegge answered that it was wholly un- necessary because he could not help them and he had no idea where he could listen to the BBC (which was a crime at that time). Weidner never- theless told him to listen for the phrase "The flower vase is on the table" on the BBC the following Tuesday. Aan de Stegge said he certainly would not risk arrest for such a frivolous reason. With that, Weidner decided that the priest was exactly the sort of overly careful man they needed.

Aan de Stegge remained undecided about his visitors until the follow- ing Tuesday, when he heard the designated sentence on the BBC. When Chait appeared at the rectory with one of Weidner's calling cards the next morning, the priest showed him around Toulouse and found him a trust- worthy family with whom to stay when he was in the city.[91] Aan de Stegge continued to help all sorts of people in Toulouse while also serving Dutch- Paris as a top-security safe house and as a distributor of welfare allotments to Dutch refugees. Weidner's prudence in recruiting the priest as part of the network would more than pay off a few months later, in May.

Weidner was also looking for couriers and postboxes for a proposed Switzerland-Spain leg of the Swiss Way intelligence relay. For the most part the Dutch embassies in Bern and Madrid communicated by telegrams that went through London. But the Dutch authorities did not trust the security of these transmissions for every message. Furthermore whenever they changed the code they needed couriers to deliver the new codebook across occupied territory. In addition Weidner sometimes had microfilm that he wanted to send directly to London because they came from contacts outside of the Swiss Way or contained urgent information.

These microfilms needed to go over the Pyrenees with someone who would be able to personally hand them to the proper officials in Madrid or London. For lack of an alternative in early January 1944, Weidner had to give a microfilm hidden in a flashlight to an economics student who had made his own way to Toulouse. After checking his identity and story through the embassy in Bern, Weidner put him on a Dutch-Paris convoy. The Dutch officer who interviewed the young Engelandvaarder when he arrived in England thought his "story about the papers…sounds somewhat fantastical," but the microfilm reached its destination.[92] Weidner recruited a French family in Carcassone and a young French woman in Toulouse to act as couriers and a postbox for messages and microfilms.[93]

The Dutch Bureau Inlichtingen (Intelligence Bureau) in Madrid sent Van Wijhe's son to Geneva as a courier, but he fell into a crevasse in the mountains. Local people rescued him, and his cousin Lulu Balfet escorted him to Switzerland for medical care. He recovered, but his trekking days were over.[94] After that they sent couriers to Gabrielle Weidner in Paris, with mixed success.[95] Weidner did manage to establish an overland courier connection between Madrid and Bern, but it never functioned as well as the link between Geneva and Amsterdam.

By January 1944 Weidner had built a functioning escape line and courier network between the Netherlands, Spain, and Switzerland. When he started helping Jews escape to Switzerland in the summer of 1942, he could personally recruit most of the members of his network between Lyon and Geneva because he and Cartier had grown up in the region. He knew the geography, the customs, and the patois. But even there he did not necessarily know everyone involved, nor did they know him.

The farther Weidner went from the Haute-Savoie, the less easily he could recruit people. Outside his home region he approached potential candidates not as a neighbor but as a stranger. When looking for people whom he could trust and whom he could convince to trust him, he drew on two aspects of his own identity: his religious beliefs and his Dutch nationality. As a believer Weidner moved easily among Catholic priests, Protestant pastors, and other Christians. He used his own contacts in Amitié Chrétienne and Visser 't Hooft's in other Protestant resistance groups to help Dutch refugees and expand his own network. They led him, for example, to Gabriel Nahas. In May 1944 his willingness to discuss theological points at great length even helped him escape from a *Milice* prison. Being Dutch brought Weidner two-thirds of the people he helped and much of the line's funding. Indeed he expanded his network beyond Lyon only at the request of the Dutch authorities in Switzerland. It was the reason Benno Nijkerk looked for him in May 1943 and the reason Herman Laatsman decided to cooperate with him six months later in November.

Weidner personally knew all the leaders and long-distance couriers, most of whom were Dutch, but he did not know many of the three hundred or so helpers whom those leaders recruited from among their own neighbors and relations. Indeed the line's membership expanded without Weidner's knowledge or control. When a helper accepted a task, he or she took responsibility for enlisting whoever else was needed to accomplish it. Everyone else just had to hope that the helper would choose carefully and not endanger them all with an agent provocateur or a gossip. This pattern of personal recruitment created a few noticeable lines of affiliation within Dutch-Paris.

The most prevalent was Dutch citizenship or heritage. Not every member of the line was Dutch; in fact the majority were French or Belgian. Even among the Dutch expatriates, some, such as Jean and Gabrielle Weidner and Catherine Okhuysen, had grown up in France as the children of Dutch parents. Still the French and Belgian members tended to be connections of Dutch expatriates who belonged to the line, and the links in the group went through the expatriates, including the second-generation Dutch.

The balance of nationalities working in Dutch-Paris shifted over time and as the line moved south from the Dutch border. In Brussels almost all members who had not been recruited for a specific function were Dutch. But Brussels lies close to the Dutch border and had a large and well-established Dutch colony. It was the first stop for both Dutch fugitives and Dutch resisters searching for a change of place.

Fewer Dutch expatriates lived in France, although they often knew each other or of each other. Even if they did not, sharing a language and a nation gave them reason to work together. When Weidner and Rens wanted Father John aan de Stegge's help in Toulouse, for example, they introduced themselves as "compatriots." There are also signs of circles of religious affiliation in the line. The Dutch farmers outside Paris from whom Brother Rufus bought black market food for aviators, for example, were Catholics. One couple had met the brother over coffee after a monthly Dutch-language mass in Paris.

Weidner's active involvement in the Seventh-day Adventist Church also brought some Adventists into Dutch-Paris.[96] For instance, he and Cartier first met Pillot at church in Lyon. Weidner may have hired her as his secretary because of that connection, but he asked her to help with his resistance work several months later because he had come to know her personally. Likewise Weidner and Cartier probably would not have known Pastor Paul and Marthe Meyer well enough to rely on them for illegal help in Lyon if they did not attend their church. The couple also recruited personal friends at the very conveniently located Adventist seminary in Collonges-sous-Salève, where Weidner had lived as a boy.

Nevertheless there was nothing expressly Catholic or Adventist or even religious about Dutch-Paris. The Catholics and Adventists worked side by side with Calvinists, Jews, and atheists. Pastor ten Kate in Brussels, for example, does not appear to have recruited from his congregation. Instead many of the members who did the behind-the-scenes work in the Comité were businessmen with sons of draft age. These men may have known one another through their children or approached each other because of their common fear that their sons would be deported as slave labor, pressed into the military, or shot in the street.

University students made up another social circle. Many of those who worked in Dutch-Paris in Brussels had also worked together in Dutch resistance groups in the Netherlands, such as the Utrechtse Kindercomité, before moving to Belgium. And of course many of the Engelandvaarders whom Dutch-Paris helped were students who found the line through their university friends who belonged to it. Students in Toulouse also recruited among themselves.

There are also signs of professional affiliation in Dutch-Paris. A number of helpers, such as Weidner, Wisbrun, and Veerman, as well as some of the fugitives, such as the man who wrote to Weidner from the French prison in 1942, were involved in the textile trade. There are also connections through the Dutch insurance company Utrecht Vie. The fathers of David Verloop and J. P. Bol in Brussels founded the company, and Consul Maurice Jacquet in Lyon worked for it. That may have been purely coincidental, although Weidner used the address of the Utrecht Vie office in Paris for at least one mysterious errand. There were undoubtedly professional connections among the police and customs agents and civil servants who worked for Dutch-Paris on the Swiss border and in the prefectures in Lyon and Annecy and the town hall of Etterbeek, Brussels.

Nonetheless the overall membership of Dutch-Paris is more noteworthy for its diversity or ecumenism than it is for any particular commonality found among a circle within the larger group. The only characteristic that every man and woman in Dutch-Paris shared was a willingness to help other men and women escape the Nazis and their collaborators despite the risks to themselves. Those dangers were about to increase exponentially when Weidner opened the escape line to downed Allied aviators who were hiding in the Netherlands, Belgium, and northern France.

Hollandsch Spoor Train Station in The Hague, 1950.

5

Over the Mountains

EVEN AS THE MEN AND WOMEN OF DUTCH-PARIS established the connections and routes of their escape line, military developments changed the demographics of the people who needed their help. They had started by rescuing Jews during the great crisis of the mass deportations in 1942. By the summer of 1943 most Jews had been captured or had found hiding places. In the meantime German losses on the Eastern Front, especially the defeat at Stalingrad in February 1943, deepened the labor shortage on the German home front. The Nazis responded with greater and more aggressive demands for manpower from occupied territories. Young men in the Netherlands, Belgium, and France went into hiding to escape the labor draft or tried to join the Allies. In September 1943 the Italian capitulation and subsequent German seizure of the Italian occupation zone in France spurred Jews hiding there to attempt the journey to Switzerland, provoking a new wave of Jewish refugees needing help.

While young men searched for ways to escape the labor draft and Jews kept trying to survive in occupied territory, the U.S. and British air forces ramped up their bombing campaign over Germany. The sheer number of aircraft involved, the distances they flew to reach their targets, and the German air defense meant that over the course of 1943 an increasing number of airplanes did not make it back to their bases in England. By the end of the year Allied aviators were literally falling out of the sky over northwestern Europe. Those who survived bailing out or crash landing joined the civilian fugitives trying to get out of occupied territory. In response the men and women of Dutch-Paris did not change the nature of their resistance, but they did change the details of the way they carried it out.

Main Routes of Dutch-Paris

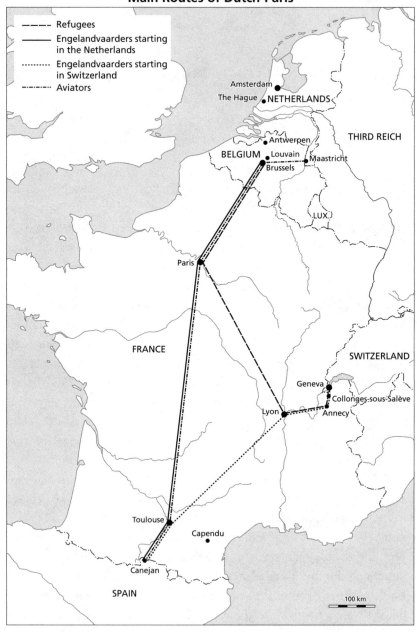

No matter what else happened, however, they did not forget the Jewish refugees they were hiding in occupied territory. When Gestapo agents arrested Consul Jacquet in Lyon in early September 1943, prudence dictated that his resistance colleagues take cover. Some did, but others could not leave the refugees who depended on them just when German troops were taking over what had been the Italian occupation zone. As Weidner put it, the Germans were "hunting Jews."[1] He, Edmond Chait, or Raymonde Pillot made the rounds of refugees they had established in legal residences in Haute-Savoie and Savoie to encourage them to leave France altogether and to make plans for their escape. One multigenerational family left their hiding place with a pharmacist in Cruseilles mere hours before the warrant for their arrest arrived. Their hosts' fifteen-year-old son led them the twelve miles to the border. Paramilitary collaborators in the *Milice* searched their hosts' home twice after the refugees left.[2]

After September 8, 1943, German troops guarded the Swiss frontier more closely than their Italian counterparts had, setting up observation posts on the slopes above the valley. They also revoked the border passes that the Swiss helpers at the Adventist seminary in Collonges had used on a regular basis. Jean Zurcher, for example, could no longer bicycle to his graduate classes in Geneva, with or without clandestine documents. Around the same time the guide Ernest Bouchet had to shift his activities away from the Genevois because French police were looking for him. Weidner therefore lost guides on the Swiss border at the very time he needed them more than ever. Once or twice circumstances forced him to hire professional *passeurs*. He received complaints of theft and greed but, thankfully, not betrayal.[3]

Jewish refugees who had been living in the Italian zone were not the only ones to attempt the journey to Switzerland after September 1943. Hiding anywhere in France was becoming increasingly untenable. For example, the Dutch farmers Jaap van der Post and his wife, Johanna Schuylenburg, hid Jews from eastern Europe, an Italian, several Frenchmen avoiding the labor draft, and eleven Dutch refugees, including a little girl and her mother, at their farm in the Jura, north of Lyon. They weathered at least one raid by the Feldgendarmerie (German military police) without incident thanks to timely warnings by French police. In fact they colluded with several local officials to hide these refugees in plain sight. In late 1943, however, Van der Post received a warning that three of his Dutch guests were going to be arrested.

He called Jacquet in Lyon for advice. The consul had returned to his illegal work after being released from prison, despite being warned not to meddle in "Dutch affairs." A few days later Chait arrived at the farm to escort the three Dutchmen to Lyon. There Weidner gave them cash from the military attaché's account and sent them to Toulouse so they could go to England via Spain and volunteer with the Allied armies.[4] Unfortunately one of them was captured during the German raid on the Panier Fleuri on December 31, leading to his death in Buchenwald sixteen months later.[5]

In the months after the German occupation of the Italian zone, the young couriers Pillot and Bouchet escorted entire families across southern France to Annecy. Bouchet took advantage of his youthful looks to convince both the fugitives and the police of his harmlessness.[6] For her part, Pillot tried to look older when she traveled for Dutch-Paris by wearing her mother's wedding ring and reading a book in the crowded trains.[7]

By this time Dutch refugees in Switzerland had started asking Elisabeth Cartier to bring their relatives in occupied territory to safety. To give one example, a Dutch refugee in Geneva whose last name was Simon asked Cartier to help his brother and his family escape occupied territory. Weidner asked Suzy Kraay to contact the brother, Julius Simon, at his hiding place in the Netherlands when she returned to Amsterdam to see her mother. A few weeks later Weidner met Kraay in Brussels to give her false documents for the Simon family and instructions for their escape.

On January 24, 1944, Kraay brought the two Simon children from their hiding places to the Dutch border near Bergen-op-Zoom to rendezvous with their parents and escort them all to Switzerland. They spent one night at the Dutch-Paris safe house at 19 rue Franklin in Brussels. The next day customs officials detained them on the Franco-Belgian border, but only briefly. In Annecy, Kraay left the family with Mademoiselle Meunier, who hid them at a café for two days until a guide took them to St-Julien by bus. From there they walked into Switzerland. The entire journey across occupied Europe took seven days in what counted for the time as an easy trip with few difficulties.[8] It was to be Kraay's last trip through the Netherlands and Belgium.

Also in late 1943 and early 1944 Weidner escorted the children of at least three resisters from France to Switzerland to protect them from reprisals for their parents' clandestine activities. Both the Germans and the Vichy French announced that they would use resisters' families as well as local dignitaries as hostages. The Germans would, in fact, take Weidner's sister Gabrielle as a hostage. Before that happened, Weidner helped two families as favors to French resistance networks with whom he was in contact in Haute-Savoie.[9] The third family were personal friends of his, the four daughters of the Dutch consul-general in France. The girls had gone into hiding with their mother when Vichy authorities imprisoned their father in December 1942. Their mother asked Weidner to take them to Switzerland a year later because the papal nuncio to Vichy warned her that the oldest two were going to be arrested.[10]

To their lifelong dismay, Weidner and his colleagues were not able to rescue all their clients. Simon Eliasar, for example, had been arrested at the customs barrier at Le Chable on his way to Switzerland, served a month in prison in Annecy, and was transferred to the internment camp at Gurs. Weidner had organized his release from Gurs and his legal establishment as a non-Jewish foreigner in a Savoyard village. He visited Eliasar there in October 1943 in order to introduce him to a guide to Switzerland.

But when German troops cordoned off the village before dawn on December 1, 1943, Eliasar and another refugee were still there. The Dutchmen were held on suspicion of being Jews, which they were, and transferred to Paris. A French friend followed them there, doing everything possible to find and help them. Weidner expected to secure the men's release through the intervention of the regional prefect in Lyon, but the prefect was himself arrested. Nonetheless Weidner remained hopeful, and Cartier encouraged André Eliasar not to despair about his father. They did not find out until after the war was over that Simon Eliasar had been deported from Drancy on December 17, 1943, and had perished at Auschwitz within a month of being captured, on December 30.[11]

Dutch-Paris continued to use the route to Switzerland until the end of the occupation, but more and more of the people they helped in 1943 wanted to go to Spain so they could get to England. Weidner and his colleagues had been taking Dutch Engelandvaarders, the occasional Belgian or French civilian, and a few Allied servicemen from Switzerland to Spain since 1942. After establishing the entire network of Dutch-Paris in

October 1943, they started taking more such civilians and began to bring some of them all the way from cities in the Netherlands to villages in Spain. The most significant change to the escape line, however, happened in January 1944, when they began taking Allied aviators to Spain from the north rather than from Switzerland.

The crews of U.S. Army Air Force (USAAF) and Royal Air Force (RAF) aircraft who had been shot down over enemy-controlled territory but not been apprehended were called "evaders" because they were evading capture by the enemy. Aviators had been crashing onto occupied territory since 1940, but the number of such men hiding in occupied territory increased sharply in March 1943, when the Allies started round-the-clock bombing of the Third Reich. By late 1943 and early 1944 much of the Ruhr Valley lay in rubble, and Frankfurt had been all but leveled.

The flight paths between the U.S. and British air bases in Great Britain and Germany took the vast formations of bombers and their fighter escorts over the Netherlands, Belgium, and northern France. If an aircraft was hit by German air defenses or experienced mechanical failure, the pilot tried to nurse it along until his crew could bail out over occupied territory. They had every reason to fear a hostile reception from the

Graffiti scratched onto the wall of the Drancy transit camp by Simon Eliasar and Dolf Klein: their names and the Dutch resistance slogan, "OZO," Oranje Zal Overwinnen (The Dutch House of Oranje shall be victorious), December 1943.

German people whose homes they were bombing, but they could hope for help from Dutch, Belgian, or French civilians.

Propeller aircraft such as the B-17 bomber made so much noise the entire neighborhood could hear a plane in trouble. Both the German occupation authorities and the civilians under the flight paths watched the skies for parachutes and for the landing site. The survivors, who may have been injured or disoriented in the crash, had no way of knowing whether the police or helpers would find them first. Often civilians found aviators in the bushes or the barn and had to make the difficult decision of whether to turn them in or find a way to pass them to the resistance.

The German occupation authorities showed no mercy to anyone who extended a hand to the men whom they called *Luftterroristen* (air terrorists) in response to the steady bombing of the German homeland. German military intelligence, the Abwehr, and secret military police, the Geheime Feldpolizei, devoted considerable resources to infiltrating and destroying resistance escape lines that helped aviators evade capture. They usually succeeded.[12]

Some civilians caught helping airmen received a trial in Luftwaffe courts for aiding and abetting the enemy, a capital crime. Other civilian helpers were condemned without benefit of trial and deported to the concentration camps as slave labor.[13] An estimated 150 to 175 Dutch men and women lost their lives for helping pilots, meaning that for every two aviators who returned to their bases from the Netherlands, one Dutch helper was killed. Indeed in 1943 the Dutch Council for the Resistance instructed illegal workers not to help airmen because the risks were too high.[14]

As part of their training all Allied aircrew were coached in evasion tactics. They were told, for instance, to bury their flight suits and to obey the instructions of civilians who helped them. Military intelligence officers interviewed every airman who made it back to England about his experiences in an attempt to piece together the escape lines such as Dutch-Paris that might help aviators in the future. But the fact was that once a crew bailed out of a burning plane or crawled out of a crashed one, the survivors had to think for themselves and respond to whatever circumstances arose. To that end, all aviators were issued evasion supplies: high-energy food, passport-size photographs meant for false documents, maps printed on silk scarves, and an escape purse with Dutch, Belgian, or French

currency in it. Yet it was still difficult to move through a densely popu-
lated country such as the Netherlands without attracting attention.
Airmen hoped that attention would come from the resistance.

Helping aviators counted as an extremely high-risk branch of resistance. In addition to the intensity of the German search for downed aviators and the fury with which they punished helpers, the airmen themselves
were harder to hide than civilian fugitives. Americans, Australians, and
New Zealanders tended to be taller and healthier-looking than Europeans.
They walked differently, smoked their cigarettes differently, and handled
their silverware differently than Europeans. They did dangerously un-
European things like jingle change in their pockets or whistle. Some of
them simply did not understand the realities of life in occupied Europe
and acted in ways that endangered the lives of themselves and their
friends, such as calling out to a crewmate across the street or writing down
the names and addresses of helpers.[15]

Even the most conscientious American could make a dangerous mistake.
Few aviators spoke French or Dutch, making it impossible to leave them
alone and forcing anyone helping them to speak English in public places. In
fact both Jacques Rens and Albert Starink told the Engelandvaarder Rudy
Zeeman that they had had to do just that. It was only a matter of luck that
no collaborator had overheard them. When guides had to check on the
train schedule in Toulouse, they left four Americans who did not speak
French under the care of Zeeman and another Engelandvaarder at the station café. The Americans pretended to be reading the newspaper, but
Zeeman had to turn one of their papers right-side up.[16]

Despite all this, Weidner and his colleagues did take a few Allied military men from Switzerland to Spain in 1942 and 1943. Such men had either
escaped from POW camps and made their way to Switzerland or successfully evaded capture between being shot down and making their own way
to Switzerland. They could be vetted, briefed, and outfitted with the appro-
priate false documents, gear, and food by the Dutch military attaché's office.
They left Switzerland in good health. In France itself they needed to walk or
take a bus to Annecy, take a train to Toulouse via Lyon, and then follow
whatever instructions the *passeur* gave them while walking over the mountains. These men were well-prepared for the short journey to Toulouse.

When Weidner arrived in Brussels in October 1943, however, he discovered that his new colleagues in the Comité wanted to send Allied

airmen on the more complicated journey from the Netherlands to Spain via the new line. These aviators had crashed in the Netherlands or northern Belgium and been rescued by local people who passed them on to people they trusted, who in turn passed them on to the young man who had jumped out of a deportation train and was running the Comité's daily operations, Paul van Cleeff, or one of his colleagues. At that time the Comité was passing the aviators to two Belgian escape lines, one of which was the famous Comet Line.[17]

Weidner hesitated to accept aviators on the new line because of the danger involved not only for the helpers but for everyone associated with them, including the families they were hiding. Furthermore Dutch-Paris would have to vet aviators coming from the north for German spies masquerading as Americans, as did happen more than once. Indeed an Engelandvaarder who crossed the Pyrenees with the escaped secret agents Dourlein and Ubbink in November 1943 later claimed that three of the twenty-nine men in their international convoy were shot as German spies in Gibraltar or England.[18] The line would also have to equip any aviators from Brussels with food, documents, and sturdy footwear. Weidner's new colleagues in Paris also wanted the expanded network to take aviators, as did the Dutch military attaché in Bern, General van Tricht. Weidner agreed in January 1944.

Doing so strengthened a number of alliances. On the international level, the Dutch government in exile could do a favor for its American and British allies by returning their military personnel to them. The Dutch would take care of the details and bear the risk, while the British and American military attachés paid the costs for their men. On average it took 30,000 French francs to get an airman to Spain: 10,000 for the *passeurs* in the Pyrenees, 10,000 for black market supplies, and 10,000 for false documents, train fare, and other travel expenses.[19] These were formidable sums. Before he went underground Weidner had been doing very well for himself earning 8,000 to 10,000 French francs per month. The British and Americans, however, were willing to spend that much on their aircrew. When Weidner told Van Tricht that he needed money for aviators, the general got 30,000 Swiss francs, about enough to pay for ten escapes, in cash from his British counterpart in Bern and took it to Weidner in Geneva on the morning train.[20] On a more immediate level Dutch-Paris strengthened its alliances with other resistance groups by taking their dangerous guests out of occupied territory.

The inclusion of aviators on the line was not the only change in Dutch-Paris in January 1944. Early in the month German police in Brussels found the trail of the Comité board member and rescuer of Jewish children, Benno Nijkerk, forcing him to abandon his new wife, infant son, and resistance work there. Before he left he recruited another Dutch expatriate, Jacob Knoote, to replace him as an intermediary between management and daily operations in the Comité. Knoote reported directly to Pastor ten Kate, the banker Verhagen, and the businessman Regout on the board. The helpers, particularly the brilliant student in charge of the *transportwerk* David Verloop and Henri Vleeschdrager, who had jumped off the deportation train with Van Cleeff and was now in charge of the *sociaalwerk*, reported to him. Knoote, who had experience managing hotels and tours, rationalized the Comité's accounts and lowered costs. Although they balked at the changes in protocol, Verloop and Vleeschdrager finally handed the books over to Knoote in a café on February 25, 1944, mere days before a German raid on their safe house. Knoote found the accounts to be in order but thought they contained far too much information.[21]

By that time the *sociaalwerk* and the *transportwerk* had been compartmentalized. Responsibility for delivering money and ration cards to more than eighty Jewish families in hiding fell to two young Dutchmen, Paul Sayers and Yves von der Möhlen.[22] Both had arrived only recently in Brussels, on the run from forced labor. Another Dutch student, Greta Roselaar, and an expatriate, Ernest Lifman, assisted them.[23]

Verloop and his student colleagues ran the "grapeline," as they called the escape line in English, out of the pension at 19 rue Franklin in a leafy residential neighborhood not far from where the European Commission stands today. Anyone passing through Brussels stayed there, including Kraay and the Jewish family she took to Switzerland. American evaders described its Belgian owner, Lydia Ogy, as a thin, red-haired woman who complained loudly about the additional housework and danger aviators caused her. As far as they could see, she hated Germans but helped Americans mainly for the money Dutch-Paris paid her for their room and board.[24] Dutch Engelandvaarders who stayed there, on the other hand, found the landlady to be friendly and helpful. At least one of them moved to other lodgings because of the carelessness of the aviators there at the time, who were walking in and out of the house speaking English to each other loudly enough for anyone to hear.[25]

At the same time that the Comité reorganized its procedures, Weidner attempted to improve security for the entire line by establishing a base in the Netherlands itself. He and the other leaders continued to worry about agents provocateurs infiltrating the line. They wanted someone to first verify the bona fides of fugitives before they learned enough to cause everyone's arrest. They also needed someone to pace departures according to conditions farther south. A snowstorm in the Pyrenees or an arrest anywhere on the line could cause a logjam that would pile fugitives up in a town where the helpers did not have enough hiding places. Pastor Visser 't Hooft enlisted a Dutch policeman who had fled to Switzerland in February 1943 to return to the Netherlands to act as the line's anchor there. Weidner introduced him to the Dutch-Paris station chiefs on his way to the Dutch border in mid-January 1944, but the man accomplished nothing beyond sending a message that he was sick.[26] Engelandvaarders continued to arrive in Brussels at an unpredictable rate.

Weidner may have had trouble recruiting helpers for his escape line, but there was never any shortage of candidates to leave occupied territory along that line. Engelandvaarders joined Dutch-Paris in the Netherlands in one of two ways. Either the government in exile summoned the potential Engelandvaarer to London and requested that Dutch-Paris take him to Spain, or the fugitive found the line through his personal connections. The medical student Willy Hijmans, for instance, proposed several candidates for the trip to Spain and vouched for them to Weidner.[27] In a typical example of how a fugitive might get from the Netherlands to Brussels via Dutch-Paris, Hijmans met three men at the Hollands Spoor station in The Hague on January 24, 1944. All three were older than the average Engelandvaarder and, as a police captain, an experienced pilot, and a lawyer, had specific skills of value to the government in exile. One was a good friend of Hijmans's father; the other two were connections of one of Hijmans's Dutch resistance colleagues.[28]

Hijmans escorted the three men on the train from The Hague to the southern city of Bergen-op-Zoom, where he passed them to another student, Piet Henry. Henry took them by taxi to Putte and then had them fan out to walk over the border into Belgium on the outskirts of the village. Crossing the border in the village itself required climbing over barbed wire, which Henry considered too dangerous because the barbs could trap a man by snagging his clothing. Once in Belgium the group took a tram to Antwerp and then an electric train to Brussels. In Brussels, Henry passed the men to Verloop.

At least as many fugitives joined Dutch-Paris in Belgium as in the Netherlands. Following the same pattern as Jewish refugees had a year earlier, some Engelandvaarders made their own way to Brussels, where friends or family introduced them to a member of Dutch-Paris. A few had personal connections to the line. The courier Chris ten Kate, for example, brought his cousin, an engineering student named Christiaan van Oosterzee, from the Netherlands to Brussels. Like many Engelandvaarders, Van Oosterzee had an international background. His father was Dutch, his mother was English, and he spent much of his childhood in the Netherlands East Indies. In Brussels Ten Kate and Van Oosterzee's uncle, Pastor ten Kate, lodged his nephew with an expatriate family, Henri and Maria Timmers Verhoeven. Three days later their son Sam decided to leave for England with their guest.

Chris ten Kate arranged false papers and train tickets for his cousin and his traveling companion. The documents identified them as white-collar employees of a company that worked on the German coastal fortifications near Dieppe who were returning from home leave. Such a disguise gave them permission to travel through Paris because all the trains between Brussels and the Atlantic Coast went through the French capital. When they arrived at the Belgian border, the pair made sure they were the last in line. As they approached the guard, one of them dropped his papers and fumbled around until the harried German told them to just keep moving.[29]

Independently of the Engelandvaarders, a number of aviators who had crash landed in the Netherlands, eastern Belgium, or northern France came into Dutch-Paris's care in Brussels. On occasion aviators arrived through the personal connections of Comité members. The Dutch teenager Joke Folmer, famous in Holland for her courage and exploits, passed aviators to her school friend Verloop eight times.[30] Similarly Belgian resisters in the town of Hasselt passed aviators to Dutch-Paris because their leader's husband worked in the same government office as a relative of the Comité's currency trader, Joseph Haenecour.[31]

Indeed so many of the Comité's connections among Belgian resisters wanted to pass aviators to them that they assigned the job of liaison for airmen to Joachim "Jo" Jacobstahl. A stateless German Jew whose family had moved from Berlin to Amsterdam in 1928, Jacobstahl found

his own way over the Dutch border and to
Pastor ten Kate's doorstep in June 1943. Once
established with a false Belgian identity,
Jacobstahl made an impressive array of contacts among Belgian and Dutch resisters, particularly those near Maastricht and in the
Ardennes. He met some of them when an
Engelandvaarder in Brussels introduced him
to the *passeurs* who had shown him over the
border near Maastricht.[32] Similarly his search
for a hiding place for his sister Hilde led him
to a resistance leader in the province of Namur

Hilde Jacobstahl, 1944.

who was looking for an escape route to Spain. Hilde Jacobstahl dedicated herself to caring for children, but did on occasion help her
brother as a courier for Dutch-Paris.[33]

Most of the aviators who came to Dutch-Paris from the Netherlands
were passed from what was known as the Groep Vrij, named after the
Dutch traffic inspector who led it, Jacques Vrij.[34] His job gave Vrij a vehicle
and a reason to be on the roads around Maastricht.

The border city offered a number of advantages to escape lines. It had
regular train service and was large enough that strangers could pass unremarked. More important, it lay within walking distance of a border with
no natural obstacles. In other parts of the southern province of Limburg,
the River Maas serves as the border between the Netherlands and
Belgium, but Maastricht lies on both sides of the river, forcing the border
to run overland in a wide, jagged arc around the western side of the city.
During the war an unofficial no man's land lay between this political
border and the physical barrier of the Albert Canal, which the Belgians
dug to the west of Maastricht to bypass the city. As in the Genevois, a
regular stream of local traffic crossed this border every day as people who
lived in Belgium went to their jobs in the nearest city, Maastricht.

Starting in the early autumn of 1943, Vrij and his colleagues hit upon
relatively easy ways of getting from Maastricht into Belgium, such as by
having an airman walk behind the customs house while a guide distracted
the guards with conversation. Sometimes aviators simply walked through
the busy checkpoint. The American aviators Norman Elkin, who worked
in the shipyards in Baltimore before the war, and Walter Snyder, an

electric plater from San Diego, had a close call there early one morning in January 1944. A German guard asked them, "Where were you born?" in English. They pretended not to understand convincingly enough that the guard let them pass into Belgium.[35]

Groep Vrij couriers met with the Comité's representatives at one of two cafés in Brussels: the Cheval Gris near the gare du Bruxelles-Nord or Le Duc de Brabant on the avenue d'Anvers.[36] As a security measure Groep Vrij couriers were supposed to take up to ten aviators per week to the Hotel Oud-Antwerpen, a ten-minute walk from the gare de Bruxelles-Nord, from where Dutch-Paris guides would fetch the men. Sometimes the aviators slept at the hotel, but at other times the guides just took them directly to the rue Franklin.[37]

Before Dutch-Paris accepted an aviator, Jacobstahl first traveled to wherever the Comité's allies on the Dutch border and in southern Belgium were hiding him in order to interview him. Jacobstahl usually took a geology student named Robert Bosschart with him. Verloop recruited Bosschart in January 1944 as a courier and guide. His father, Leopold, had already been involved with the Comité for some time. When interviewing prospective evaders, Jacobstahl and Bosschart used a standard questionnaire written by Allied officers to weed out German impersonators. It asked for personal information that a spy could not guess, such as the names of the aviator's parents.[38] Verloop then reported the replies to a Dutch woman who lived in Brussels and had radio contact with London because she worked with the Comet Line.[39] Once the Allied authorities had verified the airman's identity, Jacobstahl and Bosschart returned to the hiding place to escort him to Brussels.[40]

At the rue Franklin aviators were stripped of all their belongings except for their identity discs, which would give them the status and protection of POWs if they were captured. The Americans, it turned out, had a penchant for seemingly trivial souvenirs such as Dutch coins or tram tickets that would betray their disguise as Belgians. Some of them even carried photos and letters addressed to Queen Wilhelmina given to them by earlier helpers in the Netherlands.[41] They had been lucky to get that far with such compromising documents; the resisters of Dutch-Paris were not going to count on that luck continuing all the way to Spain. Instead they outfitted the airmen in the clothes and heavy boots worn by Belgian workmen and took them to have new passport photos made. Hans

Wisbrun escorted airmen to the Bon Marché department store on this errand several times.[42]

J. P. Bol, the student turned forger, used the photos to make false documents identifying the aviators as Belgians employed in France. He made similar documents for Engelandvaarders because all men of military age needed a war-related job to explain why they were not in uniform. He gave the Engelandvaarders, who were mostly middle class, white-collar jobs that were close to their real identities. But he made the aviators blue-collar workers to explain why they moved in groups and did not speak for themselves. In fact many aviators pretended to be deaf-mutes to disguise their inability to speak any language other than English. This ruse worked surprisingly well. The one time a French guard challenged the men's papers, one of the guides upbraided the man for his shameful discourtesy so forcefully that the guard apologized and let the aviators pass.[43] Bol's documents were so good they withstood the scrutiny of being held up to the light to check for the proper watermark used on authentic German forms.[44]

The next challenge was to take the aviators over the Franco-Belgian border to Paris. On January 19, 1944, Verloop left Brussels for Paris with the first group of clandestine travelers, or convoy, as they called it at the time. He took with him a friend from his student days at the University of Utrecht, the accomplished musician F. H. Iordens. Like several of the other students in Dutch-Paris, including Bol, Verloop, and Hijmans, Iordens had rescued Jews in 1942 as part of the Kindercomité. He and his girlfriend Anne Maclaine Pont then helped aviators in the Netherlands before joining Dutch-Paris in Brussels.

Jacobstahl had found this first group of Allied airmen hiding with Belgian partisans near Chimay, not far north of the French border. James Hussong of Maryland had bailed out of his B-24 with a bullet in his foot on December 30, 1943, and come down near St. Quentin. Sergeant Harold Bailey of the RAF had been the navigator of his aircraft. The rest of the men—Frank Tank of Wisconsin, Ernest Stock of California, Eric Kolc of Rhode Island, Russell Gallo of Pennsylvania, and Leonard Cassady, an electric welder by trade—belonged to the crew of the B-17 Sarah Jane that made an emergency landing near Wimy, France, on December 30, 1943. The Frenchmen who hid them after the crash passed them to their Belgian counterparts on the assumption that the Germans would respect the international border and restrict their search to France even if they themselves did not. The crew's pilot and ball turret gunner were also in the care of Dutch-Paris but traveling separately.[45]

Verloop and Iordens intended to take the seven airmen over the border at the Belgian town of Mouscron, north of the French town of Tourcoing, by disguising them as cigarette smugglers. But the first men to make the attempt were stopped by a German guard who was hiding behind some bushes in the field where they tried to cross. Lieutenant Tank, who spoke German fluently, did not quite convince the guard that they were smugglers despite the large quantity of cigarettes they were carrying. The guard took their identity documents for confirmation and told them to report back in a few hours. Needless to say, the aviators did not return. Instead a café owner in Mouscron hid the men overnight while their guides returned to Bol at the rue Franklin to make new documents.

The next day a French policeman launched into a long and distracting conversation with some of the German guards during their lunch. He had recognized the men as Americans when his German counterpart had not. Iordens and Vleeschdrager, who had come in Verloop's place, made a fuss going through the legal checkpoint while the aviators crossed the border by jumping a stream. Once in France the guides took the airmen to Lille on a tram. They spent the rest of the afternoon walking the streets in pairs until it was time to board the 5:20 p.m. train to Paris.[46]

After that Verloop and his colleagues hid the aviators and their guides in plain sight, mixing them into the crowds on the Berlin-Paris express that left Brussels at 11:30 p.m. to arrive in Paris around 7:30 a.m. The tensest part of the journey came at the Belgian border when all passengers exited the train and walked through long sheds so that Belgian agents could search their cases for contraband and German and French officers could inspect their documents.[47] If they were in Brussels for a meeting, Rens, Chait, or Weidner would escort Engelandvaarders. Otherwise Jacobstahl, Bosschart, Wisbrun, Verloop, or Vleeschdrager accompanied both aviators and Engelandvaarders on the night train. Once in Paris the Brussels guides passed their charges to their Parisian colleagues at some public place, such as the gare du Nord or a café. Although the night express worked well, Dutch-Paris continued to send some civilian fugitives over the border at Mouscron.[48] If they had more fugitives at the rue Franklin than they could care for, the Comité passed some aviators to Belgian escape lines as they had in 1943.

While in the French capital, Engelandvaarders and aviators remained segregated. For the most part the young engineer Albert Starink, the student Anna Neyssel, and Catherine Okhuysen, who had already been fired from her secretarial job because of her resistance activities, took care of Engelandvaarders in Paris. Starink provided French documents for them, although Chait complained that at least one set was missing a crucial number. The diplomat in hiding Herman Laatsman, the Sorbonne student Suzanne Hiltermann, the translator Leo Mincowski and their colleagues took care of aviators.

As elsewhere along the line, new fugitives came under the group's care in Paris from a variety of sources. A number of Engelandvaarders, for instance, rode the German military train between Maastricht and Paris on—amazingly enough—Sicherheitsdienst (SD) papers furnished by a contact of Starink's in Amsterdam.[49] At least one such set of false papers identified the bearers as translators hired to interrogate Dutch and Flemish prisoners for the SD in Pau. They gave the bearers the right to ride on Wehrmacht trains, protected them from being questioned by anyone other than a superior officer, and even made the other passengers on the train, all Wehrmacht personnel, wary of them. When they arrived, these Engelandvaarders took the Métro to the home of a personal acquaintance or to Starink's hotel in the Latin Quarter. Starink gave them ration coupons and told them which restaurants to patronize. If they did not have personal friends in the city who would put them up, he, Okhuysen, and Neyssel found them hotels. Some of the men waited for weeks before continuing their journey.

Engelandvaarders rarely stayed hidden in Paris. They wanted to see the sights or to visit Dutch or French acquaintances, which could lead to trouble. To give one example, Rudy Zeeman and Robert van Exter came to Paris in January 1944 on false SD papers arranged through Van Exter's father, an expatriate engineer who knew Starink. Wehrmacht officers arrested Zeeman because they overheard him speaking English at a fancy restaurant. Both young men spoke some French, but their luncheon companion, a friend of one of their mother's, wanted to speak English. The obvious conclusion for any eavesdropper to draw was that the two strangers were Allied airmen.

Van Exter managed to slip away before he could be arrested. Luckily for Zeeman, the Wehrmacht officers decided to let the SD verify his

papers. As the Wehrmacht driver searched for the road to Gestapo headquarters, the Dutchman opened the side door of the car, rolled out onto
the sidewalk, and ran away through the blacked-out streets of Paris, leaving behind his false papers made out with his authentic photograph.
When he came to a boulevard, an older woman took his arm and walked
him calmly to the Métro, which made him blend into the crowd. The
police watched for individuals running, not gentlemen escorting old
ladies. That night Starink hid Zeeman in a bitterly cold garret room of the
Hotel Medicis.

After a couple of days Starink gave him glasses and directed him to a
barber and an instant-photo booth. When his new false documents were
ready, Starink moved Zeeman to the home of an expatriate artist who
hosted many Engelandvaarders in Paris.[50] He rushed both young men out
of Paris at the first opportunity. The incident angered Dutch officials in
Switzerland and England, but nothing appears to have come of it. The
Wehrmacht officers may have decided to forget the entire incident rather
than report that they allowed what they thought was an Allied airman
with false SD papers to escape.[51]

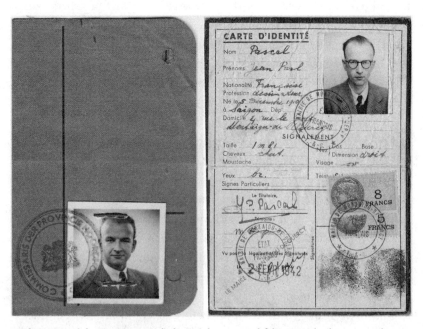

Rudy Zeeman's legitimate Dutch driver's license and false French identity card, 1943.

Aviators were harder to hide in hotels than civilian fugitives because the police monitored hotels on a daily basis. Many of them were too tall and too unfamiliar with European customs to pass unnoticed. Laatsman hid some airmen at the farm of the Dutchman Huitema in the village of Gazeran, over an hour by rail southwest of the city, but that exposed the men to extra trips on local trains. Within Paris a handful of men could hide in the neighboring apartments of the widow Fernande Goetschel and the Swiss translator Jean Milleret at 11 rue Jasmin. Goetschel nursed sick or injured aviators until they could continue. But the apartments were too small to hide more than a couple men.

At the suggestion of a Dutch priest, Laatsman found a large, very private hiding place close to the gare d'Austerlitz: the physics laboratories of the prestigious Ecole Normale Supérieure in the Latin Quarter near the Sorbonne. Brother Rufus, who lived next door, enlisted the help of the building's concierge, Emile Prilliez. Prilliez lived with his wife and three children across the narrow, cobbled rue Lhomond from the laboratories. He set up a hiding place with cots in one of the school's subterranean electrical rooms. German police missed it more than once because it did not have its own door onto the corridor.[52]

The first aviators to stay there were not entirely sure where they were when they arrived in late January 1944. Many described it as the basement of a hospital; some recognized it as an educational institution. Sergeant Elkin from Baltimore described it as a student hospital and recalled, "The caretaker kept us in an underground dungeon nearby motors" with "high voltage wires everywhere." Back in England he reported, "We slept on mattresses on the floor with the rats."[53] Other aviators described the space as cramped but not as a dungeon.

Brother Rufus took responsibility for feeding the men. He arranged for the concierge's wife, Julia Prilliez, to cook beans for their lunch every day because he himself had too much to do to stay in the kitchen that long. He bought most of their food at very low cost from Dutch farmers on the outskirts of Paris. When one of these compatriots had to kill a horse after an accident, Brother Rufus carried more than 750 pounds of fresh and salted horsemeat back into Paris in several trips by hiding it under his cape. Somehow he managed to avoid the rationing inspectors who haunted the trains and Métro. After a worker denounced the farmer to the French rationing authorities, he naturally preferred to pay a hefty fine rather than admit that the meat went to the RAF.[54]

Julia and Émile Prilliez, 1943.

Hiltermann, who spoke English very well, and Leo Mincowski, who spoke it haltingly despite his fluency in several other languages, visited the aviators on the rue Lhomond, often with cigarettes as well as supplies they would need for the Pyrenees, such as shoes, sweaters, overcoats, and food. Hiltermann also gave the men French identification documents in place of their Belgian documents and 1,000 French francs each as pocket money for the journey. Not that the men would be doing any shopping, but it would have looked odd for a man not to have some cash in his pockets.

The supplies came through Milleret, who had found enough black market grocers and restaurateurs to put together packages of food to last each man the three days it was supposed to take to get from Toulouse to Spain.[55] Footwear, however, posed a problem. The aviators had all been wearing excellent boots when they left England, but most had taken them off with the rest of their flight gear when they landed, for fear the boots would give them away. No civilian had such high-quality shoes in 1944, and no European would wear such boots in a city. Helpers provided what they could, but they were usually too small and of poor quality. At least one American complained that his French "pasteboard" shoes disintegrated in the snow, causing him frostbite in the Pyrenees.[56] Milleret found a cobbler to make high-top, lace-up walking shoes for the aviators.[57]

Laatsman also ordered sturdy shoes made to measure from a French cobbler in Versailles.[58]

In addition Milleret found the group a meeting place at a café in the
working-class arrondissement of Belleville in northeast Paris. The café
owner allowed aviators to hide there for short periods, and Laatsman,
Milleret, Hiltermann, the courier Lucie Comiti, and their French ally
from the town hall of Drancy, Miguel Duchanel, to use a backroom as a
meeting place. He himself provided the risky but fairly passive postbox
services of accepting calls and messages. For anything more active needed
by Dutch-Paris, he recruited a friend of his daughter's, a Jewish girl whom
he had rescued from the transit camp at the Velodrome d'Hiver and certain deportation.[59]

Duchanel provided the French documents for the aviators. He also introduced Hiltermann to another Frenchman whose group was hiding fifteen aviators in Livry-Gargan, not far from Paris.[60] In early January 1944
Hiltermann and Mincowski visited those aviators in their hiding places on
what the locals were now calling the "rue Yankee" and the "rue Américain."[61]
Hiltermann made copious notes about each of the men's personal details
(including their shoe size) and what they needed. The most important, she
felt, were new identification documents because the ones they had were all
issued by the same town hall. If the Germans caught one American on the
train to Toulouse with false papers issued in Livry-Gargan, they would
simply arrest everyone else on the train with documents from there.[62]

Laatsman and his colleagues preferred to take fugitives to Toulouse on
the night train on Tuesdays and Fridays because, for unknown reasons,
inspectors rarely checked passengers' documents on those nights.[63] Those
trains were also very crowded.[64] Fugitives or guides might have to stand
for the entire journey, but the crush made it difficult for any police agents
to move through the train.

On the day of departure guides brought the aviators and Engelandvaarders from their hiding places by light rail or Métro to the gare d'Austerlitz
in time for the 7:30 p.m. train to Toulouse. At least once Mincowski and
Hitlermann brought a small group of aviators from Livry-Gargan to Paris in
the morning and hid them in the back of a cobbler's shop for the day so they
could be fitted for the necessary footwear.[65] After dark the airmen in the
basement on rue Lhomond split into small groups for the ten-minute walk
and short Métro ride to the station.

Once everyone was assembled on the platform for the train to Toulouse, guides usually introduced Engelandvaarders to the convoy's leader, either Rens or Chait. They did not introduce the airmen because the language and cultural barriers might lead to misunderstandings and confusion. In addition to the designated leader, at least two of the young women in the line, Hiltermann, Comiti, Okyhusen, or Houry, usually accompanied the fugitives on the train.[66] The guides distributed them among different compartments and moved through the train periodically to check on them. They preferred to use the middle carriages, which were less likely to be damaged in case of sabotage or even aerial bombardment than those at the front of the train. Weidner was on at least one train between Toulouse and Paris that was derailed by sabotage.[67] Furthermore police inspections generally began at the front or the back, giving passengers in the middle time to react. On at least one occasion Starink supplied his Engelandvaarders with ration coupons for the dining car. As instructed, the Dutchmen scattered themselves among the tables. Those who spoke French talked to the Germans with whom they were seated. The others kept quiet.[68]

The night train usually arrived at Toulouse's gare Matabiau around 8:30 a.m. Despite the heavy presence of German police, French *Miliciens*, and French gendarmes in the station, none of Dutch-Paris's protégés were stopped there. One Engelandvaarder could scarcely believe that the blue or gray workers' overcoats, workmen's boots, and deep blue berets that the aviators wore fooled the Germans.[69] If any of the French police suspected the disguise, they made no protest.

If the students Gabriel Nahas, Simone Calmels, or Andrée Moulouguet did not meet the convoy outside the station, the guides from Paris took the men to their next meeting place. They usually went to the restaurant Chez Emile on the place St-Georges, a twenty-minute walk. After breakfast Rens or Chait would dispatch the men to various hiding places. Occasionally Calmels and her friends took aviators to a private home or to an apartment right by the police station because that neighborhood tended to be searched less often than others.[70] Usually, however, the men hid in hotels or in dingy rooms on the upper floor of a narrow building in the old part of town (which some Engelandvaarders identified as a brothel). A few men stayed at the *passeurs* Treillet and Marot's apartment in the old town. They remained there for a few hours or a few days until it was time to return to the gare Matabiau to move farther south into the Pyrenees.

Occasionally resisters from southern France passed aviators to Dutch-Paris in or near Toulouse itself because they did not have their own connections to a reliable *passeur*. Some Engelandvaarders and even aviators joined the line after making their own way that far. Rens and Chait accepted such fugitives once they had verified their identities, though they did not always have enough cash on hand to pay the 10,000 French francs fee up front. Caught short in late January but unwilling to miss the chance of sending fugitives to Spain, Chait collected almost enough money from the Engelandvaarders and aviators themselves. Fortunately that particular group had older Engelandvaarders who traveled with money and aviators who had not yet spent everything in their escape purses. Chait reached a deal with the *passeur* to pay the balance at a later date. Chait also equipped Engelandvaarders who did not bring their own gear because they had been on the run for a long time or had escaped imprisonment. It could be expensive. A rucksack cost 1,000 French francs in Toulouse in early 1944. He also bought packages of food from Chez Emile for both Engelandvaarders and aviators before they left for the mountains.[71]

The details of the rest of the journey depended on the *passeur* whom Chait or Rens was able to engage for the convoy. The Spanish Republican Caparros's line had been rolled up at Christmas time, leaving Dutch-Paris with only two other *passeurs* to take Engelandvaarders and aviators to Spain in 1944. Because the guides had a long and arduous trek through the mountains and back again with every convoy and because heavy snowfall often closed the passes that winter, two weeks might easily pass between departures.

The team of Treillet and Marot fetched fugitives from Toulouse itself. They always took the more old-fashioned trains that did not have access between the carriages rather than the newer trains because German police rarely patrolled a train if they could not walk from one end to the other between stations.[72] If necessary the fugitives spent the night in the village of Cazères in an unfinished house belonging to Treillet's future in-laws. From there they took the bus to the village of Mane and then walked eight miles through undulating country to the hamlet

Pierre Treillet, 1944.

The Franco-Spanish Border in Haute-Garonne

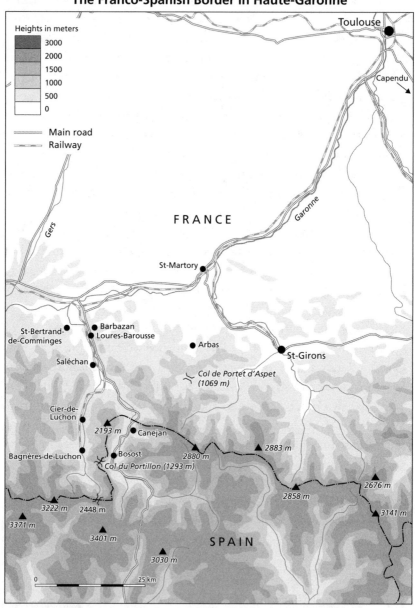

Heights in meters

- 3000
- 2000
- 1500
- 1000
- 500
- 0

Main road
Railway

Toulouse

Capendu

FRANCE

Gers

Garonne

St-Martory

St-Bertrand-de-Comminges
Barbazan
Loures-Barousse

Arbas

Saléchan

St-Girons

Col de Portet d'Aspet (1069 m)

Cier-de-Luchon

2193 m Canejan

2883 m

Bagnères-de-Luchon
Bosost
Col du Portillon (1293 m)

2880 m

2858 m

2676 m

3222 m 2448 m

3371 m

3401 m

3141 m

SPAIN

3030 m

0   25 km

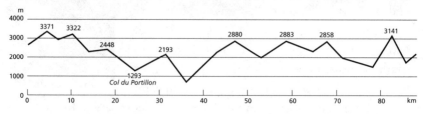

of Arbas. On occasion they covered part of this leg by taxi or private vehicle and then gathered in a meadow. After Arbas they walked in the dark through the mountains to the village of Canejan in Spain, resting in the daylight hours if possible. Marot and Treillet kept revolvers hidden somewhere in Arbas, which they carried only for the final portion of the approach to Spain. They personally accompanied their convoys all the way to the border.[73] It usually took three days to get there but much less time for the *passeurs* to return on their own.

The Armée Secrète *passeur*, Bazerque (aka Charbonnier), on the other hand, did not pick fugitives up in Toulouse. Instead Chait and Toulouse-based couriers escorted them to the village of Lannemazan, which aviators later said they understood to be under the control of armed *maquisards*.[74] From there they rode in a truck farther into the hills.[75] Although the driver's name was Joseph Barrère, aviators called him "Frisco" because he had been born in California. He had moved to France at sixteen to work on the family farm and had driven an ambulance in the campaign of 1939–40.

The Pyrenees near the Spanish border, 1944.

Bossòst, Spain, seen from France, 1944.

Bazerque took convoys of thirty or more fugitives from different sources. At least one with Dutch-Paris fugitives also included a Jewish family with children. Bazerque used a relay of guides along a less rigorous route slightly farther west than Treillet and Marot's. They often arrived in Bossòst, along the Garonne River in the valley below Canejan. Sometimes Frenchmen armed with the British submachine guns known as Sten guns that had undoubtedly been dropped by parachute to the *maquis* rode in the truck. They openly guarded parts of the route while the convoy walked in daylight, suggesting how well Bazerque's intelligence network of forest wardens and shepherds functioned.[76]

Even if the weather was clear, however, everything did not always go according to plan. Problems began in Toulouse when large groups of foreigners had to be spaced out on different trains into the foothills. There were not enough guides to accompany every group, and some fugitives who did not speak French well or at all missed their trains or buses. One group got lost in the foothills of the Pyrenees because they got off at the wrong stop. They included the British flier Bailey and the German-speaking American Lieutenant Tank who had tried to pass as cigarette smugglers on the French border. In order to reduce suspicions Treillet and Marot had split up their convoy for the bus and train journey between Toulouse and the meadow where they would begin their trek.

Bailey, Tank, and five other Americans were traveling with two Yugoslavians and a young French woman who had guided many refugees into Switzerland for a French Protestant rescue group and may have been accompanying the Yugoslavians from Switzerland. She was on her way to Spain with Dutch-Paris because the Germans were looking for her in the Alps. Although she was unfamiliar with the Pyrenees, she installed the aviators in a restaurant to wait and then went in search of their contact. What she found was Polish *passeurs* who agreed to take her and the evaders to Spain on their own route through Andorra to Barcelona.[77]

Meanwhile Treillet and Marot took the other six men in the convoy—Zeeman, Van Exter, and four Americans—on the slow train to Boussens in the foothills of the Pyrenees. Two of the Americans, Cassady of the B-17 Sarah Jane and Hussong, who had bailed out with a bullet in his foot, had been with Dutch-Paris since Brussels. The other two, Ernest Grubb, who bailed out of his bomber in early November 1943, and Charles Downe, the navigator of a plane that crashed in northern France in early September 1943, had been hiding on the rue Yankee in Livry-Gargan before joining Dutch-Paris.

Leonard Cassady, James Hussong, Charles Downe, Rudy Zeeman, Robert van Exter, and Ernest Grubb in Lérida, Spain, in February 1944.

While they were waiting for the bus from Boussens to Mane, a car rolled into town. By that time cars usually meant trouble, and sure enough this one belonged to the SD. Treillet told two of the Americans to ride around on bicycles until the bus arrived because they looked too "Nordic" to pass unnoticed. When the wheezing bus with a wood-burning engine finally arrived, the six fugitives filed into seats in the back. A German police officer boarded the bus but took a seat rather than questioning anybody. Treillet sauntered up to the front and engaged the policeman's attention with all sorts of bombast about how he had worked in Germany and couldn't wait to get back. The evaders got off in Mane and ate a meal of eggs and sausages in a basement café. They made it to Spain without incident, but the next convoy to follow that route did not.[78]

On that next convoy twenty-six aviators and Engelandvaarders left Toulouse with the *passeurs* Treillet and Marot, but only half of them made it to Spain. For this particular convoy Dutch-Paris brought aviators and Engelandvaarders from Brussels to the French capital in batches. Once everyone had reached Paris, they split the fugitives into two groups, which they escorted to Toulouse on two consecutive nights. None of the men spent any time in Toulouse, which was part of the problem. The first group of aviators in the ill-fated convoy left Brussels for Paris during the evening of January 23. It included the American crew mates Victor Ferrari and Omar Roberts; another American, Nicholas Mandell; Phil Brown, who was the pilot of a Mosquito fighter plane; and two other RAF men, a Sergeant Harris who had hid in Livry-Gargan, and George Watts, who injured his leg when the Lancaster on which he served as bombardier was shot down over Groningen in late September 1943. An unidentified Frenchman on his fourth escape from German POW camps joined them as far as the French capital. The seven men and their guides took the usual Berlin-Paris express that crossed the Franco-Belgian border in the night. At the station in Brussels, German police searched the party for guns but did not check their papers. At the frontier Belgian agents looked through their cases and German guards inspected their papers. Once again the false travel documents held good.

They arrived in Paris the next morning about 9:00 but spent a hungry day waiting for their Brussels guide to make contact with their Paris guide. After he finally reached someone at an emergency number, a young woman, possibly Lucie Comiti, came to take the aviators to a farm outside the city.[79] They waited there for the next group of evaders to arrive from the north.

One man in the second group, an Australian named John McLaughlin, was the pilot of an RAAF Typhoon that was shot down over Holland on January 14, 1944. He had been passed to the Groep Vrij, who took him over the border near Maastricht with two Americans, Frank McGlinchy and William McDonald. They belonged to the crew of a B-17 that had been shot down in Friesland three months earlier. Once in Belgium they were passed to Dutch-Paris guides who took them to Brussels with four other Americans: Snyder, Elkin, and two of their crewmates from their bomber that was shot down earlier that month, Clyde Mellen and Harry Kratz.

These seven aviators spent only one day at the rue Franklin, during which Bol made documents for them. Someone who struck the aviators as the "chief of the house" gave Snyder and Mellen "movie strips" to hand to the Allied authorities in England. These were probably microfilms with military intelligence, possibly concerning bomb targets.[80] Late on the same day that they arrived in Belgium, January 28, Jacobstahl and Bosschart took them to Paris on the 11:30 p.m. train, arriving on the morning of January 29. Hiltermann and Mincowski, who one of the Americans described as a "heavy-set girl" and a "dark man in a black beret," met them at the gare du Nord. They took them to have passport photos made for their next set of false documents and then to the basement of the physics laboratories.[81]

Hiltermann then took the light rail out of Paris to Huitema's farm to bring the six aviators who had been hiding there for the previous five days to join the new arrivals. The next day the pilot and ball turret gunner of the B-17 Sarah Jane, a textile designer from South Carolina named Campbell Brigman, and Harold Boyce, came from Brussels to join their crewmates in the laboratory basement. There were now fifteen Allied aviators on the rue Lhomond.[82]

When Ferrari, a schoolteacher from Philadelphia, developed what he called a "skin infection which hampered [his] walking," Hiltermann took him across town to stay with Goetschel at her apartment. A French doctor visited him, and Goetschel nursed him until he was able to walk well enough to attempt the Pyrenees a couple weeks later.[83]

In the meantime Starink and Okhuysen had been collecting young Dutchmen in Paris whom Weidner agreed to take to Spain via Dutch-Paris.

One of them, Jan Langeler, had already been captured once in the Pyrenees and escaped with bullet wounds in his hand and arm; he had been hiding in a farm outside Paris for the past few months.[84] Four more—Van Oosterzee, Timmers Verhoeven, Ferry Staverman, and Gijs den Besten—had arrived in Paris with the assistance of the Comité in Brussels.[85] Like so many of the other students involved with Dutch-Paris, Staverman and Den Besten had been active in the resistance at home.

For the next two weeks the Engelandvaarders waited, but they did not hide in their hotel rooms. Instead they made the rounds of the Dutch colony. On one of these visits Timmers Verhoeven met a French banker who knew the banker and Comité member Jacques Verhagen in Brussels. The Frenchman asked the young Dutchman to visit a certain Belgian, who gave him a tube of toothpaste that contained "instructions for dropping weapons over the Ardennes" to arm the resistance there. The Belgian told him to hand it over to the Dutch intelligence officers in Madrid because he did not trust the Belgian authorities in Spain.[86]

On the night of February 2 Rens escorted another four civilian fugitives from Brussels to Paris. One was a middle-aged Belgian, Roger Bureau, who traveled at the expense, and probably at the request, of the Dutch government in exile. The other three were young Dutchmen whom the medical student Willy Hijmans had found through his contact at a German shipyard. Many years later he still remembered this particular group. They were standing on the back deck of a train as it made its way toward the border when Jacobus Hijmans introduced himself with his real name. Willy Hijmans was so surprised they shared the same surname that he forgot his usual exemplary caution and blurted out his own real name.[87]

After passing the four Engelandvaarders to his colleagues in Paris the next morning, Rens met Weidner to give him Swiss Way microfilm he had picked up in Louvain. He intended to return to Geneva with Weidner, but they decided that his papers were not good enough to get him through the Haute-Savoie at that time. Tensions between the paramilitary collaborationist *Milice* and the armed *maquisard* resistance were escalating toward a state of civil war there. Instead Rens agreed to accompany a convoy to Toulouse with Okhuysen that very night, February 3. The Engelandvaarders and the Australian aviator would leave that evening, followed by the rest of the airmen the next evening.

One of the young Dutch-Paris women took mountain clothes to the rue Lhomond for McLaughlin and escorted him to the gare d'Austerlitz for the evening train. Starink made sure that the eight Engelandvaarders in Paris had the necessary papers as well as ration coupons for the dining car on the train to Toulouse. Like most trains at the time, this one was packed full. The ten fugitives and their two escorts arrived at Toulouse's gare Matabiau at 9:00 a.m. on February 4.[88] Okhuysen returned to Paris immediately, while several guides took the fugitives to a café in a poorer part of town. That evening at 7:00 Treillet took the Australian, the Belgian, and the eight Dutchmen to Cazères by train to spend the night in the empty house belonging to his fiancée's family.

As night fell the next day, around 5:00 on February 5, guides divided the men in the unfinished house into two groups to walk to the station in Cazères so they could catch a local train to the village of Mane. A bicyclist saw some of them while they hid in the shadow of a wall near the station. With the eye of a man who had been living under occupation for years, Timmers Verhoeven recognized that the bicyclist was not French because he was fat and well-shod. But the bicyclist did nothing obvious about his discovery. Wood-burning vehicles soon arrived to drive the men to a field outside the village at about 3,280 feet to wait for the rest of the convoy.[89]

While that group shivered in Cazères, the other aviators at the rue Lhomond rode the night train from Paris.[90] The previous day, February 4, Mincowski, Hiltermann, and Okhuysen had escorted the aviators in small groups from the rue Lhomond to the gare d'Austerlitz. French gendarmes stopped two of the Americans, Elkin and McGlinchy, in the Métro and searched one of their suitcases, possibly for black market items. The aviators had the definite feeling that the gendarmes knew who and what they were but chose not to say anything.[91] That was the only document inspection they encountered on the entire journey from Paris to the Pyrenees.[92]

The thirteen aviators arrived in Toulouse early enough on February 5 to breakfast at Chez Emile with Rens and Chait, who was acting as the Dutch-Paris station chief in Toulouse. At least some of them waited in an empty building in the old part of town until it was time to take the 2:00 p.m. train to St-Girons. The *passeurs* Treillet and Marot solved the problem of transporting a large group of strangers of military age by disguising them as a soccer team. It is debatable whether it fooled anyone other than the Germans, who were themselves strangers, but it did offer a ready explanation for anyone who was willing to give the resistance the benefit of his or her silence.

After getting off the local train, the *passeurs* arranged for a taxi to take eight of the aviators farther south to Arbas and instructed the other four to take the bus. They missed it. While they were waiting for the next one at an inn, a German patrol came in. Brigman, the pilot from the Sarah Jane, thought the Germans were "too stupid to notice" the aviators.[93] After reaching the village of Mane, the airmen waited in the back room of a restaurant for another hour or so until a taxi took them farther into the foothills. Three more Dutchmen appear on the convoy list here. They may have been waiting for the others in Toulouse, but they probably came from Belgium on January 30 with Brigman and Boyce and then took the train from Paris with either of the other two groups without attracting any attention.[94]

The ten Americans, three Brits, one Australian, one Belgian, and eleven Dutchmen who rendezvoused in the meadow outside of Arbas during the early evening of February 5 made up an exclusively Dutch-Paris convoy.[95] They carried sufficient provisions for the journey, but none of them began the trek well-rested. The Engelandvaarders and the Australian had slept badly in a freezing, unfinished mountain house the night before. They had all spent the night before that on the crowded train from Paris. Four of them had spent the night before that on the train from Brussels to Paris. The American and British aviators had come directly from Paris on the night train and may not have slept at all. Before leaving Paris they had all been cooped up in the basement on the rue Lhomond for four or even five days.

The convoy started out into the dense darkness of a cloudy winter night at about 10:00 on February 5. After filing through a hamlet, the evaders started along a trail through three feet of snow. On the second mountain it started to snow heavily. The men walked across the slope to keep from sliding down, but it cost them time. The wind picked up, gusting snow into their faces. As the men struggled to climb the mountain without adequate boots, the stragglers got farther and farther behind. One of the British airmen who had been on the move for several nights broke down, but other aviators helped him along.

When they reached a valley at daybreak, they found shelter in a building various evaders described as a hut, a cabin, or a barn. They ate and tried to rest but were too cold and wet to sleep. After a couple of hours the *passeurs* decided to keep moving. One of the Dutch students took Timmers Verhoeven's backpack so he could help another Engelandvaarder who was just not strong enough to climb through the snow and wind. About 10:00 a.m. they arrived at the Col du Portet d'Aspet, hours behind schedule because of the storm. They had climbed about 2,625 feet in altitude over a little more than six miles in ten hours. They still had eight miles to go up and down even higher peaks before they would reach Spain. Exhausted, they took shelter in a low stone hut used by shepherds about three hundred yards west northwest of the pass itself and only minutes away from the village of Portet d'Aspet by motorized vehicle.

The storm cleared early on February 6, leaving a crystalline visibility that exposed anyone moving in the forbidden border zone. The guides decided that if the men were too cold and wet to sleep, it was pointless to stay crammed in the small building. They warned everyone that there was a German border post in the vicinity and told them that if they saw a German somewhere on a mountainside, they were to ignore him and keep walking single file. Treillet went first.

Scene of the ambush at the Col du Portet d'Aspet.

He had not gone far when he noticed the ears of a German shepherd poking above a boulder. He waved his hat and ran for his life through the heavy snow up the mountain as shots rang out behind him. Marot ran behind the hut, shouting for the others to follow him. The first half of the line did just that and then fanned out to head back up the northern slope. But the sun was coming up over the mountain at an angle that made it hard for the men coming out of the hut's door to see properly. The men at the back of the line misunderstood the shouting and went back inside. Treillet saw ten Germans on skis surround the hut and a bus arrive on the nearby highway.

From hiding places above the hut, the Engelandvaarders Den Besten, Bureau, Van Oosterzee, and Timmers Verhoeven and the aviators Brigman, Elkin, Kratz, Mandell, McLaughlin, Snyder, and Watts could see their unlucky companions being boarded onto the bus as prisoners. Brigman had been evading with Boyce since December 30, and Elkin, Kratz, and Snyder had been hiding with their crewmate Mellen since they crashed almost four weeks earlier. McGlinchy and McDonald had successfully evaded capture together since their plane went down in northern Friesland four months earlier, only to be caught together almost at the Spanish border. The Engelandvaarder Langeler had already escaped from the Germans in the Pyrenees but was now once again in their custody.

The men on the hillside could also see that a German officer and an enlisted man with a dog had caught Marot. The Germans relieved the *passeur* of the francs and pesetas he was carrying to pay the last local guides in the relay and to distribute to the evaders when they reached the border. They clearly wanted to take him back down the mountain, but Marot sat down as if dead tired or wounded. When the officer left, Marot either punched the enlisted man in the face or shoved him downhill and made his escape.

After the Germans had taken away their prisoners, Treillet led nine of the men he had gathered on a ledge above the hut to an inn to warm up. One of the aviators had frostbite in both feet but managed to carry on. They slept in a barn that night and went farther down the French side of the mountain the next day to spend that night in another barn, this one belonging to an old man. The next day Marot took them in groups of two to a small village, where they took a truck or a bus to Boussens. From there they caught a local train to Cazères. They hid in the unfinished house there for nine days while Chait made arrangements for them to attempt the Pyrenees again, this time with the *passeur* Bazerque. The Germans had Marot's identity card and photo. He and Treillet would have to lay low for some time.

Meanwhile Timmers Verhoeven and Den Besten decided not to go with Treillet but to return to the hut to get the backpack their friend had been carrying. It had the tube of toothpaste containing the military intelligence about dropping weapons over the Ardennes. After retrieving it, they walked west, roughly following the highway, which, fortunately, the Germans did not patrol with dogs. Frostbite, not to mention the lack of a compass, map, or guide, prevented them from reaching the Spanish border as planned. Instead they stopped at the first hamlet they found, Autrèche. The Ribis family took them in even though they had every reason to think the Germans would be searching for the fugitives. As far as Dutch-Paris was concerned, the two Engelandvaarders were lost in the mountains for several days until the Ribis reunited Timmers Verhoeven with his guides. Den Besten, however, could not walk because of frostbite in his feet. The family cared for him for two weeks before passing him to

Bart van Holk, Sam Timmers Verhoeven, Klaas Conijn, Pim de Nerée tot Babberich, Hans Langerer, Jan Weve, Rudy Regout, Cyril Gips, Dick Nederlof, René van der Stock, and Vic Lemmens in Viella, Spain, in February 1944.

French gendarmes, who took him to the hospital in St-Girons, where he had several toes amputated.[96]

The day after the disaster the prison in Foix registered the names of eight Dutchmen.[97] They were interrogated at Ruchon and Foix before being transferred to the prison of St. Michel in Toulouse. A couple weeks later the Germans removed all Jews from the prison to be deported. Two Jewish men from the Dutch-Paris convoy, Langeler and Lemmens, jumped out of the truck taking them from the prison to the train station as it slowed in the city. They made their way to Chez Emile on the place St-Georges, where they had eaten when they first arrived in Toulouse the previous month. French helpers whom they did not know hid them. Three weeks later they joined another Dutch-Paris convoy to Spain.[98] This time Langeler made good on his escape. The other six captured Dutchmen were deported as political prisoners and died in the concentration camps.[99]

The aviators captured at the Col du Portet d'Aspet were sent to POW camps, although not before being roughly interrogated. Snyder got rid of the "movie strip" he had been given in Brussels when the enemy attacked on the mountain. He thought that Mellen still had his when he was captured, which may or may not explain why the Germans did not abide by the Geneva Convention when questioning them. Nonetheless they all survived the war.[100]

What went wrong? The aviators who escaped felt that the guides "were good and trustworthy and the episode was no fault of theirs."[101] Years later Treillet himself thought the men in the barn were "too fatigued.... [They] preferred to let themselves be captured, thinking that the end of hostilities was close."[102] That may have been true for the Allied aviators, who could expect to be taken to a POW camp. It seems unlikely, however, that the Dutchmen allowed themselves to be captured for any other reason than that they were trapped in a barn and surrounded by the enemy. None of them could hope for the clemency of a POW camp, especially not the Jews among them.

Did the German mountain patrols simply have a lucky break? Did they see the tracks of so many men leading from the highway to the hut? Or did they have a superior intelligence network? Did one of those German spies that the Engelandvaarder reported had crossed into Spain with his

Sam Timmers Verhoeven and Chris van Oosterzee in Spain, February 1944.

group in December inform his superiors about that route before the English exposed him? Or perhaps the Germans who came into the inn in Boussens or Mane where the aviators were waiting for the bus were not as stupid as the pilot thought they were. They may have pretended not to notice the Americans so as not to arouse their suspicions and then alerted the border patrol. Or perhaps they went for reinforcements.

Timmers Verhoeven offered another explanation. According to him, the bicyclist who saw the Dutchmen hiding behind a wall as they made their way to the rendezvous reported them. Zeeman had seen two German policemen in Boussens and Mane only a few days earlier. The Germans controlled the telephones and could easily have called the border patrol stationed in the village of Portet d'Aspet, not far from the hut. Even without phones the Germans could have sent a messenger in a motorized vehicle to alert the ski patrol in far less time than it took for the fugitives to arrive there.[103]

No network that covered as much territory, involved as many different people, and interacted with outsiders as frequently as Dutch-Paris did could hope to avoid police attention for long. Indeed individual members, such as Paul van Cleeff in Brussels, Consul Maurice Jacquet in Lyon, and Jean Weidner himself, had already been arrested and in some cases released. Benno Nijkerk had had to leave Belgium. So far such events had been brushes with disaster without further consequences. But in January 1944 Weidner, Laatsman, and their colleagues could feel the net tightening around them.

That month the truncated Dutch embassy in Paris received an anonymous denunciation written in block letters that accused Starink, Laatsman, Weidner, Okhuysen, and two other Dutch civil servants who did not participate in Dutch-Paris of having an "un-Dutch attitude."[104] Denouncing Dutchmen to the Dutch embassy was far less malicious, of course, than denouncing them to the French or Germans, but it did serve as notice that Dutch-Paris had enemies within the Dutch colony.

Around the same time Laatsman warned Weidner that a certain Dutch expatriate had been asking for him at the Dutch Chamber of Commerce. The young man had helped Dutch refugees in Lyon before November 1942 and had given the Eliasars, father and son, good advice. But in 1944 he was known to be living with a woman who worked for the Gestapo, which was more than enough to put him beyond the pale of trust.

More disturbing, in mid-January Gestapo officers arrested the more senior of the last two Dutch civil servants working in Vichy, apparently because of the activities of a Dutch agent provocateur. The arrest was worrisome enough at the time without Weidner and his colleagues knowing that the Gestapo in Paris had tortured the civil servant for four days, asking specifically about Weidner, Jacquet, Laatsman, and the acting consul in Toulouse, Antonius Aarts, among others.[105] The civil servant was then deported to the concentration camps, from which he returned broken in health. It seems that in January 1944 German police had identified members of Dutch-Paris as resisters without having yet pieced together the existence of Dutch-Paris itself.

But that was not all. There were other disturbing events along the line. At the end of January, Swiss intelligence officers passed Weidner over the border in full view of French gendarmes. The French arrested Weidner but allowed him to go "on his mission" after he demonstrated that he carried neither contraband nor weapons.[106] It looked as if the Swiss wanted the French to arrest Weidner, but he could not think of a reason why they would have changed their attitude about him so completely. He and his colleagues were soon to learn about the capture of the convoy near the Spanish border. Although the resisters had no reason to suspect any cause other than bad luck, the Germans now had fifteen men who knew, at the very least, what several Dutch-Paris couriers looked like. It was only reasonable to assume that the Germans would torture some information about the line out of their captives.

None of this was enough to cause Weidner and the others to end or even pause their illegal work. In addition to the families in hiding who needed regular deliveries of cash and documents, Dutch-Paris had aviators and Engelandvaarders hiding in Brussels and Paris who needed to be evacuated to Spain. They did take what precautions they could. Weidner, for instance, warned a courier from Brussels to tell the Comité to cut off contact with a certain Dutchman who was "too dangerous because he talked too much."[107] But otherwise they continued with the *sociaalwerk*, the *transportwerk*, and the courier relay. Dutch-Paris would flow through western Europe as long as it was occupied.

Gare d'Austerlitz, Paris, 1942.

6

Catastrophe in Paris

ON FEBRUARY 11, 1944, DUTCH-PARIS'S SECOND IN COMMAND, Jacques Rens, was in Paris for one of their regular meetings. The main actors involved with the dispatch of a convoy of aviators and Engelandvaarders to Toulouse that night gathered at a Chinese restaurant for lunch. The diplomat Herman Laatsman and his associates, the student Suzanne Hiltermann and the translator Leo Mincowski, had been hiding aviators in the basement of the physics laboratories on the rue Lhomond. The engineer Albert Starink had been taking care of Engelandvaarders. Rens would lead the convoy on the train, assisted by the couriers Lucie Comiti, who declared she would rather die than work for the Germans, and Suzy Kraay. Kraay had recently escorted a Jewish family from the Netherlands to the Swiss border and was now working for Dutch-Paris as a courier at large.

During lunch tensions arose over security protocols. Laatsman, for example, did the bookkeeping during the meal in full view of everyone else in the restaurant and anyone passing by the window. He asked his colleagues to sign receipts and stored them in a folder. Both the public nature of the transactions and the creation of a paper trail irritated and alarmed Starink and Mincowski.

After lunch Kraay went to Jean-Michael Caubo's apartment near the gare du Nord, where Laatsman gave her three packages of food for the aviators to take on their trek over the Pyrenees. Kraay protested that she did not want to take the packages because Mincowski had already explained that the police were looking for black marketeers carrying food. But Laatsman insisted. Because the packages were big, as long as her shoulders were wide, Kraay borrowed a valise to carry them. She then left for a 4:00 p.m. meeting with Mincowski at the Métro station at the Place des Fêtes, located on the same northeastern side of the city as the town where the aviators were hiding, Livry-Gargan, and the town of Drancy, where their colleague made false documents at the town hall.

Because she arrived early, Kraay went to a brasserie called l'Arc-en-ciel, located on the corner of the rue des Fêtes and the rue des Solitaires, where she could easily see the entrance to the Métro station.[1] While she was waiting, two French policemen asked to see her papers and demanded to know what was in the valise. The inspectors belonged to a special unit of the French police called the Brigade d'Interpellation that operated in train stations, the Métro, and cafés looking for Jews, foreigners, and communists. It had a reputation for zealous collaboration.[2]

Kraay gave them her false French documents made out in the name of "Suzanne Melinand" and told them the valise contained food parcels meant for a prison camp in the Pyrenees. Recognizing that she was not French, they accused her of being Jewish, which she denied. She tried to talk her way out of being arrested by telling the officers that she was afraid of being put into an internment camp as a foreigner, but the inspectors insisted that she go with them.

Kraay dropped her notebook by the entrance to the Métro, but a passerby, thinking he was doing her a kindness, returned it to her. Naturally the inspectors confiscated it. When they arrived at the police prefecture around 5:30 p.m., Kraay insisted on speaking to the police commissioner, Lucien Bizoire. Weidner had told her that if the French ever arrested her, she should tell the superior officer that she worked for the Resistance, although he probably meant the regular French police rather than a collaborationist unit, which this one happened to be.

An hour after she arrived at the prefecture, Commissioner Bizoire took Kraay into a small room. He opened one of the packages, finding a knife, hard-boiled eggs, sugar cubes, a small flask of cognac, bread, butter, and sausage. He asked her if she was Jewish or a refugee. She replied again that she was not Jewish but had left her native Holland because of the Germans. Was there anything she could do to regain her freedom?

Commissioner Bizoire hesitated, telling her that he had to be careful because the Germans had arrested a subprefect for helping someone out of a similar situation. Still under the mistaken assumption that French police would not want to alienate the Resistance so late in the war, Kraay then said that her real name was Ratgeer and offered to prove her bona fides as a resister. She told him about the convoy of aviators leaving from the gare d'Austerlitz that very evening. The commissioner looked up the train schedule, looked at the clock, and rushed out of the room. Kraay was taken into the hallway where about thirty-five police agents were waiting. One of them asked her to come with them to point out the resisters and the aviators, but she refused.

The police squad returned around 8:30 that evening without any prisoners.[3] It is not clear whether they intentionally overlooked the fugitives, could not identify them in the crowd, or were on the wrong platform.

Comiti, Hiltermann, and Mincowski had indeed brought seven men of the USAAF and two of the RAF as well as seven Engelandvaarders to the gare d'Austerlitz that very evening of February 11.[4] When Kraay did not show up, Hiltermann took her place on the night train to Toulouse. The airmen, the Engelandvaarders, and their guides all arrived the next morning without incident.

After he returned from the train station that evening, Commissioner Bizoire asked Kraay which parts of her story were true. Changing her strategy, she now told him that it was all lies meant to hide simple black marketeering. Then he asked about the names in her notebook. No one should have written down such compromising details as the names and addresses of colleagues, but Kraay had, and so had others. Paul van Cleeff, for example, had been arrested in Brussels with a compromising notebook, although he had either coded it or destroyed it so that it did not lead the Germans to anyone else in Dutch-Paris. The French police, however, had no difficulty deciphering Kraay's notebook, which contained the notations "Caubo 189 rue du Fg Poissonière; Melle Josette Molland; Hotel Ibis; rue Jasmin, and Mr Milleret."[5] Kraay said that Caubo was an acquaintance, Molland was a friend, and she did not know Milleret. She also claimed that she bought her false ID from an unknown person in a café in Lyon. The questioning went on until about 11:00 p.m., when the police locked her in a cell for the night.

On February 12 policemen paid a visit to Caubo at 189 rue du Faubourg Poissonière, the address in Kraay's notebook.[6] They arrived around 10:00 a.m. to find Marie Schenck, Caubo's wife, alone in the apartment. An elderly neighbor brought the Caubos' nine-year-old daughter home from school an hour later. Half an hour after that, the Caubos' twin sixteen-year-old sons returned from school to find strangers ransacking their home; only some of them wore uniforms. While preparing lunch, their mother retrieved some Dutch-Paris papers hidden behind the teacups, tucked them in her clothing, and tore them up in the bathroom. The boys ate their meal, but their sister picked at hers. The family and their unwanted guests waited for Caubo to return.

Later than expected, around 2:00 or 2:30, Caubo and Mincowski entered the building together. The neighbor lady warned the men about the police as they mounted the staircase. Caubo continued on to his family. The police asked him, "Who is leaving for Toulouse tonight?" They also questioned him about his work and some packages of food with Red Cross stamps on the wrapping that they found in the apartment. Caubo told them that the food was meant for prisoners, though they were likely more of the food parcels meant for aviators that Kraay had picked up there the day before.

Mincowksi, on the other hand, left immediately to warn their colleagues. Because Hiltermann had gone to Toulouse the night before, Mincowski met her return train at the gare d'Austerlitz. Together they went to their apartment on the rue du Laos, within sight of the Eiffel Tower, and burned most of their papers. They did, however, wrap up a packet with a list of the names of the aviators they had helped and their supplies for making false documents, which they hid securely in the bathroom. Hiltermann slept on a friend's couch for a few days but then moved back to the rue du Laos.[7]

Laatsman and Starink were also on their way to Caubo's apartment on that Saturday afternoon. They avoided arrest on the rue Faubourg Poissonière that day because either Mincowski or a French policeman they met on the stairs warned them of the danger.[8]

Once they finished searching the apartment, the officers took the entire family to the police prefecture on the Ile de la Cité. They left behind three plainclothes members of the secret police—a German, a Frenchman, and an Alsatian—as a trap to capture anyone who knocked on the door. At the police station the Caubos waited in a large room filled with other suspects. Caubo and Schenck were each taken away individually for questioning several times. After a woman came around with a cart of snacks that evening, the boys thought that they were going to be released. Instead policemen handcuffed the twins and their father and took away their shoelaces and belts. They and two other prisoners spent a restless night with bags of straw for pillows in a cell where the light burned continuously. Their mother and sister were taken to another part of the building overseen by nuns, where they slept on cots in a very cold room.

The next morning, February 13, the women were taken to mass and then to the prefecture. The men were given a lukewarm, brownish liquid to drink and allowed about half an hour of exercise before returning to the prefecture in handcuffs. The parents and twins spent the day being questioned, apparently without revealing anything that could be used against the boys or their mother even though they had certainly been involved in Dutch-Paris.

That day the secret policemen who had remained behind at the Caubos' apartment caught a Dutch priest and Brother Rufus. The priest, who had worked for Dutch-Paris in Toulouse for only a few days and done very little, arrived at the door with a bag of shoes meant for aviators. The police accepted the story that Caubo intended to buy the shoes for his sons and released the priest after he gave them the cobbler's name and address. The priest immediately went into hiding using Dutch-Paris money that he had not yet returned.[9]

Brother Rufus went to the Caubos' apartment because he had not heard from anyone in Dutch-Paris for a while. He was worried because the Gestapo had been in the physics laboratories of the Ecole Normale Supérieure twice to question a professor. When policemen answered the door, Brother Rufus claimed that he had come to give the children Dutch lessons, as he did for many Dutch families, but they took him to the police prefecture anyway. After several hours of questioning, they put him in a small room, which they left unlocked. When he heard nothing outside the door, Brother Rufus walked out of the prefecture with the calmness that befitted a chaplain on his rounds. He was even greeted politely by the policeman on guard duty. He returned to his home on the rue Lhomond. The next morning he took the early train outside the city to warn his Dutch farming friends from whom he bought black market food for fugitives not to go to Caubo's.[10]

That same day French inspectors took Kraay with them to search her room at the Hotel Ibis.[11] There they found a suitcase containing Belgian, Spanish, and English money, which would have been difficult to explain. At this time the proprietor of the hotel received only a fine for registering someone who was using a false identification card.[12] Kraay remained in custody.

The next morning Caubo was taken from the cell that he had shared with his sons for two nights. Several hours later the boys were given back their shoelaces and belts and reunited with their mother and sister. An inspector took them all back to the prefecture, where they were given back their identity documents and allowed to say good-bye to their father. Police continued to watch their apartment for some time and followed them whenever they went out.

During their ordeal at the police prefecture, the children were told that "it was nothing" and that the whole thing could have been hushed up if the collaborationist police commissioner had not alerted the Gestapo.[13] That may have been true. The French police were not obliged to report every case of false documentation or black marketeering to the Germans, and they had various ways to hide such cases if they wanted to. They could lose records or even lose suspects. They had, after all, put Brother Rufus in an unlocked room on an unoccupied corridor and then neglected to look for him at his home address. Laatsman, who found out about Caubo's arrest while the police were still in his apartment, seems to have also had a source of information at the police prefecture. He knew that Kraay had been arrested and had been carrying a notebook with Caubo's name in it, although he thought she had been caught in a raid in the Métro. He also knew that Caubo, Brother Rufus, and the priest had been arrested, although he did not know what had happened to the priest.

Finally into this growing catastrophe came Jean Weidner. When he arrived in Paris on February 13, his sister Gabrielle informed him that the Caubo family and Kraay had been arrested. The next day he, Laatsman, Hiltermann, Mincowski, Comiti, and Catherine Okhuysen held a conference about how to limit the damage. They decided to stop any traffic on the escape line until everyone already in Toulouse had reached Spain. Laatsman had already sent Starink to Brussels to warn them not to send any new airmen to Paris, although the message was not received. Comiti and Okhuysen went to Toulouse that night to help Edmond Chait with the large group of almost thirty aviators and Engelandvaarders who were waiting there for the weather to improve in the mountains.[14]

After curfew that night, Mincowski and Hiltermann went to the apartment of Fernande Goetschel, the well-traveled widow of a French military attaché. She had opened her home on the western side of the city to an RAF pilot named Robert Ellis. Ellis had been strafing trains in northern France in November 1943 when the engine of his single-seater Typhoon fighter plane cut and he was forced to land in trees. Helpers had passed him to the organization in Livry-Gargan, who passed him to Dutch-Paris on February 11. Ellis did not take the train to Toulouse that night because a childhood illness had weakened his legs enough that he could not walk over the Pyrenees. Laatsman and Rens intended to send him to Switzerland instead.[15] As a precaution, on February 13 Hiltermann and Mincowski escorted Ellis through the blacked-out streets of Paris to a new hiding place, the home of friends of Milleret's, a French veteran of World War I and his wife who lived near Les Halles in the center of the city.[16]

Mincowski visited Brother Rufus the next day, February 14, to give him some money and tell him to remain at his post unless ordered to leave it. Of course Rufus had already had plenty of opportunity to go into hiding but had chosen not to. The good brother felt he had no other choice as long as there was no one else to look after the "jongens," meaning the aviators hiding in the basement of the physics laboratories next door.[17]

As planned, Weidner left Paris for Louvain on February 15 to exchange microfilm for the Swiss Way. He improvised a new route over the Belgian border because Laatsman had told him the police had found a briefcase containing Rens's false identity documents. Because he and Rens both used false documents supposedly issued by the Belgium Chamber of Commerce, Weidner worried that the German police would be looking for such papers. As it turned out, however, Caubo had hidden the documents with his neighbor, who had had the presence of mind to burn them all after the family had been arrested.[18] On his way back to Paris, Weidner stopped in Brussels to warn his colleagues there to use extra caution. The young people involved in the *transportwerk* of the escape line duly observed a "short hiatus" but soon returned to their illegal work.[19]

When Weidner returned to Paris on February 16, Laatsman and Mincowski told him that Caubo had been delivered to the occupation authorities under suspicion of being in contact with the enemy but that Kraay was still in the custody of the French police. Weidner advised Mincowski and Hiltermann to take a holiday outside Paris. They stayed in the capital, however, because they did not have the money to leave. He also recommended that they all have as little contact as possible with the

Red Cross representative Jules Mohr in order to protect his work on behalf of Dutch prisoners. As long as they had a friend at the Red Cross, they had a chance of finding out what was happening in the prisons in France. Weidner also took steps to get Kraay and Caubo out of jail. He probably talked to a Dutch lawyer in Paris.[20] But it was too late.

Laatsman had been misinformed. Kraay, like Caubo, was already in the hands of the Germans. On February 14, three days after her arrest, Commissioner Bizoire ordered Kraay to sign a declaration that identified her as a black marketeer. Black marketeering counted as a lesser offense than resistance and was dealt with by the French courts. Although she could expect a prison sentence or a heavy fine as a black marketeer, Kraay had reason to think the charge would keep her out of the hands of the Germans and their torturers. She signed the statement. The commissioner's secretary, however, warned her not to trust Bizoire and promised to warn Caubo as well. Caubo would not have needed the warning because he knew that the police had handcuffed his wife and children and kept them in jail for two nights. That was how the police treated resisters, not how they treated black marketeers.[21]

Admitting to black marketeering did nothing to help Kraay. Late on the afternoon that she signed the statement, February 14, five or six Germans arrived at the police prefecture to take her and Caubo to the dreaded rue des Saussaies, location of the Gestapo headquarters in Paris.[22] There a man in plainclothes questioned Kraay. This time she gave her true name. Another German came into the interrogation room and told her he was glad to have finally found her. He then pulled a copy of her passport photograph out of a large book, possibly the passport photo that the agent provocateur Rouwendal had asked her for a year earlier.

After taking Kraay to an upstairs room, the second German asked her where Weidner was. She claimed that she had not seen him since escaping from Gurs, the Vichy internment camp, several months earlier. Her interrogator wanted to know how she had managed to do that and asked where she had gone from there. He did not accept her answer of "Holland" because he knew she had been in Toulouse. He sent her to the massive prison of Fresnes on the outskirts of Paris, where she remained for two days.

On February 17 Kraay was taken back to the rue des Saussaies to be interrogated again, this time by three Germans in civilian clothing. It soon became clear to her that two of them were there to "help her memory" if she should forget anything. The interrogator told her plainly that it would not help her father, who had been arrested in the Netherlands in September, if she left anything out. In the evening all three of the Germans questioned Kraay, one of them claiming not to believe anything she said, while another refused to believe selected parts of her story. Although Kraay was not aware of it, the Germans already knew everything she had told to and done with "Van den Berg" (Rouwendal) and his "resistance partner Eugène" (the Abwehr officer Christmann) between March and June 1943.

Before sending her back to Fresnes that night, the lead interrogator told her that her father had been sentenced to death for helping Jews escape, but that the death sentence could be commuted if she cooperated. The threat echoed an odd encounter near her old apartment in Amsterdam a month earlier when she was there on Dutch-Paris business. An acquaintance had told her that a stranger had been looking for her at her old address with what he said was a message from her father: he had been sentenced to death and she alone could free him.

The questioning resumed the next morning at 7:00 on the rue des Saussaies. A German in uniform came in and out during the interrogation, which now consisted of rapid-fire questioning and beating. Again and again they asked her where Laatsman and Weidner were. After a couple of hours the uniformed German returned and offered her a deal: if she told them all the names and addresses she knew, they would release her father; if she did not, it would be easy enough to have her mother arrested. It was standard practice under the Nazi doctrine of collective family responsibility to threaten and indeed punish the families of resisters in France and other occupied territories.[23] She had no reason to doubt they would do it.

When Kraay replied that she had nothing to add to her previous answers, she was taken down a flight of stairs in a different section of the building, to a room where she saw three men hanging from their wrists. All three had their hands and feet cuffed; one was covered in blood. None of them gave any sign of life. A uniformed man whom Kraay thought belonged to the SS then took her into an adjoining room. There were the three interrogators, another SS soldier, and a large bathtub being filled with water. This was the notorious *baignoire*, a form of torture in which the victim was repeatedly held under ice cold water to the point of almost drowning. The Germans told Kraay to undress, chained her feet together and her hands behind her back, and threw her into the water. The soldiers held her under. When they allowed her up for air, the others fired questions. Where was she going when she was arrested? Where was Laatsman? Where was Weidner? Who did she pass fugitives to in Lyon?

After what seemed like an hour, she was taken back upstairs and asked more questions. She did not know many of the names they asked her about. As she later remembered it, "The Germans apparently started to lose patience and self-discipline and they tried to get me to answer by being rather rude. Around three o'clock in the afternoon they ceased their screaming."[24] Two of them took her downstairs to a room where a man was stretched out naked on a table and groaning in agony as four soldiers flogged him with leather whips. Kraay fainted. Her captors revived her and held her upright, forcing her to watch.

Her interrogator told her that the same would happen to her unless she cooperated. He told her they would get to the truth one way or another. Did she want her father to be treated in the same way as the unfortunate man on the table?

Fear overwhelmed her.

She did what she herself found unforgiveable and told the Germans what they wanted to know.

According to her postwar statement, Kraay told the Germans the names and addresses of Laatsman, Hiltermann, and Mincowski in Paris; Weidner, Raymonde Pillot, and Pastor Paul Meyer in Lyon; and Mademoiselle Meunier in Annecy. She also told them the truth about the addresses on rue Franklin and rue Jasmin, which she had previously claimed belonged to friends in Liège. And she told them what she knew about the Panier Fleuri in Toulouse, which, fortunately, Dutch-Paris had stopped using in January.

She hoped to save her father. He was indeed released eight weeks later, on April 4, only to be rearrested the next morning and sent to Neuengamme concentration camp, where he died.[25]

In Paris her interrogators sent Kraay back to Fresnes that night and left her alone the next day. On February 20 two of them questioned her again at the prison. They accused her of leaving out information and asked her about someone called "Odette" and two other people whom she did not know.[26] There was no "Odette" in Dutch-Paris, which suggests that although the German security services knew a lot about the organization, they could not separate it out from the general pool of information they had about escape and evasion lines.

By this point, nine days after Kraay's arrest, Weidner and his colleagues knew that she and Caubo had been turned over to the Germans, though they still thought they were being held for black marketeering. They certainly did not know that Kraay, one of the few people to have traveled the entire Dutch-Paris route, including Brussels, Paris, Lyon, Annecy, and Toulouse, had broken under torture. Even if they had known, there was little they could have done beyond exercising extra caution. They could not go deeply into hiding because of all the fugitives who relied on them for the money and false documents they needed to survive. Their immediate problem, however, was a pile-up on the escape line to Spain.

On the morning that Kraay was arrested, February 11, three aviators arrived in Paris from Brussels. Because they did not have the proper false documents to leave for Toulouse that same night with the convoy that Kraay should have escorted, Laatsman hid them in the basement on the rue Lhomond. Even though Laatsman had told Starink to warn their colleagues in Brussels not to send more fugitives, five more Americans and a Dutchman arrived in Paris on February 14. Laatsman put them in the basement on the rue Lhomond as well. There were now eight aviators and an Engelandvaarder hiding in the laboratories' electrical room: a Brazilian flying with the RAF who spoke French fluently and seven Americans who had crashed in the Netherlands and been passed to Dutch-Paris in Brussels.[27] One of them was a pilot who had been on his twenty-fourth mission when his bomber exploded in midair over the Netherlands.[28] Three of them had been arrested by the Germans after they crashed near the North Sea in November but had made a daring escape by jumping out of a moving train.[29]

Coincidentally German and French police searched the laboratory building on the afternoon of February 14. They arrested the director of the Ecole Normale Supérieure and four young Frenchmen, but they did not find the aviators because the door to their hiding place was locked. It is unlikely that this search had anything to do with Dutch-Paris; it happened before Kraay admitted anything. Indeed there is no indication that she or Caubo even knew the address. Nonetheless, at about 10:00 that same night Brother Rufus moved the Brazilian and the Americans through a hallway, across a roof, through his quarters, and into a building in the Congregation's complex that had been condemned five years earlier. He put them in a room on the second floor, where the window gave them a view of the golden dome of what they thought was a church but that was probably the Panthéon.

Even had they known that Kraay had been tortured, Laatsman and his team could not have evacuated these men to Toulouse because Chait had nowhere to put them there. As of February 12 Chait had twenty-eight fugitives to care for in Toulouse and the surrounding area and no way to get them through the snowstorms that were closing the passes in the Pyrenees. The fugitives included the ten men who had escaped from the ambush on the Col du Portet d'Aspet three weeks earlier, some of whom were hiding in Cazères and some in Toulouse.[30] Two more aviators were staying in the city with a contact of Father John aan de Stegge.[31] And sixteen more men had arrived from Paris with Comiti and Hiltermann (but not, of course, Kraay) early that morning.[32]

The convoy that Kraay missed included seven Engelandvaarders and nine aviators. Seven of the airmen had been passed to Dutch-Paris from their allies in Livry-Gargan. Five of these were Americans who had crashed in northern France several months earlier. Two flew with the RAF. The remaining two aviators were crewmates on a bomber that crashed in the Netherlands in mid-December. Both farm boys, Loral Martin from Illinois and Herman Morgan from Missouri had made their own way through the Dutch countryside for an impressive five days before finding help from civilians.[33]

Chait took the nine airmen who arrived on February 12 to an empty house on the outskirts of the city that belonged to the *passeur* Bazerque's family. It sat on the chemin de Castellardit by the Cartoucherie, about two miles across the Garonne River from the restaurants and shops where Dutch-Paris fed and hid fugitives and collected messages around the place St-Georges and the old part of town. Chait named it the "Villa du Crime." To supply these men for the next nineteen days, Chait relied on the help of the students whose families disapproved of their resistance work: Simone Calmels, Andrée Moulouguet, and Anita Boicoran. The *passeur* Treillet may also have taken them supplies, as did Chait.[34]

The weather in the mountains appeared to clear later in the week, allowing Chait to move some of the aviators and Engelandvaarders on toward Spain. On February 16 he bought eighteen train tickets from Toulouse to the village of Lannemazan and picked up eighteen packages containing three days' worth of provisions from the restaurant Chez Emile.[35] For the time being Chait left the nine aviators at the Villa du Crime, but he and his colleagues gathered up the rest of their charges: the two aviators hiding with Aan de Stegge's contact, six of the Engelandvaarders who had come from Paris five days earlier, and the ten men who had escaped the ambush at the Col du Portet d'Aspet. They escorted these men by train from Toulouse to the hamlet of Lannemazan, where they handed off the fugitives to Bazerque.

The *passeur* told one of the Americans that Treillet had told him about the ambush at the Col du Portet d'Aspet. He assured the aviator that he and his men would get them to Spain on the trail that was the highest and toughest, but also the safest. The snow, he said, was too deep to travel for another three or four days, but he would feed them in the meantime.[36] The weather, however, got worse, and the three days turned into weeks.

In Paris on February 20, the day Kraay signed the declaration she made under torture, Laatsman, Weidner, and their colleagues had eight aviators hiding on the rue Lhomond and two agents in the hands of the German secret police. They were nervous but did not as yet have enough information to appreciate the gravity of the situation. Weidner moved about Paris freely, even managing to get money to Madame Caubo, despite police observation of her home.

The Germans were watching the addresses they had gleaned from Kraay but did nothing obvious for days. Unbeknownst to Goetschel or Milleret, for example, police had their building at 11 rue Jasmin under surveillance and had interviewed the concierge about the inhabitants.[37] Late at night on February 21 a tall blond man in his midtwenties rang Goetschel's doorbell. Calling himself "Albert," he asked for Hiltermann and gave the noms de guerre of Laatsman and Comiti. This disturbed Goetschel enough that she consulted Hiltermann the next day, who thought that it must have been Albert Starink. Hiltermann was wrong, of course—in hindsight it was clearly a German agent—but it was a comforting explanation.[38]

Caubo sent a cryptic warning to "be very careful" through one of his twin sons, who was allowed to take him food and clothing in the prison.

Weidner kept his appointments in other cities but returned to Paris in time for a dinner meeting with colleagues from Brussels and Paris on February 25. He spent the earlier part of what turned into a very long day talking to his colleagues separately or in small groups. In the morning he met with representatives of the *transportwerk* in Belgium, David Verloop and Hans Wisbrun, who had come to Paris for the meeting. They complained about the behavior of Visser 't Hooft's assistant, a man named Joop Bartels, who had shown up in Brussels. Bartels ran a secret office in Geneva in which he and a Dutch refugee with superior artistic skills made and developed microfilm for the Swiss Way. Even though he did not belong to Dutch-Paris, he strutted about Brussels issuing orders and countermanding Weidner's own instructions. As if to prove their point, Jef Lejeune arrived in Paris that day with a Dutch pastor and his wife who were fleeing to Switzerland.[39] Lejeune should not have been doing any traveling other than ferrying microfilm between Amsterdam and Louvain for the Swiss Way, but Bartels had ordered him to take the couple to Paris.

Weidner also had an unsettling interview with Starink that day. The young engineer had joined Dutch-Paris in order to move Engelandvaarders to Spain after arrests crippled the escape line he had been working with in late November 1943. But he had also continued to work with the remnants of his original group. On February 12 Starink had gone to see the woman who was now running his original group. A policeman had opened her door and marched him back down the stairs at gunpoint. He managed to get away at an intersection with shots ringing out behind him.[40] There was no reason to link that close call to Dutch-Paris, but Weidner had heard that the French police had asked Caubo whether he knew Starink. He decided to send Starink to the Netherlands. He left that night, February 25, with Verloop and Wisbrun, who got off the train in Brussels while he continued north.[41]

Before they left, however, Verloop and Wisbrun had dinner with Weidner, Benno Nijkerk, Laatsman, Mincowski, Hiltermann, and Comiti at a restaurant. The Gestapo had gotten close enough to Nijkerk in Brussels that he had had to leave his wife and baby behind to seek refuge in Switzerland. He was returning to occupied territory under a new pseudonym in order to help Laatsman with Dutch-Paris in the French capital. Dinner involved a "painful" discussion that Weidner regretted having in public. The pressure seems to have frayed Laatsman's nerves; he aired all his grievances about what he considered to be the incompetence of everyone else on the line. Nijkerk and Weidner talked to him for a long time that evening, managing despite everything to part as friends.

On his last stop of the day, Weidner visited his sisters, who were both staying in Gabrielle's rooms in the Adventist church. Annette Weidner had left their parents' home in The Hague for Paris after her twenty-first birthday in October 1943. Although she played no documented role in the escape line, she probably did the same sort of behind-the-scenes rescue work that her sister did. This quiet family gathering late on February 25 was to be the last time Weidner ever saw Gabrielle.

Around 6:30 in the early morning darkness of February 26, German police arrested Hiltermann and Mincowski at their apartment on the rue du Laos. The first thing they found was a list of the names of the aviators hiding on the rue Lhomond that Mincowski had written down when he visited the Americans the night before and that Hiltermann had left in her handbag. They did not, however, find the list of names hidden in the bathroom two weeks earlier.

Half an hour later German police raided 11 rue Jasmin. Unfortunately the British pilot Robert Ellis was sleeping in Milleret's apartment when they arrived. Hiltermann had visited Ellis at his other hiding place near Les Halles over the past two weeks to give him cigarettes and reading materials. Just the day before she had taken him to get new passport photos and moved him back to the rue Jasmin according to a plan to take him to Switzerland. The Germans did not need any further evidence against Milleret than the presence in his apartment of an enemy airman.[42]

The police beat Milleret, put him in handcuffs, and threw him and his British guest into one of the long, black Citroëns favored by the Gestapo. Twenty minutes later they put Milleret's neighbor, Goetschel, into another Citroën. After the cars left, a special SD unit removed every valuable from Milleret's and Goetschel's apartments, including typewriters, refrigerators, wines, furniture, and clothing.[43]

Shortly after, at 7:30 a.m., someone knocked on the back door of Laatsman's home west of the city in St-Nom-la-Bretèche. After the Caubos' arrest two weeks earlier, Madame Laatsman and her small daughter had moved into Paris to stay with friends. Laatsman and his fifteen-year-old son from his first marriage ate dinner with them in the evenings but slept at their house well outside the city. Laatsman knew immediately that trouble had arrived because whoever was knocking asked in French if "Monsieur Felix" was in. No one in the suburb knew him by that pseudonym, which he used for Dutch-Paris and aviators. The knocking continued, but this time the person on the other side yelled in German. Laatsman's son opened the shutters of a bedroom window that opened onto the garden. Bullets struck the outside wall but did not hit him.

Shouting "Where are the parachutists?," German soldiers with submachine guns entered the building through a window and surrounded the two Dutchmen. While searching the house, some of the soldiers pocketed a number of items, such as an electric razor, a flashlight, a leather satchel, and a bottle of cognac. With his hands cuffed behind his back, Laatsman was taken outside. The entire courtyard was filled with automobiles and the surrounding woods filled with armed men. Laatsman was put in one wagon and his son in another and both taken in the direction of Paris under the guard of German soldiers and French *Miliciens*.[44]

Meanwhile, across the city, Gabrielle and Annette Weidner were attending services at the Adventist church by the place d'Italie, not far south of the gare d'Austerlitz, as they did every Saturday morning. Around 9:30 a.m. someone in the congregation, who had somehow not grown savvy to the signs of danger even after four years of occupation, went to get Gabrielle when two plainclothes German police officers asked for her. Assuming that the strangers were couriers from Spain for whom she was holding two microfilms for her brother, Gabrielle went to talk to them. She told her sister to follow ten minutes later. But when Annette opened the door to Gabrielle's room, she knew the men were not resistance couriers. Gabrielle's face was deathly pale. She turned on her sister as if she were an impertinent maid, berating her for not knocking before entering and slamming the door in her face. Annette realized that the strangers, who were wearing boots with their suits, must be Gestapo. Because she had promised her brother never to tell anyone that Gabrielle worked with him in the resistance, she hid under the portico without saying anything to anyone at the church. Twenty minutes later she saw the men take her sister away.[45]

When Laatsman and his son arrived at an upper floor of the secret police headquarters on the rue des Saussaies, a German in plainclothes asked Laatsman if he recognized him as the man who had been shadowing him.[46] The diplomat turned resistance leader was further surprised and disconcerted to find Milleret, Goetschel, Hiltermann, Mincowski, and Gabrielle Weidner already there. These arrests had been coordinated by the Kommandatur der Sicherheitspolizei und SD (KdS commander of the Security Police and SD in Paris, section IVE, counterespionage) with the assistance of the Abwehr officer Richard Christmann, whom Kraay had met as "Eugène" in 1943.[47]

By 10:00 a.m. on February 26 the Germans had captured enough helpers to extract everything they needed to know about Dutch-Paris's work with aviators in Paris. They did not, however, restrict their investigation to torture. When it was useful, they took their prisoners on what they called "a little tour together." They began by putting Millert in the back of a black Citroën and taking him to the café in Belleville that Dutch-Paris used as a meeting place. The proprietor correctly identified the two unknown men with Milleret as German plainclothes police agents. Milleret demanded that the owner give him the papers that Laatsman kept there in such a way as to divert suspicion from his colleague. The proprietor handed over the documents, including the folder in which Laatsman had put the signed receipts at the Chinese lunch on February 11, the day Kraay was arrested. It became an integral part of the dossier against Dutch-Paris at the rue des Saussaies.

Milleret and the policemen left the café with the papers, allowing the proprietor to warn Comiti that Milleret had been arrested. He thought he had warned Hiltermann as well, although the message could not have been delivered that late in the day.[48] He may also have warned Miguel Duchanel, who went into hiding that day and escaped arrest.

Shortly after noon German police invaded the concierge's home across the street from the physics laboratories on the rue Lhomond, demanding to know where the aviators were. When they found nothing in that building, they brought Milleret in from the vehicles parked outside. According to Julia Prilliez, wife of Emile, Milleret identified her and told the Germans that he himself had given her a package of supplies for aviators.[49]

Unaware of what was going on, Brother Rufus walked into the concierge's kitchen to get the beans that Julia Prilliez was cooking for the aviators' lunch. There he found Milleret in handcuffs and no fewer than sixteen uniformed German police he assumed to belong to the Gestapo . When asked why he was there, he told them he had come for a visit. When asked if he knew what was going on, he replied that he knew nothing at all. After about fifteen minutes Brother Rufus said that he had things to attend to and wrote his address on a piece of paper in case the Germans needed him later.

At that point Milleret stood up and asked to speak to an officer. The two went outside for five minutes. When they returned, Brother Rufus was arrested. A passing neighbor, Marcelle Brousse, was so horrified by the sight of the handcuffed religious being put into a Citroën that she stopped walking. The Germans arrested her too.

At the rue des Saussaies the Germans beat Brother Rufus, then subjected him to the *baignoire*. The torture permanently damaged his back, causing him such severe chronic pain that he had to wear a brace for the rest of his life. Afterward they put him in a waiting room with Hiltermann, who was shivering with wet hair, obviously also a victim of the *baignoire*.

The Germans soon decided they had made a mistake in arresting Brother Rufus's neighbor from the sidewalk and released her. Brousse, however, was aware that Rufus had been helping aviators; she had even left packages of food for them in the confessional.[50] After leaving the rue des Saussaies she went straight to the mother house of the Congrégation du Saint Esprit, where she told the porter, Brother Mathurin Robo, what had happened. Brother Robo informed the father superior and made a "petite inspection." He started in the old building that had not been used since the war began because he had seen Rufus there several times a day. On an upper floor a man who did not seem to be alone opened a door. The brother returned to the father superior, who told him to go back for more information.

Meanwhile the Germans returned to the rue Lhomond, this time bringing Hiltermann with them. The Germans took her and the concierge Emile Prilliez to the basement of the ENS, but found no one. They left again, then returned. This time they found the electrical room that the aviators had been in, but no aviators. The Prilliez's eighteen-year-old daughter convinced them that the mattresses and cots were in the room as part of an air raid shelter.[51] The police took Hiltermann and Prilliez away.

Next door at the convent Brother Robo returned to the strangers in the empty building. The Brazilian RAF pilot, who spoke excellent French, told him they were Allied aviators and were impatiently awaiting their lunch. Brother Robo explained the danger and suggested they leave immediately.[52] The airmen replied that they did not want to lose the organization and suggested going back to the basement room instead. When Robo and the Brazilian pilot went to see if it was safe, the Prilliez's teenage daughter leaned out a window to signal that they should keep walking because the police were in the house and had arrested her father.

The men turned around. Brother Robo found maps of Paris and the southern suburbs in the Congregation's parlor and showed the RAF pilot a route out of the city. Two other brothers escorted the other fliers to the chapel and told them to leave in pairs when the service ended. They made their way out of the city going south by following the sun, probably through the Porte d'Italie, and rendezvoused at a haystack near an airfield. The men had no identification documents, neither Belgian nor French, and most of them could not speak a word of French. Nonetheless they decided to try their luck in four groups of two.[53] Half of the men made it back to England before the end of the war. Brother Robo himself went to the post office and then, feeling feverish, went to bed. First, however, he asked two others to tidy up the room where the aviators had been hiding.

Not long after the airmen left, the Germans returned to the rue Lhomond with Brother Rufus. Soldiers searched through the chapel complex and questioned the brothers and priests. But despite kicking in all the doors in the condemned building, they found nothing. Shortly after 6:00 p.m. they took Rufus with them to get Brousse from her home. She admitted that she had told Brother Robo about Brother Rufus's arrest.

An interpreter for the German police got Brother Robo out of his sick bed, told him to dress quickly, and brought him downstairs. Despite denying knowledge of any aviators, Brother Robo was handcuffed and put into one of the three cars filling the narrow street outside. He recognized the towers of Notre Dame and the Grand Palais as they drove through the dark to the rue des Saussaies. Later that night German police arrested the father superior of the order, who knew even less than Brother Robo did. They also arrested an unidentified Dutchman who had gone to get food from the Dutch farms outside Paris that morning, probably the Engeland-vaarder who had traveled with the aviators from Brussels.

On the rue des Saussaies Brother Robo's interrogation began with blows to the face and demands to know "the hiding place of those pilots that they called the assassins of women and children." Then his interrogators took him upstairs, stripped him, handcuffed him behind his back, and put him in the freezing water of the *baignoire*. Twice he was held under until he passed out. Then he was hauled out of the tub, told to dress quickly, and taken downstairs to a police vehicle divided into cells. Brother Robo found himself with a woman who rubbed his hands when she heard his teeth chattering in the heavy darkness. It was Fernande Goetschel.

When they reached the prison of Frenses, Robo stumbled out of the police van into the prison courtyard. Guards with submachine guns surrounded him, along with the Prilliezes, Milleret, Hiltermann, Goetschel, Brother Rufus, Brousse, and the assistant director of the Ecole Normale, whose laboratories had sheltered aviators. The neighbor and the director may have helped Brother Rufus in small ways, but neither was in Dutch-Paris, and it is unlikely that either knew about the hiding place in the basement.[54] Robo, Milleret, and Rufus were put in a cell with three straw mattresses and two covers. Robo vomited water all night. They could see snow falling outside the bars of their cell the next day.[55]

As a resistance leader whom the German police had wanted for many months, Laatsman was separated from his colleagues. His interrogators stripped him naked, bound his hands and feet, beat him, and subjected him to the *baignoire* for three days. Then they brought in his fifteen-year-old son and beat him again. Laatsman had warned his son that the Germans might do this and instructed him to say that he did not know anything. While making the boy watch his father being beaten, the interrogators told him that if he would simply tell them where his stepmother was hiding, they would treat his father more gently. But the boy remained, in his father's words, "heldhaftig"—heroic—and refused to give any information.

Father and son managed to sit together in the police wagon when they were finally taken to Fresnes. They shared a dark, wet cell without food or water. In the prison shower room Laatsman saw aviators whose false identity documents he had made, possibly some of the airmen who had headed out from the rue Lhomond on foot the day of the roundup. Laatsman was taken back to the rue des Saussaies the next day for further questioning. This time they asked about Brussels and Toulouse, questions he could not answer because he had deliberately refused to know anything about Dutch-Paris that was not his direct concern. When Laatsman returned to Fresnes that night, his son was not in the cell they had shared the night before.[56]

The last time Laatsman saw his son, the boy was delivering ersatz coffee to other prisoners in Frenses. A Dutch lawyer from the Mitropa rail company secured the boy's release in early March 1944, after which the Gestapo delivered him to the Dutch authorities. He paid a brief visit to his stepmother, then went to Amsterdam to stay with his mother. He disappeared there in March 1945.[57]

Before he left Paris the young Laatsman reported that the Germans tortured Mincowski so badly that his friends feared he would die. After she returned from Ravensbrück, Goetschel wrote, "The highly refined cruelty of the Gestapo knows no bounds." The fifty-year-old widow underwent seven interrogations at the rue des Saussaies and was tortured twice. The last session lasted eight hours, during which she was held under water in the *baignoire* until she lost consciousness; this happened three times. The cause of such determined and vicious interrogation was a calling card from "Thierry" that police had found in one of her pockets when they searched her apartment. Her German interrogators must have suspected that "Thierry" was a pseudonym of Colonel Thomas of the British Intelligence Service. Separate from her work with Dutch-Paris, Goetschel had indeed hidden documents and weapons in her apartment for the Intelligence Service. Her final interrogation ended with a pronouncement that she had been sentenced to death.[58]

Unlike many of her colleagues who were treated as the accomplices of *Luftterroristen*, Gabrielle Weidner escaped the torture. According to her lawyer, the Germans had no evidence against her and had simply arrested her as a hostage. They claimed they would release her the day her brother was executed. She was allowed the small privileges of unimportant prisoners and wrote a letter in pencil to one of the other secretaries at the Adventist church, asking her to bring a few things from her room: soap, clothes, and either a sleeping bag or the gray comforter from her bed. She also gave instructions for delivering a monthly package of food and asked for money.[59]

Ellis, the British aviator with the damaged legs who was arrested in Milleret's apartment, was separated from his helpers. At least in theory all he had to do was declare his true identity as a British soldier to be spared torture and sent to a POW camp. He did not, however, have his identity discs with him. He was interrogated on and off between February 26 and May 16 by Germans he identified as Gestapo but who were more likely to have belonged to the military secret police, the Geheime Feldpolizei. He spent the rest of the war in a series of POW camps and wrote a letter of thanks to Goetschel after he returned home to London in 1945.[60]

While the Germans were interrogating their colleagues in Paris in late February 1944, Weidner, Rens, and Chait did not know what was going on. Weidner found out from Annette about Gabrielle's arrest late on the day it happened. After Annette left her hiding place under the church portico, she had searched Paris for her brother without knowing where precisely he might be and finally stopped at a café where she had once met Chait. Chait appeared by chance at 7:00 p.m. and took her to another café, where they found Weidner.

Annette spent that night at the home of a Swiss friend. The next day Weidner asked her to go back to Gabrielle's room to find a false French ID and microfilm that Gabrielle had been hiding for him. When she got there Annette found a photograph of herself lying face down on the bed. The policemen had accepted the pretense that Annette was the maid because the sisters did not look alike, but they may have wondered why Gabrielle kept a framed photograph of her maid. Annette found the false ID in a book and the microfilm in the gramophone without any trouble, a circumstance she attributed to God's guidance. She took these with her to the gare du Nord for a rendezvous with her brother, an Adventist pastor, and either Rens or Chait. While they were talking, Weidner told them to split up because the Gestapo was there. Annette hurried away, finally losing the footsteps behind her in the underground maze of the Métro passages. Her brother told her she would have to go to Switzerland.[61]

At this point, February 27, Weidner still did not know for certain what had happened to anyone other than Gabrielle. All he knew was that Laatsman had missed a meeting with himself, Rens, and Chait and that everyone else connected to the aviator escape line in Paris was missing. All or some of them could have been arrested. All or some of them could have gone into hiding. Weidner did not necessarily know where anyone but Caubo lived and had to assume that the Germans were lying in wait to trap anyone who came to their homes. He had three options: he could wait for his missing colleagues to find him; he could, maybe, track them down; or he could ask the Red Cross representative, Jules Mohr, to find out if they were in the prison at Fresnes. Weidner, however, could only give Mohr a list of the names as he knew them. He may not even have known that the woman he referred to as "Anne-Marie Mermillod" was really Suzanne Hiltermann. If he did know that, he had no way of knowing which name the Germans would use to register her at the prison.

Nor could Weidner, Chait, or Rens understand how the Germans had found Gabrielle. In the meantime, however, there was enough reason to worry for Chait to take a train to Lyon to warn their colleagues there.

In Paris on the morning of February 28 Weidner tracked down Joseffa Laatsman-Bekking at her hiding place in the city. He offered to take her and her four-year-old daughter to Switzerland, but she told him she was too pregnant to travel. Weidner gave her 50,000 French francs for her expenses instead.[62] Madame Laatsman knew that her husband and step-son had been arrested two days earlier, but neither she nor Weidner could figure out how the Germans had found them. Hiltermann, Mincowski, and Kraay had all visited the Laatsmans at their hiding place. Hiltermann and Mincowski had been arrested at the same time as her husband, so they could not have given away his address. Both Weidner and Madame Laatsman thought that Kraay was too "courageous" to have betrayed him.

That same morning Wisbrun arrived on the night train from Brussels with two microfilms and four Engelandvaarders. As far as he knew, nothing was amiss in Belgium or even Paris. The next day Weidner warned the couriers Okhuysen and Anna Neyssel to find new places to live, somewhere no one knew them. He was beginning to suspect that Brother Rufus must have been arrested because he had not heard from him.

On March 1 Comiti told Weidner that three inspectors were watching the entrance to the building where she and the Caubos lived and gave him 50,000 French francs that Caubo had given her. He gave her some of it to go into hiding.

Then Weidner heard that the Gestapo had been asking for him by name at the home of Pastor Paul Meyer in Lyon four days in a row. That settled the matter for him. Less than a handful of people knew about Meyer because Weidner himself slept and ate there. Kraay was one of those people. Indeed she knew all the addresses that had been raided. People whom she did not know about, however, had not been touched by the arrests. Weidner concluded that the Germans must be getting their information about the line from Kraay.[63] He went to Annecy the next day to beg his friends whom Kraay knew to go into hiding and returned to Paris that same night.

Before Weidner left for Annecy, however, Wisbrun returned to Paris with bad news from Brussels.

Gare du Midi, Brussels, 1935.

7

The Gestapo Knocks

LONG PAST CURFEW ON FEBRUARY 27 Edmond Chait threw pebbles against Raymonde Pillot's bedroom window in Lyon. When the courier came downstairs, he told her about the arrests in Paris and warned her to hide. Pillot, however, decided to wait until after she had made her father's breakfast the next morning. Just as she was about to leave her home at 10:45 a.m., someone banged on the door. Pillot opened it to the notorious Gestapo chief Klaus Barbie, often referred to as "the Butcher of Lyon," and four of his henchmen.[1] He immediately asked whether she was Jean Weidner's secretary.

At Gestapo headquarters on the rue Berthelot, Pillot was taken into an immense office in which eight more Germans awaited her. They demanded to know about Weidner and his illegal activities. When she lied that she didn't know what they were talking about, they showed her a file of telegrams that had come from Paris with information given by Suzy Kraay. On the list she saw her own name and address as well as those of Gabrielle Weidner, Pastor Paul Meyer, Consul Maurice Jacquet, Marie Meunier, and "Moreau" (an alias of Chait). The very precise information they already had, including details that only Weidner and Kraay knew, discouraged Pillot, but she tried to at least establish the innocence of Mademoiselle Meunier. Her interrogators offered the twenty-year-old her freedom, a large reward, and a high-paying job if she would give them the information they wanted. She continued to pretend that she did not know the answers.

Impatient with her prevarications, the interrogator told her that if she would not cooperate they would arrest her father. To emphasize the immediacy of the threat, two Germans left the office. Then she was taken to an empty room, made to undress, and whipped with leather thongs.

She was then thrown into an icy bath and held under the water. After three hours of this she was dragged into a cellar. She stayed there for two days before being taken to the local prison at Fort Montluc. After she was transferred to the prison of Fresnes outside Paris, German agents questioned her again, but without the previous insistence. Her interrogators told her that her father, Weidner, and everyone else whose names they knew had already been arrested. It was not true, but Pillot had no way of knowing that.[2]

On their way from Pillot's home to their headquarters on the rue Berthelot on the morning of February 28, 1944, the Gestapo agents stopped at the Dutch consulate. They arrested Jacquet and anyone else who happened to be there, whether they were Dutch refugees looking for help from their consul or individuals who had come to pay their insurance premiums. They captured a young Jewish man and a Jewish family, all of whom perished in Auschwitz.[3] Gestapo agents remained at the insurance office that housed the consulate for some time in order to trap other resisters and then raided it sporadically until they retreated from Lyon in August.

As they did elsewhere, the Germans also ransacked and looted Jacquet's office and home. Although they did not mistreat him physically, they kept Jacquet in custody, leaving his wife and two young children in difficulties. They did not find any incriminating papers because Jacquet had burned them after the arrest of the Dutch civil servant in Vichy in January. But they did confiscate 1,295 tins of sardines that had been sent through the Dutch Red Cross in Portugal to be distributed to Dutch citizens in France. Jacquet's French secretary remained at her post for the duration. She and the French bureaucrat who bore official responsibility for social assistance to Dutch nationals in Lyon did what they could to help Dutch refugees in Jacquet's place.[4]

The Germans had one more address in Lyon on their list for February 28: Weidner's shop at 13 rue du Griffon. Weidner himself had not been there since he had gone underground five months earlier. But he, or one of his resistance allies, was using it as a hiding place. That morning the Germans captured three Jewish refugees there, none of whom survived the war.[5]

That same morning in Brussels, German civilian and military police raided the Dutch-Paris safe house on the rue Franklin. An aviator from

New Zealand named Mervyn Breed later put the invasion of twenty plainclothes "Gestapo agents" armed with pistols at about 8:30 a.m. On the top floor Robert F. Anderson, a B-17 navigator from Iowa, heard loud shouting. He dove back under his covers while his roommate hid in the armoire. Almost immediately "a large man" stuck a gun in Anderson's face, demanding to know where his companion was. Just as Anderson said he was alone, the floor of the armoire broke and a pale-looking American emerged. German secret military police belonging to Geheime Feldpolizei took the aviators into the garden and lined them up against the wall. There were ten of them in all.

As Anderson remembered it more than sixty years later, he and the other Americans had been very suspicious of a man in their group whom they thought was a Polish pilot with the RAF. They could not understand why the man kept taking walks. When "the Pole" was not lined up against the garden wall with the rest of them, they concluded that he must have been a German agent. Within the parameters of what they knew, that explanation for their arrest made sense. But they were mistaken. In 1945 Breed identified the missing aviator not as a Pole or a German but as a Dutch officer who had been taken to Paris the night before. And indeed Hans Wisbrun escorted four Engelandvaarders, including a Dutch Air Force captain, to Paris on February 27.

The GFP officers took the ten aviators captured on the rue Franklin to their headquarters on the rue Travesière.[6] Contrary to the stipulations of the Geneva Convention regarding prisoners of war, Anderson was beaten during questioning about a new bombsight on the B-17. He never understood why they thought that he, a navigator, would know about a top-secret bombing device. He was then thrown into solitary confinement, where he spent his twenty-first birthday. After a few days he was transferred to the Wehrmacht side of the local prison of St-Gilles, where he shared a cell with the New Zealander Breed. During the weeks of their imprisonment one of their German guards kept promising them a special treat of roast squab. When it finally arrived Anderson did not eat more than a single bite because whatever was on the plate had four legs. The aviators captured on the rue Franklin were all eventually transferred to a POW camp in Germany.[7]

Out of sight of the Allied aviators, German civilian policemen arrested everyone else they found at 19 rue Franklin that morning, including the leader of daily operations David Verloop, the forger J. P. Bol, and the couriers Robert Bosschart and Henri Vleeschdrager. The number of fugitives caught that morning is unknown, but it included at least one Engelandvaarder.[8] As usual the Germans left behind some men as a trap, with a young woman to answer the doorbell. The liaison for aviators Jo Jacobstahl walked right into it at 5:00 p.m. that same day.[9] The courier Chris ten Kate fell into it the next day when he returned from a dinner celebrating the completion of his theological studies at the University of Utrecht.[10] Another Dutch student, Adriaan Schmutzer, fell into the same trap on March 3 when he tried to deliver a message from Paris. He had been working with Jacobstahl and Bosschart to guide aviators but was not a regular of the house. In fact Bol did not meet him until they shared a cell in the prison of St-Gilles.[11] At least one Engelandvaarder was also captured when he rang the doorbell at 19 rue Franklin.[12]

At Gestapo headquarters on the avenue Louise, German agents interrogated the Dutch-Paris helpers whom they had caught at the rue Franklin. They did not always know their prisoners' real names and in some cases never discovered them, but they had found more than enough evidence against them at the rue Franklin: ten Allied aviators sleeping in the house and a cache of compromising papers, including the stamps and blank forms used to make false documents as well as French identity cards and Métro tickets left in two men's wallets.

On the first day, February 28, German police questioned Bol from midafternoon until early evening with only mild violence. But the next day the interrogators—whose names were Weber, Wagner, and Franz— stopped being so restrained. As Bol described it in a report he wrote in 1945, Weber accompanied every question "with kicks, then hit me with his clenched fists then used a rubber hose filled with iron wire." Not getting the answers they wanted, the interrogators put Bol in a corner of the room "with my hands locked behind my knees and kicked or punched me each time they walked past."[13] As Bol understood it, another Dutch student had told the Germans that Bol knew the code to a document they had found, when in fact the other student knew it but Bol did not.

As a stateless German Jew and the chief guide for aviators, Jacobstahl had every reason to expect harsh treatment. But he had been captured with false documents under the name of Lambert, which was neither a Jewish name nor the name he usually used with aviators, which was

Stranders. Because the Germans had found French train tickets in their wallets, he and Bosschart agreed on a story. They had escorted three aviators to Paris twice and nothing more. Not realizing who they had, Jacobstahl's interrogators—Barth and Weber—restricted their questioning to those two trips to France.[14] Bosschart was not registered at the prison of St-Gilles until March 6, meaning he was at Gestapo headquarters for a week.[15] Vleeschdrager was tortured there five times.[16]

A week or so after their arrests Verloop put an end to the interrogations. First he claimed to be the mastermind and leader of the entire organization in Belgium, then he threw himself over the third-floor railing in the prison stairwell. The twenty-three-year-old survived long enough to be taken to a German military hospital, but not much longer.[17] Suicide was a drastic measure for a devout Christian like Verloop, but one that his comrades honored as the ultimate heroic sacrifice made for their sakes. Verloop's action spared his colleagues from further torture. After his death Bol and Vleeschdrager, who knew what had happened, could blame everything on Verloop with a clear conscience.[18] All the known Dutch-Paris prisoners captured in Brussels were transferred to the Wehrmacht section of St-Gilles. Bosschart, at least, was allowed to receive packages in May.

From the German point of view, the raid on 19 rue Franklin was a success. Whether or not they knew it, they had captured the leader of the *transportwerk* (Verloop), the man who gathered Allied airman from other resistance groups (Jacobstahl), the organization's forger (Bol), and a number of couriers (Bosschart, Schmutzer, Chris ten Kate). They also extracted enough information to begin rolling up Dutch-Paris's many trails over the Dutch border. For instance, the arrest in the Netherlands and subsequent death of the student Adriaan van Haaften appears to be linked to the arrests in Brussels. Van Haaften was last seen in Zeist on February 29, bicycling with an RAF aviator.[19]

The death of Frits Iordens, who had taken part in the attempt in January to pass aviators over the French border disguised as cigarette smugglers, was probably also tied to the February 28 raid. On March 2 Iordens, two *passeurs* from the Groep Vrij, and two Allied pilots missed a train connection in Hasselt on their way from Maastricht to Brussels. When they tried to leave the station, the German soldiers who inspected their papers arrested Iordens and one of the other *passeurs*. These might have been especially sharp-eyed Germans who saw something awry in the usually excellent false documents used by Dutch-Paris agents. However, it is more likely that they were looking for them because of information that came out of the raid on the rue Franklin. Iordens broke free but was shot and killed while trying to escape. The third *passeur* and the two pilots managed to slip away in the confusion.[20]

Despite the use of torture, the interrogators on the rue Louise and the rue Travesière did not uncover Dutch-Paris's *sociaalwerk* in the city, or even all the couriers associated with the *transportwerk*. Jan Nauta and Piet Henry, for instance, received warnings about the arrests in enough time to go into hiding. They remained underground for six weeks, then joined another resistance group in the Netherlands. Unfortunately a notorious traitor betrayed that organization, leading to both men's arrest and deportation.[21] Henry's partner in escorting Engelandvaarders to Belgium, Willy Hijmans, also received a warning to stay away from Brussels. He continued his resistance work in the Netherlands until a V-2 rocket misfired on its launch and crashed into his family home in The Hague in January 1945. He sustained an injury to his face so serious that he spent the rest of the war in the hospital and then qualified for reconstructive surgery and a rest period in England after the Liberation.[22]

At twenty-three Wisbrun was the most senior member of the leadership of the Comité's daily operations still at liberty in Brussels. He had missed the roundup on rue Franklin because he was escorting fugitives to Paris that day. He then escaped the trap there either by luck or his own prudence. Wisbrun spent most of March traveling between Brussels and Paris and training new volunteers for the *sociaalwerk*. Weidner and Jacques Rens considered him to be an excellent and dependable agent but worried that his stiff leg made him too memorable and too easy to pick out in a crowd. They arranged for him to go to Switzerland at the end of the month. Just two days before his departure, however, Wisbrun, like so many men in occupied Europe, was rounded up from the street, deemed fit enough for slave labor, and deported to Germany as a worker. He spent that long last year of the war in a factory near Berlin, terrified the entire time that the Germans would discover that he was Jewish.[23]

While the German police in Brussels followed the leads from the raid on the rue Franklin, their counterparts in Paris continued to unravel Dutch-Paris in France. On March 3 the Lyon Gestapo arrested Kraay's friend Josette Molland, who had traveled with her in France and the

Netherlands. Molland later said she thought she had been betrayed when a warning that Kraay sent to her was sold to the Germans by a third party.[24] In fact the Germans had found Molland's name in the notebook that Kraay was carrying when French police detained her almost a month earlier. Molland, along with a grocer on the rue Bon Pasteur in Lyon, was arrested because of her association with Kraay rather than because she belonged to Dutch-Paris.[25]

In Paris at 8:00 the next morning, March 4, German agents arrested two women, Louise Roume and Anna Neyssel, who had helped Okhuysen shelter and care for fugitives.[26] The next morning they found Okhuysen at her parents' farm in Briis-sous-Forges, twenty-five miles southwest of the capital.

In Annecy, German police arrested Marie Meunier at her ribbon and souvenir shop around closing time on March 7.[27] They also detained her shop assistant, Paul Lacôte, and Alice Charroin, who unwittingly entered the shop to deliver secret documents at exactly the wrong time while the Germans were there.[28] The documents may or may not have been for Dutch-Paris; both women had strong ties to local resistance groups. The three prisoners spent over a week at the makeshift jail in the Franciscan school in Annecy before being transferred to regular prisons in Lyon and Paris.

Friends cared for Charroin's nine- and ten-year-old daughters after her arrest because her husband, the inspector who had helped Weidner and Laatsman cross the border in St-Julien, had been arrested three weeks earlier in connection with a different resistance line. That arrest almost spread to Dutch-Paris when the courier and guide Jean Zurcher went to the Charroins' home that afternoon. Luckily a neighbor warned him to stay away from the house.[29] As it happened, the roundup of Dutch-Paris did not spread to the Adventist seminary in Collonges. The helpers there, such as Zurcher and his wife, Anna, played no part in the aviator evasion line and had never met Kraay. Those who did know them and were arrested—Pillot, Meunier, Alice Charroin, and Gabrielle Weidner—did not give them away.

After the first big raids on February 26 Weidner, Rens, and Chait exercised extra caution but did not go into hiding. Rens had his suit cleaned and changed his appearance with eyeglasses and a new haircut. Then he took a day trip from Paris to Brussels and another trip to Lyon in order to escort four unidentified Engelandvaarders to a safer place. He also spent the relatively modest sum of 5,000 French francs on what he described as a bribe.[30] He may have used it to buy information about his imprisoned colleagues or to persuade jailors in Paris or Brussels to treat them a little less harshly.

The possibilities for assistance to any particular prisoner depended on the charges laid against that prisoner and his or her nationality. The courts and legal procedures still operated under German occupation, if not in quite the same way as before the war. Friends and family could even engage legal representation for some prisoners. A Dutch lawyer arranged the release of Laatsman's fifteen-year-old son. Separately, Gabrielle Weidner's lawyer met with a high-ranking Gestapo official on her behalf; he reported back to her brother that the Germans had no case against Gabrielle but were holding her as a hostage. As late as June 1944 Elisabeth Cartier expected Mademoiselle Meunier to be released.[31] It was even possible to arrange one's own release through connections or bribes if the charges were vague or minor enough. One of the Dutch farmers outside Paris who hid aviators and supplied food was arrested in late February but quickly released because he knew the right people. Of course as a farmer he could also offer deeply persuasive "gifts" of food.[32]

As a matter of bureaucratic procedure, French authorities interceded on behalf of some prisoners, for example Jean Milleret, Fernande Goetschel, and, later, Madeleine Larose-Reinaud. First, the French police investigated the circumstances of the arrest. If they did not find anything objectionable, such as evidence of communist activity, the French Delegate to the German Occupation Authorities wrote an official objection to the arrest. His representations may have ameliorated the conditions of the prisoners' incarceration or delayed their deportation, but they did not secure their release.[33]

It goes without saying that it was better not to be arrested for any reason, including being taken as a hostage, in the first place. Rens escorted Annette Weidner from Paris to Switzerland on March 6 so she could not be taken as a hostage like her sister. Because he had to assume that every regular Dutch-Paris address was compromised, he could not take her on the easy route, through Lyon, Annecy, and Collonges. Instead they took trains from Paris to Monnetier-Mornex, a village east of Collonges high on the Salève, where Weidner, Chait, and Rens had a safe house at the home of two Adventists.[34] It was part of the secret layer of infrastructure of Dutch-Paris, places known only to the leadership, where they could eat, sleep, or leave messages for each other. From there Rens and Annette skied into Switzerland, where she arrived in a state of exhaustion.

Rens reported to General van Tricht and Pastor Visser 't Hooft on the dire events in occupied territory. He was able to say with certainty that Verloop, Vleeschdrager, Bosschart, Bol, and Jacobstahl (whom he knew only by one of his noms de guerre, Lambert) had been arrested in Brussels. He knew about the arrests in Paris of Laatsman and his son, Gabrielle Weidner, Jean-Michael Caubo, and Okhuysen's co-conspirator Roume. He had also learned of the arrests in Lyon of Pillot (whom he knew by her nom de guerre, Raymonde Raviol), Jacquet, and a Jewish family whose name he did not know. He feared that Brother Rufus as well as Leo Mincowski and Suzanne Hiltermann, whose real names he did not know, had also been captured in Paris, as indeed they had. And he suspected that the following addresses had been compromised: Pastor Meyer's in Lyon; Mademoiselle Meunier's in Annecy; Weidner's parents' in The Hague, which Kraay had visited; and the Café Hulstkamp in Brussels, which was a postbox and meeting place for the Comité. Except for two of the addresses, his information and suspicions were correct. Neither Weidner's parents nor the widow at the Café Hulstkamp were arrested, although they may have been under surveillance.

The German authorities continued to make arrests. While Rens was still in Switzerland, they launched another roundup in Paris. On March 9 they arrested the cobbler in Versailles who had made the shoes for aviators that the priest was carrying when he was briefly detained at Caubo's apartment on February 13. The shoemaker did not belong to Dutch-Paris and may not have known for whom his work was intended, but he was deported to the concentration camps nonetheless. German police also returned to the Hotel Ibis, where Kraay had been staying in Paris in early February, in order to arrest the proprietor. This man too did not belong to Dutch-Paris, although he was sympathetic enough to charge Laatsman a "derisory price" to lodge fugitives without entering them in the register, as he was legally obliged to do. German police also raided the Parisian home of the Dutch artist who hosted several Engelandvaarders for Albert Starink, including Rudy Zeeman after he escaped from the Wehrmacht car.[35] All three of these people who helped Dutch-Paris on the peripheries of their mission without belonging to the line died in the concentration camps.

On that same day, March 9, German police raided a hotel in Paris used by a different Dutch escape line, capturing fifteen men and women.[36] They were not part of Dutch-Paris, although it is possible that the Germans mistakenly thought there was only one Dutch expatriate escape line. The raid may also have been part of a separate investigation. It might have resulted from a message that Abwehr officers in the Netherlands sent to their counterparts in Paris on March 3. The message requested assistance in finding seven men traveling to a neutral land—meaning Spain or Switzerland—with false *transportführer* (travel supervisor) documents purportedly issued by a German firm and authorizing workers to travel to a job site in France. The message claimed that a Dutch secret agent was among the seven, who were traveling at that moment, and that such papers had already been used by many others.[37] It did not say how the Abwehr had stumbled upon this particular ruse, but more than one Dutch group, including Dutch-Paris, had certainly been using it for some time.

In an interview with a ranking Gestapo officer a week later, Gabrielle Weidner's lawyer ascertained that Weidner and his colleagues were wanted for passing Dutchmen and Allied *Luftterroristen* to Switzerland and Spain.[38] This was good news because it implied that the German police did not know about the Swiss Way microfilm relay. It also suggested that they did not know, or perhaps did not care, about Dutch-Paris's *sociaalwerk*. Indeed there is no evidence that the roundup spread outside the *transportwerk* except in the case of the Dutch police inspector Gerrit ter Horst, who had helped Kraay arrange the escape of the Simon family in January 1944.[39]

The Abwehr and their colleagues, however, were not done with Dutch-Paris. On March 17 German police arrested the French couple who had sheltered the English pilot Ellis after Caubo's arrest. They had found the address among Milleret's papers on February 26. It is not clear why they waited so long to arrest these French helpers. Perhaps the police had been watching their home and finally decided that these people played only a minor role and had no further information to offer. They did not consider them so minor, however, that they did not eventually deport them to the concentration camps, which they both survived.[40]

By March 27 the Gestapo in Lyon had wearied of watching the home of Pastor Meyer and carried out their threat to arrest him if they did not find Weidner.[41] Like Gabrielle, Meyer appears to have been arrested as a hostage rather than as a resister. If the Gestapo had searched their house, they may have found the forms and rubber stamps the Meyers used to make false travel documents for Weidner and the fugitives he asked them to help. Indeed if the German authorities had appreciated how deeply engaged the Meyers were in helping the persecuted, they would have arrested Marthe as well.

While incarcerated in France, some of the prisoners were allowed to receive visitors or packages. Jules Mohr sent Red Cross packages to Dutch-Paris prisoners, which had the added benefit of providing information about their location. One of Caubos twin sons had permission to bring him food and visit him very briefly at Fresnes. The Adventist pastor Oscar Meyer was able to inquire about, and perhaps visit, the Adventist prisoners Gabrielle Weidner, Pillot, and his own brother, Paul. Similarly the members of the order of the Congregation du Saint-Esprit on the rue Lhomond took food and other small comforts to their father superior and Brothers Rufus and Robo at Fresnes until May. The sudden end to this privilege caused the priests and brothers some anxiety because it suggested their prisoners had been transferred elsewhere.[42]

There was very little that could be done for Laatsman, however. Because he had been wanted as a resistance leader for more than a year before he was captured, Laatsman was categorized as a "Night and Fog" (NN, Nacht und Nebel) prisoner. Like all such prisoners he was held under the strictest security and segregated from non-NN prisoners. He could not send letters to friends, nor could he receive visitors. As the NN decree intended, Laatsman disappeared into the maw of Nazi power without a trace.[43]

With Laatsman and his circle as well as Okhuysen and the other couriers in prison and Starink in hiding, Dutch-Paris had almost collapsed in the French capital. Yet the line could not abandon the city. People hiding in the region relied on them for money and other support, which was partially distributed by Mohr at the Red Cross. Furthermore the trains from the north still stopped in Paris, and the trains to the south and the east still left from there. Couriers and fugitives would have to keep traveling through the city. Benno Nijkerk, who had come to Paris a couple of days before the big raid to assist Laatsman, took on the task of rebuilding Dutch-Paris there. He did not have the sort of personal relationships in Paris that he had in Brussels, but Weidner had contacts among the Protestant community whom he had kept separate from the escape line and who would not be compromised by the arrests. Weidner and Nijkerk had already recruited a Swiss woman who worked at a bookshop in the fifteenth arrondissement to act as a new Dutch-Paris postbox the day before Laatsman's arrest.[44]

In early March a French doctor introduced Nijkerk to a French nurse named Madeleine Larose-Reinaud. She had been helping fugitives since 1942 and had even weathered a French police investigation after someone denounced her, anonymously, for hiding Jews. Nijkerk asked her to help rebuild the network by finding lodgings for Engelandvaarders and recruiting other women to act as guides and to provide ration tickets.[45] He also asked her to host a Dutch Air Force officer and instructor at her apartment, beginning on March 13. Hijmans had put the captain and three of his trainees onto Dutch-Paris in the Netherlands. Wisbrun took them from Brussels to Paris on February 27 so that they arrived in the French capital on the morning of February 28, narrowly missing the raid on the rue Franklin.[46] This was the man the American airman Robert Anderson and his compatriots suspected of being a German agent because he kept going out for walks. He certainly did not stay quietly in his hiding place in Paris. At his request, Larose-Reinaud gave him a set of keys to her apartment so he could visit acquaintances among the Dutch colony.

At 7:00 a.m. on March 23 the doorbell rang at Larose-Reinaud's apartment, followed by the chilling announcement "Police Allemande!" Calling back that she was dressing, she roused the captain and put him and his suitcase on the balcony, the only other exit from the apartment. Two German plainclothesmen broke down the door and rushed in, followed by several more in and out of uniform. They demanded to know where the man was. When she claimed innocence, one of them hit her hard enough that she was thrown across the room. She heard shots from the street below.

While being put into a long, black car an hour later, Larose-Reinaud was amazed to see that dozens of uniformed Germans had closed off the street. Apparently they expected more than a single Dutchman and a middle-aged nurse. They drove from her apartment on the rue du Trésor in the Marais neighborhood across the Seine to a small hotel near the place d'Italie. After a short time policemen emerged with four unidentified young men who did not speak French and whom Larose-Reinaud assumed to be Dutch. When they arrived at Gestapo headquarters on the rue des Saussaies, Larose-Reinaud saw Nijkerk and her houseguest getting out of a car. The Germans compared her keys to those carried by the Dutch captain. They were, of course, the same.

At 1:00 p.m. the prisoners were transferred to Fresnes without serious interrogation. There Nijkerk and Larose-Reinaud had a few unsupervised minutes to plan a story. In whispers they decided to say that she had met the captain at the cinema and to pass the whole thing off as an *aventure sentimentelle*. Larose-Reinaud spent the next three and a half months in cell 422 without any opportunity to communicate with the men or find out what was going on. She had been part of Dutch-Paris for less than one month.

Then, on June 9, she was taken for questioning. Before her interview with a German who spoke fluent French, she exchanged a few hushed words with Nijkerk, who had lost a considerable amount of weight, and a sympathetic young Dutchman. Larose-Reinaud tried the story of a movie theater romance, but the German showed her a statement signed by the captain in which he had confessed everything. She acquiesced and signed the statement provided for her. Back in the holding cell the young Dutchman told her that he had known the captain before Paris and that he "lacked prudence." Nijkerk told her to "stand fast" because he thought he had been arrested as part of a separate investigation.[47]

In a case similar to Paul van Cleeff's, Nijkerk was arrested because he was in the wrong place at the wrong time. He had gone to speak to Baron Jacob Brantsen, an experienced Dutch intelligence officer, on Dutch-Paris business when German police came to Brantsen's home on the avenue Victor Hugo.[48] They had found Brantsen's name and address among the things the Dutch Air Force captain abandoned at Larose-Reinaud's. The Germans were following up that lead, not looking for Nijkerk, but they arrested everyone in the apartment as a matter of course. Nijkerk was arrested and incarcerated under the name on his false documents: Bernard Smits. The Germans never realized they had captured the man they had wanted in Brussels for months.

Weidner did not know that anything had gone wrong with Nijkerk until the latter missed a meeting on March 31. When he inquired, the Swiss woman at the bookshop told him she had not seen Nijkerk since March 22. The fact that Nijkerk was being held under a false name would have made it even more difficult to find out if he had been captured or gone into hiding. After Nijkerk's arrest someone, probably Rens, gathered up the Engelandvaarders still waiting in Paris.[49] The Paris part of Dutch-Paris never recovered from this latest blow.

Even after the Allies landed in Normandy in early June 1944 and as they began to battle their way across France and Belgium, the Germans continued their investigation into Dutch-Paris. On June 14 German police arrested the courier Jacqueline Houry and her mother at their home outside Paris. Houry had lost contact with Dutch-Paris after the roundup in February but had continued to guide French fugitives from Paris to Toulouse, where she passed them to Simone Calmels. Her interrogators at the rue des Saussaies, however, made it quite clear that they had arrested her for her involvement with Dutch-Paris and showed her remarkably complete dossiers on the passage to Spain. When she refused to cooperate, they tortured her with the *baignoire*.[50]

Three days later three men from the Gestapo broke into Lucie Comiti's apartment with revolvers drawn, demanding "Mademoiselle Comiti" rather than using her nom de guerre, Marie-France Paoli. She had gone into hiding after the roundup in late February but had continued to work for Dutch-Paris as a courier and had eventually returned to her home. The secret policemen ransacked her apartment before taking her to the rue des Saussaies. Like Houry, she reported that her interrogators knew "absolutely everything" about her activities, down to the smallest details. They showed her photographs of Milleret and Mincowski, asked her if she knew Starink, and demanded to know where "Jean" was. When she said, "Which Jean?" a man she described as a "giant" replied, "Your leader," and hit her so hard that she lost her balance. One of the others kicked her while she was on the ground. They put her in a police wagon and sent her to Fresnes without further mistreatment.[51]

In Toulouse, Calmels had also continued to work for Dutch-Paris as a courier after the wave of arrests. She ran several errands for Chait, such as delivering money to a Dutch-Paris associate in Monaco. The Gestapo found her on June 22, arrested her, and ransacked her home. Despite her involvement in more than one resistance network, Calmels had no doubt that they arrested her for her work with Dutch-Paris. Over the course of seven interrogations, German police asked her specifically about Dutch-Paris and showed her what she later remembered as a report of Kraay's interrogation that gave the names of the medical student Gabriel Nahas, the Paris-based courier Houry, Rens (but not his first name), Lil van

Wijhe, who could send people to Spain on a freight train, and her own name but not her address. She was also questioned about a meeting she had had with Laatsman six months earlier in Paris.[52]

How did this devastating series of arrests happen? In a certain sense they were inevitable. Dutch-Paris involved so many people in so many places that it could not go forever undetected. The French and German police had been looking for Weidner, Laatsman, and others for months before February 1944. They had, in fact, interrogated a Dutch civil servant about them in January.

Nor could Dutch-Paris control those whom they helped, even though the helpers' safety depended in part on how they acted. The arrests of Nijkerk, Larose-Reinaud, and Brantsen resulted directly from the carelessness of an Engelandvaarder who treated his trip to Spain as a holiday and refused to stay hidden or even act circumspectly.

The roundup was also a matter of bad luck. One of the few people who had traveled the entire length of the line and knew the closely guarded addresses of Laatsman and the Meyers was arrested by collaborationist French police merely because she arrived early for a meeting and happened to be carrying a valise. A different French police unit might have accepted Kraay's story of black marketeering without any further consequences. But the policemen who detained her turned her over to the Germans.

The German police knew what to ask Kraay because they had her photograph and a dossier on her made up in 1943, when an acquaintance introduced her to a Dutch agent provocateur in the pay of the occupation authorities, who in turn introduced her to an intelligence officer of the Abwehr. Because they knew roughly what Kraay had been doing, her captors also knew how to interrogate and relentlessly intimidate her both physically and psychologically until, as a British report put it after the war, she "went to pieces at the Gestapo torture house."[53] They then used the information they had pressed out of her to extract more names and addresses from other prisoners.

No one expected resisters to withstand repeated torture. The general rule among Dutch resisters was that a prisoner should try not to talk for the first twenty-four hours in order to give his or her colleagues time to hide.[54] The courageous and intelligent Verloop decided that the only way to prevent himself and maybe others from breaking under torture was to kill himself. It is less a question of blaming those who broke under torture than it is of admiring the fortitude of those who did not. Weidner, who used his postwar position in the Netherlands Security Service to investigate the arrests, did not himself blame Kraay. As he put it in his postwar investigation summary, she did "good work," and though she faltered when under arrest, he would not judge her psychological reaction to the Gestapo. However, Weidner did remove her name from "the lists for any proposals for decorations or any expression of thanks for her work."[55] Even decades later Weidner did not fight a civil law suit against him because it would have involved bringing up accusations against Kraay, which he refused to do.

Weidner blamed himself for having trusted Kraay too much.[56] It would undoubtedly have been safer, he realized, to have had nothing to do with her after she had escaped from Gurs, but he needed someone in Toulouse and she had volunteered. It would have been safer to refuse to take her back into Dutch-Paris after she had gone to the Netherlands in December 1943 against his wishes. But while she was there she had delivered false passports and brought a Jewish family to safety in Switzerland. By that time she had been rescuing people without losing anyone for over two years. And again Weidner's problem was not too many volunteers but too few.

After the war, Hiltermann blamed Weidner for what happened because she thought that he did not take Kraay's and Caubo's arrests seriously enough.[57] It is true that if everyone else had gone under in mid-February, they may not have been arrested. But then again, they might have been. Several Dutch-Paris couriers escaped the roundups in February and March only to be arrested when they emerged from hiding in April and even June.

Besides, Weidner did not dismiss the arrests. He told Hiltermann and Mincowski to take a holiday, although he did not give them money to do so. He did, however, give money to other couriers to hide. Chait took the train to Lyon to warn Pillot, who chose not to leave home until it was already too late. Weidner himself went to Annecy to beg Marie Meunier to go into hiding.

But a resistance network that was dedicated to rescuing the persecuted, as Dutch-Paris was, could not simply melt away into the hills the way saboteurs could. What would have happened to the hundreds of Jews hiding in Belgium and France if all their helpers suddenly disappeared? How would the Allied aviators and Engelandvaarders have gotten to Spain without their guides? Weidner, Rens, and Chait could have kept the microfilm relay of the Swiss Way going on their own, but they could not run the *sociaalwerk* or the *transportwerk* without the help of many other men and women. Most of their colleagues engaged in *sociaalwerk*, especially in Brussels, remained at their posts, but they still needed more help. In particular the line needed new couriers to keep the different sections in communication and take money and documents to refugees hiding across France and Belgium.

General van Tricht found two Dutch refugees in Switzerland for the job. The first recruit, Paul Veerman, had left Amsterdam in the summer of 1942 and made his own way to Switzerland. He then went back, again on his own, to bring a friend to safety. While waiting for his turn to go to England, Veerman had made the acquaintance of both Rens and the military attaché.[58]

In early April 1944 Visser 't Hooft's assistant, who had returned from Brussels to his regular administrative duties in Geneva, arranged for Veerman's disappearance from Switzerland. Veerman was to let other Dutch refugees think he planned to attend classes on silk weaving at a technical school in Zurich. He also needed to write a letter to the Swiss police requesting permission to leave the country for family reasons because when the Swiss authorized an official *réfoulement* they took the individual concerned off the refugee registers. That would allow Veerman to come in and out of the country under the aegis of the Swiss Intelligence Service, as Weidner and Rens did. Rens took Veerman on his first mission across the border on April 13, 1944. Then Veerman spent the next few weeks traveling across France and Belgium with Rens, Chait, or Weidner so he could learn their routes and meet their contacts.[59]

Van Tricht also enlisted Nico Gazan's younger brother Henri as a courier.[60] Nico had left for England several months earlier. Weidner intended to take Henri with him to Paris and Brussels when he left Switzerland on April 22. As usual, the Swiss Intelligence Service would supervise his departure from the country in the person of Paul Frossard de Saugy. Weidner had noticed that de Saugy's attitude toward him had deteriorated but could not explain it. This time he arrived at the border two hours late. Weidner wanted to delay the trip until the following evening because they did not have enough time to brief Gazan on the crossing or his new documents. De Saugy, however, insisted on doing it then.

After going under the barbed wire around 4:00, Gazan walked onto the road that runs parallel to the border without first checking his surroundings. Bumping into a French gendarme, he proceeded to babble, as Weidner put it, which made them both look suspicious. The gendarme let them go, but then thought better of it and told the two men to follow him. Weidner pointed out that their papers were in order and did not justify any regrettable excesses of zeal. When he lost hope in the gendarme's better nature, Weidner signaled to Gazan to run. But the rookie courier made no move. Weidner shouted, "Save yourself Henri!" then jumped back through the barbed wire into Switzerland. The gendarme arrested Gazan.

After Weidner returned to Geneva, he set to work to free Gazan. De Saugy tried to have a chat with his French counterparts about the matter, but the Dutchman had already been booked at the jail in St-Julien. The next day Weidner crossed the border in the mountains rather than in the valley. French gendarmes appeared to be looking for someone, possibly him, but he nevertheless arrived in Annecy with enough time before catching the train to Paris to ask a contact to intervene on Gazan's behalf.[61] Veerman delivered the relatively minor sum of 2,000 French francs, which may have been intended to pay a fine rather than a bribe, to the sympathetic clerk of the civil court in St-Julien, and Gazan regained his liberty. This cheered Weidner enough to write, "There are still good Frenchmen in France." He felt, however, that it would be "useless" to send Gazan back over the border.[62]

In view of the obvious dangers they were running on behalf of the government in exile while delivering microfilm and escorting Engelandvaarders and in view of their increasing anxiety because of the ongoing arrests in occupied territory, General van Tricht, Ambassador Bosch van Rosenthal, and Pastor Visser 't Hooft decided that Weidner and his colleagues should have official recognition. Working within the available bureaucratic forms, the military attaché and ambassador received permission to incorporate Weidner and the top tier of his colleagues into the military pay structure if they could be considered to be based in Switzerland and volunteering for hazardous duty.

Of course everyone involved in Dutch-Paris was a volunteer. Some of the younger people, particularly couriers, were paid a small stipend so that they had the means to pay their rent and buy groceries while working for the line full time. In a few instances of less affluent colleagues who devoted themselves completely to the line without any compensation, Weidner offered them small gifts of 500 to 5,000 French francs. It is not clear from the accounts whether he gave them the cash or used it to buy new shoes, a coat, or other useful but scarce items for them.

The older people who had jobs and homes did not expect any sort of compensation for their resistance work. Weidner himself had abandoned his business and thus his livelihood in September 1943. In the fourteen months before that he had neglected the business and drained his bank account to help refugees and fugitives. He and Cartier were living on what remained of their savings, and those were dwindling fast because of Weidner's habit of emptying his pockets whenever a refugee asked for a loan, most of which were never paid back.[63]

Many Dutch-Paris helpers simply paid for things needed by fugitives, such as food, from their own funds. Some men, especially in Brussels but also Caubo in Paris, even loaned the line large sums without solid guarantees of repayment. For the most part, however, the line paid for the daily expenses of supporting refugees and fugitives as described earlier. Weidner, Rens, and Chait delivered the cash to pay for train tickets, hotels, food, boots, and the like, and recorded the expenses in ledgers kept in Switzerland.[64] The government in exile required an accounting of how its money was spent, although in the case of Dutch-Paris's clandestine work it did not require receipts.

Considering the very high cost of living in Switzerland, both Weidner and Rens had been receiving an unofficial per diem for the time they spent there along the lines of the money the Dutch embassy allotted Dutch refugees there. It paid for meals and other small purchases. Both men lived with family when in Switzerland, Weidner at his mother-in-law's and Rens with his parents.

As of April 16, 1944, however, Weidner and his lieutenants received a regular salary and a per diem when in Switzerland. They and their wives, if they were married, would also be reimbursed for clothing, shoes, and medical expenses. Wives would receive the same allotment as military wives in Switzerland. In his official letter General van Tricht also promised to do everything in his power to ensure that the wives would receive a military pension if their husbands were killed.[65] At that time the provisions for wives applied only to Cartier. Weidner told Van Tricht that the formalized financial arrangements put him and Cartier much more "at ease."[66]

This new arrangement gave Weidner, Rens, Chait, and Veerman a more formal status as soldiers of the government in exile. It also recognized the standing of Dutch-Paris and all its members as a Dutch resistance network even though it operated outside the Netherlands with many non-Dutch members. That would be important after the war, for those who survived that long.

Gare Matabiau, Toulouse, France, 1950.

8

Sociaalwerk in the Chaos of War

THE LOSS OF SO MANY HELPERS AND RELIABLE ADDRESSES in February and March 1944 hampered but did not end Dutch-Paris's illegal work. The Germans who supervised the roll-up of Dutch-Paris, particularly the Abwehr counterespionage officer Richard Christmann, were primarily interested in stopping Allied airmen from evading capture. They appear to have limited their investigation to the escape lines to Spain and to Switzerland. Dutch-Paris's own security measures that separated the *transportwerk* from the Swiss Way microfilm relay and the *sociaalwerk* also limited the damage. Weidner and his colleagues continued to assist those in hiding and deliver documents. The only thing Dutch-Paris stopped doing altogether in March 1944 was escort Allied airmen from Brussels or Paris to Spain.

Nonetheless almost everyone based in Paris had been captured, including Nijkerk and those he had recruited to help him rebuild the line there. In Brussels most of the young people who had done the daily work of rescue had been arrested, as had the men and women who bore the daily responsibilities for the line in Lyon and Annecy. Dutch-Paris's leaders—Jean Weidner, Jacques Rens, and Edmond Chait—would have to both restructure certain aspects of their illegal work and recruit more helpers to make up for these losses. They themselves took on even more responsibility and travel than before. They needed to keep moving in any case because they had no way of knowing what information the Germans might have tortured out of their prisoners. They did know that Weidner had a price on his head: 5 million French francs, as Pillot remembered it; 1 million according to Weidner himself.[1] Either one counted as a small fortune.

At the same time as the men and women of Dutch-Paris reorganized the network, the battle was returning to western Europe. Despite German censorship, people in the occupied territories knew that the Soviets had been inflicting heavy losses on the Wehrmacht and pushing it back toward the German homeland since their crushing victory at Stalingrad in February 1943. They knew the Allies had landed in Italy in September 1943. In late 1943 and early 1944 a civilian on the ground in the Netherlands and Belgium could see hundreds of bombers heading toward Germany at a single time. Towns that were not officially in the warzone, such as Paris, Maastricht, Toulouse, and Annecy, suffered aerial bombardment, sometimes by mistake. Occupied and occupier alike expected an Allied invasion somewhere in western Europe in 1944.

These signs of the Third Reich's weakness emboldened the armed resistance. Partisans sabotaged trains, roads, and bridges and assaulted collaborators. Such attacks made the German occupation forces and their collaborators more anxious and more likely to commit the kind of atrocities they had previously confined to the East. Indeed the Haute-Savoie had been in a state of civil war between the resistance Armée Sècrete and the collaborationist *Milice* and occupation forces since January 1944.[2] Rens had changed his travel plans because of the tensions in Annecy as early as December 1943.[3]

Those who favored the Allies could find hope in the deteriorating situation. At the end of March 1944 a conversation with Wehrmacht officers on a train gave Weidner cause for optimism. One of them remarked, "If they keep bombing Germany like this, it won't be able to hold out past May."[4] Even if the officer's prediction was off by a year, the enemy's low morale would have given those who were risking so much to rescue Allied airmen reason to believe that their sacrifices were indeed contributing to winning the war.

In recognition of the deteriorating situation at the end of April, Weidner suggested that General van Tricht reduce the number of Engelandvaarders leaving Switzerland to the absolute minimum, as the bombardments and the general tension in France made traveling there ever more difficult.[5] As he said, "Everyone is expecting the invasion." He also issued orders that when the Allies invaded Dutch-Paris, helpers should continue to support those they were hiding. He suggested giving clients three months' financial support in advance, though he worried they would spend it all at once and ask for more the next month.[6]

The arrests of their colleagues and general increase in military tensions affected Dutch-Paris in Belgium as well as in France. Over the spring of 1944 the Comité saw a drastic changeover in personnel doing the daily work of supporting fugitives in hiding. Before March 1944 most of the couriers within the city and over the borders were young and unmarried, either students or just starting out in their careers in textiles or other businesses. In the summer of 1944, however, the helpers tended to be slightly older and more established, with families and businesses of their own.

In late March, German labor officials seized Hans Wisbrun, the last of the young leaders still at liberty, to work in the Third Reich during a neighborhood roundup. A few weeks later, in April, German police raided the *sociaalwerk* headquarters at 73 rue du Trône. That raid had nothing to do with the arrests on the rue Franklin in February. One of the Comité's clients was arrested during a document inspection on the street and panicked, giving the address and several names. The young men who had taken over responsibility for daily operations just a few weeks earlier, Paul Sayers and Yves von der Möhlen, narrowly escaped capture and had to disappear. Chait took them to a farm in France run by a Dutch couple, where they joined the *maquis*.[7] The Dutch student Greta Roselaar briefly took over their job overseeing the *sociaalwerk*.[8]

German police arrested Pastor ten Kate on May 15 because two Dutchmen mentioned his name during what they thought was a private conversation.[9] Scandalized, members of Ten Kate's church sent official letters of protest to the highest levels, specifically German intelligence chief Admiral Wilhelm Canaris. Their letter had no immediate result.[10] The banker Jacobus Verhagen took on the pastor's daily responsibilities, in particular coordinating couriers.

Roselaar left the Comité in May 1944, to be replaced by Philip Polak, who had fled Amsterdam in the summer of 1943 with his wife, Jetta Pool. As a merchant in meat and groceries and an Orthodox Jew, Polak had worked for the Jewish Council in the Dutch capital. When the young couple received an order to report for deportation, they dressed themselves as if they were taking the baby out for some air, put their toddler in his stroller, and simply walked away from the ghetto. Van Cleeff welcomed Polak into the Comité before his arrest in November 1943. Van Cleeff's successors, Verloop and Vleeschdrager, however, thought that a family man should take his wife and child to Switzerland rather than put himself at risk on the streets of Brussels. While waiting for that to be arranged, the Polak-Pools started delivering money and ration tickets to families in hiding. Before his arrest Pastor ten Kate helped the Polak-Pools find a Belgian family to take care of their son so that both husband and wife could devote themselves to the *sociaalwerk* full time. When Roselaar left the Comité in May 1944, Polak stepped into her place as the leader of daily operations in Brussels.

After the Liberation the Comité board noted that Polak was "the first and only one among the leaders of the *sociaalwerk* after Paul van Cleeff who would follow the advice of the Comité and who worked according to a system."[11] Polak trained Edouard van Kempen as his second-in-command so that none of the people they were hiding would be lost if he himself were arrested. An expatriate businessman with a son of military age, Van Kempen joined the group through a distant relation by marriage, the board member Edouard Regout.[12] Around the same time, the Comité enlisted another expatriate, Tom Oostendorp, to reestablish their account books because some of them had been confiscated during the raid on the rue Franklin. As a professional accountant with a Jewish wife and a small child, Oostendorp had the skills and the motivation to help the Comité's rescue work.[13]

Knoote, Oostendorp, and Polak's top priority in June 1944 was to implement a new security system, one conceived in principle by Roselaar. They needed a way to both protect the identities of the helpers and to make sure that no clients were abandoned if their helper was arrested. The new system used numbers in place of names. Every Comité member who delivered money and ration tickets was assigned a single-digit number. Every family for whom he or she was responsible was assigned a number beginning with the same numeral as the helper. A courier, for example, would be known to his clients and many of his colleagues as "Number 5," and every family to whom he delivered money and documents would be known by a number beginning with 5. Knoote hid the key to the numbers and all the account books. As it turned out, women did the courier work during the last months of the occupation of Brussels. The women went by more friendly and unremarkable-sounding pseudonyms such as "Madame Josée" and "Madame Hélène."[14]

After the raid on the rue du Trône, the Comité returned to an earlier arrangement in which clients made appointments to meet their helper at a public place, often a café. They could also send letters addressed to "Mej de Coster" at a particular café. "Miss de Coster" was actually Van Kempen, who knew the café owner through his Belgian resistance group, the Organisation Militaire Belge de Résistance. He received about ten letters a day from clients who were afraid of being abandoned. Van Kempen excused the tone of some of these letters on the understandable grounds that the authors had been shut up in hiding places for months, afraid of meeting the Gestapo on the street and being deported.[15]

To make false documents now that their forger Bol was in prison, Polak recruited a Belgian who had provided him with a legal work card when he had first arrived in Brussels. Georges Moussiax also allowed the showroom of his toy factory to be used as a postbox for the organization. Couriers deposited and retrieved documents from a cardboard horse that Moussiax later presented to Pastor ten Kate as the "Paard van Troye der Nederlanders" (Dutch Trojan Horse). He, in turn, enlisted a Belgian acquaintance as a courier and involved his secretary in accepting messages in his absence.[16] For ration tickets, Polak recruited a Belgian secretary at the administrative offices of the rationing service named Rosa Pouillon. She began pilfering ration tickets at her workplace early in the year and later expanded her illegal work to include delivering money and false documents to fugitives.[17]

The number of families being helped meant they also needed more couriers. Polak found a Jewish woman in her late twenties who was willing to help after she fled Amsterdam in February 1944. He also recruited a Belgian couple after being introduced to them by a Dutch family in hiding whom they were helping. The Comité's currency trader, Joseph Haenecour, enlisted another expatriate husband-and-wife team. Oostendorp himself invited an old friend from The Hague, a young widow named Johanna van Helden-Hus, to join the *sociaalwerk*. All of these people had helped the persecuted before joining the Comité. The Belgian couple had assisted Spanish Republicans and German and Italian refugees before the war, and the others had helped Jews during it.[18]

Van Helden-Hus had actually tried to work with Vleeschdrager in 1943, but Van Cleeff had vetoed her involvement because he thought the work was too dangerous for women. By the time her friend Oostendorp asked her to help in 1944, however, no one took exception to women in the resistance. Of course by the summer of 1944 the Comité had little choice but to accept the help of women because the streets of Brussels were too dangerous for men of military age. The occupation troops there increased the number of patrols and actions in the streets after the Allies landed on the beaches of Normandy in early June. Every man was treated as a potential threat because he might be in the resistance or as a candidate for slave labor in the Third Reich. Women, however, were less likely to be stopped or arrested, although it did happen.

On one occasion during that summer, when air raids made the trams infrequent, crowded, and dangerous, Van Helden-Hus found herself with a suspiciously large roll of bills and two false identity cards when a German patrol boarded her tram. The forgers had put her birth date down as 1901 instead of 1910, and the Germans who were inspecting the passengers' identity cards refused to believe that the thirty-three-year-old was forty-three. The Dutchwoman put on her most charming smile, which she later said she had never yet shown to a German, and "asked in a friendly way if they didn't think that we Belgian women knew how to keep our looks."[19] They let her go on her way. Van Helden-Hus took care of thirty families, including one located in the town of La Hulpe, between Genval and Brussels, which took a full day of bicycling to visit. She also took care of all the refugees' medical needs by paying any bills and escorting those who did not speak French to sympathetic clinics or doctors' offices.[20] Van Kempen regularly visited twenty families. Other couples took on the responsibility for forty or even forty-five clients.

During the final days of the occupation of Belgium, in August 1944, the Comité was supporting four hundred people at 150 addresses at the cost of about 400,000 Belgian francs per month. They could help so many people only because they had resolved their ongoing financial crisis. Money kept coming in from the Dutch expatriate community in the form of donations and unsecured loans. In early March, for example, the Comité collected enough money in private donations to establish a sick fund for refugees. But the key to the problem of how to pay for rescue came from the Dutch government in exile in the late spring.[21]

Because it was so hard to exchange and transfer foreign currency, the ambassador in Switzerland gave the Comité a government guarantee for loans raised in Belgium itself to be paid back after the war. This was an attractive offer for potential investors because by that point the Allies seemed sure to win and the government in exile was almost sure to pay back the loan. Furthermore the financially savvy could predict postwar currency reform and/or currency regulations to punish black marketeers, all of which would make the amount paid back after the war more valuable in real terms than the same amount of francs was during the occupation. Once they had a government guarantee, the Comité had no trouble at all in raising very large loans.[22]

Communication delays between London and Geneva, however, meant that the ambassador effectively authorized a much larger loan than the government in exile intended: 4.5 million Belgian francs in place of 2 million. They sorted out the confusion with a typically convoluted Dutch-Paris exchange. In April, Chait reestablished contact with a Jewish group with which Benno Nijkerk had been connected before he left Belgium. At their request Weidner pleaded their case for funds with Jewish aid organizations in Switzerland, but those organizations could not transfer money across enemy lines. Instead the Comité gave 2 million Belgian francs from the loans they raised to Nijkerk's colleagues in Brussels, and the Jewish donors in Switzerland reimbursed the Dutch embassy there the equivalent in Swiss francs. In this way the Dutch embassy in Switzerland retrieved its money and the Jewish organizations in Switzerland sent money to Jewish resisters in Belgium.[23]

The government money allowed the Comité to increase its monthly allotments to its clients and expand its services. In principle clients who were in hiding in the summer of 1944 received 1,000 Belgian francs per month for adults and 500 for children, as well as ration coupons, a supplement for coal, and medical care.[24] The cash delivered by the helpers was meant to pay for rent, food, and other necessities. Clients signed a receipt for each payment, which meant the helpers were constantly carrying around incriminating pieces of papers.[25] The Comité also paid for food packages to be sent to Dutch Jews interned in a transit camp north of the city.[26]

As businessmen, the financial managers of the Comité understood that shortages and risk drove up prices, but they would not succumb to extortion. They also kept track of prices on the black market and put a ceiling on what they, or their clients, would pay. Nor did they confuse business with resistance. If a landlady charged a high rent to lodge Jews, for example, they considered the arrangement to be strictly business and did not consider the landlady to be a member of Dutch-Paris. They did have one case, however, of a landlady who charged so little that it was clear that she hid Jews for purely altruistic reasons. Indeed it seemed that she charged anything at all only because she did not have enough money to pay for everything herself. The financial managers concluded that she was a bad businesswoman but a good resister and put her on the official roster of helpers.[27]

In France, Weidner continued to run the clandestine social welfare system with funds provided by Ambassador Bosch van Rosenthal. Covering a much larger territory than Brussels and its region, the *sociaal-werk* in France was never as tightly organized as the Comité's. It had grown out of the diplomatic system of delivering assistance through regional consuls and continued on that model. Dutch-Paris couriers took cash to Dutch consuls to disburse to the needy as long as they were at liberty and willing to participate in illegal activities.

The arrests of Consul Maurice Jacquet in Lyon and the diplomat Herman Laatsman in Paris in February 1944 disrupted this distribution system but did not put an end to it. Weidner diverted the money to other individuals in the network of Protestant resisters to which Visser 't Hooft was tied and to humanitarian organizations such as the French Protestant group CIMADE and the Quakers.[28] For example, on one brief visit to Paris in early May, Weidner delivered mail to two Protestant pastors. He also paid a visit to Jules Mohr at the Dutch Red Cross, giving him cash for care packages for Dutch-Paris helpers in prison and for their families, including Madame Laatsman and her small children and the Caubo children, whose father was still in prison. Their mother, Marie Schenck, had died of a heart attack during a bombing raid in April 1944, leaving the twin boys and their younger sister on their own in occupied Paris.[29]

In Annecy, Chait gave money to a French contact at the prefecture to distribute to needy Dutch, especially those in prison. In Toulouse he made regular deliveries of cash to Father aan de Stegge to distribute to several families.[30] Chait also worked with the Quakers in Toulouse to assist Dutch citizens in the prisons and internment camps in the region. In return he carried reports to Switzerland that they had written on such topics as the psychological effects of internment on children, the efficacy of vitamin biscuits donated by the Swiss, and the convoy of political prisoners deported from Toulouse that included the elderly and much respected archbishop of Montauban.[31] In some cases Dutch-Paris couriers took money and false documents directly to individuals or families hiding in small villages in southern France. Raymonde Pillot and Ernest Bouchet did much of that work. After Pillot's arrest, Chait, Paul Veerman, and possibly others filled in for her.

Paul Veerman, 1945.

Dutch-Paris also continued to smuggle Jewish refugees into Switzerland. Chait made a number of trips across southern France during the summer of 1944 to check on Jewish families in hiding, deliver money to them, and ask if they were ready to risk the journey to Switzerland. At each address he had a password, such as "Loulou" or "Germaine," to let the refugees know that he came on behalf of friends in Switzerland. If they agreed, Weidner and Elisabeth Cartier prepared the escapes and sent Chait back to the hiding place with money, false documents, and instructions. By that time, however, Dutch-Paris was no longer using its own route through Lyon, Annecy, and Collonges. Instead Chait made arrangements with CIMADE helpers in Valence to take Dutch Jews into Switzerland. The route from Valence was more rugged and mountainous than the path under the barbed wire in the Genevois, but in the summer of 1944 it was considered safer.[32]

Dutch-Paris had other obligations, of course, in addition to the *sociaalwerk*. The government-in-exile relied on the line for the microfilm relay and to bring men whose skills it needed from the Netherlands to Spain. The early decision to compartmentalize the Swiss Way courier route from Dutch-Paris's other work bore fruit in March 1944. The few people who knew about it and could have identified the people and places involved were not captured. So nothing needed to change on the Swiss Way in response to the arrests unless Weidner and Rens chose to alter their routes or identities as a precaution. However, Visser 't Hooft's assistant, Joop Bartels, had gone to Amsterdam after his disruptive visit to Brussels just before the coordinated arrests in Paris. He took it upon himself to reorganize the route. Much to Weidner's surprise, Bartels ordered the courier Jef Lejeune to move to Brussels in order to run a station there for Engelandvaarders and microfilm. In this plan Lejeune's assistants, A. L. A. Borst and Nico van Dorp, would replace him as the liaisons in Louvain. Weidner had no cause for complaint about Borst and Van Dorp's portion of the Swiss Way, but he did not think that Lejeune had the organizational talents for the job in Brussels.

Lejeune, however, saw himself as prudent. He and an unnamed colleague in the Netherlands concluded that Engelandvaarders who were not physically fit enough to keep up on the journey or astute enough to blend in in Belgium and France put everyone else involved in the line at risk. They therefore refused all candidates except those who had been condemned to death in the Netherlands or whom the government in exile called to London. This policy meant, in effect, that a mere ten men traveled officially from the Netherlands to Spain on Dutch-Paris between March and September 1944.[33]

Despite this unwelcome meddling, Weidner, Rens, and Chait continued to evacuate fugitives from occupied territory wherever they found them. But circumstances forced them to change the way the escape line operated. Instead of a relay across western Europe in which guides handed fugitives off to colleagues in other cities, the initial guides took them all the way. Chait, for instance, picked up Engelandvaarders in Brussels and took them from there to Toulouse himself rather than passing them to new guides in Paris.

Chait also took over in Toulouse, evacuating aviators and Engelandvaarders to Spain as quickly as the weather and the *passeur* Bazerque's schedule would allow. Dutch-Paris still used the restaurant Chez Emile but added a few new addresses, such as a restaurant called Au Truffe de Quercy, deeper in the winding maze of the old town, and a flower shop near the gare Matabiau. And they now had a postbox at a drycleaner's on the rue de la Trinité, a few doors down from their meeting place at the Protestant Foyer de la Jeunesse.[34]

Somewhat surprisingly no arrests troubled Dutch-Paris operations in Toulouse until Simone Calmels was captured at the end of June. German investigators may not have been following up their leads in Toulouse, but they were most certainly tracking down Dutch-Paris's allies on the Spanish borderlands. Jan Langeler, who had been captured by Germans on skis in the ambush at the shepherd's hut in early February and then escaped by jumping out of a truck in Toulouse, managed to make contact with Dutch-Paris again. Chait paid for him, two other survivors of the Col de Portet d'Aspet—Lemmens and Timmers Verhoeven—and an American and a Canadian who were staying with friends in Toulouse to join a convoy that left for Spain on March 25. Langeler had a nasty surprise when he walked into a bar in Viella, Spain, to find the German officer who had arrested him in the mountains dressed in civilian clothes. He was chatting with Allied aviators in English about the last town they had seen in France and the first they had come to in Spain. Without being recognized, the Dutchman quickly explained to as many Americans as he could find who this friendly chap really was.[35]

Aviators who arrived in Spain a few days earlier reported similar activities by German officers there. Chait used that convoy to evacuate the seven Americans and two Brits from the "Villa du Crime," a Canadian he came across in Toulouse, the six aviators and one of the Dutchmen who escaped the ambush at the Col du Portet d'Aspet, and two other Americans who had been with Dutch-Paris since Brussels. They made it to Spain safely, but not without divisions in the group.[36] At least one American saw two Czech fugitives who had trekked across the mountains with their convoy draw a detailed map of their route for a civilian in a Spanish bar, possibly the same or another German officer. Another aviator in that same group reported that the Spanish authorities had a wall map with pins of escape routes, including one very close to the one they had taken.[37]

It is doubtful that Chait or any of his colleagues knew about the German presence in Spain. They heard nothing about their protégés after their guides saw them over the border. If they had known that the Spanish Guardia Civil routinely confiscated all valuables carried by foreigners, they would not have gone to the trouble and expense they did to provide each of their men with Spanish pesetas before he left Toulouse. As it was, there were no immediate repercussions to the German mapping of the evasion lines in the Haute-Garonne for either Dutch-Paris or its allies in the Pyrenees. On April 10 Chait sent another twenty Allied fugitives from Toulouse to Spain with Bazerque without incident.[38]

Soon after that Weidner, Chait, and Veerman escorted Dutch-Paris's most famous fugitive across Belgium and France. The government in exile called the Dutch resistance leader Gerrit Jan van Heuven Goedhart to London to take up the portfolio of minister of justice. After the war he would become the United Nations' first high commissioner for refugees and a Nobel Peace Prize laureate. During the occupation Van Heuven Goedhart exerted so much influence as editor of the underground newspaper *Het Parool* that the German authorities offered an astronomical reward for his capture. The London Dutch wanted Weidner and his colleagues to bring Van Heuven Goedhart out of occupied territory with the utmost caution and sparing no expense. In their telegrams back and forth about this escape, the Dutch authorities in London and Bern referred to him as the "zeer buitengewoon mens" (very, very important person), or ZBM.

Weidner made sure that Van Heuven Goedhart traveled by a new route that could not have been betrayed to the Germans through the earlier arrests.[39] Lejeune brought him from Amsterdam to Brussels on April 25, 1944, rowing across the River Maas to Belgium and then taking a series of trams. Lejeune had not made any further preparations and intended to share a hotel room with the ZBM. Weidner considered a hotel altogether too risky but had no other option.

He did, however, decide that Chait would take the ZBM farther south on an indirect route. They took a zigzagging path of local trains, long walks, and a lift from a passing truck, crossing the Belgian-French border in Chait's usual spot by creeping along the outside of the footbridge in Quiévrain. They rendezvoused with Weidner in Paris in the early evening of April 28. Weidner had stayed in Brussels an extra day on Dutch-Paris business, then brought the ZBM's suitcase with him on the direct, international train.

After a night's rest in Paris, Chait and Veerman escorted their guest farther south. Again Weidner carried Van Heuven Goedhart's suitcase on a separate train. They were much better prepared in Toulouse than they had been in Brussels. Veerman had rented a small apartment and equipped it with cleaning supplies, an ashtray, and dishes. More private and reliable than a hotel, it offered as much security as possible. They could not be certain of the neighbors, of course, but that was a constant risk throughout occupied Europe. The apartment also served as a meeting place and depository for papers and money. It was large enough that three other Engelandvaarders stayed there at the same time as Van Heuven Goedhardt: two other Dutchmen called to London—a physician and a jurist with colonial expertise—and a young man who had escaped the arrest of his companions in Paris in March and found his way back to Dutch-Paris in Toulouse in April.[40]

In Toulouse, Dutch-Paris equipped the ZBM with a rucksack, a beret, a book, a fountain pen, a handkerchief, and some French and Spanish cash.[41]

Veerman took Van Heuven Goedhart to the mountain city of Foix, ate lunch with him, and introduced him to the *passeur* Treillet. On his way back German police questioned Veerman, but without detaining him.

Dutch-Paris paid the extraordinary sum of 50,000 French francs, five times the going rate for taking aviators across the border, for the ZBM's passage over the Pyrenees. It should have taken him into Spain quickly and safely, but two separate sets of guides abandoned him in the mountains, leaving him to find his own way back to his local contact in the mountains beyond Foix. The third set of guides, found by the local contact, took him to Spain via Andorra. Weidner received a message from Dutch authorities in Spain acknowledging the ZBM's arrival, which he passed on to his wife in the Netherlands. Despite the near debacle in the Pyrenees, Van Heuven Goedhart later thanked Dutch-Paris publicly for their help and testified that he could not have made the trip without their assistance.[42]

Soon after, Weidner made arrangements to cross the Pyrenees himself in order to deliver microfilm and make inquiries about going to England. On one of his trips to Toulouse to check on Van Heuven Goedhart and to talk to the Quakers about Dutch prisoners in French internment camps, Weidner found what he considered to be a "pretty good way" to Spain. For the trek he would use false documents made out in his mother's maiden name, Linschoten. He paid the escape line broker Gabriel Nahas with a wristwatch to leave Toulouse on May 21, 1944, and return on an undetermined date.[43] The form and value of the payment, almost twice the usual rate, suggest that Weidner intended to go by a different path than other Dutch-Paris Engelandvaarders took.

On the evening before his scheduled departure, May 20, Weidner, Rens, Veerman, and Nahas met at a restaurant in Toulouse. During their conversation about religious sectarianism, Nahas gave Weidner a pocket-size New Testament. As they left the restaurant five minutes later, around 9:30 p.m., they walked straight into six plainclothes French policemen holding revolvers.[44] Nahas fled when the man searching him dropped his papers. The policeman told his companions that he could not shoot the fugitive because his revolver jammed, but later he told Weidner that he just did not have the heart to do it. They took Weidner, Rens, Veerman, and a passerby to the police station but soon let the passerby go.

Because the men who arrested them were not in uniform, the Dutchmen did not immediately understand that they had fallen into the hands of the paramilitary, collaborationist *Milice* rather than the regular French police.[45] In the previous few months the *Milice* had been given greater powers and escalated their offensive against their countrymen in the resistance. Weidner and the others admitted to being Dutch resisters traveling secretly through France. Weidner gave his true name, though Rens and Veerman did not. The inspectors repeatedly asked their prisoners about the man who gave the book to Weidner. They showed them photographs of Nahas and of a communist who bore a striking resemblance to Weidner. Indeed when they arrested Weidner, the *Miliciens* thought they were apprehending the communist, whom they accused of shooting twenty of their comrades.

At 11:30 p.m. the inspectors took their prisoners in handcuffs to the apartment Dutch-Paris had rented in the old part of town. They found no Engelandvaarders or resisters, but they did uncover a pair of false IDs, an expense sheet, and a message confirming the ZBM's arrival in Spain. They did not find the three microfilms hidden there.[46] Weidner considered the discovery of the apartment and the papers to be a "catastrophe," as he later put it. It was certainly a financial setback; the *Milice* confiscated more than enough money to get eleven aviators to Spain.[47] After that they took the Dutchmen to a *Milice* prison in the old part of town, not far from the place St. Georges and the restaurant Chez Emile where Dutch-Paris guides and fugitives ate so many meals.

On May 22 Weidner asked to see the commanding officer, Pierre Marty, who had gained a notorious reputation. Weidner explained the situation quite frankly, admitting to being a Dutch resister but pointing out that he never carried a weapon and had done nothing against France. He also made it clear that he refused to give the names of any French people who had helped him because doing so would be cowardly and against his honor. Marty told Weidner that he liked his attitude and ordered that the three Dutch prisoners be treated "correctly." He gave his word that neither the men nor the documents found with them would be released to the Germans if Weidner's story held up to inquiries. Although both he and Marty knew the Germans had offered a reward of 1 million francs for him, Weidner found cause to hope from this interview.[48]

Taking advantage of an open window at the prison, Veerman escaped at 10:30 that night. Within five minutes he was at the restaurant Chez Emile. He picked up 5,000 French francs, enough for several train tickets, and made sure that someone would meet Chait at the station the next morning with the news. Then he took a train to Paris via Marseille. Two days later he took the train from Paris to Annemasse, right on the Swiss border.[49]

Veerman's escape worried the *Miliciens* in Toulouse because they were sure that, without money or documents, the Germans would capture him. They feared that once they got the story out of Veerman, which inevitably they would, the Germans would punish them for not handing over Weidner. The two *Miliciens* whom Weidner and Rens saw the most asked Weidner if he could find Veerman before the Germans did. They worked out a deal whereby one of the *Miliciens* would accompany Weidner through the streets of Toulouse to make sure that he would not be arrested, but would not go up to the door of any house with him. In Weidner's recollection his twenty-two-year-old warden made an effort not to know exactly which houses he visited.

On that tense walk through Toulouse, Weidner visited Father aan de Stegge at his parish. The priest thought he looked healthy but nervous, constantly looking over his shoulder. Weidner told him that he had convinced the *Milice* chief to let him out for half an hour on the understanding that Rens would pay if he did not return. He gave the priest what he thought might be his last letter to his wife because he expected to be turned over to the Germans despite Marty's promises. When he returned to the prison, Weidner could reassure his jailers that Veerman had escaped to Switzerland.

Weidner and Rens had been cultivating the friendship of these two *Miliciens* since their arrest. When the younger *Milicien* told them that he admired people who read the Bible, Weidner, who was himself a devoted reader of the Bible, took advantage of the opening. Likewise, when they found a receipt from a garage in Toulouse where Weidner had stored his personal automobile at the beginning of the war, he offered it to the older *Milicien* and officially signed it over to him. He figured that the car, a Chevrolet, was a small price to invest in their liberty and that, anyway, the *Milice* could requisition it at any time, with or without his approval. In exchange Weidner asked the *Miliciens* not to bother any of the French people whom they could track down through Weidner's papers. Weidner believed they kept that promise. They also treated their Dutch prisoners far better than many others, whose screams of pain they heard in that prison.

Three days after arresting Weidner and his colleagues, the *Milice* chief left for Vichy to consult with his superiors. Almost a week later, on May 29, one of the friendly *Miliciens* informed Weidner that Marty had received orders to transfer them to a prison under German control. Again Weidner spoke freely. He explained that the Germans would surely torture and kill him and Rens. He also expected that the Germans would kill all their Dutch-Paris colleagues in prison once they could no longer blame everything on Weidner without fear of cross-examination. Weidner assured his jailers that he would rather risk being shot while escaping than fall into the hands of the Germans. Finally he offered the two *Miliciens* the significant sum of 300,000 French francs and the chance to flee with him and Rens to Spain or Switzerland if they would let them go. The *Miliciens* accepted neither offer but did agree to have the Dutchmen moved down from the third to the second floor. They were willing to make conditions favorable for an escape as long as they would have no direct responsibility for it.

Rens and Weidner decided to wait until the curfew lifted at 6:00 the next morning, when they would be less likely to be arrested simply for being on the street. They spent the night carefully dismantling the lock to their cell. At 5:00 they opened the cell door and, shoes in hand, tiptoed past the guard sleeping outside their cell with his submachine gun on his lap. A second guard slept at the end of the hallway. They then slipped into an office with windows running along the street that Weidner had noticed a few days earlier. As soon as the curfew lifted and the sentinel outside reached the farthest point of his circuit, Weidner and Rens jumped out the window and ran to the corner. Right up until the last minute, Weidner feared an ambush. But no one sounded the alarm.[50]

Weidner and Rens then adopted a natural walking pace so as not to attract any attention and made their way to Father aan de Stegge's rectory. The priest hurriedly brought them in and made up beds for the two fugitives on chairs. Then he took an early tram to arrange money and false documents with the organization. When he returned from saying mass at 8:00 a.m. his guests were awake and eager to be gone from Toulouse.

First, however, they needed new false documents, which required passport photographs. The place to obtain instant photos lay far enough away that walking there posed too great a risk. Instead they decided to go to the photographer across the square from the church, though it involved passing a police post. Chait, who had just arrived from Paris, crossed the square at the same time they did and followed them into the photographer's.[51]

It took a couple of days to make the necessary false documents and plans to get Rens and Weidner out of Toulouse. Because the Germans and the *Milice* were hunting for them in the Pyrenees, they chose to leave the city through the north and head to Switzerland instead of Spain. Chait used his contacts with other resisters in town, including a French engineer named Roger Nougarède, who was a regional scout leader and director of a trade association.[52] "Nougat," as Chait dubbed him, had been helping Andrée Moulouguet hide aviators sponsored by a French escape line since November 1943. Knowing full well that the police and *Milice* had set up road blocks throughout the city to find Rens and Weidner, Nougarède volunteered to drive them out of town. On the evening of June 1 he drove them to an outlying train station that was not being watched. The next day, after great anxiety, they returned to the safety of Geneva using cash given to them by Chait for train tickets and tips.[53]

Chait himself stayed in Toulouse to get more fugitives out of town. He found two Dutch Engelandvaarders at Aan de Stegge's rectory on the day Weidner and Rens escaped from the *Milice* prison. Rudi Schreinemachers, an agent of the London-based Dutch Intelligence Service, the Bureau Inlichtingen, and Father Lodewyk Bleys, a well-known personality in the Dutch Catholic resistance, had made their own way from the Netherlands to Switzerland. They had left Geneva with instructions for the Dutch-Paris route but lost their way between Lyon and Toulouse. It was only by chance that their Catholic connections had led them back to Dutch-Paris in Toulouse.[54] Chait arranged for them and three aviators to cross into Spain with Bazerque.

Two of the aviators were Americans whom resistance allies in southern France passed to Chait.[55] The third aviator was a Dutch RAF pilot, Bram van der Stok, who had escaped from the POW camp at Sagan, Stalag Luft III, as part of the famous "Great Escape." He was one of only three aviators to make it to Britain—the proverbial "home run." Van der Stok had been shot down in April 1942 and escaped from the high-security POW camp on March 24, 1944. He headed straight to the Netherlands but left home via Maastricht on April 21. He came into the care of Dutch-Paris in Brussels, probably through Joseph Haenecour, who had family in Maastricht. Chait took him to Paris, where he passed the pilot to an unidentified young woman who escorted him to Toulouse. For the next two weeks Van der Stok stayed with Chait at 9 rue du Puits Vert, in the old part of Toulouse, not far from Chez Emile.

On June 9 a guide took the priest, the secret agent, and the escaped pilot by local train to a village fifty miles south of Toulouse, different from where the *passeur* Bazerque usually marshaled convoys. They spent the night in the small Hotel Moderne, where Germans were quartered. The next day two guides armed with Sten guns drove the Dutchmen farther south into the Comingeoise. On June 11 they settled into a rat-infested farmhouse that already sheltered a large number of fugitives. Schreinemachers remembered twenty Jews; Van der Stok mentioned several other airmen, a Russian, a French officer, and the Frenchwoman who had brought him from Paris.[56]

Bazerque did not stay in the farmhouse with the fugitives but made a daily visit to bring them bread. On the day they were to start walking to Spain, however, either June 13 or 14, Bazerque did not show up. He, the truck driver called Frisco, and one of their colleagues had been ambushed by Germans as they drove over a mountain bridge and been killed, some said by flame thrower, some said by execution.[57] Two days later new guides and four men with automatic weapons took the group from the farmhouse to Spain. They walked for two and a half days in beautiful weather without a German in sight, arriving on June 18 at the Spanish village of Canejan, like so many other Dutch-Paris fugitives before them.[58]

While Van der Stok had waited in Toulouse, the Allies had landed on the Normandy beaches. Armed resisters had sabotaged bridges and telephone and telegraph wires in western Europe, upsetting the occupation forces and drawing down reprisals. The war had returned to France and Belgium both on the traditional battlefields, where the German and Allied armies fought, and behind the lines, where armed resisters fought against paramilitary collaborators and German troops.[59] Although Allied soldiers would not land in southern France for another two months, the region was not at peace.

Dutch-Paris had lost its *passeur* in the Pyrenees, Bazerque, and one of its most dedicated couriers in Toulouse, Calmels. Her colleague Moulouguet had gone into hiding. Nahas had joined the *maquis* after escaping the policemen waiting outside the restaurant on May 20. As an organization Dutch-Paris scarcely existed in Toulouse, but Chait would keep sending fugitives to safety through the city until its Liberation in August.

Four days before the Normandy landings, on June 2, Weidner crossed into Switzerland and turned himself in to the first Swiss guard he encountered as a political refugee rather than taking the time to make arrangements to cross the border as a member of the Swiss Intelligence Service, the SR, as he usually did. He stayed with his wife and mother-in-law outside Geneva and returned to the business of Dutch-Paris. But at the end of the month the Swiss authorities changed his status, which curtailed his freedom of movement. Unbeknownst to Weidner, this move came at the request of his contact at the Swiss SR, Paul Frossard de Saugy. A month later authorities in Geneva requested that Weidner be transferred away from the frontier to the canton of Fribourg, where the Swiss monitored all his communications and kept him under house arrest.[60]

Swiss suspicions of Weidner created difficulties for General van Tricht and Pastor Visser 't Hooft. They needed to maintain both the goodwill of their hosts and their clandestine connections to the Netherlands. Because the Swiss did not want Weidner to be involved in those connections anymore, Visser 't Hooft's assistant Bartels took over the dispatch of Dutch-Paris couriers from Switzerland. From the perspective of the resisters, he was an unfortunate choice. Weidner had fielded more than one complaint about his high-handed attitude. Now Bartels ignored Weidner and sent Veerman and Rens on missions without even notifying him, let alone consulting him. Weidner, who felt a deep personal responsibility for every member of Dutch-Paris, was livid. He would put his own life at risk for Holland, he wrote, but he would not allow his French friends to be endangered by the incompetence of someone who did not understand the realities of occupation.[61]

Weidner could not explain how he had fallen so far in the esteem of the Swiss and assumed that it must have something to do with political infighting among the Dutch. However, it appears the Swiss authorities lost confidence in Weidner because of a series of letters of denunciation sent to police officials in Bern and Zurich. The first, anonymous denunciation, signed "ein guter Schweizer" (a good Swiss citizen), arrived in Bern in July 1943, at the time the Dutch embassy was trying to arrange a visa for Weidner, months before anyone had proposed any sort of official role for him. The anonymous author warned the police that the Dutch national Johann Weidner, whom they had approved to enter Switzerland, was only doing so to bring nine refugees into the country. The writer was well-informed but not closely enough involved to know that Weidner went by the French form of his name, Jean. Swiss police investigated the letter and its claims but took no action.[62]

Several months later, in February 1944, a secretary who worked at the Hotel Victoria in Geneva sent a letter to a major in the Swiss security services in Zurich. The author described Weidner as having the trust of the

Dutch military attaché in Bern and the protection of the Swiss military authorities, which was true. He also claimed that the Gestapo was arresting all men between eighteen and fifty in Haute-Savoie, which was not true. He pointed out that Weidner traveled freely in and out of Switzerland without encountering any difficulty from the Germans. From this the author concluded that Weidner must work for the Gestapo. Furthermore, he claimed, Weidner was bringing Jews into Switzerland for profit. The author concluded that he had no proof of his accusations but felt obliged to notify the authorities. And he signed his name and address.

Because this was not an anonymous letter of denunciation, the Swiss took it seriously enough to investigate and to put Weidner under surveillance. But they also investigated the author of the letter. All they discovered at that time was that he was a German citizen who had come to Switzerland in 1941. He had been questioned by the police regarding an espionage case in Stuttgart in October 1943 but had done nothing noteworthy in Geneva since then.

Over the following weeks the same man continued to send handwritten updates to the Swiss security services. He announced that Weidner had appeared in Geneva for one day and then returned to France and that his sister Anne-Marie (Annette) would soon be at liberty in Geneva. He also warned, in an express letter, that Weidner would enter Switzerland from France on March 17 and that he appeared to be a middleman in an international diamond-smuggling operation. The details of Weidner's movements were correct, although the accusations of diamond smuggling and other war profiteering had no basis in truth. Illegal financial gain, especially made from the sufferings of refugees, however, were crimes the Swiss would not tolerate even if they might overlook some clandestine comings and goings.

Once the investigating officer found out that Weidner worked for the Swiss SR, he took no action against him. But it was apparently almost impossible to believe that Weidner could do what he did without being a German agent. If the author of the letters of denunciation was a German agent, he did a masterful job of manipulating the Swiss into stopping a man the Germans could not capture themselves. This well-placed and cleverly conceived series of denunciations explains the change in de Saugy's attitude that Weidner noticed in the late winter of 1944 and why the Swiss effectively put him under house arrest in the summer of 1944. It also suggests that Weidner's activities had become an open secret in Geneva.[63]

Weidner's change of status in Switzerland did not affect Dutch-Paris as much as it would have a few months earlier because he had planned to be in Spain then anyway. He had already briefed Rens to take over the *transportwerk* and Chait to take over the *sociaalwerk*. Veerman had enough experience at this point to take on part of the courier work.

After he escaped from the *Milice* prison in Toulouse, Veerman took refuge at the home of Rens's parents in Lausanne. A week later, on May 31, he slipped over the border en route to a rendezvous at the Café Vieille Heidelberg in Louvain to pick up Swiss Way microfilm coming from Amsterdam on June 5. As was typical for Dutch-Paris couriers, Veerman traveled the complete circuit on his way to Louvain. Disguised with new glasses, he returned to Toulouse on the very day the *Milice* were scouring the streets of the city for Weidner and Rens. He spent one night there, then passed through Paris on his way to Brussels. He had to fall back on the emergency contact in the Belgian capital because no one in Switzerland knew that Pastor ten Kate had been arrested on May 15. Veerman picked up the Swiss Way microfilm as scheduled. The password at the café was "1918," to which the contact would answer "1944." The Germans lost the First World War in 1918; resisters hoped they would lose the Second World War in 1944.

Veerman left Belgium on June 7, heading straight into the sabotage of the communications network triggered by the Normandy landings and the delays caused by German troop trains rushing to the battlefield. Because the trains were running sporadically and likely to be patrolled by police, Veerman decided to walk from Lyon to Geneva. To avoid the fighting between the *Milice* and the armed resistance in the Forces Françaises de l'Interieur in the Alps, he chose a route through a region known to be controlled by the *maquis*. Not surprisingly *maquisards* stopped him and took him to their headquarters high in the mountains. The fabled partisan commander Colonel Henri Romans-Petit questioned Veerman and then gave him an escort most of the way to Geneva.[64]

The end of the occupation was close but would not come for many long weeks. France would not be liberated until late August. Belgium and the southern Netherlands would not be free until September. In the meantime Dutch-Paris had refugees to support in hiding, fugitives to move to safety, and documents to deliver.

Gare de Lyon, Paris, 1946.

9

Waiting for News

DUTCH-PARIS COURIERS HAD ALWAYS HAD TO CONTEND WITH delays caused by sabotage and Allied bombing of the rail system, but after D-Day civilian travel involved so many risks and disruptions that the face-to-face communication on which the line relied became almost impossible. The breakdown in reliable communications caused by the battles for liberation meant that Weidner and his colleagues in Switzerland knew even less than usual about what was going on in France and Belgium. At the end of June they lost track of both Paul Veerman and Edmond Chait.

Weidner had already recognized the need for another courier and recruited Armand Lap from among the refugees in Geneva. Weidner had first met Lap in July 1942 in Annecy's prison, where he was serving the usual one-month sentence for illegal border crossing with Nico Gazan. Weidner and Elisabeth Cartier had arranged Lap's second, successful crossing into Switzerland. They also helped his fiancée disappear from a Vichy internment camp a few months later. Once Lap had a written guarantee that his family would be taken care of should he be arrested, he prepared to return to France.[1]

Jacques Rens and Lap left Geneva on their bicycles at noon on July 7 to find Veerman and Chait, deliver money to contacts in Paris, and exchange microfilms in Louvain. Crossing the border without difficulty, they stopped for a rest at the farm of Cartier's family. Her uncle welcomed them with the news of the region, full of "shootings and crimes just about everywhere." When they stopped at a bistro along the route for a cold drink, a German patrol passed by, but when they pedaled through the village of Cruseilles on the same road they saw a car full of *maquisards*.

Damage to the rail lines meant Rens and Lap had to patch together a route from Annecy to Lyon. They arrived in St-André-le-Gaz to find that *maquisards* had occupied the town the day before and derailed a train. German troops had arrived in the evening, seized the first thirteen young men they found, and simply shot them. The Germans were still in the town, terrorizing the population with what Rens described as a "very brutal attitude." The couriers made it to Lyon but could not find Chait or hear any word of him.

Rens and Lap boarded a train that, remarkably, was running on time and arrived in Paris on July 10 less than four hours late. Rens found the atmosphere in Paris a few weeks before its liberation to be "very unpleasant." When they inquired at the bookshop that served as the line's new postbox, their contact had seen Chait on June 30, but not Veerman. They could not get in touch with the Red Cross representative Jules Mohr. When the couriers went to the station to inquire about trains, they were told that there were no more trains to Brussels. The closest anyone could get to Belgium was Nancy, in Alsace Lorraine.

Rens and Lap boarded the 6:30 a.m. train for Nancy on July 12 with the intention of finding some way to get to Brussels from there. The train covered only nine miles in three hours. Because other passengers in the single carriage designated for civilians warned them that Nancy was heavily guarded and entrance there required a special pass, the Dutchmen returned to Paris.

That afternoon they located Mohr, who had not seen Chait for the past twelve days. Chait had told him that Veerman and many others had been arrested in Brussels. Rens found this disturbingly vague and had to suppose that the Swiss Way courier from Amsterdam, Jef Lejeune, and others in Dutch-Paris had also been arrested. From an Adventist pastor Rens learned that the courier Raymonde Pillot had been deported and that Pastor Paul Meyer had been transferred from Fresnes to the transit camp at Compiègne, the first stop on the way to the concentration camps. Gabrielle Weidner, however, was doing as well as could be hoped and still in the prison of Fresnes.

That night Rens and Lap boarded a train to Lyon. It crawled eastward, delayed by three bombardments and other unexplained stoppages. In Chalon-sur-Saône, about eighty miles north of Lyon, they were told the train would go no farther. After searching for hours, Lap, Rens, and another passenger, a Frenchman, found a taxi to share. Because the driver insisted on a minimum of five passengers, Rens found two more respectable-looking men who wanted to go to Lyon. The driver told them a hair-raising story about the Germans discovering weapons in a taxi and killing everyone in it, including the innocent driver, and more stories about a big battle between resisters and German soldiers the night before. He apologized that his car was still so dirty after being requisitioned by the *maquis* for two weeks.

On that morning of July 14, 1944, they saw the French tricolor flying all along the route in celebration of either Bastille Day, which had been suppressed for the previous four years, or imminent liberation. At the entrance to the village of Tournus, about eighteen miles south of Chalon, they stopped at a barricade manned by a unit of young, well-armed German soldiers in uniform and many Germans disguised as French peasants. Everything at the roadblock was going normally until one of the "peasants" gave orders in German to one of the soldiers to inspect the interior of the taxi in which Rens and Lap were riding. The five passengers, the driver, and a boy who was the driver's assistant exited the vehicle.

Suddenly there were cries of "Ammunition! Hands up! *Maquis!*" Every German cocked his weapon and shoved it into their faces. Rens, stunned, saw nothing suspicious, but Lap noticed cartridges on the floor of the taxi. The Germans took everyone from the taxi to a nearby villa, hurling their captives face first up against the wall as they entered. Lap carried the marks of their brutality on his face for weeks. Rens was sure they would all be murdered. While the men and the boy stood against the wall with their hands in the air, the Germans yanked off their jackets, pulled down their pants and emptied all their pockets. They screamed insults at the prisoners, kicking and hitting them.

After two hours of this, when Rens did not think he could hold his hands up much longer, the Germans started interrogating the prisoners. A lieutenant in uniform and three Gestapo agents in plainclothes questioned Rens about his identity. Fortunately his false documents were well made and gave him some cover for his movements by identifying him as a supply inspector. The interrogator furiously demanded to know if a certain letter in which a man in Paris thanked his wife in Collonges for some ration cards for bread belonged to him. The Germans believed the letter proved that Rens had been carrying a packet of 1,000 to 1,500 ration tickets for bread and a bundle of 5,000 French franc notes, which would make him look like either a black marketeer or a resister. Rens managed to talk his way out of both accusations.

After forty-five minutes the Germans remarked that all the rest of the prisoners were bandits, and asked how well he knew his companion. Rens replied that Lap was his superior in the putative supply office. They called in Lap, releasing him again fifteen minutes later. Lap's smile reassured Rens, "because Armand is very shrewd and very resourceful" (*très débrouillard*). The two "inspectors" were given back their papers and allowed to pick up their belongings from the floor. Rens was not surprised that their gold watch chain, cigarette case, and cigarettes were missing, "because," as he later put it, "those gentlemen are great thieves."

Announcing that they were taking them to be shot, the Germans pushed Rens and Lap out of the building and let them leave on foot. They fired into the air to scare the others. Days afterward Rens had trouble expressing how grateful they were to have escaped death. Had they been killed, it would not have been because of their very real resistance work against the Germans but simply by an unlucky coincidence and for the sake of a few cartridges on the floor of a taxi.

As they walked, their taxi drove by with some of the Germans in it. Rens hailed it and the Germans politely drove them the final twenty or so miles into Mâcon. The couriers took a train into Lyon the next evening. Traveling by train when possible and bicycle when it was not, they reached Collonges without trouble. Amy Mae Charpiot escorted them from the Adventist seminary down the hill toward the border, using her trick of signaling with her scarf when she saw a German patrol. Trying again a few hours later, they returned to Switzerland. Despite twelve days of exhausting and dangerous travel they had neither found Chait or Veerman nor reached Louvain.[2]

A postcard solved the mystery of what had happened to Veerman. He had left Switzerland in mid-June for the regular biweekly Swiss Way microfilm exchange. As usual he made the Dutch-Paris rounds to deliver money and messages. In Brussels, for instance, the banker Jacobus Verhagen gave him the names and birthdates of a Jewish family who were interned at a nearby transit camp to put on the exchange list for Palestine.[3] Soon afterward, on June 22, Veerman and Lejeune were walking from the gare du Nord to the gare de Luxembourg in Brussels in search of a functioning train connection to Paris. German plainclothes police, who were randomly inspecting the documents of men on the streets near the station, stopped them. They arrested Veerman because one of the numbers on his false documents had not been filled out correctly in Geneva. Lejeune, however, was still carrying his legitimate student identity documents from the University of Louvain. The police let him go after Veerman said they were not together.[4]

Veerman spent two days in a jail in Brussels without the Germans asking enough questions to discover that he was Jewish, let alone a resister. Like Wisbrun and the thousands of other men they had rounded up on the streets of Brussels, the German authorities sent him to the Third Reich as a forced laborer. Veerman made a break for freedom when they were already in Germany by leaping from a moving train, only to be recaptured yards from the Swiss border and spend the rest of the war in punishment prisons.[5] In July he sent a postcard to Rens's parents in Lausanne, telling them that he was with "other Belgian" workers. He signed it with one of his aliases, Paul Vermeer. With a purple 6-pfennig Hitler stamp and the censor's blue stripe across it, the postcard made it safely to Switzerland, where the Germans could take no measures against those who received it. His friends there could read between the lines that his arrest had nothing to do with Dutch-Paris.[6]

The postcard Veerman sent from a German prison.

Unbeknownst to Rens and Lap, their meeting with Mohr in mid-July would be the last contact between him and Dutch-Paris outside the concentration camps. German police arrested him at the Dutch Red Cross offices in Paris on July 18.[7] His detention appears to have been connected not to Dutch-Paris but to a woman from the Red Cross in The Hague who had been staying with the Mohrs until the previous day. She belonged to another escape line between the Netherlands and Switzerland. A Dutchman at the Dutch Chamber of Commerce whom she asked to get her false French documents gossiped about her to a Dutch collaborator, who told the Gestapo.[8]

Chait, on the other hand, remained at liberty and very busy with Dutch-Paris affairs. As he made his deliveries of cash and messages, he accommodated himself and his routes to the tensions and disruptions caused by the ongoing battles for the liberation of France and Belgium. His accounts show large purchases of cigarettes during that last summer of the occupation.[9] He may have used them as bribes or gifts to ease his way through borders and checkpoints.

While Rens and Lap had been looking for him in Lyon and Paris, Chait had been preparing another convoy to cross the Pyrenees. Unusually Dutch-Paris purchased the release of three Dutchmen from the Vichy internment camp at Noé through the intercession of the Quakers. On July 7 Chait gave his Quaker contact 10,000 French francs to pay for the release of the three prisoners and walked nearly ten miles in "crushing heat" to meet them at the local train station with food and clothing. He escorted them to a hiding place in the village of Cazères and went to fetch more Engelandvaarders from the north.[10]

Chait met two men in Brussels, a member of the Dutch national police force, the Marechaussée, and a member of a national resistance organization that protected people in hiding and their helpers, the Landelijke Knokploegen. He escorted them to Toulouse using his own slow, circuitous route through the battle zone in northern France. Two more Engelandvaarders arrived on their own from Switzerland: a Dutchman whom the ambassador sent to England to fulfill the mission that the *Milice* had stopped Weidner from carrying out, and a Belgian sent by his own embassy. These four plus the three men rescued from the camp at Noé left for Spain on July 17. While in the mountains the marechausée and the Dutch partisan elected to join the local *maquis* to fight the Germans instead of completing the trek to Spain.[11]

On his way to Lyon three days later, Chait made a quick trip to Nîmes, either to deliver cash to a resistance ally or to speak to Dutch refugees about leaving for Switzerland. Then he went to Switzerland for the first time during the occupation.[12] While he was there Chait and Weidner talked to the representative of the American Joint Distribution Committee, an American Jewish charity, on behalf of Benno Nijkerk's former colleagues at the Comité de Défense des Juifs in Brussels to beg him to send the money he had promised them.[13]

Chait left the safety of Geneva on August 6. Delayed by air raids and sabotage to the rail lines, he made his way by train, taxi, and bicycle to Lyon, Dijon, and Nancy, over the Belgian border and through the Ardennes, to arrive in Brussels twelve days later. Fear of what the Germans might do before they retreated gripped the city as Allied soldiers fought their way through southern Belgium. Chait expected to exchange microfilms for the Swiss Way, but Lejeune was in the Netherlands.

When he returned to Brussels on August 24, Lejeune was astonished to see his counterpart from Geneva. Radio messages from London had led him to believe that the Germans had captured Chait. He immediately sent the microfilms Chait had brought from Switzerland to Amsterdam, but had brought none himself. In fact he had sent the microfilms from earlier in the summer back to Amsterdam when no one had come to get them.

Meanwhile, on August 13, Lap left Geneva for what turned out to be the last mission to the north on General van Tricht's behalf. Lap rode his bicycle most of the way to Lyon but could get no farther. Mass arrests in nearby towns to the north, the lack of trains and buses, and the refusal of drivers to leave the city convinced Lap to heed several people's advice and turn around. On his way back he followed the longer route that took him slightly south and east to Chambéry before turning north to Annecy and Geneva.

At the Beauvoisin Bridge, Lap waited at the Hotel du Commerce for the Forces Françaises de l'Interieur commander of the *maquis*, the Armée Secrète, and other armed resisters in the region to advise him on the safest route through the mountains. The hotelkeeper asked him to offer moral support to an older Dutch Jew who took his meals there. As a representative of Dutch-Paris, Lap offered to pay the man's bill, but the hotelkeeper told him not to worry, he could pay after the war or not at all. The Dutch gentleman told Lap that Rens had loaned him money and two other men had come to check on him. He did not need money, but he did need documents to get back home to the Netherlands when the war ended. Lap promised to do whatever was necessary in Geneva.[14]

The courier continued his bicycle journey without any difficulties at the FFI checkpoints because they had been told he was coming. But German confiscations, arrests, and executions forced him to take shelter in a village outside Chambéry for two nights. On August 21 the road was safe enough for him to ride the twelve miles north through the mountains to Aix-les-Bains and then another twenty-five miles northeast to Annecy. Annecy had been liberated, which must have made a happy contrast to the bloodshed near Chambéry. Lap waited with Dutch-Paris friends at the Hotel Bel Abri for the local FFI commander to return to the prefecture to sign a safe conduct for him. No one doubted that he would get the pass: the secretary who filled them out had been helping Weidner for years. Lap pedaled back to Switzerland the next day, stopping at Cartier's uncle's farm along the way. Eleven days after he left Geneva, Lap returned without having accomplished most of his mission. He had delivered messages and money in Annecy and Lyon but had not managed to get any farther north, let alone to Belgium.

By this time the Allies had landed on the Mediterranean coast in Provence as well as Normandy. The German garrison in Paris surrendered on August 25, 1944. In Switzerland, Weidner worried about his imprisoned colleagues and the refugees and fugitives who depended on Dutch-Paris in occupied territory. What was happening to political prisoners in France during the German retreat and the turmoil of liberation? What would happen to the Dutch fugitives who would be free to come out of hiding when the Germans left but would not have valid identity documents in their true names or enough money?

Weidner, still under house arrest in Switzerland, proposed that he return to France himself in order to protect the interests of Dutch refugees and political prisoners there until an official representative of the Dutch government in exile arrived. The Dutch authorities in Bern agreed. In preparation Cartier used her connections with the French consulate in

Geneva to arrange documents and safe conducts for her husband in liberated France. Van Tricht asked the American and British military attachés
to issue safe conducts for Weidner for the war zone.[15] On September 8
an officer of the Armée Territoriale in Geneva, with whom Cartier had
worked on behalf of so many refugees, discreetly escorted Weidner over
the border. Two weeks later Swiss federal authorities, who had been investigating the letters denouncing Weidner, ordered his internment. He had
arranged his official *refoulement* and disappearance from Switzerland
just in time.[16]

On the French side of the border, Weidner encountered the Dutch-
Paris courier and guide Ernest Bouchet, who had joined the local *maquis*.
He took Weidner to their headquarters, where the *maquis* commander
put a car at his disposal to take him to Annecy. Later Bouchet saw Weidner
in the area in a car with "Mission Hollandais" written on the side in big
letters.[17] Weidner made his way to Paris, where he found the Dutch
consul-general, Ate Sevenster. Vichy officials had interned Sevenster in
December 1942, and Weidner had taken his daughters to Switzerland a
year later. Resisters liberated him and other diplomatic prisoners in late
August. Weidner gave Sevenster enough cash to resume his duties assisting Dutch citizens.[18]

The people Weidner most wanted to find, however, were his sister and
colleagues who had been arrested. But the Germans had already started
deporting their Dutch-Paris prisoners to the concentration camps in
April 1944, quite soon after their arrests and without trial.[19] The first to
be deported was Consul Maurice Jacquet, on April 6, followed twelve
days later by Suzanne Hiltermann, Anna Neyssel, Suzy Kraay, the concierge on the rue Lhomond Julia Prilliez, and the neighbor lady Marcelle
Brousse. More followed in May and June in small groups of between one
and four Dutch-Paris prisoners in larger convoys, without any obvious
pattern as to who was deported when.

Most of the remaining captured Dutch-Paris helpers were loaded onto
deportation trains in August 1944 in the final days of the German occupation of Paris. Lucie Comiti was deported on August 8, followed by
Jacqueline Houry and her mother three days later. A large group, including Marie Meunier from Annecy and, from Paris, Hermann Laatsman,
Jules Mohr, and Gabrielle Weidner, were locked into cattle cars and taken
east on August 15. Leo Mincowski followed three days later, and Baron

Jacob Brantsen was deported on August 20.[20] By that time the FFI was battling the Germans on the streets of Paris.

Only a handful of Dutch-Paris prisoners in France escaped deportation. Alice Charroin and Paul Lacôte, both of whom had been arrested by happenstance at Meunier's shop in Annecy, were released from Fresnes in mid-August because of illness. Catherine Okhuysen also was deemed too sick to be deported and was released through the intervention of the Swedish consul on August 19.[21] More dramatically the citizenry of Toulouse liberated Simone Calmels and other political prisoners from the city's prison of St. Michel that same day.[22]

As a Red Cross representative, Mohr had found out about a few of these deportations before his own arrest in July, but the whereabouts of some Dutch-Paris prisoners remained unknown. The occupation authorities did not notify the family when a prisoner of any status was transferred to another prison or out of the country. A few prisoners nonetheless managed to send messages. Raymonde Pillot got a message to her father while she was still incarcerated in Lyon and was later able to write a note on one of the small scraps of paper hidden by railway workers in the train that carried her to Germany. An unknown resister delivered it to her father.[23] The cobbler Gabriel Piveteau threw a message out of his deportation train in mid-June, which someone found and delivered to his family in Versailles.[24] Similarly Mohr dropped a note out of one of the last deportation trains to leave France. A stranger found it on the tracks and took it to his wife in Paris.[25]

A few deported prisoners whom the German authorities did not deem important enough to classify as incommunicado under the Nacht und Nebel decree were able to send postcards from the Third Reich. These were plain rectangles of white card stock. A prisoner could write on both sides, but only in German so the censors could read it. Brother Rufus sent one from a "salt mine in Austria" to his congregation on the rue Lhomond, which confirmed their worst fears about why they had not been able to take food to him at the prison of Fresnes since May.[26]

Nijkerk also managed to send a sign of life. Mohr had been able to locate him in Fresnes under a false name several weeks after he disappeared in Paris. No one knew anything else until September, when his cousin received a standard-issue postcard from "B. Smits" at Konsentrationslager Hamburg-Neuengamme. Nijkerk may have sent it to his cousin instead of his brother, who was also in Switzerland, in order to avoid any association between his assumed identity of "Bernard Smits" and the wanted resistance leader Benno Nijkerk. The cousin could tell who "B. Smits" really was because in bland, censored German Nijkerk sent greetings to a list of names that included those of his brother, wife, and infant son. He gave his regrets that he would miss his little boy's first birthday on September 30, 1944.[27]

There was very little that Weidner or anyone else could do for any prisoner once he or she was deported to the Third Reich. In October 1944 the International Committee of the Red Cross in Geneva officially requested that the German Red Cross send a delegate to visit Mohr in Buchenwald and to determine if he could receive packages. The response from the German Red Cross, which ended with "Heil Hitler!," was not encouraging.[28]

In Belgium, unlike in France, most Dutch-Paris prisoners escaped deportation. After David Verloop's suicide in March, they were not questioned again until July, and then without the earlier ferocity. Robert Bosschart reported being taken before a Luftwaffe tribunal. His fellow guide on the aviator escape line Jo Jacobstahl, however, was told to expect the death sentence without a trial.[29] In August the Dutchmen arrested at the rue Franklin were transferred from St-Gilles prison in Brussels to the prison camp at Beverloo, Belgium, but not taken out of the country.

Their Belgian landlady Lydia Ogy, on the other hand, followed the more usual trajectory of resistance prisoners. The Allied aviators captured at the rue Franklin heard that she had been executed in the prison of St-Gilles, just like the First World War heroine Edith Cavell. More emblematic of the Second World War, however, she had actually been deported to the concentration camp at Ravensbrück, where she perished in a makeshift gas chamber in January 1945.[30]

Why were the Dutchmen who were caught at the rue Franklin not deported to Germany? Henri Vleeschdrager ascribed the Dutch resisters' deliverance, including his own, to three factors: Verloop's death, infighting among German agencies, and "external influences."[31] However, Verloop's assumption of all responsibility may well have caused the Germans to stop torturing his colleagues, but it would not have stopped their deportation. The occupation authorities deported men and women to the concentration camps for the most minor infractions, including having the misfortune of being taken as a hostage. Being captured in the presence of Allied aviators should have guaranteed deportation, if not execution. Infighting among German agencies may indeed have played a part simply because it was so common, and the businessmen in the Comité may have found a way to play the military authorities in Belgium against the Nazi Party officials there.

By "outside influences" Vleeschdrager probably meant bribery. The young men who had been arrested in Brussels, some of whom were the sons of wealthy executives, belonged to a highly organized network of expatriates. The older generation in the Comité had the means and certainly the will to save their prisoners. In fact the fathers of two of the young men arrested on the rue Franklin and another member of the line worked through personal connections in Antwerp to do so. They would have followed every opportunity. One of the Comité's more resourceful members, Joseph Haenecour, reported that one of their contacts knew a German judge in Maastricht who would release prisoners for twenty pounds of real coffee.[32] During the occupation civilians drank various forms of ersatz coffee made of roasted chicory root and other ingredients. It would have taken a considerable sum and serious connections in the black market to get hold of twenty pounds of actual coffee. If the men looking out for Dutch-Paris's prisoners in Brussels could not find someone to bribe, they could hire lawyers to stall the case indefinitely.[33]

The same mysterious influences appear to have helped save Paul van Cleeff and the widow Petronella van Gellicum-Kamps from deportation as well. They had been arrested in November 1943 at a meeting with members of a separate escape line held at her home. A Luftwaffe court pronounced them all guilty in February 1944. But unlike their codefendants, who were deported, Van Cleeff and Van Gellicum-Kamps remained in custody in Belgium. Van Cleeff was transferred to Beverloo. In the final hours of the occupation Van Gellicum-Kamps was loaded onto the last deportation train to leave Brussels. Fortunately, Belgian railway workers managed to delay this last train of political prisoners and Allied airmen long enough for local officials to negotiate their release.[34]

British troops liberated Brussels that same evening, September 3. American soldiers liberated Maastricht on September 14. Members of the Dutch military government (Militair Gezag) arrived in Brussels from

London with the Allies. The war was not over, but it was safe for refugees and fugitives to come out of hiding in Brussels.

In recognition of the happy military situation, the banker Verhagen called a meeting of the Comité a few days after the liberation of Brussels. Chait attended, as did Pastor ten Kate, who had been released from prison without explanation in mid-August. Other former prisoners whom Allied troops had liberated from St-Gilles and Beverloo in early September also came. The helpers voted unanimously to turn over responsibility for the support of the four hundred or so people they had been hiding to the newly reestablished Dutch embassy in Brussels.[35] The following week the board submitted a "Report on the Activities of the Committee for the Support of Dutch War Victims in Belgium, 1942–1944."

As a member of the board, Edouard Regout held a dinner party for those who had worked with the Comité that last spring and summer. Finally they could introduce themselves by their real names and meet their colleagues.[36] The expatriate social club, the Nederlands Vereeniging, also held a liberation party, during which they toasted their political prisoners Ten Kate and Van Gellicum-Kamps. The wording suggests that members of the club had taken measures to protect them while they were in custody.[37]

After the celebrations many of the young people in the Comité continued the work they had done in the resistance; now, however, they were wearing Allied uniforms. Some pursued the fight against the Germans in the Dutch Princess Irene Brigade or as interpreters for the Americans or British. Others continued their rescue work in Allied welfare units. Hilde Jacobstahl, for example, joined the United Nations Relief and Rehabilitation Administration as a nurse.[38] Van Cleeff served as a liaison officer for the Netherlands Repatriation Mission.[39]

For his part Chait agreed to wait in Brussels to speak to Major Somers from the government in exile's intelligence service, but after almost three weeks he gave up waiting and left for Paris on September 22. It took him three

Jo Jacobstahl in the uniform of a Dutch repatriation unit, 1944.

days to get there. He arrived in Geneva without further incident two weeks later.[40] By that time Dutch-Paris had lost its raison d'être. The Netherlands below the River Maas, all of Belgium, and most of France had been liberated. Resisters from the still occupied north of Holland could now contact the queen's government by slipping through the German lines and crossing the river to reach the Allied lines. Dutch authorities no longer needed a clandestine courier service for microfilm through France and Belgium or an escape line across the Alps or the Pyrenees. Dutchmen could volunteer for military service without traveling to England. Likewise Jews and other fugitives whom Dutch-Paris had been supporting could emerge from hiding because their persecutors had retreated into Germany.

Weidner and his colleagues still had some responsibilities toward the families of prisoners and refugees, but these could be fulfilled openly and were quickly shifting into bureaucratic tasks. Weidner did what he could for his colleagues who had escaped deportation, many of whom left prison ill or at least malnourished. He gave them back pay for their monthly stipend to cover the time spent in prison so they could buy new clothes and pay for rent and the like. If they were sick, he gave them money for doctors and medicine. If necessary he used his personal funds to address their immediate needs.[41]

The government in exile, however, had another use for Weidner. In November 1944 he flew to London for a private audience with Queen Wilhelmina and a meeting with Prime Minister Gerbrandy. At their request he wrote reports on the situation of Dutch citizens in Belgium and France and the work of his resistance group. Weidner left London as a captain in the Dutch Army, with orders to establish and run the Netherlands Security Service in Paris and to disband his resistance organization.

The Netherlands Security Service, also called the Bureau de rencensement néerlandais (Dutch Census Bureau) and Bureau Nationale Veiligheid, Bureau IIIA (Bureau of National Security, section IIIA), had the delicate task of vetting all Dutch nationals in France and Belgium to unmask any collaborators trying to pass themselves off as refugees or resisters. Anyone applying for a Dutch passport in France or Belgium needed clearance from the Netherlands Security Service. Weidner staffed it with men he knew or knew of from Dutch-Paris, either his resistance colleagues, such as Rens and Chait, or men they had helped get to Switzerland, such as

André Eliasar. They drew their supplies, including two jeeps, fuel and maintenance for the jeeps, tickets to the mess and PX, and typewriters, from the American Army.[42]

At the same time that they investigated suspected Dutch collaborators, Weidner and his lieutenants used their position as the Netherlands Security Service to look after the interests of Dutch-Paris. According to Weidner's instructions, that included seeing to the health and well-being of their resistance colleagues or their survivors; discharging any debts, such as loans contracted to pay the allotments to people in hiding; and making sure their colleagues were acknowledged as resisters. Such recognition brought very practical benefits, including food packages and medical care. Weidner took this part of his orders as a solemn duty laid upon him as the *chef du réseau* (network chief) and fulfilled it for the rest of his life. He also assisted several Dutch and Swiss men and women whom he knew had been resisters in other networks but who had no *chef du réseau* to represent them.[43]

Weidner, Rens, and Chait used their rank and their jeeps to interview helpers who knew the details of what had happened during the occupation and to look for Dutch-Paris deportees. For the most part, however, they had to wait for the Allied armies to liberate the concentration camps and bring the political prisoners home in the spring of 1945.[44] Veerman returned to the southern Netherlands on April 17. Of the Dutch-Paris prisoners who had been arrested for their resistance work, Laatsman was the first to return, arriving in Paris on April 28. He had a harrowing story to tell of his arrest, torture, deportation journey, and incarceration in Buchenwald, Dora, and Bergen-Belsen.[45] It could not have reassured those who were waiting for others to return.

Laatsman was understandably anxious about his teenage son, whom he had last seen in the prison of Fresnes more than a year earlier and who had disappeared in Amsterdam in March 1945. Desperate to make sense of things, Laatsman had also come to an erroneous conclusion about who had betrayed Dutch-Paris, one that was based on incomplete and circumstantial observations and that resulted in his accusing an innocent person. It took Weidner many months and quite a lot of written evidence to convince Laatsman to drop his demands that this person be punished.

Dutch-Paris women who had been sent to Ravensbrück began to return to Paris in May 1945. A month earlier the Swedish Red Cross

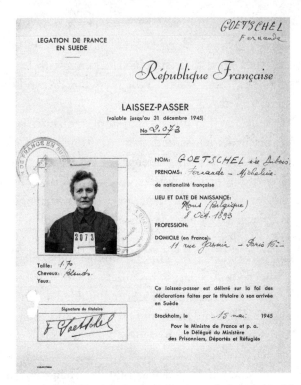

The safe conduct passes used by Fernande Goetschel and Madeleine Larose-Reinaud to return to France from Sweden.

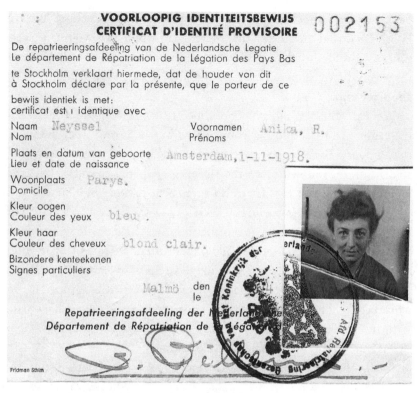

VOORLOOPIG IDENTITEITSBEWIJS
CERTIFICAT D'IDENTITÉ PROVISOIRE   002153

De repatrieeringsafdeeling van de Nederlandsche Legatie
Le département de Répatriation de la Légation des Pays Bas

te Stockholm verklaart hiermede, dat de houder van dit
à Stockholm déclare par la présente, que le porteur de ce

bewijs identiek is met:
certificat est i identique avec

Naam   Neyssel   Voornamen   Anika, R.
Nom   Prénoms

Plaats en datum van geboorte   Amsterdam, 1-11-1918.
Lieu et date de naissance

Woonplaats   Parys.
Domicile

Kleur oogen
Couleur des yeux   bleu .

Kleur haar
Couleur des cheveux   blond clair.

Bizondere kenteekenen
Signes particuliers

Malmö   den
        le

Repatrieeringsafdeeling der Nederla...
Département de Répatriation de la léga...

Fridman Sthlm

Temporary identity papers issued to Anna Neyssel after her rescue from Ravensbrück.

negotiated the release of seven thousand western European women from that notorious concentration camp and drove them to safety in the famous white buses. The women received medical care in Sweden and returned home when they were strong enough for the journey.[46]

But not all Dutch-Paris women were still at Ravensbrück when the white buses arrived. Gabrielle Weidner, for example, had been transferred to one of its subcamps, Klein Konigsberg, near Koningsberg-am-Oder, about forty-seven miles northeast of Berlin in what is now Poland.[47] Already sick when she arrived, she was in and out of what passed as an infirmary there. When the German guards started deserting the camp at the end of January 1945, some of the prisoners left. Others risked being shot by the remaining guards in order to get food from the storehouse. In early February SS soldiers returned to the camp, throwing grenades into the cell blocks and machine-gunning inmates to force the remaining prisoners to leave with them. When they stormed into the infirmary to demand that the sick prisoners also start marching westward, a brave Polish nurse told the SS men that they all had typhus. The Germans, who generally dreaded such diseases, allowed the women to remain. None of them could have survived the forced march through the winter cold to another camp.

Very early the next morning, hours before dawn, the Russians attacked the camp. Gabrielle and her companions watched from the window of the infirmary. To their great joy, they were woken up the next day by Soviet soldiers. In the following days the Soviets gave them rice and slaughtered animals for them to eat. They also gave them mattresses, blankets, and pillows and buried those who had been shot by the SS or who had died of their illnesses. That Sunday the former prisoners held a community worship service, something the SS had not permitted. Despite being in good spirits, Gabrielle never recovered enough strength to leave the infirmary. She died there within days of being liberated. Her friends wrapped her in a blanket and buried her between a Polish woman and a French woman, with more dignity than she would have received under the SS.[48] No official record was made of her death or burial.

Comiti had also passed through Ravensbrück but spent most of her captivity as a slave laborer in a factory connected to the minor concentration camp of Apteroda. At the end of February 1945 all the slaves there were transferred to Buchenwald because of the Soviet advance. On April 13 Comiti left Buchenwald on one of the infamous death marches. The exhausted inmates walked for ten long days "almost without rest and without food." On the tenth day Comiti and four others escaped from the column and "after many difficulties" met up with some French POWs. Their compatriots gave them uniforms to wear so they could sneak into their POW camp, where at least they had a roof over their heads and something to eat. But the French soldiers were also forced to evacuate their camp. Comiti marched an entire night under "a battering rain" but was liberated the next day, May 7, by American troops.[49] Pillot, who had been sent from Ravensbrück to a different subcamp, was also liberated by American soldiers that day.[50]

In all, thirteen Dutch-Paris resisters returned to Paris from the concentration camps between April 28 and July 20.[51] News of deaths in the camps arrived slowly and mostly through the goodwill of survivors. At government welcome centers, deportees were asked what had happened

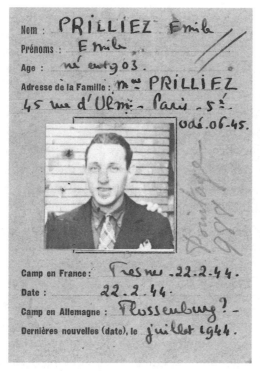

Nom : PRILLIEZ Emile
Prénoms : Emile
Age : né en 1903.
Adresse de la Famille : m.me PRILLIEZ
45 rue d'Ulm - Paris - 5e.
odé.06-45.

Camp en France : Fresnes .22.2.44.
Date : 22.2.44.
Camp en Allemagne : Flossenburg ? –
Dernières nouvelles (date), le juillet 1944.

Missing persons card filled out for Emile Prilliez.

in the concentration camps, whom they had seen there, and whom they had seen die. The Dutch Red Cross used this information to trace missing persons. Families and friends also posted notices at reception centers or town halls or ran newspaper ads asking about an individual. Many deportees felt an obligation to tell families about the deaths of their companions in the camps.

But it could take determination and a lot of paperwork and luck to discover what happened to someone who disappeared in the Third Reich. After Weidner found out that Marie Meunier had died in Ravensbrück in February 1945, he wrote to several women who returned from there until he found someone who could tell him about her death. Her friends felt that the immediate cause was "internal pains" that she suffered from a beating by camp guards. But at age fifty-four it would have been hard for her to withstand the starvation, exposure, and slave labor of Ravensbrück even without the beatings.[52]

Even Weidner, with his military, police, and resistance connections, could not get solid information about his own sister. Although the family learned of her death from another deportee quite early, in April 1945, they did not know the details until 1947. At that time Weidner placed an ad in a French newspaper asking for information about the location of Gabrielle's grave. One of her companions in misfortune wrote to him with the story of his sister's final days.[53]

Some families were unable to get any news at all about their deported prisoner. Even with the reports of survivors and the efforts of the Red Cross and other welfare agencies, several factors made it difficult to find a missing person. The transfer of prisoners, the death marches between camps, and the bombings all meant that prisoners simply disappeared without proper notice being taken of their deaths. As long as there was no news of a death, there was hope that the prisoner was in a hospital somewhere or waiting for the Soviets to repatriate him or her. Notification of a death could take some time to arrive, even when the prisoner died in an Allied hospital from an illness contracted while an inmate of a concentration camp. The wife of the proprietor of Suzy Kraay's hotel in Paris, for example, was still filling out missing persons forms for her husband in August 1945 without knowing that he had died at the end of June.[54]

When Hiltermann returned from Ravensbrück via Sweden in July 1945, she found the list of aviators and supplies for making false documents that she and Mincowski had hidden in their apartment, but she could not find Mincowski. Another deportee told her that he had seen Mincowski near Ebensee after their liberation, but that was the only trace. In January 1946 one French bureau wrote to another requesting information about Mincowski on her behalf. But it appears that she never did know what happened to him. In fact Mincowski was officially listed as *disparu* (missing) until 1948. Three years after the war, a rumor in their Parisian neighborhood led his wife to a deportee who had witnessed Mincowski's death in Buchenwald in April 1945. It is not known whether she shared the information with any of his former colleagues in Dutch-Paris.[55]

Nijkerk also vanished in the Third Reich. His wife and brother searched for him through their private connections and every available public office in the Netherlands, Belgium, and France. In August 1945 they succeeded in finding a French deportee who had known "Bernard Smits" in the concentration camps and could describe with confidence and in great detail why Nijkerk must have died in a bombing raid around November 1944. Weidner found this convincing enough to issue a notice of his death in November 1945.

Unfortunately, around the same time the Dutch Foreign Ministry notified Nijkerk's wife that they had received a telegram from the embassy in Moscow telling them that the Soviets had turned a deportee named "B. Nijkerk" over to the Allies on October 28, 1945. She waited, but he did not come home. Weidner and the family launched a new round of inquiries. It was not until August 1946 that the Soviet Ministry of Foreign Affairs sent a note acknowledging that they had misspelled the name of the deportee who had been handed over to the Allies the previous year. It was not Benno Nijkerk. Finally a Belgian court declared Nijkerk to be legally deceased in 1950, six years after his presumed death in the bombing raid.[56] Similarly the Caubo children were not able to get the death certificate that they needed to close their father's estate until 1948, three years after learning of his death. It might have taken even longer if the children's uncle and Weidner had not been so unrelenting in their efforts to settle the children's affairs.[57]

In addition to aiding his resistance colleagues and their families, Weidner deployed his position as commanding officer of the Netherlands Security Service until early 1946 and his status as *chef du réseau* of an officially recognized Resistance network to contribute to the postwar purge of collaborators who had harmed Dutch-Paris. He shared information with the French prosecutor in charge of the purge trials of the French policemen who arrested Kraay and turned her over to the Germans. He even testified against the men at their trial. They were convicted of collaboration by the Cour de Justice in October 1945 but amnestied in 1951.

The Caubo twins also testified in a purge trial, this time of the police agents who arrested their family, leading to their father's deportation and death. The policemen were executed.[58] Similarly Jo Jacobstahl reported that he had caused the arrest of two of the Germans who interrogated and tortured him and his colleagues from the rue Franklin.[59] In Toulouse Marie Combes, who escorted Engelandvaarders from the city to the foothills, accused a neighbor of denouncing her based on the public rumor surrounding her arrest at the end of 1943 and subsequent deportation. The court found the neighbor not guilty of that particular crime.[60]

In his dealings with the French purge, Weidner wanted justice rather than vengeance. He wrote a character testimonial for the younger of the two *Miliciens* who had helped him and Rens when they were in prison in Toulouse in May 1944. That young man and five others from his *Milice* unit had been convicted of collaboration and sentenced to death. Weidner's letter may have influenced the judge's decision to commute the young *Milicien*'s sentence to hard labor for life. Weidner could not write a similar letter for the older of the two men. His superior officer had blamed the man for Weidner and Rens's escape and had him deported. Other inmates in the concentration camp recognized him as a *Milicien*, held a kangaroo court, and hanged him.[61]

Altogether, including those caught in the roundups in February and March 1944, couriers swept up in street raids, and individuals taken in for questioning for more than one night, eighty-two men and women of Dutch-Paris were arrested during the war. Sixteen of them were tortured. Some forty-nine were deported to the concentration camps because of Dutch-Paris. Twenty-seven died because of German mistreatment. Several of those who survived the concentration camps died young because their health had been irrevocably undermined in the camps. More than one suffered from nightmares or other psychological discomforts as a result of his or her illegal work in the resistance. Some returned home to empty apartments, stripped bare by German agents after their arrest.

These numbers are minimum estimates. Some names were undoubtedly lost in the concentration camps when Dutch-Paris helpers died. Meunier, for example, may well have recruited other helpers without telling anyone their names in order to protect them. If they did not speak up on their own behalf, there would have been no one to acknowledge them. In addition German police cast their nets very wide in the Dutch-Paris roundup, but the records proving how wide are missing. We do not know how many people who assisted on the peripheries without belonging to Dutch-Paris, such as the grocer in Lyon and the cobbler in Versailles, were arrested and deported. Nor do we know how many of the line's resistance allies, such as the Dutch policeman who hid the Jewish family whom Kraay took to Switzerland, were arrested because of their contact with Dutch-Paris.

Weidner himself contributed to the confusion in his postwar reports. For example, he included the men and women arrested in a hotel in Paris in March 1944 among the victims of the Dutch-Paris roundup even though they did not belong to the line. He may have done this because the French investigator gave him undocumented reason to believe that the two were connected. Or he may have done it because those arrests would not otherwise have been included in postwar court cases. He also put concentration camp survivors and the widows and orphans of resisters from other networks on the Dutch-Paris rolls so they could claim the benefits to which they were due but for which they would not have been able to apply without the sponsorship of a recognized Resistance network.

At the end of his Liberation-era research as head of the Netherlands Security Service and *chef du réseau*, Weidner concluded that Dutch-Paris helped 1,500 persons escape occupied territory and supported 1,500 persons in hiding, 500 of them in Belgium. In addition Dutch-Paris couriers crossed borders clandestinely 1,000 times in Belgium and 750 times in France.[62] He reflected, "This work and its results have cost us blood and tears."[63] Was it worth it?

In his November 1944 report to Queen Wilhelmina, Weidner wrote, "We have held the honor of the Netherlands high whenever it was possible by doing what we could for our country and our countrymen." The men and women of Dutch-Paris had, they believed, contributed to the ultimate defeat of Nazism by returning Allied aircrew to their bases and taking Engelandvaarders to Spain so they could volunteer for the Allied armies. More important, they had defied Nazi racism and hatred by rescuing people whom the Nazis intended to kill, thereby defending the dignity of all human beings. Despite the years of fear, the deprivation, even the torture and imprisonment, they believed they had fought the good fight and upheld *een rechtvaardige zaak* (a righteous cause).[64]

When she returned from torture at the rue de Saussaies, imprisonment at Fresnes, deportation in cattle cars, exactly one year of punitive slavery at Ravensbrück, and three months of recuperation in Sweden, Suzanne Hiltermann concluded about the Germans, "Everything I saw in the camp made me very glad to have worked against them."[65]

Americans at the liberation of St-Julien-en-Genevois on the Swiss border, August
1944.

Conclusion

The Helper's Courage

THE BREADTH OF ITS OPERATIONS, the diversity of its tasks, and the extent of its social network give Dutch-Paris a privileged place in the history of the Second World War. The line operated across four borders and two mountain ranges, using five currencies and three languages in six occupation zones, each of which required different identity documents and travel passes. Its members hid Jewish families in Belgium and France or escorted them to Switzerland while also guiding political opponents of the Nazis, Engelandvaarders, and Allied airmen to Spain. At the same time they relayed microfilms between the Dutch Resistance and the London Dutch as a link in the Swiss Way and acted as a clandestine courier service for a number of individuals, underground organizations, and humanitarian aid workers. They also gathered intelligence collected by others as well as from their own observations while crisscrossing the occupied territory between the Netherlands and the neutral countries of Switzerland and Spain.

The 330 men and women who risked their lives as part of Dutch-Paris came from different nations, religions, political opinions, and social classes. Many of them did not even share a common language. They earned their livings as businessmen, shopkeepers, farmers, customs officers, translators, railway supervisors, civil servants, clergy, and teachers. Many were university students. Just as many were housewives or widows.

When the war began all of them were leading ordinary lives. Nothing particularly set them apart among the general population or suggested that out of the millions of people living in the Netherlands, Belgium, and France these few hundred would ever belong to the same organization, let alone an illegal one. Under German occupation they had to find ways to cope with the same shortages of food, fuel, and clothing that plagued all civilians' daily lives. Like everyone else, they had to show their documents on street corners, in public transportation, and at borders. Like everyone else, they rode in crowded trains that were targets for aerial bombardment or sabotage. Their mail and telephone calls, like everyone else's, were censored and monitored. The young men in the group were just as likely to be rounded up off the streets of Brussels and sent to Germany as slave labor as any other young men. In fact that was the fate of two of them, Hans Wisbrun and Paul Veerman. And yet somehow these few individuals found the courage and resources to resist by protecting the persecuted.

Inevitably, in the context of the time, protecting the persecuted meant compromising their prewar standards of behavior. Now they had to lie as a matter of course. The guides and couriers among them gained a considerable amount of experience in bluffing their way past police inspectors of all sorts. Three of them jumped out of the upper-story windows of a prison. One of them regularly sidled along the outside of a bridge covered with barbed wire.

But the men and women of Dutch-Paris did not court danger. They tried to stay within the law, even if only by exploiting the loopholes. For example, they determined which evenings the police did not usually inspect passengers' documents on the night train from Paris to Toulouse and sent their convoys south on those days. Once Weidner learned that foreigners were banned from the Haute-Savoie except for medical reasons, he obtained legitimate passes for Jews to travel through the restricted zone to spas near the Swiss border for the treatment of fictitious ailments. In Brussels the Comité tot Steun voor Nederlandsche Oorlogschlachtoffers in België (Committee for the Support of Dutch War Victims in Belgium), known as the Comité, took full advantage of the provision allowing Dutch citizens to transfer a small sum of money to Belgium each month.

When it was not possible to stay within the law, they skirted it while staying as close to the edge as possible. The line's leaders—Jean Weidner, Edmond Chait, and Jacques Rens—circulated almost constantly in the guise of businessmen. They bought first-class train tickets and berths in sleeping cars. They even deposited 1,000 Belgian francs with Belgian officials as required when leaving the country, although they did so under false names. The courier Raymonde Pillot moved constantly between Lyon and Annecy on business for Weidner's two shops in those towns, though the nature of her job had changed radically, from selling textiles to saving lives. They also camouflaged groups of young men of military age among the mass of legitimate passengers by disguising them as contract laborers on their way to work for the Germans in the mines and forests of the Pyrenees.

Nevertheless Dutch-Paris's primary goal of protecting fugitives from the occupation authorities as well as their later tasks of smuggling documents and aiding and abetting enemy soldiers were indisputably illegal. Every time they transferred large sums of currency without filling out the proper paperwork or falsified someone's identity they broke the law. And they did it in a remarkably businesslike fashion.

Like the good businessmen that many of them were, they kept track of and limited their expenses. Circumstances may have forced them to engage in the black market, but they refused to pay exorbitant prices themselves or allow the refugees under their protection to do so. As men with international trade experience, the line's managers also pursued a policy of seeking out relationships with other groups and accepting opportunities. They welcomed alliances with other like-minded people no matter where they fell on the political or religious spectrum. In Brussels, for instance, the Comité invited men to join the board who belonged to the Left-leaning Front de l'Indépendance as well as men who belonged to the Right-leaning Mouvement National Royaliste. Weidner was himself an Adventist, though he took money to ministers of other churches for Pastor Visser 't Hooft at the World Council of Churches and gladly sought the cooperation of Catholics. For his part, Chait established connections with an array of aid organizations and resistance groups, such as the Quakers, the Red Cross, and the underground Comité de Défense des Juifs.

The men and women of Dutch-Paris drew the line at carrying weapons but were otherwise remarkably flexible about what they would and could do. They started by helping Jews because, at that time and place, those were the people who needed help. When other people needed to escape occupied territory, they helped them to do so. It did not matter to them if the fugitive was a child of a Resistance leader in danger of being taken as a hostage or an Allied airman shot down by the Luftwaffe. Nor did it matter if fugitives found the line themselves or through one of Dutch-Paris's many allies. The fact that two-thirds of the people they helped had some connection to the Netherlands derived entirely from the ways that people could ask for and find help under the occupation. As Weidner said, the helpers in Dutch-Paris did not see Dutchmen. They saw human beings.[1]

He and his colleagues responded to requests for other types of help as well. Sometimes their contacts among the clandestine world of resistance needed a way to get someone to safety, but sometimes they needed a way to get something across or out of occupied territory. Many other people gave Dutch-Paris couriers intelligence reports of all sorts to take to the Allies or the governments in exile. These ranged from directions for dropping weapons for *maquisards* to eyewitness accounts of atrocities and reports on public health. Doing so helped the Allies, of course, but it also strengthened Dutch-Paris by creating bonds of cooperation.

In effect, Dutch-Paris served as a clandestine courier and guide service for the occupied territories of the Netherlands, Belgium, and France with pathways to the unoccupied lands of Switzerland and Spain. As such it linked together a shadow, transnational community that stood in opposition to the official New Order that Hitler imposed by force.

Why did these otherwise ordinary men and women risk their lives to oppose Nazism and the German occupation? Several decades after the war, political scientists and psychologists interviewed rescuers of Jews about their motives. Generally speaking, they concluded that rescuers had an "altruistic personality" and considered themselves members of the human race rather than of any narrower grouping. Many rescuers thought of themselves as too ordinary and their actions as too normal to be worth mentioning.[2]

Historians have rarely had enough documentary evidence to draw any conclusions on the subject. Indeed very few members of Dutch-Paris explained why they joined the line, if only because no one asked them that question for any of the reports or documents written at the end of the war. Most considered their reasons either too unimportant or too obvious to include in their own summaries of their resistance activities.

In hindsight, three members of the line offered some reasons for their resistance. In 1945 the Dutchman Joseph Haenecour wrote that he had always been vehemently anti-German because of the suffering that his grandmother and aunt endured under the German occupation of Belgium in the First World War. As the son of an officer he felt obliged to act during this war.[3] In an interview almost fifty years after the event, Raymonde Pillot also mentioned the First World War to partly explain why she had resisted: three of her brothers were killed in the trenches, and her fourth brother was killed in the campaign of 1939–40. In addition Pillot felt that she had a duty as a Christian to help the persecuted.[4]

Jean Weidner too had a deep sense of his resistance work as a Christian obligation. Indeed he felt that God's direct protection enabled him to do that work. Patriotism also played a role. Speaking on behalf of all his colleagues in November 1944, Weidner wrote in his official report to Queen Wilhelmina that relaying messages, hiding Jews, and guiding fugitives to safety had cost them blood and tears, but they were supported by their faith in a just cause and in the liberation of their country.[5]

The political scientist Jacques Semelin describes the process of engagement as a "tipping into disobedience."[6] A resister slid further and further into disillusionment until finally seizing the opportunity for action when it arrived. That describes Weidner's own path. He worked legally on behalf of refugees and belonged to a Christian charity that assisted refugees, but it was not until he received a direct request for help from a fugitive that he and Elisabeth Cartier started the escape line between Lyon and Geneva.[7] Their disobedience evolved in reaction to Vichy's policies. The more persecutory French laws became, the further the two slid into illegality.[8] Some newcomers to the group received a more formal invitation than others, but every single man and woman had to make the choice of whether or not to leave behind the apparent safety of self-preservation and act.

For those who were cast outside of legal society by the Nazi racial laws and the occupation laws, that choice presented itself more clearly than for others, but even they could have taken a safer path than resistance. Jo Jacobstahl and his sister Hilde, for example, were stateless German Jews. Paul van Cleeff and Henri Vleeschdrager had escaped from the deportation train carrying them to Auschwitz. They could not stay in their homes and go about their everyday lives. But, like all of the other Jews in the line, including Edmond Chait, Benno Nijkerk, Philip Polak, Jetta Pool, and Hans Wisbrun, they had the option to hide or go to Switzerland but rejected it. Others in the line, including Ernest Bouchet, had disobeyed orders to report for work in the Third Reich. They too could have gone into hiding but chose to actively resist instead.

Most of the men and women in Dutch-Paris, however, were neither Jews nor fugitives from the forced labor laws. They could have followed the lead of the overwhelming majority of their neighbors and focused on their own survival and that of their families. After all, the occupation authorities did not persecute young Dutch women like Suzanne Hiltermann and Catherine Okhuysen if they followed the rules. Nor did they usually pay attention to respectable older widows like Fernande Goetschel and Petronella van Gellicum-Kamps. Long before any one of them helped a single fugitive, they had all rejected the sudden imposi-tion of tyranny in their formerly democratic countries. When the victo-rious German Army established occupation regimes run by Nazis and their collaborators, they and all civilians lost their civil liberties and many of their human rights. While most of their neighbors adjusted to the times, the men and women of Dutch-Paris stubbornly maintained the habits of free citizens, such as thinking for themselves and interact-ing with strangers.[9]

They did not accept the slogans and whitewash of propaganda but searched for the facts and judged them against the standard of truth as they knew it rather than as the Nazis defined it. For instance, the Germans and their collaborators might have said they were deporting Jewish men, women, and children for resettlement in the East, but Weidner and his colleagues knew better. Even though it was forbidden, they listened to the BBC and Swiss Radio and read the underground press instead of the of-ficial propaganda outlets. They talked to people. They observed with their own eyes and drew their own conclusions. They knew that the human beings being herded into trains were on their way to Poland to die. And because they believed in the age-old truth that murder is wrong rather than the new-fangled explanations of Nazi propaganda, they had enough conviction to act.

The members of Dutch-Paris also maintained the social habits of free men and women. They did not sink into their own shells, as the pervasive fear and daily effort to find food led most people to do. Instead they kept in touch with friends and family even when the mail was censored and, at times, prohibited across international borders. They looked others in the eye and made small talk. Weidner even chatted with German officers he met on trains. That was how he and his colleagues found out useful information and, in a few cases, how they recruited new members.

Being friendly in the way that people had been before the war served them all well, especially Chait, who had every reason to be afraid during the occupation. His mother and sisters were deported to Auschwitz. He himself was arrested on the street in Lyon and spent several weeks in a French prison on the grounds that he was a foreign Jew. After that he constantly broke the laws of several countries while carrying incriminating papers. The safety of many people depended on him. If he had been caught with the list of the names and hiding places of Jewish children in Brussels, all those children would have been caught as well. And yet his colleagues in Dutch-Paris adored him for his sense of fun. It was Chait who gave his young colleagues in Toulouse a way to think of their very dangerous conspiracy as an adventure by calling the aviator hideout the "Villa du Crime." And it was Chait who always knew where to get good food no matter how severe the shortages and invited his colleagues to dinners of lighthearted fellowship.

There is no doubt that Chait's gift for personal connection helped him avoid arrest during all the long months that he circulated through occupied territory. Indeed mundane friendliness cast a safety net of goodwill around everyone in Dutch-Paris. Small talk among strangers crowded together in a bus or standing in a line or anywhere else in public builds fellow feeling. It protected the men and women of Dutch-Paris many times when a stranger warned one of them that he was walking into a Gestapo trap or a German search on the other side of a border. Consider the elderly lady who took the Engelandvaarder Rudy Zeeman's arm on a street in Paris so that he could pass unnoticed by the Wehrmacht officers from whom he had just escaped. Would she have done that if she lived shut up in her own worries, isolated from the people around her?

Most important, the men and women of Dutch-Paris found the courage within themselves to stand out among the crowd. Like all resisters, they took risks to defend the values of democracy at a time when the fearful majority let those values go. Armed resisters fought the foreign invader. Intellectual resisters risked torture and death for the sake of intellectual freedoms. Other resisters conspired to bring civil liberties back to their countries. Rescuers and helpers put themselves in danger for the sake of human rights.

The men and women of Dutch-Paris and all of its allies shared a common belief that the laws enforced by the occupation authorities and their collaborators did not reflect natural justice or basic morality, let alone decency. On the contrary, those laws were being used to commit injustices. For the sake of justice, they acted outside the law, voluntarily becoming outlaws. As the messengers between these many circles, Dutch-Paris spread the culture of the outlaw from rural areas where villages supported *maquis* bands into the cities of Belgium and France.[10]

As the couriers and guides of this imagined community of resistance, the men and women of Dutch-Paris subverted the extremely nationalistic political order of the day on both the practical and theoretical levels.[11] On the workaday plane they denied the prerogatives of the nation-state every time they forged an official document, transferred money without following the proper procedures, and slipped over an international border without having their passports stamped. In fact, from their perspective, they redrew the map of western Europe, from a collection of nation-states into a simple dichotomy of occupied and unoccupied territory.

Yet they went beyond flouting the laws of the day to reject the fundamental concept on which the Nazis and their collaborators claimed legitimacy. Nazism was based on the assumption that biology determined nations as well as the characteristics and place of the men and women who belonged to each nation. According to Nazi ideology, Aryan Germans were superior to all other ethnicities and therefore the natural overlords of all other ethnic nations. Nazis scorned democratic ideas such as equality and human rights. They did not shy from using violence to implement their radically nationalist vision of society.

Under Nazi domination the nation-state failed to uphold human rights. That fell to the outlaws in the resistance. The men and women of Dutch-Paris defended human rights every time they helped a person for the straightforward reason that he or she was a human being in need of help. These otherwise ordinary people stood up to violent oppression without resorting to violence. With every refugee and fugitive they protected and every link they forged between like-minded resisters and helpers across international borders, Dutch-Paris built a moral alternative to Hitler's New Order.

The men and women of Dutch-Paris were ordinary before the war but remarkable during it because they refused to accept what passed for

Edmond Chait, Jean Weidner, Paul Veerman, Elisabeth Cartier, and André Eliasar in the Netherlands, 1948.

"ordinary" during the occupation. It became ordinary under the occupation for individuals to withdraw into self-imposed isolation. Civilians focused on surviving. They did not make eye contact with strangers for fear of attracting attention to themselves or even of seeing something that might make their consciences uncomfortable. This attitude bolstered the regime's power and made it easier to carry out its agenda.

Suzanne Hiltermann and daughter in 1946.

It became "ordinary" under the occupation for Jewish men, women, and children to be separated from their fellow citizens, impoverished, imprisoned, and deported to their deaths. It became "ordinary" for young men to work in slave-like conditions on behalf of Hitler's war effort. The usual response to such events was to look away or to think that somebody else should do something about them. At that time, with the Gestapo and collaborators watching for dissent, ordinary people did not break the law to help a stranger. They did not risk trouble for themselves or their families.

The men and women of Dutch-Paris, on the other hand, did chat with strangers. They did voluntarily put themselves at risk to help others. They stepped up to defend the dignity and value of every human being when the government failed to do so. That defense cost all of them their respectability, even if it preserved their moral integrity. They had to learn to lie to almost everyone, to forge official documents, and to sneak around the law and its officers. The authorities of the time considered the members of Dutch-Paris to be criminals and traitors. Some of them were tortured and some died because they refused to accept the Nazis' new definitions of right and wrong.

And then, after the war, the survivors went back to their ordinary, respectable lives in their restored democracies. The time for their heroism ended when the postwar governments reestablished human rights. And so the men and women of Dutch-Paris were both ordinary people and great heroes. They stand as an inspiration to us all.

Appendix I

List of Dutch-Paris Members

Even though this list represents every member of Dutch-Paris whose name appears in the archival documents, it is probably incomplete. Some people who played minor roles were undoubtedly forgotten after the war because the person they helped did not survive the concentration camps to tell anyone else what they did. In other cases resisters themselves may not have survived the war and no one knew their real name to record it.

The list includes individuals whom the leaders recognized as members of the organization. A few individuals played a critical role in a group that later joined Dutch-Paris but were arrested before the merger. For example, Maurice Bolle and A. G. B. ten Kate created the Comité that joined Weidner's new organization in October 1943. Bolle was arrested before then, in July 1943, but there would not have been a Comité to join Dutch-Paris without him. The category of Resistance allies includes men and women who belonged to other organizations but worked closely with Dutch-Paris, mostly on the evasion of Allied airmen. It also includes a small number of men and women who were not resisters but whom German police arrested during the roundups of Dutch-Paris, imprisoned, and deported to the concentration camps because they considered them to be members of Dutch-Paris.

Many other men and women made contributions of one sort or another, such as food, information, or silence, without being members of Dutch-Paris. Jean Weidner considered someone who spontaneously helped a fugitive out of common decency to be a good person, but not a resister. A resister made a conscious and premeditated effort to help the persecuted despite obvious risks. And a resister did not profit from helping others. Landladies who rented rooms to Jews, for example, ran a risk and made it possible for those persecuted individuals to survive, but if they charged enough money to make the risk worthwhile, then the leadership of Dutch-Paris did not consider them to be resisters.

Although many of the men and women in Dutch-Paris moved around and performed many tasks, the list categorizes them by their resistance home base and main job. The categories have been vastly simplified into leadership; couriers, guides, and border crossings; postboxes; shelter; and supplies. Toulouse includes the additional category of *passeurs* and their assistants to accommodate the French *filières* on which Dutch-Paris relied to get Engelandvaarders and aviators over the Pyrenees. It includes only the members of those *filières* who played an important (and known) role for Dutch-Paris fugitives. Again, if Weidner and his colleagues thought a *passeur* took fugitives for the money, the *passeur* does not appear on the list of resisters. The catch-all category "supplies" includes false documents, information, money, provisions of any sort, and any other supply besides shelter.

The resisters have been organized alphabetically, followed by their birth date and their nationality during the war. Where applicable, the list includes the date of their arrest. "Released" means that the individual was released from prison by the authorities, probably due to illness. "Liberated" means that resistance or Allied forces freed the individual from German imprisonment. "Repatriated" means the individual was deported to the concentration camps but survived to return. If the individual died in the concentration camps, the list gives the name of the camp and the date of death.

Leadership

Chait, Edmond Salomon (1912, Belgian)

Rens, Jacques (1916, Dutch; arrested May 20, 1944; escaped June 1, 1944)

Weidner, Jean (1912, Dutch; arrested October 1942; released after three days; arrested May 20, 1944; escaped June 1, 1944)

Brussels

Leadership of Comité

Bolle, Maurice (1890, Dutch; arrested July 13, 1943; repatriated)

Nijkerk, Benjamin (1902, Dutch; arrested March 22, 1944; died at Wedel November 1944)

Regout, Edouard (1898, Dutch)

Ten Kate, Pastor Antoon G. B. (1897, Dutch; arrested May 15, 1944; released August 20, 1944)

Van Cleeff, Paul (1919, Dutch; arrested November 18, 1943; liberated September 1944)

Van Schaardenburgh, Cornelis (1892, Dutch)

Verhagen, Jacobus (1896, Dutch)

Verloop, David (1921, Dutch; arrested February 28, 1944; died in German custody March 1944)

Couriers, Guides, and Border Crossings

Bloemist, Betsy (1916, Dutch)

Borst, A. L. A. (Dutch)

Bosschart, Robert (1918, Dutch; arrested February 28, 1944; liberated September 4, 1944)

De Bie family

De Haan, Hildegonda (Dutch)

De Wit, Michiel (1921, Dutch; arrested February 1944; died Mauthausen April 17, 1945)

Ilegems, Carolina Hellemans (1907, Belgian)

Ilegems, Gaston (1905, Belgian)

Israel, Philip (Dutch; died Auschwitz May 22, 1944)

Jacobstahl, Hilde (1925, stateless)

Jacobstahl, Joachim (1921, stateless; arrested February 28, 1944; liberated September 4, 1944)

Lalieu, Joseph N. E. L. (1907, Dutch)

Lalieu-Wagemans, Elisabeth (1923, Dutch)

Lemaître, D. (Belgian)

Mirgaut, Jules (1893, Belgian)

Polak, Philip (1917, Dutch)

Polak-Pool, Jetta (1920, Dutch)

Pouillon, Rosa (1921, Belgium)

Roselaar, Greta (1919, Dutch)

Sayers, Paul (1918, Dutch)

Schmutzer, Adriaan (1925, Dutch; arrested March 3, 1944; liberated September 4, 1944)

Souren, Pierre (Dutch)

Spierings, C. A. M. (Dutch)

Swaab, J.

Ten Kate, Chris (1917, Dutch; arrested February 29, 1944; liberated September 4, 1944)

Van den Bogaerden

Van der Most van Spijk, Daan (Dutch)

Van Dorp, Nico (Dutch)

Van Helden-Hus, Johanna (1910, Dutch)

Van Kempen, Edouard (1890, Dutch)

Vleeschdrager, Henri (1923, Dutch; arrested February 28, 1944; liberated September 4, 1944)

Von der Möhlen, Yves (1920, Dutch)

Wisbrun, Hans (1920, Dutch; arrested in a raid March 22, 1944; forced labor in Germany until April 22, 1945)

Zellerhof, G. (Dutch)

Postboxes

Dronsart, Mr. (Belgian)

Flinal, Jane (Belgian)

Mahillon, Pierre (Belgian)

Moussiaux, Georges (1904, Belgian)

Richmond-van Witzenburg, Weduwe (1879, Dutch)

Van Gellicum-Kamps, Petronella (1881, Dutch; arrested November 18, 1943; liberated September 3, 1944)

Veron, André (1895, Belgian)

Verteneuil (Belgian)

Shelter

Anciaux, Mademoiselle (Belgian)

Ballian, Madame (Belgian)

Bolle, Hélène (1918, Dutch)

Bontemps, Madame (Belgian)

Brabant, Monsieur and Madame (Belgian)

Dans, Madame (Belgian)

Davignon, Mevrouw (1890, Belgian)

De Cuyper, F. Georges (Belgian)

De Haan, Pastor Pieter (Dutch)

Delpierre, Guillaume (Belgian)

Derckx, Albert (Dutch)

Derckx, Madame

Devis, Madame (Belgian)

Devis, Lucienne (Belgian)

Devriendt, Antoine (Belgian)

Goudsmit, Esther (Dutch; arrested July 1943; fate unknown)

Goudsmit, Helene (Dutch)

Grenez, Madame (Belgian)

Henriquez de Castro, Elisabeth (1884, Dutch)

Henriquez de Castro, Ines (1917, Dutch)

Krauss, Mary (1910, Belgian; arrested November 1943; repatriated)

Laymarie, Madame (Belgian)

Lever, Josephine (1905, Belgian; arrested and jailed for two days in June 1944)

Lifman, Ernest (1890, Dutch)

Milaire-Engels, Jane (1886, Belgian)

Nieulant Pelkman, Arie (1890, Dutch)

Nieulant Pelkman, Wies (Dutch)

Nieulant Pelkman-van den Ende, G. L. (Dutch)

Ogy, Lydia (1889, Belgian; arrested February 28, 1944; gassed at Auschwitz January 28, 1945)

Oostendorp, Thomas (1907, Dutch)

Pateyn, Mr. (Belgian)

Rosier, Mr. (Belgian)

Snethlage, Hendrik C. (1893, Dutch)

Timmers Verhoeven, Henri (Dutch)

Timmers Verhoeven-Keuchenius, Maria (Dutch)

Van Altena, Elisabeth (1894, Dutch; arrested November 18, 1943; liberated September 3, 1944)

Van den Wijcer

Van Oberghe, Jeannette (Belgian)

Van Vrecken, Robert

Wibbens, Pastor Jacob

Supplies

Allard, Dr. (Belgian)

André, Carl (Belgian)

Bol, Jan Pieter (1917, Dutch; arrested February 28, 1944; liberated September 4, 1944)

Bosschart, Leopold (1888, Dutch)

Buffy, Alice (1893, Swiss)

De Thomaz de Bossierre (1908, Belgian)

Detien, Edmond (Belgian)

Dulier (Belgian)

Gold, Dr. (Belgian)

Haenecour, Joseph C. E. (1910, Dutch)

Knoote, Jacob (1904, Dutch)

Nijkerk-Marienko, Marina (1914, Russian)

Snoek, Dr. Jean (Belgian)

Somerhausen, Dr. Jacques (1905, Belgian)

Spaanjard

Ten Kate-Vandenbroek, Johanna (Dutch)

Van Coevorden (Dutch)

Van Dalen, Jacob (1919, Dutch)

van der Donck, J. (Belgian)

Van Win (Dutch)

Wulffaerl

Lyon and the Haute-Savoie

Couriers, Guides, and Border Crossings

Bernard, Emile (French)

Bouchet, Ernest (1923, French)

Charpiot, Amy Mae (1898, Canadian)

Charroin, Alice Coste (1911, French; arrested March 6, 1944; released August 11, 1944)

Charroin, Arthur (1906, French; arrested February 19, 1944; died Bergen-Belsen February 1945)

Dreyfus, Dr. Vital (1901, French; died in Pyrenees December 1942)

Faber, Lykele (1919, Dutch)

Fasnacht, D. (Belgian)

Fasnacht, Roger (1919, Swiss)

Jacques, Pierre (French)

Kahn, René (1922, Dutch)

Kraay, Suzanna (1921, Dutch; arrested February 11, 1944; repatriated)

Lavergnat, Jeanne (French)

Lavergnat, Robert (French)

Mathy, Maurice (French)

Merckling, Alfred (1920, French; arrested October 1942; served sentence)

Pillot, Raymonde (1923, French; arrested February 28, 1944; repatriated)

Poney (French)

Stoppleman, Hélène (Dutch)

Tièche, Jacques (1924, Swiss)

Toureille, Dr. Pierre (arrested, escaped)

Voisin, Madame (French)

Zurcher, Jean (1918, Swiss)

Postboxes

Gambrillon, Yvette (1909, French)

Groll, Agnes Riga (1886, French)

Groll, René (1893, French)

Jolivet, Father Marius (French)

Meyer, Marthe Schlegel (Swiss)

Meyer, Pastor Paul (1886, Swiss; arrested March 27, 1944; died Dachau
    January 24, 1945)

Shelter

Beausoleil, Monsieur and Madame (French)

Beausoleil, Madame (French)

Bouchet, André (French)

Chapal, Odette (French)

Chapal, Pastor Paul (1898, French)

Charpiot, Pastor Frederic (1893, French)

Crespy, Pastor Georges (French)

Folliet, Father Camille (French)

Harry, Maurice (French)

Harry, Madame (French)

Jaccoud, Lea (1889, French)

Jaccoud, Pierre (1888, French)

Lacôte, Paul (1897, French; arrested March 7, 1944; released August 11, 1944)

Langlade, Annie Beaujolin (1908, French)

Lavranchy, Jean

Mathieu, Francia Roset (1900, French)

Mathieu, François (1903, French)

Mercier, Madame (French)

Meunier, Marie (1890, French; arrested March 7, 1944; died Ravensbrück February 1945)

Meylink, Bernard (1885, Dutch)

Stocker, Valentine Chaland (1893, Swiss)

Stoppleman, Helena (Dutch)

Stoppleman, Moritz (Dutch)

Tièche, Maurice (1895, Swiss)

Van der Post, Jacob (1909, Dutch)

Van der Post-Schuylenburg, Johanna (1910, Dutch)

Verdoye (French)

Weber, Max (1914, Swiss)

Zurcher, Anna

Supplies

Ambre, Joannes (French)

André, M. (French)

Balland, Marguerite (1894, French)

Bergeat, Inspector (French)

Bouchet, Madame N. (French)

Brunet, Maître (French)

Castaign, Henri (1895, French)

Claparède, Mr.

Colpart, Simone (French)

Delaporte, Mr. (French)

Delaunay, Robert (French)

Dubost, Mr. (French)

Dupont, Nicolas (1900, French; arrested March 31, 1944; died Lübeck May 3, 1945)

Falconnet (French)

Fayolle, Mr. (French)

Floquet (French)

Gambrillon, Luisette (1912, French)

Gerlier, Renée (French)

Grand-Clément, Renée (1915, French)

Jacquet, Maurice (1897, French; arrested September 1943 and February 28,
    1944; repatriated)

Janse, Marius (1901, Dutch; arrested January 13, 1944; repatriated)

Kolkman, Joseph (1896, Dutch; arrested January 1943; died Lublin
    February 8, 1944)

Marcher, Intendant de police (French)

Marx, Colonel P. (French)

Massendès, Jean (1915, French)

Metzger, Pastor (French)

Mouwen, Gustava (1908, Dutch; arrested March 27, 1944; repatriated)

Naeff, Peter (1903, Dutch)

Naudet (French)

Ordioni, Jean-Pierre (French)

Pinochet (French)

Rizet, Marcel (1899, French)

Roset (French)

Sauveur (French)

Sessler, Marius (1880, Swiss; arrested August 9, 1942; released August 20,
    1942)

Sevenster, Ate (Dutch; arrested December 9, 1942; liberated June 8, 1944)

Sevenster-Lindenbergh, P. N. (Dutch)

Terpend, René (1912, French)

Testers, Josephus (1903, Dutch; arrested January 13, 1943; died Buchenwald
    May 14, 1944)

Toussaint, Commissaire (French)

Travard (French)

Van Tricht, Dr. Barend (1885, Dutch)

Netherlands

Contact/Postbox

Furth, Mevrouw (Dutch)

Niclaes, Madame

Couriers, Guides, and Border Crossings

Eikeboom, Giel (Dutch)
Henry, Piet (1920, Dutch; arrested April 9, 1944; repatriated)
Hijmans, Willy (1921, Dutch)
Iordens, F. H. (Dutch; shot trying to escape March 1, 1944)
Lejeune, Joseph G. (1914, Dutch)
Maclaine-Pont, Anne (Dutch)
Meiers, Mr. and Mrs. (Dutch)
Nauta, Jan (1922, Dutch; arrested May 1944; repatriated)
Sijen, Father
Van Haaften, Adriaan (1920, Dutch; arrested March 1, 1944; died Buchenwald January 29, 1945)
Vogel, Frits

Supplies

De Ruyter (Dutch)
Ten Cate, Wilhelmus (1889, Dutch)
Van der Wilt (Dutch)

Paris

Leaders

Caubo, Jean-Michael (1891, Dutch; arrested February 12, 1944; died Dautmergen, subcamp of Natzweiler, February 13, 1945)
Hiltermann, Suzanne (1919, Dutch; arrested February 26, 1944; repatriated)
Laatsman de Bailleur, Johan Herman (1903, Dutch; arrested February 26, 1944; repatriated)
Mincowski, Leo (1913, Romanian; arrested February 26, 1944; died Buchenwald April 10, 1945)
Starink, Albert (1917, Dutch)

Couriers

Caubo, Hubert Joseph (1927, French; arrested February 12, 1944; released February 14, 1944)
Caubo, Jean Henri (1927, French; arrested February 12, 1944; released February 14, 1944)

Comiti, Lucie (1922, French; arrested June 17, 1944; repatriated)

Houry, Jacqueline (1922, French; arrested June 14, 1944; repatriated)

Laatsman, J. H. Jr. (1929, Dutch; arrested February 26, 1944; released March 1944)

Neyssel, Anna (1918, Dutch; arrested March 5, 1944; repatriated)

Okhuysen, Catherine (1919, Dutch; arrested March 5, 1944; released August 1944)

Postboxes

Caubo, Marie Schenck (1895, Luxembourgian; arrested February 12, 1944; released February 14, 1944; died in a bombing raid April 1944)

Collomb, Simone (1902, Swiss)

Labois, Marcel (French)

Meyer, Pastor Oscar (Swiss)

Weidner, Gabrielle (1914, Dutch; arrested February 26, 1944; died Konigsberg sur Oder February 15, 1945)

Shelter

Brantsen, Baroness Eloise (1875, Dutch; arrested April 1944; released August 1944)

Chanoinat, Louis (1893, French; arrested March 17, 1944; repatriated June 1945)

Chanoinat, Marguerite (1889, French; arrested March 17, 1944; repatriated May 1945)

Goetschel, Fernande (1893, French; arrested February 26, 1944; repatriated July 1945)

Holweg, Ellen (Danish)

Langhout, Pastor Adolf (1915, Dutch)

Larose-Reinaud, Madeleine (1900, French; arrested March 23, 1944; repatriated July 1945)

Mériot, Raymond (1897, French; arrested March 9, 1944; died Ravensbrück June 23, 1945)

Mériot, Yvonne (French)

Prilliez, Emile (1903, French; arrested February 26, 1944; died Kalmels January 31, 1945)

Prilliez, Julia Richet (1906, French; arrested February 26, 1944; repatriated)

Prilliez, Mauricette (1925, French)

Roume, Louise (1905, Belgian; arrested March 4, 1944; repatriated)

Ruys, John (1891, Dutch; arrested March 9, 1944; died Dachau February 12, 1945)

Tourné, Brother Hironymus "Rufus" (1901, Dutch; arrested February 26, 1944; repatriated)

Van de Bogaard, J. C. (Dutch)

Van Exter, Bertus (Dutch)

Supplies

Beillard, Mr. (French)

Brantsen, Baron Jacob K. J. (1877, Dutch; arrested April 1944; died Buchenwald December 9, 1944)

Brousse, Marcelle (1895, French; arrested 26 February 26, 1944; repatriated)

Chelti, Mr. (French)

Choureau, Mr. (French)

Duchanel, Miguel (1908, French)

Duchemin, Madame (French)

Evenou, Dr. Yves (French)

Graeve, Alice (French)

Hooymans, Farmer (Dutch)

Huitema, Homme (1893, Dutch)

Juillet, Mr. (French)

Jurius, Farmer (French)

Lesieur, Henri (French)

Merle d'Aubigne, Robert (1900, French)

Milleret, Jean (1903, Swiss; arrested February 26, 1944; repatriated)

Mohr, Josephus Julius (1893, Dutch; arrested July 18, 1944; died Buchenwald February 6, 1945)

Piveteau, Gabriel (1917, French; arrested March 9, 1944; died Flossenburg January 17, 1945)

Reveyrand, Marguerite (1913, French)

Rod, Jacques (1920, French)

Ströbel, Mr.

Van de Kamp (Dutch)

Van Doorn, Father Kees (Dutch)

Weidner, Annette (1921, Dutch)

Switzerland

Couriers Based in Switzerland

De Jong, Dirk (Dutch)
Gazan, Henri (1918, Dutch; arrested and released April 1944)
Lap, Armand (1911, Dutch)
Veerman, Paul (1918, Dutch; arrested May 20, 1944; escaped; arrested in
a raid June 20, 1944; repatriated)

Supplies

Bartels, Joop (Dutch)
Bouchardi (Swiss)
Cartier, Flavie (1889, French)
Cartier Weidner, Elisabeth (1915, French)
Demierre, Ferdinand (Swiss)
Ferrin (Swiss)
Freudenberg, Pastor A. (German)
Frossard de Saugy, Paul (Swiss)
Gazan, Nico (1905, Dutch)
Guillon, Pastor Charles (French)
Monnard, Georges
Nijkerk, Dolf (1910, Dutch)
Van Niftrik, Jacobus (1893, Dutch)
Van Tricht, General Aleid Gerhard (1886, Dutch)
Visser 't Hooft, Pastor Willem (1900, Dutch)
Wertheim (Dutch)

Toulouse and Pyrenees

Couriers and Guides

Balfet, Louise (1922, French)
Boucoiran, Anita (1920, French)
Calmels, Simone (1920, French; arrested June 22, 1944; liberated August
19, 1944)
Delrue, Charles
Moulouguet, Andrée (1922, French)

Passeurs and Their Assistants

Barrère, Jean (1912, French)
Barrère, Joseph (1913, American; killed in ambush June 13, 1944)
Battault, Victor (1895, French)
Bazerque, Jean-Louis (1905, French; killed in ambush June 13, 1944)
Bordes, Louis (1901, French; arrested January 1944; escaped)
Bordes, Marcelle (1907, French; arrested January 3, 1944; repatriated)
Caparros-Muñoz, Audaine (1912, Spanish)
Combes, Marie Barthes (1888, French; arrested December 24, 1943; repatriated)
Lucas, Georges (1908, French; arrested June 28, 1944; liberated August 19, 1944)
Marot, Henri (1916, French)
Nahas, Gabriel (1920, French)
Sabadie, Pierre (1914, French; killed in ambush June 13, 1944)
Soum, Paul (French)
Treillet, Pierre (1918, French)
Verdier, Emile (1891, French)
Verdier, Pierre (1930, French)

Postboxes

Aarts, Antonius J. C. H. P. (1890, Dutch)
Billot, Geneviève (French)
Billot, Madeleine (1914, French; arrested July 11, 1944; repatriated)
Bovis, Jean (1905, French)
Germain, Mr. (French)
Mossaz, Blanche (French)

Shelter

Aan de Stegge, Father John (1906, Dutch)
Baert, Madame J.
Collaine family (French)
Drach family (French)
Dupias family (French)
Lejeune, Gaston (1911, French)
Lejeune, Joan Tuke (1911, British)

Mataigne family (French)
Meige family
Nougarède, Roger (1898, French)
Serment, Prof. and Mrs. (French and English)
Vila, Dolores Guillaume (1887, Spanish; arrested April 12, 1943; repatriated)
Van Wijhe, Marthe Pietman (1892, Belgian)

Supplies

Derrac, Roger (1905, French; arrested February 4, 1944; repatriated)
Dupré, Jacques (1890, French)
Groseiller, Emile (French)
Van Praag, Jacob (Dutch; killed 1943)
Riguet, Mademoiselle (French)
Veron, Charles (1914, French; arrested July 17, 1944; liberated August 19, 1944)

Resistance Allies of Dutch-Paris

Barot, Madeleine (French)
Bas Backer, Johan (1906, Dutch; arrested November 23, 1943; repatriated)
Beaujolin, Gilbert (French)
Belvaux, Robert (French)
Benoit, Monette (French)
Biernaux, Leon Florent (Belgian; arrested August 6, 1944; repatriated)
Biernaux, Raymond (Belgian; arrested August 6, 1944; died Neuengamme March 3, 1945)
Biernaux-Doby, Olympe (Belgian; arrested August 6, 1944; repatriated)
Brichard, Emile (Belgian; executed March 6, 1944)
Bruat, Mr. (French; arrested February 26, 1944; died in deportation)
Cacheux, Arthur (Belgian)
Chabot, Elise (Dutch; arrested November 18, 1944; repatriated)
De Graaff, Eva (1887, French; arrested February 16, 1944; died Ravensbrück)
De Wit, Jean-Marie (1907, Dutch; arrested November 23, 1943; repatriated)
Fety, Jacqueline (1923; arrested May 23, 1943; released September 1943)
Fety, Jean (1892, French; arrested May 23, 1943; repatriated)
Fety, Louise née Hellio (French)

Folmer, Joke (Dutch)

Gielens, Harry (Dutch)

Gielens, Tonny (Dutch)

Glasberg, Father Alexander (1902, Ukrainian)

Jaspar (Belgian)

Lamy, Pierre (French; executed July 1944)

Mengin, Georges (French)

Molland, Josette (1923, French; arrested March 3, 1944; repatriated May 2, 1945)

Mouchon, Violette (French)

Muller, Father Emile (1869, German; arrested February 28, 1944; died Bergen-Belsen November 19, 1944)

Nicolas, Camille (French)

Nizet (Belgian)

Pedérizet, Mademoiselle (French)

Pouls (French; arrested February 26, 1944; repatriated)

De Pury, Pastor Roland (French)

Robo, Brother Mathurin (1910, French; arrested February 26, 1944; repatriated)

Schoenmaeckers, Paul (1886, Dutch; arrested November 1943; died in deportation)

Simmons (Dutch)

Smeets, Eduard (Dutch)

Smit, Karst (Dutch; arrested March 18, 1944; repatriated)

Smits, Eugène (Dutch)

Stadler, Georges (1908, Swiss; arrested July 1943; repatriated)

Strengers, Jan (1914, Dutch; arrested November 22, 1943; repatriated)

Swane, Victor (1920, Dutch; arrested March 9, 1944; died Buchenwald October 8, 1944)

Symonds (Dutch)

Ter Horst, Gerrit (1908, Dutch; arrested April 14, 1944; died Dachau January 7, 1945)

Van der Heijden, Eugène (1920, Dutch)

Van der Vliet, Dr. Koos (Dutch)

Van Moorleghem, Ernest (1914, Belgian; arrested November 18, 1943; executed 1944 or 1945)

Van Nes, Adrianus (1918, Dutch)

Van Roggen, Matthys (1919, Dutch; arrested November 14, 1943; died
    Buchenwald February 9, 1945)
Verspyck, Mathilde (1908, Dutch; arrested April 11, 1944; died Ravensbrück
    February 11, 1945)
Vrij, Jacques (1916, Dutch; arrested May 1944; escaped August 1944)
Wyssogota-Zakrzewski, André (1905, Polish; arrested November 14, 1943;
    repatriated)

Appendix II

List of Dutch-Paris Pseudonyms

This book refers to the men and women of Dutch-Paris by their real names, although few of them used their real names during the war. In many cases resisters who had worked together for months or years had to tell each other their names after the Liberation. Archival documents and postwar memoirs often use the resisters' wartime pseudonyms rather than their real names. The following pseudonyms appear in the documents.

Barrère, Joseph aka Frisco, California
Bazerque, Jean-Louis aka Charbonnier, Lebrun, l'Aigle, Sanglier
Bolle, Maurice aka Meneer Albert, Meneer Marius
Bordes, Louis aka Paul Blanchard
Boucoiran, Anita aka Melusine
Calmels, Simone aka Sim, Claudie Sael, Francette, Jacqueline Dumoilin
Caparros-Muñoz, Audaine aka Carlos
Chait, Edmond Salomon aka Edmond, Moen or Moun, Pierre Mathieu, Moreau
Charroin, Arthur aka Georgette
Combes, Marie aka Mme Arnaud
Comiti, Lucie aka Marie-France Paoli
Delrue, Charles aka Charles de la Rue, Karel van Straaten, Peter Street
De Thomaz de Bossiere aka Didier
Duchanel, Miguel aka Paul
Frossard de Saugy, Paul aka Rochat
Gambrillon, Luisette aka Cani
Gambrillon, Yvette aka Dico
Goetschel, Fernande aka Micheline
Goudsmit, Esther aka Madame Demaret

Haenecour, J. C. E. aka Jacobs

Henry, Piet aka Frits van Os

Hijmans, Willy aka Emile

Hiltermann, Suzanne aka Anne-Marie Mermillod, Toetie

Houry, Jacqueline aka Jacqueline, Darville

Ilegems, Carolina Hellemans aka Madame Helene

Ilegems, Gaston aka No. 5

Israel, Philip aka Olyslagers

Jacobstahl, Joachim aka Jo, Jo Staal, Jerry Stranders, Jean Paul Lambert

Knoote, Jacob J. A. aka de Smet

Kraay, Suzanna aka Erna, Susy Claes, Suzanne Melinand, Raatgeer

Laatsman de Bailleur, Johan H. aka Felix II, Mr. Bekking

Lalieu, Joseph M. E. L. aka Heer Sanders

Langhout, A. N. aka Michiel

Lautman, Albert aka Lucien Perrault, Georges, Lucien

Lejeune, Joseph G. aka Jef, de Jong

Lejeune, Gaston aka Maurice, Gustave

Lucas, Georges aka Lakanal

Marot, Henri aka Mireille

Massendès, Jean aka Morin, Sylvain, José

Milleret, Jean aka Able

Mincowski, Leo aka Pierre, Michel, Mermillod

Moulonguet, Andrée aka Teuteur

Nahas, Gabriel aka Gaby, Georges, Dr. Brantes, Georges Prontas, Georgette

Nauta, Jan aka van Ryswyck

Neyssel, Anna aka Anika, Anita

Nijkerk, Benjamin aka Nestor, Marcel, Armand Smit, Bernard Smits

Nougarède, Roger aka Jean-Marie

Okhuysen, Catherine aka Okkie

Pillot, Raymonde aka Raymonde Raviol

Polak, Philip aka de Waele

Rens, Jacques aka Jacques, Jacques Thierry, de Vis

Roselaar, Greta aka Maggy de Coninck, Madame Vermeer

Spierings, C. A. M. aka Toke, Marianne

Stadler, Georges aka Lecordonnier

Swane, Victor aka van Ryswyck, van Landschot, Peter Jurgens, Jean-Pierre

Ten Kate, Chris aka van Dongen

Treillet, Pierre aka Palo, Palau, Etienne Ferrand, Pierre Palo

Van Cleeff, Paul aka Meneer Paul, van Caneghem, Mertens, Charles Moermans

Van der Heijden, Eugène aka Meneer Vos uit Brabant

Van Doorn, Kees aka Kees Lepine, Ome Kees

Van Dorp, Nico aka Hugo

Van Helden-Hus, Johanna aka Madame Josée

Van Kempen, Edouard aka Leclerq

Van Roggen, Matthys aka Mathieu Rolin, van Ryswyck

Van Tricht, Barend aka L'Autruche

Van Wijhe, Marthe aka Lil, Cam

Veerman, Paul aka Paul Vermeer, Pierre Paul Valmont, André

Verloop, David aka Vermaas

Vleeschdrager, Henri aka Vermaat, Monsieur Hans, Henri Paul Meertz, Pierre van Aarden

Vrij, Jacques aka Leo van den Brink, Henk

Weidner, Jean aka Jean Cartier, Louis Segers, Henri Meunier, Jean Lins, Jean Linschoten, Mr. Vernet, Jean-Jacques, Paul Rey

Wisbrun, Hans aka Leon, Seegers, Michel

Wyssogota-Zakrzewski, André aka André Martins, André Gotha, Oncle Georges, Mathieu de Busse

Appendix III

List of People Helped by Dutch-Paris

After the Liberation, Jean Weidner estimated that Dutch-Paris escorted 1,000 to 1,500 people out of occupied territory to Switzerland or Spain and helped support between 1,500 and 3,000 more hiding in Belgium and France. The great majority of these people passed through Dutch-Paris anonymously or under pseudonyms. Except for Allied airmen and to some degree Engelandvaarders, the resisters had no need to know anyone's name. In fact common sense warned everyone to avoid names and keep no lists. Therefore the following lists represent only a fraction of the men, women, and children helped by Dutch-Paris during the war. The resisters themselves reported these names during or immediately after the war in documents that have survived in archives. Because some of the people on the lists received help from more than one organization, they may appear in the accounts of other humanitarian resistance organizations as well. Only the list of Allied military personnel can be considered to be close to complete. Other than the Allied airmen, all individuals are presumed to be Dutch unless otherwise noted.

Engelandvaarders

Alexandre, Georges
Auping, Leo
Bamberger, Harry
Bartmann, Antonius
Beukers, Alfred
Blanes, David
Bleys, Father Lodewijk
Blok, Albertus Frederik

Bollee, G. C.
Boon-Hartsinck, Ariane
Borel-Rinkes, Hilbrand
Born, Joop
Bosch, Leonard
Bottenheim, Jack
Bureau, Roger (Belgian)
Cassé
Conijn, N. H.
De Bakker, L.
De Besancon, Guillaume
De Jonge, Henk
Den Besten, Gijsbert
De Nerée tot Babberich, Pim
De Veer, Johan
De Vos, Pieter
Devries, A.
De Zwaart, M.
Dito, Father
Dourlein
Erwteman, Jaap
Fehmers, Jan
Fetter, Emile
Frank, Max
Gans, Alexander
Gips, C. G.
Goes
Glukman, Ludri
Godfrin, Robert (Belgian)
Goedhuis, D.
Greidanus, Johan
Groen, G. F. J. A.
Guyt, Harry
Hagen, J.
Hartog, A.
Hartog, Philip A.
Hijmans, Jacobus A.

Hox, Charles (Belgian)
Hudeley, V.
Hymans, Henry J.
Idema, Kornelis G.
Isings, Bruno
Janse
Janssen, Wilifried
Kahn, Hans
Kaspers
Klausner, J.
Klein, Hugo
Klijzing, J.
Kobus, Willem
Koch, A. B.
Krijger, G.
Kroone
Langeler, Jan Willem
Lannoy
Laureijssen, Father Leonardus J. A.
Laverge, G.
Lemmens, Victor
Mantel, A. S.
Milborn, H.
Nederlof, D.
Pahud de Mortagnes, Charles
Perlstein, Hugo
Philipp, E.
Post, Hendricus W.
Postma, Sierp
Prokop
Regout, A. L.
Rens, Dr.
Roesing
Sandberg, Henri
Schiff, Eric
Schipper, Gerald
Schreinemachers, Rudi

Simons
Sinnige, Johannes Martinus
Spetter, Mathew
Spijker, T. W.
Staverman, Ferdinand
Swaab, J.
Ten Brink
Ten Have, P.
Timmers Verhoeven, Samuel
Trichtchriff
Tuts, Philip
Ubbink
Uiting, Dick
Valck Lucassen, Theo
Van Alphen, Johannes
Van den Ende
Van der Helde
Van der Heyden, Arie
Van Doornik
Van Exter, Robert
Van Gich, Bernard
Van Goor, Dr.
Van Gullink
Van Hasselt, B.
Van Heuven Goedhart, Gerrit J
Van Holk, Lambertus
Van Houten Dekker
Van Hutten, F.
Van Nouhuys, Herman
Van Oosterzee, Christiaan
Van Os, Frits
Van Rossum, Carel
Van Veeze, J. J.
Visser, Hugo
Weisglas, Max
Westhof
Weve

Wiersma, Sijtje
Willebeek le Mair
Wins, Henri
Wins, Max
Zeeman, Pieter Rudolph
Zeggers, J. H.
2 Algerians

Allied Military Personnel

Anderson, Robert F., USAAF
Arp, Elwood, USAAF
Bachman, Carl E., USAAF
Bailey, Harold, RAF
Boyce, Harold, USAAF
Breed, Mervyn, RNZAF
Brenden, Arden, USAAF
Brigman, Campell C. Jr., USAAF
Brown, Cecil, USAAF
Brown, Philip H., RAF
Buckner, John R., USAAF
Cassady, Leonard, USAAF
Cohen, Simon, USAAF
Davenport, RCAF
David, Clayton C., USAAF
Downe, Charles O., USAAF
Dutka, John A., USAAF
Elkin, Norman, USAAF
Ellis, Robert O., RAF
Ferrari, Victor, USAAF
Flores, Leopold, USAAF
Gallo, Russel, USAAF
Grubb, Ernest, USAAF
Hargest, James, NZMF
Harris, RAF
Hicks, Chauncey, USAAF
Horton, Jack O., USAAF

Hussong, James, USAAF
Koenig, William, USAAF
Kolc, Eric, USAAF
Kratz, Harry, USAAF
Krengle, Robert, USAAF
Lock, William B., USAAF
Mackie, N. M., RAF
Mandell, Nicholas, USAAF
Martin, Loral, USAAF
McDonald, William H., USAAF
McGlinchy, Frank, USAAF
McLaughlin, John G., RAAF
Mellen, Clyde, USAAF
Miles, Reginald, NZMF
Miller, Karl D., USAAF
Miller, William J., USAAF
Morgan, Herman, USAAF
Morley, Henry, RAF
Morphen, Jeffrey, RAF
Mullins, Charlie, USAAF
Newton, James, USAAF
O'Welch, Paul, USAAF
Page, Fred, RAAF
Roberts, Omar, USAAF
Shaffer, Edward R., USAAF
Schuman, Donald C., USAAF
Settle, James, USAAF
Shaver, Kenneth, USAAF
Sherman, Howard, USAAF
Smith, Sydney, RAF
Snyder, Walter, USAAF
Steel, Henry, USAAF
Stern, Albert, USAAF
Stock, Ernest, USAAF
Tank, Frank A. Jr., USAAF
Tracy, James E., USAAF
Trinder, Wallace, USAAF

Trnobransky, Jan, RAF
Van der Stok, Bram, RAF
Vass, John, RAF
Wallinga, Jacob, USAAF
Wardle, Hank, RCAF
Watlington, RAF
Watts, George, RAF

Civilians and Resisters

Bengers, Felix
Blitz, Gerard
Blitz, Maurice
Byron family (Polish, 4 persons)
Cahen Salvador, Georges (French)
Cahen Salvador, Jean (French)
Calff, Mevrouw
Cauveren
Classens, Alphonse
Clercx-van de Velde, Mr. and Mrs.
Coppens, Willie
Corolla, Helen
Davids family
De Jong, Dr. and daughter
De Jong, David
De Leeuw-Kleinkramer, Eddy and Sophie
De Menthon, François and family (French)
Duchamps (Belgian)
Eliasar, Joseph André
Eliasar, Simon
Elzas family
Epstein
Fajgenbaum
Fichman, Rolande (Polish)
Fisel, Ferdinand
Fourcade children (French)
Gazan, Nico

Gazan, Mary Stibbe
Grun, Mr.
Hakkert family
Hartog, Henri
Hertz, Alexander
Hoekendijk-Laman, Pastor and Mrs.
Israels-Cohen, Henriette
Kammerlid, Frans
Kloppenburg-Hendrikse, Mevrouw
Koeleman, Dirk and family
Koster, Regina
Kuyper, Jacques
Langendijk, H., Mr. and Mrs.
Lap, Armand
Laverge, G.
Lecocq, Simone and husband (Belgian)
Legros, Madame (French)
Levy, Monsieur and Madame (French)
Ludolph
Magnus, K., Dr. and Mrs.
Magnus, O., Dr. and Mrs.
Mendel, Madame
Montesinos, Madame (French)
Montesinos, Mathilde (French)
Moppes-Goudsmit, Madame
Nathans, A., Mr. and Mrs.
Neter, Magnus
Neter-Stad, Helen
Pels, Emile and family
Peterfreund family (Polish, 3 persons)
Piller-Polak, Mr. and Mrs.
Polak Daniels, Ans
Polak-Winkel, Mr. and Mrs.
Rademakers, Fons
Rosenthal, Saul
Rosenthal-Frank, Jeanette and infant
Rosican, Carla

Rosican, Isja
Rudelsheim family
Scheindlinger, Edith
Scheindlinger, Fritz
Scheindlinger, Sara
De Schotten, Mr.
Schumann family
Sevenster, Gisele
Sevenster, Madeleine
Sevenster, Nieltje
Sevenster, Suzanne
Simon, Julius and family
Simon, Rudi
Simon, Sonja
Smit family (3 persons)
Stoppelman, Helena
Stoppelman, Hélène
Stoppelman, Moritz "Maurice"
Taub, Benjamin
Taub, Hendel Silberzahn
Taub, Sonja
Troostwijk, S. I.
Van der Burg
Van der Touw, To
Van Hoof, Fanny
Van Gelderen, Lex and parents
Van Straten family (4 persons)
Verveer, Emmanuel
Vogel, Antonius A.
Vogel, Denise
Warrendijn family
Weill, André and family
Werlingshoff, Rudolphe
Zonnlicht

GLOSSARY

Abwehr	German military intelligence.
Amitié Chrétienne	"Christian Friendship," an ecumenical Christian group based in Lyon, France, that offered legal assistance to refugees as well as engaging in illegal spiritual and humanitarian resistance.
Armée Sècrete	Secret Army of the French Resistance.
Ausweis	German identity document.
Bureau Inlichtingen (BI)	Dutch Intelligence bureau.
chef du réseau	The leader of a resistance group.
CIMADE	French Protestant group that offered both legal and illegal aid to refugees and evacuees in Vichy France.
douaniers (*douanes*)	Customs agents, some of whom had the authority to patrol the borders.
Engelandvaarder	A Dutch man (or woman) who left the Netherlands during the war with the intention of getting to England to join the Allied effort.

Filière	A local group that smuggled fugitives over the Pyrenees into Spain.
Grüne Polizei	Common name for German policemen of the Ordungspolizei who wore green uniforms.
Guardia Civil	Spanish militarized police, similar to the French gendarmerie.
maquis	French partisans, armed resisters who lived in the hills.
maquisard	A member of a maquis unit.
Marechausée	The Dutch militarized police, similar to the French gendarmerie or American state troopers.
Milice	French paramilitary police created by Vichy that collaborated with the Germans.
Onderduiker	Dutch man, woman, or child who has "dived under" to hide from the occupation authorities.
passeur	A clandestine guide over a border. In the Pyrenees the *passeur* was the leader of a team that smuggled fugitives into Spain. Some *passeurs* were volunteer resisters; others demanded payment.
Passierschein	Safe-conduct pass.
préfecture	Administrative offices of a French department or region.
réfouler	To turn someone back over the border or deport. During the war Swiss authorities could *réfouler* someone over the border secretly or openly, meaning directly into the custody of French, Italian, or German officers.
Renseignements generaux (RG)	Security branch of the French police, gathers intelligence.

SD	Sicherheitsdienst, Nazi Party and SS intelligence agency.
sociaalwerk	"Social work," referring to illegal efforts to support Jews and others in hiding.
transportwerk	"Transport work," referring to illegal work to help fugitives of all sorts get across Belgium and France to neutral Spain and Switzerland.
Vertrauensmann or V-mann	A local man (or woman) who worked for the German occupation police, particularly to infiltrate the Resistance
zone interdite	Forbidden zone in France along the Spanish border. German border guards could arrest anyone they found inside it without any other cause than their being there.
zone reservée	Reserved zone in France along the Swiss border, included the entire department of Haute-Savoie. No one could move about in the zone without a special pass.

TIMELINE

Dates in roman are events in the war or occupation that were important for Dutch-Paris. Dates in italics are events within the history of Dutch-Paris.

1940

May 10: German Wehrmacht invades the Netherlands and Belgium.
May 15: The Netherlands surrender; German occupation begins.
May 28: Belgian Army surrenders.
June 24: Vichy France signs the Armistice with Nazi Germany.
September 27: Creation of worker brigades for foreigners (GTEs) in France.
October 4: Vichy law permits the internment of foreign Jews.

1941

January 15: Swiss authorities create a military zone 200 to 600 yards deep along border.
May 14: Foreign Jews arrested in Paris
June 22: Hitler invades the Soviet Union.
December 7: Japan bombs Pearl Harbor. The United States enters the war.

1942

January: Jean Weidner and Elisabeth Cartier are married.

January 17: Occupation authorities in the Netherlands begin to concentrate Jews in Amsterdam.

January 20: Nazi authorities hold the Wannsee Conference about extermination camps.

March 26: First deportation train from western Europe leaves Drancy with Jews destined for Auschwitz.

April 5: The Gestapo is officially at work in the unoccupied zone of France.

May 30: The first RAF Thousand Bomber Raid takes place over Germany.

July: Jean Weidner receives a letter from a Jewish acquaintance in a French prison. He and Elisabeth Cartier construct an escape line between Lyon and Geneva.

July 4: Vichy authorizes the deportation of Jews from the unoccupied zone of France.

July 4: First draft notices for labor service in Germany are sent out in the Netherlands.

July 15: Deportations begin from the transit camp at Westerbork, the Netherlands, to Auschwitz.

July 16–17: Massive arrests of Jews in Paris take place, called "Rafle du Vel d'Hiv."

August 4: The first deportation of Jews from Belgium occurs.

August 15: Vichy police arrest 4,000 foreign Jews in the unoccupied zone of France.

October 14: Weidner detained and beaten by French gendarmes for two days on suspicion of passing refugees over the Swiss border.

November 8: Allies land in North Africa.

November 9: Vichy law forbids Jews to leave their official residence without special authorization.

November 11: Germans invade unoccupied zone of France; Italians occupy the Alpine departments.

December 6: Vichy's minister of the interior decides to evacuate all foreign Jews from the Pyrenees and Mediterranean coast.

December 9: Vichy arrests the Dutch consul-general Sevenster.

1943

January 27: Eighth USAAF launches its first bombing raid on Germany.

February 16: Creation of the obligatory labor service (STO) in France that drafts men for labor in Germany.

February 27: Germans surrender at Stalingrad.

March 1: Demarcation Line in France is suppressed; the *zone interdite* is created in the Pyrenees.

March 1: First group of labor draftees departs from France as part of the STO.

March 13: The German occupation authorities require that Dutch university students sign a loyalty oath (*Loyaliteitsverklaring*) or report for labor in Germany. Only about 15 percent of the students sign, closing the universities.

March 23: Weidner talks to the Dutch ambassador in Bern for the first time.

March 24: Weidner meets Pastor Willem Visser 't Hooft.

April: In Lyon, French police question Weidner about the disappearance of Dutch Jews.

April 29: German Occupation authorities order Dutch POWs to report for internment, triggering a wave of strikes across the Netherlands.

May: On his way to Switzerland, Benno Nijkerk visits Weidner in Lyon; Edmond Chait begins regular courier service between Lyon and Brussels.

June: Suzy Kraay is arrested on the Spanish border, spends one month in prison in Pau, and is then transferred to the Vichy internment camp at Gurs.

August 11: Weidner turns himself in to Swiss border guards for his first official meeting at the Dutch embassy. From now on he crosses the border as part of the Swiss SR.

September 3: Allies invade Italy.

September 6–8: In Lyon, the Gestapo arrest Jacquet and warn him not to interfere in Dutch business. Elisabeth Cartier goes to Switzerland.

September 8: Italy surrenders.

September 9: Germans occupy the Italian zone in France.

September 17: Weidner and Peter Naeff take refuge in Switzerland following Jacquet's arrest.

Late September: Weidner accepts a clandestine mission to distribute money to Dutch refugees in France, take Engelandvaarders from Switzerland to Spain, and carry microfilm for Visser 't Hooft and the Swiss Way.

September: The Comité reorganizes; Nijkerk and Pastor ten Kate ask Edouard Regout and Cornelis van Schaardenburgh to join the board.

October 13: Weidner leaves Switzerland for the first of many clandestine trips to organize Dutch-Paris.

October 15–16: Weidner travels to Brussels for the first time to coordinate with the Comité.

November 1: Kraay escapes from the Vichy internment camp at Gurs.

November 3: In Paris, Weidner and Herman Laatsman meet for the first time.

November 18: German police arrest Paul van Cleeff with several of his resistance allies.

December: Comité rents the pension at 19 rue Franklin as a safe house.

December 24: Marie Combes is arrested at the gare Matabiau in Toulouse; the Caparros filière stops functioning.

December 31: Germans raid Panier Fleuri in Toulouse.

1944

January 21: The first Dutch-Paris aviator convoy leaves Toulouse for the Pyrenees.

January 25: The second Dutch-Paris aviator convoy leaves Toulouse for the Pyrenees.

Late January: Kraay escorts a Jewish family from the Netherlands to Lyon, spends the night at the rue Franklin.

February 4: The third Dutch-Paris aviator convoy leaves Toulouse for the Pyrenees.

February 6: A German ambush at the Col du Portet d'Aspet captures half the evaders in the third aviator convoy.

February 9: A fourth convoy of aviators leaves Paris, stays in "Villa du Crime" in Toulouse until the weather clears in the mountains.

February 11: French police arrest Kraay in Paris.

February 12: French police arrest the Caubo family in Paris. Brother Rufus is arrested but released.

February 26: In Paris Germans arrest Gabrielle Weidner, Laatsman and his son, Fernande Goetschel, Jean Milleret, Suzanne Hiltermann, Leo Mincowski, Brother Rufus, Marcelle Brousse, and Julia and Emile Prilliez.

February 28: In Lyon Gestapo agents arrest Raymonde Pillot and Maurice Jacquet. In Brussels German police raid 19 rue Franklin, arrest ten aviators and David Verloop, Henri Vleeschdrager, Robert Bosschart, Jo Jacobstahl, J. P. Bol, and Lydia Ogy.

February 29: Chris ten Kate is arrested.

March 1: F. H. Iordens is shot; Adriaan van Haaften is presumed arrested.

March 3: In Brussels Adriaan Schmutzer is arrested. In Paris, Louise Roume is arrested. In Lyon Josette Molland is arrested.

March 4: Anna Neyssel is arrested in Paris.

March 6: In Annecy, Marie Meunier, Paul Lacôte, and Alice Charroin are arrested. Jacques Rens takes Annette Weidner from Paris to Switzerland.

March 7: David Verloop throws himself down a stairwell while in German custody to protect his colleagues.

March 9: In Paris and environs, Gabriel Piveteau, Raymond Meriot, and John Ruys are arrested. Hotel Montholon is raided.

March 17: Louis and Marguerite Chanoinat are arrested in Paris.

March 22: Hans Wisbrun is caught in a street raid in Brussels and deported to Germany as a forced laborer.

March 23: Benno Nijkerk, Jacob Brantsen, and Madeleine Larose-Reinaud are arrested in Paris.

March 27: Pastor Paul Meyer is arrested in Lyon.

March 29: The maquis *battle the Germans and* Milice *on the Glières pla-teau in Haute-Savoie.*

Late March: German police raid the sociaalwerk office on rue du Trône, Brussels.

May 15: Pastor ten Kate is arrested in Brussels.

May 20: Jean Weidner, Jacques Rens, Paul Veerman, and Gabriel Nahas are arrested by French Milice in Toulouse. Nahas escapes immediately.

May 22: Veerman escapes from the Milice prison in Toulouse.

May 30: Weidner and Rens escape from the Milice prison in Toulouse.

June 6: D-Day: Allies land in Normandy.

June 13: Jean-Louis Bazerque and Joseph Barrère are ambushed and killed in the Pyrenees.

June 14: Jacqueline Houry and her mother are arrested at home outside Paris.

June 17: Lucie Comiti is arrested.

June 20: Paul Veerman is arrested on the street in Brussels and deported to Germany as a forced laborer.

June 22: Simone Calmels is arrested in Toulouse.

July 18: Jules Mohr is arrested in Paris.

August 11: Alice Charroin and Paul Lacôte are released from prison due to illness.

August 15: Allies land in Provence.

August 16–22: Most of the Pyrenees are liberated.

August 19: Annecy is liberated.

August 19: Citizens free political prisoners in Toulouse, including Calmels.

August 19–25: Paris is liberated.

August 20: Toulouse is liberated.

August 20: Herman Laatsman, Marius Janse, and Jules Mohr are deported to the concentration camps.

August 24: Lyon is liberated.

September 3: Brussels is liberated.

September 4: Dutch-Paris prisoners are liberated from the prison camp at Beverloo, Belgium.

September 8: Weidner leaves Switzerland for France.

September 14: Maastricht is liberated.

September 17–25: Operation Market Garden fails to liberate the Netherlands.

October 27: Bergen op Zoom is liberated.

November: Nijkerk is killed in a bombing raid on his concentration camp.

November: Weidner flies to London for a private interview with Queen Wilhelmina and discussions with Prime Minister Pieter Gerbrandy.

1945

December 16–January 25: Battle of the Bulge takes place in Ardennes, Belgium.

January: Weidner establishes Netherlands Security Service in Paris.

January 27: Soviet troops liberate Auschwitz.

February 6: Mohr dies in Buchenwald.

February 13: Jean-Michael Caubo dies in the concentration camp of Dautmergen.

February 15: Gabrielle Weidner dies in a subcamp of Ravensbrück a few days after her liberation.

April 13: Lucie Comiti leaves Buchenwald on a death march.

April 15: British troops liberate Bergen-Belsen, the first concentration camp to be liberated in the West. Herman Laatsman is there.

April 17: Veerman returns to the Netherlands from imprisonment as a forced laborer.

April 21: Soviet troops reach Berlin.

April 25–26: The Swedish Red Cross evacuates French and Dutch women prisoners from Ravensbrück, including Kraay, Larose-Reinaud, Hiltermann, Anna Nyssel, Julia Prilliez, and Marcelle Brousse.

April 28: Laatsman returns to Paris from the concentration camps.

April 29–30: Soviet troops liberate Ravensbrück.

May 1: Julia Prilliez and Molland return from the concentration camps.

May 4: Neyssel returns to Paris.

May 4: German troops in the Netherlands, Denmark, and northern Germany surrender.

May 5: Amsterdam, The Hague, and the rest of the Netherlands are liberated.

May 7: American soldiers liberate Pillot from a concentration camp and Comiti from a second death march.

May 8: Germany surrenders.

May 14–31: Larose-Reinaud, Milleret, Jacqueline Houry, Marguerite Chanoinat, Comiti, and Brother Rufus return from the concentration camps.

June 3: Brother Robo returns to Paris.

July 2: Goetschel returns to Paris.

July 20: Hiltermann returns to Paris.

November: Nijkerk's wife is mistakenly notified that the Soviets are sending him home.

1946

August: The Soviets acknowledge that they made a spelling error and had not released Nijkerk.

1947

Weidner finds a political prisoner who can tell him about his sister Gabrielle's death in a subcamp of Ravensbrück.

1948

Mincowski's widow is able to prove that he died on April 10, 1945, in Buchenwald.

1948

The Caubo children are able to get a death certificate for their father, Jean-Michael Caubo.

1950

A Belgian court declares Nijkerk legally dead.

1953

Weidner has brain surgery to repair the lingering effects of being beaten with rifle butts by French gendarmes in October 1942.

ARCHIVES CONSULTED

Belgium

AJB	Archives of the Ministry of Justice, Belgium
ARB	Algemeen Rijksarchief, België
CEGESOMA	Center for Historical Research and Documentation on War and Contemporary Society, Brussels
DGO	Dienst Archief en Documentatie, Directie-generaal Oorlogsslachtoffers
NEDVER	Private archives of the Nederlands Vereenigen, Terruwe, Belgium
PROKER	Private archives of the Protestante Kerk, Brussels

France

AADV	Archives historiques de l'Adventisme en Europe, section Collonges-sous-Salève
ADHG	Archives départementales de la Haute-Garonne
ADHS	Archives départementales de la Haute-Savoie
ADR	Archives départementales du Rhône
AN	Archives nationales, Paris
APP	Archives de la préfecture de Police, Paris

CADAN   Centre d'archives diplomatiques à Nantes
CDJC   Centre de documentation Juive contemporaine, Paris
CHRD   Centre de l'histoire de la Résistance et de la Déportation, Lyon
SHD   Service historique de la Défense, Vincennes
SHDC   Service historique de la Défense, Caen
SHDLB   Service historique de la Défense, Le Blanc

Germany

BAMA   Bundesarchiv, Abteilung Militärarchiv, Freiburg-im-Breisgau
CGR   Captured German Records

Netherlands

NA   Nationaal Archief
NIOD   Nederlands Instituut voor Oorlogsdocumentatie
NRK   Nederlands Rode Kruis, Den Haag
ST4045   Stichting '40–'45 (limited access granted)
VA   Verzetsmuseum, Amsterdam

Switzerland

AEG   Archives de l'Etat de Genève
SBAR   Schweizerisches Bundesarchiv
WCC   Archives of the World Council of Churches, Geneva

United Kingdom

NAUK   National Archives of the United Kingdom

United States

NARA   National Archives and Records Administration
ROSS   Rossiter Papers, University of Michigan, Ann Arbor

WA   Weidner Center Archives (now the John Henry Weidner Papers, Hoover Library & Archives, Stanford University)

WA AS   Weidner Center Archives, Alberto Sbacchi Collection (now the John Henry Weidner Papers, Hoover Library & Archives, Stanford University)

WA BR   Weidner Center Archives, Belgian Resistance (now the John Henry Weidner Papers, Hoover Library & Archives, Stanford University)

WA EC   Weidner Center Archives, Edmond Chait Collection (now the John Henry Weidner Papers, Hoover Library & Archives, Stanford University)

WA WC   Weidner Center Archives, Weidner Collection (now the John Henry Weidner Papers, Hoover Library & Archives, Stanford University)

NOTES

Introduction

1. The renowned signer Ré Koster and her husband, David de Jong. Weidner Center Archives, Weidner Collection (hereafter WA and WC, respectively), now at the Hoover Library & Archives, Stanford University, 29 testimonies; WA WC 17 Koster; WA Ré Koster; Weidner Center Archives, Alberto Sbacchi Collection (hereafter WA AS), Ré Koster interview with Alberto Sbacchi, May 12, [1994?], summarized by Janet Carper. Also see van der Heijden, "Oorlogsherinneringen: Jean Weidner."

2. WA WC 10 Dutch-Paris History, 1.

3. For Jews in wartime France see Marrus and Paxton, *Vichy France and the Jews*, 56–70;165–73; Poznanski, *Jews in France*.

4. See Burleigh and Wippermann, *The Racial State*.

5. There are not many studies of the Dutch experience of the war available in English. See Van Galen Last, "Netherlands"; Hirschfeld, *Nazi Rule and Dutch Collaboration*; de Jong, *The Netherlands and Nazi Germany*; Moore, "Nazi Masters and Accommodating Dutch Bureaucrats"; Moore, *Victims and Survivors*; Warmbrunn, *The Dutch under German Occupation*.

6. Very little has been published in English about Belgium during the war. See Lagrou, "Belgium"; Schrijvers, *Liberators*; Warmbrunn, *The German Occupation of Belgium*. For the First World War see McPhail, *The Long Silence*.

7. Willy Hijmans, personal conversation with the author, April 2, 2010.

8. For overviews in English of France during the Second World War, see Burrin, *France under the Germans*; Diamond, *Women and the Second World*

War in France; Fogg, *The Politics of Everyday Life in Vichy France*; Gildea, *Marianne in Chains*; Jackson, *France*; Vinen, *The Unfree French*.

9. Weidner Senior told this story to Willy Hijmans during the war when Hijmans went to visit him at Jean Weidner's request (Willy Hijmans, email to the author, October 23, 2010). For other examples see Bennett, *Under the Shadow of the Swastika*, 83–84, 97; Fogelman, *Conscience and Courage*, 73, 80; Monroe, *The Hand of Compassion*, 229–30.

10. Semelin, "Introduction," 10; Vinen, *The Unfree French*, 247–77; Wieviorka, *Histoire de la Résistance*, 209–24.

11. For civil versus military resistance see Semelin, *Unarmed against Hitler*. For recent studies of resistance see Carr et al., *Protest, Defiance and Resistance in the Channel Islands*; Gildea, *Fighters in the Shadows*; Moore, *Survivors*; Semelin, "Introduction"; and Wieviorka, *Histoire de la Résistance*.

12. For the sociology of the resistance see Marcot, "Pour une sociologie de la Résistance"; Marcot, "La Résistance dans ses lieux et milieu"; Wieviorka, *Histoire de la Résistance*, 410–37.

13. François Marcot in "Pour une sociologie de la Résistance" distinguishes between "intentional" resisters, who resisted in order to oppose the occupation, and "functional" resisters, who were recruited into resistance organizations for the skill or good they could provide.

14. For recent summaries see Gildea, *Fighters in the Shadows;* Van Galen Last, "Netherlands"; Wieviorka, *Histoire de la Résistance*.

15. See Bennett, *Under the Shadow of the Swastika*.

16. In southern France the French and German authorities pursued organized networks of Jews but not primary shelterers of Jews. Andrieu, "Assistance to Jews and to Allied Soldiers and Airmen in France."

17. Jean Weidner, November 1945, WA WC 11 Dutch Resistance in France. That number agrees with historians' estimates of the percentage of the population actively engaged in resistance in western Europe: one in fifty, or 2 percent. No one knows how many men and women actively engaged in resistance before the Normandy landings, and few historians will hazard a guess. Robert Paxton famously estimated that 2 percent of the adult French population were resisters (*Vichy France*, 295). Henry Rousso in *Où en est l'historie de la Résistance* estimates that between 1 and 1.5 percent of the adult population of France were resisters, based on the number of individuals officially recognized as resisters by the French administration. Lynne Taylor puts the number for the Nord-Pas-de-Calais at six thousand resistance fighters out of a population of 3 million (*Between Resistance and Collaboration*, 63). John Sweets, however, uses a broad definition of resistance in his estimation that in the mountainous Puy-de-Dome between 7 and 17 percent of the population resisted (*Choices in Vichy France*, 224–25). Considering only the resistance specialty of escape lines, Emilienne Eychenne estimates that 0.14 percent of the people in the department of Haute-Garonne and 0.12 percent of the population of the

city of Toulouse were involved in providing illegal passage over the Pyrenees (*Montagnards de la liberté*, 139). Lou de Jong discusses the difficulties of arriving at a satisfactory count of Dutch resisters in *Het Koninkrijk der Nederlanden in de tweede wereldoorlog*, 7:1040–47. Thanks to Diego Gaspar Celaya, Lynne Taylor, and Peter Romijn for their thoughts on the matter.

18. See Caestecker and Moore, *Refugees from Nazi Germany and the Liberal European States*; Dwork and van Pelt, *Flight from the Reich*.
19. See Diamond, *Fleeing Hitler*; Risser, *France under Fire*.
20. According to Vinen, twenty thousand Dutch and Belgian Jews fled to France in 1940 (*The Unfree French*, 135). Citing de Jong (*Koninkrijk* 9:547) Moore puts the number of Dutch refugees in Vichy after the repatriation in 1940 at two thousand (*Survivors*, 29). The postwar parliamentary commission calculated the number after November 1942 as 1,200 to 1,300 (Enquêtecommissie Regeringsbeleid, *Enquêtecommissie Regeringsbeleid 1940–1945*, Dl. 6a en b: *De vertegenwoordiging van Nederland in het buitenland*, 6a–b, 163–64).
21. Dessing, *Tulpen voor Wilhelmina*.
22. See Hallie, *Lest Innocent Blood Be Shed*.
23. See de Graaff, *Stepping Stones to Freedom*; Ottis, *Silent Heroes*.
24. See Lazare, *Rescue as Resistance*; Menager, "Roundups, Rescue and Social Networks in Paris"; Moore, *Survivors*; Zuccotti, *Holocaust Odysseys*, 42–45, 219–21.
25. Andrieu, "Assistance to Jews and to Allied Soldiers and Airmen in France," 56.
26. Eychenne, *Montagnards de la liberté*, 139.
27. See Conway and Romijn, *The War for Legitimacy in Politics and Culture*.
28. For the history of the memory of the war see Lagrou, *The Legacy of Nazi Occupation*; Rousso, *The Vichy Syndrome*.
29. Inspecteur Arthur Charroin, Archives départementales de la Rhône (hereafter ADR), 3808W1503.

Chapter 1

1. Wieviorka, *Histoire de la Résistance*, 242–43.
2. For the Weidner family, see Carper, "The Weidners in Wartime." For details of J. H. Weidner's biography see WA WC 3 Biographical Information.
3. Between 1939 and 1942 the number of Jews in Lyon quadrupled; one third of the newcomers were foreign Jews (Menager, "Roundups, Rescue and Social Networks in Paris," 424).
4. Gilbert Beaujolin, who worked with the French intelligence network Alliance. The two men went to high school together. Weidner often stayed at the Beaujolin homes in Paris and Lyon during the war. He also took the children of Alliance's leader to safety in Switzerland. WA WC 2 Beaujolin, WA WC 11 DP member biographical information. For Amitié Chrétienne see Delpech, "La persecution des Juifs et l'Amitié chrétienne." Also see Moore, *Survivors*.

5. Service historique de la Défense (hereafter SHD), Bureau central de renseignements et d'action (hereafter BCRA), no catalog number, a list of names of "very sure" addresses given by Henri Sandberg, written on "Honneur et Patrie" letterhead, dated Lisbonne, 14 Mai 1942.

6. WA WC 10 Dutch-Paris History 1.

7. Centre d'archives diplomatiques à Nantes (hereafter CADAN), Consulat de France à Geneve, série B, box 84; Nationaal Archief (hereafter NA) 2.13.71(MvOL), 413; WA AS, Elisabeth Cartier Jolivet interview with Alberto Sbacchi, July 26, 1994, Geneva, transcribed and translated by Janet Carper; WA WC 3 Biographical Information, November 17, 1944; WA WC 11 Dutch Resistance in France.

8. See Meyer and Meinen, "La Belgique, pays de transit."

9. Among the vast literature on the deportations, see Klarsfeld, *Vichy-Auschwitz*; Luijters, *In memoriam*; Moore, *Victims*; Presser, *Ashes in the Wind*; Steinberg, *La Persécution des juifs en Belgique*.

10. Neither Jacquet nor his secretary Renée Grand-Clement spoke Dutch; NA 2.13.71 (MvOL) 413; NA 2.05.48.02 (BZ) 81; NA 2.05.57 (BuZaAmFr) 998; NA 2.05.57 (BuZaAmFr) 956; NA 2.05.48.02 (Commissie Cleveringa) 81 Jacquet; ADR 3335W24 and 3335W18; SHD 17P 115; WA AS Jacquet; WA WC 9 Dutch Ministry Foreign Affairs. Vichy changed the name and status of the Dutch consulate in Lyon several times during the war. For the sake of clarity, I refer to it as the consulate throughout. For the history of Dutch diplomats in France during the war see Plantinga, "Joseph Willem Kolkman (1896–1944) en de Engelandvaarders."

11. WA WC 15 Jacquet.

12. Intendant de la police de la préfecture du Rhône, Marcher (NA 2.13.71 (MvOL) 2523); commis greffier au tribunal civil à Lyon, Pinochet (NA 2.05.57 956; WA WC 15 Jacquet); chef du service des étrangers à la préfecture du Rhône, Travard (NA 2.13.71 2523; WA WC 15 Jacquet, Service historique de la défense, Caen (hereafter SHDC) 21P 542960); Colonel P. Marx, Commissaire du gouvernement près le tribunal militaire de Lyon (NA 2.05.57 (BuZaAmFr) 956; NA 2.13.71 (MvOL) 2523; WA WC 15 Jacquet, and WA WC 9 Dutch-Paris).

13. See, for example, WA WC 30 van der Post; WA WC 4 Castaing [*sic*]. For the Demarcation Line see Alary, *La Ligne de démarcation*.

14. For the Franco-Swiss border see Boulet, *Les Alpes françaises*; Lundi, "Dwindling Options"; Munos-du Peloux, *Passser en Suisse*; Fivaz-Silbermann, "The Swiss Reaction to the Nazi Genocide."

15. Dwork and van Pelt, *Flight from the Reich*, 207; Fivaz-Silbermann, "The Swiss Reaction to the Nazi Genocide."

16. Fivaz-Silbermann puts the rate of "racial refugees" *refoulé* into Haute-Savoie at 9 percent ("The Swiss Reaction to the Nazi Genocide," 240–41), but she does not include incidences of Swiss guards turning refugees back without filling out the paperwork. Boulet puts the rate much higher, considering

25 percent to be an underestimation. He notes that the prefect of Haute-Savoie requested extra police to take away the *refoulés* in October 1942 (*Les Alpes françaises*, 216–17). Anecdotal evidence from the Dutch-Paris archives supports Boulet's conclusions. Also see Munos-du Peloux, *Passer en Suisse*, 41; Yagil, *La France terre de refuge et de désobéissance civile*, 2:300–304.

17. Schweizerisches Bundesarchiv BAR (hereafter SBA) 6351(F)1 522 1942, letter dated September 16, 1942.

18. SBA 6351(F)1 522 1942, letter dated October 21, 1942. For the exponential escalation of illegal crossings between July and September 1942, see Boulet, *Les Alpes françaises*, 213–18.

19. Report of February 1943, quoted in Munos-du Peloux, *Passer en Suisse*, 31.

20. Munos-du Peloux, *Passer en Suisse*, 42.

21. U.S. Bureau of Labor Statistics, "Wage Trends and Wage Policies," 12.

22. Centre de l'histoire de la Résistance et de la Déportation, Lyon (hereafter CHRD), *Témoignage* Mme Raymonde Perrier neé Pillot, 11 Mars 1992.

23. Pastor Paul Chapal of Amitié Chrétienne and Abbé Camille Folliet, of the Comité inter-mouvements auprès des évacués (CIMADE, Ecumenical Committee to Aid Evacuees), with whom he helped fifty refugees get into Switzerland in 1942. For Chapal: WA WC 5 Chapal; WA WC 11 Dutch Resistance in France, WA WC 9 Dutch Ambassador. For Folliet: WA WC 3 Biographical Information; NA 2.05.57 (BuZaAmFr) 998; NA 2.13.71 (MvOL) 413. For both: Fabre, *God's Underground*; Lazare, *Le Livre des justes*; Yagil, *Chrétiens et Juifs sous Vichy*.

24. WA WC 19 Meunier; WA WC Beaujolin 2; WA WC 11 Dutch Resistance in France; SHD 17P 115; SHD 16P 414737; SHD Caen 21P 515930; Schulten, "*Zeg mij aan wien ik toebehoor*," 112; National Archives of the United Kingdom (hereafter NAUK) WO 208/5882.

25. These civil servants belonged to French *réseaux* but also helped Weidner: Luisette and Yvette Gambrillon (WA WC 12 Gambrillon; WA WC 10 DP Lists members 1; WA AS Cartier Jolivet; NA 2.05.57 (BuZaAmFr) 998; SHD 17P 115; AD 3808 W 1374); Jean-Pierre Ordioni (WA WC 11 Dutch Patriotic Association 1; NA 2.05.57 (BuZaAmFr) 998); Pierre Lamy (ADR 3808 W 1374; SHDC 21P 68700); René Terpend (WA WC 10 DP lists members 1; SHD 16P 565148; NA 2.05.57 (BuZaAmFr) 961); Marguerite Balland (NA 2.05.57 (BuZaAmFr) 961; NA 2.05.57 (BuZaAmFr) 998; SHD 16P 222004; WA WC 12 FFCI; WA WC 4 Chait); and Renée Gerlier (NA 2.05.57 (BuZaAmFr) 998).

26. In the absence of Weidner or Cartier, Lea and Pierre Jaccoud ran the shop and its clandestine hostelry. SHD 17P 115; SHD 16P 302956; SHD 16P 302957; Nederlands Instituut voor Oorlogsdocumentatie (hereafter NIOD) 187 49R; NA 2.05.57 (BuZaAmFr) 998; WA WC 10 DP lists members 1.

27. Abbé Marius Jolivet, WA AS. Also see Lazare, *Le Livre des justes*, 102; Yagil, *Chrétiens et Juifs sous Vichy*, 189.

28. "Témoignage of Roger Fasnacht," given during the Céremonie de la paix, November 2007, Archives historiques de l'Adventisme en Europe, section Collonges-sous-Salève (hereafter AADV), don de R. Lehman 2008.

29. At the seminary Pierre Toureille, Raymond Meyer, Jean Lavanchy, Maurice Mathy, Anna Zurcher, and Maurice Tièche also helped the escape line. Mr. Charpiot spent most of the war in Paris rather than in Collonges with his wife and son. WA WC 12 FFCI; NA 2.05.57 (BuZaAmFr) 998; SHD 16P 571196.

30. Later in the war Jacques Tièche traveled far outside the Haute-Savoie to bring Jewish refugees from their hiding places to the border and sometimes over it. WA WC 12 FFCI; WA WC 10 DP lists members 1; NA 2.05.57 (BuZaAmFr) 998; SHD 16P 571193; Archives de l'Etat de Genève (hereafter AEG) JetP Ef/2 no 2849.

31. Anna Zurcher and Frederic Zurcher in discussion with the author, January 31, 2011, Gland, Switzerland; AADV don de R Lehman 2008.

32. WA AS, Cartier Jolivet.

33. WA WC 29 Testimonies; WA WC 17 Koster; WA AS, Ré Koster interview with Sbacchi; Van der Heijden, "Oorlogsherinneringen: Jean Weidner."

34. Denise and Antonius Vogel, WA WC 32 Vogel; WA WC 29 Testimonies; WA AS Vogel.

35. Zurcher interview with author, January 31, 2011.

36. AADV don de R Lehman 2008.

37. After the war Fasnacht estimated that he and his colleagues at the seminary had helped 150 Jews in this way. AADV don de R Lehman 2008. Anna Zurcher, like other rescuers, felt that her contributions were too "normal" to mention. AADV don de R Lehman 2008. For resistance as "normal" see the work of Fogelman, *Conscience and Courage*; Klempner, *The Heart Has Reasons*; Monroe, *The Heart of Altruism*; Monroe, *The Hand of Compassion*; Oliner and Oliner, *The Altruistic Personality*.

38. Munos-du Peloux, *Passer en Suisse*, 62.

39. Munos-du Peloux, *Passer en Suisse*, 62–64.

40. Boulet, *Les Alpes françaises*, 218.

41. Munos-du Peloux, *Passer en Suisse*, 73

42. CIMADE was also able to do this (Munos-du Peloux, *Passer en Suisse*, 22). Other escape lines tried to fit their clients to Swiss policy; see, for instance, Fivaz-Silberman, "The Swiss Reaction to the Nazi Genocide," 240–41; Lazare, *Rescue as Resistance*; Moore, *Survivors*.

43. WA WC 3 Beaujolin.

44. WA WC 3 Beaujolin; WA AS Cartier Jolivet; NIOD 244 1074; NA 2.05.48.02 (BZ) 15; NA 2.05.48.02 (BZ) 29.

45. The list went into effect on October 9, 1942, but was kept highly secret. SBA 6351(F)1 522 1942.

46. WA WC 24 Rosican; WA WC 11 Dutch-Paris Members Biographical Information.

47. NIOD 244 1074; WA WC 3 Bouchet; WA AS Emile Bouchet interview with Alberto Sbacchi, August 3, [1994?], transcribed by Janet Carper; CHRD *Témoignage* Mme Raymonde Perrier neé Pillot, 11 Mars 1992.

48. For example, NA 2.05.57 (BuZaAmFr) 998; NA 2.13.71 (MvOL) 413; NA 2.05.57 (BuZaAmFr) 998; Yagil, *Chrétiens et Juifs sous Vichy*, 139.

49. *Nieuw Israelisch Weekblad*, January 6, 1950, with thanks to Maarten Eliasar and Rudy Zeeman for the translation.

50. After the war Weidner calculated that of the approximately 1,000 people he and his colleagues helped to escape occupied territory, all were Dutch except 200 French, 100 other nationalities, and 118 Allied aviators (Weidner, "De Weg naar de Vrijheid," 3:737.

51. Guillon, "'Talk Which Was Not Idle.'"

52. Captain Vallette at the prison and the Moos family helped the Stoppelmans in Annecy. WA WC 29 Testimonies, Helene Stoppleman Cornelisse, January 27, 1992; SBA E4264 1985/196 12968.

53. SBA E4264 1985/196 12572. They traveled with Armand Lap, Lex van Gelderen, and Henri Hartog. WA WC 30 van Gelderen.

54. Gazan and Lap were taken to the court in St-Julien, France, to testify in the trial of the two *passeurs*, both of whom were found guilty of complicity in illegal border crossing. *Journal de Gèneve*, August 4, 1942.

55. NIOD 244 1074; WA WC 30 van Gelderen.

56. M et Mme J Beausoleil of Les Petits Bois welcomed many Dutch refugees to their farm to await the trip over the border. NA 2.05.57 (BuZaAmFr) 998.

57. NIOD 244 1074.

58. The list included two couples, a family of four, a family of three, and three individuals, including the Gazans' traveling companions, Lap and Hartog. SBA E4264 1985/196 15818. Also see NIOD 244 1074; WA WC 30 van Gelderen.

59. WA WC 11 Dutch Resistance in France.

60. Munos-du Peloux, *Passer en Suisse*, 42–43. The French *police speciale* also suspected the Dutch at the Office néerlandaise in November 1942. Centre de documentation Juive contemporaine, Paris (hereafter CDJC) xxxiii–24.

61. Eliasar, "Zwitserlandva(ar)der"; WA WC 12 Eliasar Family; WA WC 19 Merckling.

62. A third Dutch Jew hiding at their hotel escaped at Le Chable. Their guide, Alfred Merckling, was conscripted into the Wehrmacht as a result of this arrest but managed to serve as a nurse among the *Malgré Nous* on the Eastern Front. A postwar ordinance of June 6, 1945, erased his wartime condemnation for complicity in crossing the frontier, See WA WC 19 Merckling; SHD 17P 115; SHD 16P 411999.

63. NIOD 244 1074.

64. WA AS Cartier Jolivet; WA WC 26 Sevenster.

Chapter 2

1. Rodogno, *Fascism's European Empire*, 393–416.
2. Fasnacht remembered that the Italians did not hesitate to shoot fugitives in the no man's land between Haute-Savoie and Switzerland. AADV don R Lehman; NA 2.05.57 (BuZaAmFr) 998.
3. Between three thousand and five thousand refugees left the German occupied parts of France for the Italian zone after November 1942, Rodogno, *Fascism's European Empire*, 397.
4. NA 2.05.49 (GzZw) 853. See also Laffitte, "Was the UGIF an Obstacle to the Rescue of Jews?"
5. NA (2.13.71) 413; NA 2.05.80 (BuZaL) 3777; NA 2.13.71 (MvOL) 2571; SHD 16P 439025; WA WC 20 Naeff; WA WC 30 van Lennep; WA WC 29 Toulouse.
6. For the process see Moore, *Survivors*, 125.
7. Eliasar, "Zwitserlandva(ar)der"; WA WC 29 Toulouse; WA WC 3 Bouchet; AEG PetJ Ef/2 3995; SBA E4264 1985–195 1039.
8. Dr. Pierre Toureille, captured while escorting fugitives into Switzerland. AADV don R Lehman; NA 2.05.57 (BuZaAmFr) 998.
9. NA 2.05.57 (BuZaAmFr) 998.
10. Chait's father owned a lumber business; he was not a rabbi, as erroneously reported in other books. His mother and sisters perished at Auschwitz. WA Edmond Chait Collection (hereafter EC); WA WC 28 Spetter; Stichting '40–'45, "Verslag over de werkzaamheden van de Nederlandsche Verzet-Beweging in Brussel gedurende de Bezettingsjaren 1942–1944," signed A. Nijkerk, December 5, 1944, and September 10, 1945 (hereafter ST 4045 Verslag). See also Steinberg, *Le Comité de défense des Juifs en Belgique*, 150.
11. Such as the Families Hakkert, Rosenthal, Van Straten, de Leeuw, Biron, Peterfreund, Rosican, Magnus, and Van Moppes. WA WC 4 Chait.
12. U.S. National Archives and Records Administration (hereafter NARA), RG 498, HQ ETO US Army WWII; MIS-Y, French Evasion Organizations and Networks, Dutch-Paris Dossier; National Archives Identifier 6005919 (hereafter NARA MIS-Y Dutch-Paris), and NARA; RG 498, HQ ETO US Army WWII; MIS-X, French Evasion Organizations and Networks, Dutch-Paris; National Archives Identifier 6005918 (hereafter NARA Dutch-Paris dossier); NARA, RG 498, HQ ETO US Army WWII; Office of the Assistant Chief of Staff G-2 Awards Branch, MIS-X Files, French, National Archives Identifier 5682722, (hereafter NARA, MIS-X, French), Box 71, Chait.
13. For Vichy as mental chloroform see Semelin, *Unarmed against Hitler*, 54–56.
14. George Stadler, an Alsatian refugee living in Annecy with his three children, was arrested in July 1943. NA 2.05.57 (BuZaAmFr) 998; SHD 16P 555985; WA WC 28 Stadler.
15. ADR 3808 W 1503; WA WC 10 Dutch-Paris Lists Members 1; WA WC 5 Charroin; NA 2.05.57 (BuZaAmFr) 998; SHD 17P 115; SHDC 21P 435358; SHD 16P 144379; SHDC 221200862.

16. WA Beaujolin 2; WA WC 11 Dutch Resistance in France; WA WC 5 Charroin; SHDC 21P 435458. For de Menthon's role in the Mouvement de Libération Nationale see Wieviorka, *Histoire de la Résistance*, 70, 95.

17. Jean Massendès, a member of several French resistance groups. WA WC 19 Massendès; SHD 16P 401558; Archives départementales de la Haute-Savoie (hereafter ADHS) 14 W 27.

18. Emile Bernard, father of four. WA WC 3 Bernard; SHD 16P 51008; Zurcher, January 31, 2011.

19. In Annecy: Mme N. Bouchet at the Café du Marché on the rue du Pont Neuf, Mr. and Mrs. Maurice Harry at the Hotel Bel Abri, and the widow Mercier at the Maison Pierfetti (WA WC 3 Bouchet, WA AS Bouchet; WA WC 13 Harry; WA WC 10 Dutch-Paris lists members 1; NA 2.05.117 [BuZaCode Archief] 20893). In Les Cruseilles: The hotel of Mr. Brandt and the pharmacy of André Bouchet (not related to Ernest) (NA 2.05.57 [BuZaAmFr] 998; WA AS Bouchet).

20. WA WC 10 Dutch-Paris lists of members 1; WA WC 3 Bouchet; NA 2.05.57 (BuZaAmFr) 998.

21. Among others, Bouchet guided André Eliasar, two of the de Menthon children, and the Azkenazy, Nathans, and Pels families. He worked with his brother Georges, who burned their records before being arrested in February 1944. WA AS Bouchet; WA WC 3 Bouchet.

22. Marrus and Paxton, *Vichy France and the Jews*, 148, 302, 307.

23. After Consul-General Ate Sevenster was arrested on December 9, 1942, and incarcerated at Evaux-les-Bains, only two Dutch civil servants remained in Vichy to work in the Dutch bureau of the French ministry in charge of foreigners, mostly on technical matters pertaining to the distribution of official monies. Marius Janse: SHD 16P 306417; NA 2.05.49 (GzZw) 853; NA 2.05.80 (BuZaL) 3577; NA 2.05.57 (BuZaAmFr) 1199; NA 2.05.48.02 (BZ) 81; WA WC 14 Janse; WA WC 10 Dutch-Paris History 1; NRK 186.496. Gustava Mouwen: WA WC 20 Mouwen; NA 2.05.49 (GzZw) 853.

24. The short-lived committee consisted of Heren Asscher, Duizend, Appelboom, Jacquet, Weidner, Naeff, and Janse. See Naeff's report of July 1943: WA WC 20 Naeff.

25. WA Gazan.

26. Dutch-Paris reimbursed the 100,000 French francs at the end of the year. WA WC 9 Dutch-Paris Finances, Visser 't Hooft. Visser 't Hooft's colleague was the Swiss pastor Roland de Pury, delegate for Pastor Marc Boegner to Amitié Chrétienne. See Wagner, *The Righteous of Switzerland*, 150; Yagil, *Chrétiens et Juifs sous Vichy*, 141.

27. The appeal was signed by I. de Bruyn, P. Kerdel, R. Polak, W. A. Visser 't Hooft, J. W. J. Baron de Vos van Steenwijk, and R. C. M. Wertheim Salomonson. NA 2.05.49 (GzZw) 853.

28. WA WC 24 Rosican. Only one refugee contributed, Mr. D. Koeleman, who spontaneously gave half of everything he had. NA 2.13.71 (MvOL) 1393; WA WC 31 van Tricht.

29. The *Devizienschutzkommando*. See Meinen, "Face à la traque."

30. Both the official and black market exchange rates fluctuated over the course of the war. For instance, in May 1943 Gazan reported an official exchange rate of 1.80 Swiss francs to 100 French francs. In December 1943 Visser 't Hooft and Weidner used a rate of 1 Swiss franc to 55 French francs. WA WC Gazan; WA WC 9 Dutch-Paris Finances Visser 't Hooft.

31. By December the committee had collected 508,400 French francs. WA WC 9 Dutch-Paris Finances, Visser 't Hooft.

32. WA BR Haenecour.

33. Between June and December 1943 Weidner collected the equivalent of 41,880 Swiss francs in French francs in Lyon from the representative of Pastor Charles Guillon, who was working with the Red Cross in Switzerland. WA WC 23 People 2. See also WA WC 9 DP Finances Visser 't Hooft.

34. The original contact was Pastor Roland de Pury. Instead the money went through CIMADE channels to "Monnette" in Lyon, from whom Weidner received it in two bundles of 50,000 French francs. WA WC Gazan.

35. WA Gazan; WA World Council of Churches Archives.

36. NA 2.05.49 (GzZw) 853; WA Gazan.

37. NA 2.05.49 (GzZw) 853.

38. NA 2.05.49 (GzZw) 853.

39. WA WC 11 Dutch Resistance in France; NA 2.05.80 (BZL) 3603.

40. He was, however, unable to contract a loan for the second 100,000 Swiss francs in January 1944, after the first installment was spent. NA 2.05.49 (GzZw) 853.

41. For example, WA WC 24 Rosenthal Family; WA CIMADE Archives; WA WC 4 Chait 1. CIMADE donated 100,000 French francs to help Dutch refugees, which Weidner paid back in late summer 1943 from money collected by expatriates in Switzerland. WA Gazan; WA WC 5 CIMADE; WA WC 9 Dutch-Paris Finances, Visser 't Hooft. For the CIMADE see Fabre, *God's Underground*; Moore, *Survivors*, 125–35.

42. Visser 't Hooft, *Memoirs*, 142.

43. For the Engelandvaarders see Dessing, *Tulpen voor Wilhelmina*; Visser, *De Schakel*.

44. Van Galen Last, "Netherlands," 199–202.

45. NA 2.13.71 (MvOL) 2571; NA 2.09.06 (MvJL) 11994.

46. NA 2.13.71 (MvOL) 2508.

47. Pastor Chapal in Annecy was particularly inundated with these Engelandvaarders. For Van Niftrik see NA 2.13.71 (MvOL) 1301; NA 213.71 (MvOL) 413; NA 2.05.48.02 (BZ) 29; WA WC 32 Visser 't Hooft; WA WC 3 Biographical Information; Enquêtecommissie Regeringsbeleid, *Enquêtecommissie Regeringsbeleid*, 4cII:1504, and 6a-b:70.

48. He seems to have sent them to a CIMADE pastor, de Crespy, in Lunel with two guides, "Pierre" and "Poney." WA WC 3 Biographical Information. Consuls J. W. Kolkman and J. C. A. M. Testers.

49. NA 2.05.49 (GzZw) 853; WA WC 30 van Rosenthal.

50. Marius Sessler, NA 2.05.57 (BuZaAmFr) 998, WA WC 30 van Rosenthal; SBA E4320B 1990/266 4703; SBA E 2001–8 1978/107 1609; ADR 182W100, 3335 W 28, and 3335 W 19.

51. WA WC 12 Financial Records Misc.

52. WA WC 26 Segers; WA EC; WA WC 5 Chait 5. Also see Croquet, *Chemins de Passage*, 97–98 ; Yagil, *La France terre de refuge et de désobéissance civile*, 2:314, 304.

53. AEG JetP Ef 2 4157.

54. Fanny van Hoof, fiancée of Armand Lap. WA Gazan.

55. WA WC 18 and WA WC 25 Sanders.

56. For denunciation see Fitzpatrick and Gellately, *Accusatory Practices*; Diamond, *Women and the Second World War in France*, 87–89.

57. ADR 45 W 38.

58. WA WC 4 Chait 1.

59. NA 2.05.57 (BuZaAmFr) 998.

60. WA WC 15 Jacquet.

61. WA WC 15 Jacquet; ADR 3335 W 24; ADR 3335 W 18.

62. CHRD Lyon, *témoignage* Perrier.

63. NA 2.13.71 (MvOL) 257; WA WC 31 van Wijhe; WA WC 8 Delrue.

64. Emile Bernard, WA WC 3 Bernard.

65. SBA E4264 1985/196 19872.

66. After Janse's arrest in January 1944, Weidner returned to Vichy several times to retrieve the cash. WA WC 26 Sevenster 2; WA WC 26 Segers; WA WC 9 Dutch-Paris Finances Visser 't Hooft; WA WC 13 Groll; WA WC 14 Janse.

67. NA 2.13.71 (MvOL) 413. Also see van Borssum Buisman, *Agent van de Zwitserse Weg*; de Jong, *Het Koninkrijk der Nederlanden in de Tweede Wereldoorlog*,7:2, 892–915.

68. WA WC 9 Dutch-Paris Finances.

Chapter 3

1. For the French railways see Richardot, *Héros et salauds pendant l'Occupation*.

2. Willy Hijmans in discussion with the author, June 4, 2010.

3. WA WC 24 Rens.

4. When in Belgium, Chait stayed with Josephine Lever and her husband and son. Weidner Archives, Belgian Resistance (hereafter WA BR) Lever; WA WC 4 Chait 1.

5. January 1944, NIOD 187 46 R.

6. Chait's contact in Quiévrain was Jules Mirgaux. WA BR Mirgaux; WA WC 2 Birgand; WA WC 4 Chait 1.

7. Chait demonstrates the crossing in Verkijk, "Weg naar de Vrijheid, Meer dan 1080."

8. Weidner kept carbon copies of these reports, found in WA WC 26 Segers; parts can also be found in NIOD 187 46R.

9. WA WC 26 Segers.

10. WA WC 11 Dutch Resistance in France.

11. The pastor had sent his two young Dutch assistants in the Swiss Way, Jan van Borssum Buisman and Joop Bartels, on exploratory missions to the Netherlands that included stops in Brussels. The contacts they made there, however, were kept out of Dutch-Paris and reserved as last resorts. WA WC 7 Decorations, recommendations. Enquêtecommissie Regeringsbeleid, *Enquêtecommissie Regeringsbeleid*, 4a: *Zwitserse Weg*; van Borssum Buisman.

12. For the CDJ see de Lathouwer, "Comité des défense des Juifs"; Moore, *Survivors*, 175–86; Steinberg, *Le Comité de défense des Juifs en Belgique*. Also see Vromen, *Hidden Children of the Holocaust*.

13. The Swiss turned Nijkerk back over the border after his first attempt, on May 26, 1943, on the grounds that his mission for a children's aid society did not qualify him for asylum. WA Gazan; NA 2.13.71 (MvOL) 413; AEG JetP, Ef/2 3325. See also WA BR Nijkerk; WA WC 22 Nijkerk Family; Liagre, "De Zwitserse Weg en de Dutch-Paris line."

14. After the war Chait complained that the international Jewish organizations collected money for the Jewish refugees but did not disburse it. WA WC 4 Chait 3. See also Boudin, "Les lignes d'évasion."

15. WA WC 4 Chait 1.

16. Maurice Bolle, who ran his own escape route between the Netherlands and Brussels and served in the leadership of the CDJ and FI, approached Ten Kate about working together to help refugees in spring 1942. WA BR Bolle; Steinberg, *Le Comité de défense des Juifs en Belgique*, 29, 45–46, 123–32. For resistance in Belgium see Lagrou, "Belgium."

17. For Ten Kate see WA WC 3 Belgian Resistance; NA 2.13.71 (MvOL) 413; NA 2.02.20 (Kabinet der Koningin) 9480; Liagre, "De Zwitserse Weg en de Dutch-Paris line"; Boudin, "Les lignes d'évasion."

18. In early 1942 the FI contributed as much as 500 Belgian francs per month to support an individual in hiding, 750 per month for a family of two, and 1,000 per month for three people. In October 1942 Bolle told Ten Kate that the Dutch expatriate community would have to take on the burden of hiding Dutch Jews. WA BR Bolle; WA BR van Cleeff; WA BR Goudsmit; WA WC 3 Belgian Resistance; NA 2.13.71 (MvOL) 413; ST 4045, Verslag.

19. ST 4045, Verslag; WA BR van Cleeff; WA BR Vleeschdrager.

20. In addition to Devriendt, J. van der Donck and Georges de Cuyper obtained or registered false documents at the Etterbeek *mairie*. WA BR van Cleeff.

21. Enquêtecommissie Regeringsbeleid, *Enquêtecommissie Regeringsbeleid*, 6c:553.

22. The Flam Breton on the chaussée d'Ixelles run by Mme Verteneuil; the café du Tunel at 55 boulevard Waterloo; the "salon" of Mlle Jane Flinal at 17 rue de la Tulipe in Ixelles; and the home of Mme Devis, a laundress on rue de la Verrerie in Boitsfort, whose "intrepid" seventeen-year-old niece, Lucienne, helped with errands. WA BR Davignon.

23. In her report Mme Davignon wondered if it was necessary to give the names of all those who helped Jews but mentioned Mlle Anciaux, Mme Jeanette van Oberghe, Mme Victoria, M et Mme Brabant, Mme Bontemps and M Jules Bontemps, M Pateyn, and Mme Laymarie as willing hosts for Jews and other fugitives. For merchants she listed as the most "patriots et complaisants" the butcher Dulier, the Maison Noël, Guillaume Delpierre, the grocer Edmond Detien, the grocer Maison Hukt, and Mme Valet, "rexiste, mais non antisemite" (collaborationist but not anti-Semitic). WA BR Davignon.

24. WA WC Belgian Resistants.

25. Pastor de Haan and his daughter cared for those hiding in Antwerp. WA BR Vleeschdrager.

26. The Comité had the cooperation of Drs. Allard and Snoek at the Hospital St Pierre as well as Sister Buffy at the Hollandsche Kliniek. Joanna ten Kate-Vandenbroek had directed the clinic before her marriage to Pastor ten Kate in 1939.

27. André Carl printed documents for several réseaux. ST 4045, Verslag.

28. For example, NA 2.13.71 (MvOL) 2524.

29. Jan Strengers and Thijs van Roggen worked with a Polish officer, André Wyssogota-Zakrzewski, who ran the Visigoths-Lorraine Line. He charged Dutchmen more in order to underwrite the passage of Poles. See SHD 16P 295767, SHDC 100114151, WA WC 36 Wyssogotha [sic], NA (2.13.71), 2571; NAUK WP 208/5459; NARA Dutch-Paris dossier; WA WC 28 Strengers; WA WC 30 van Cleeff.

30. The most notable was a gift of 80,000 Belgian francs from the Synod of the Dutch Reformed Church delivered to Pastor ten Kate in November 1943 by the Dutch banker Jan Strengers, who worked for Van Mierlo's bank in Brussels. NA 2.13.71 (MvOL) 413.

31. The Dutch government repaid the loan after the war. Bosschart sheltered refugees, laundered money, and sent several men from his shipyard to Spain via Dutch-Paris. WA BR Bosschart; WA WC 32 Verhagen; WA WC 9 Dutch Ambassador.

32. NA (2.13.71) 2571; WA BR Haenecour.

33. WA BR Haenecour.

34. Haenecour began helping Allied evaders and Jews to escape and hide in the early days of the war. The Comité valued his contributions highly. WA BR Haenecour; NA 2.13.71 (MvOL) 413.

35. Regout was the secretary-general of the Compagnie des Mines, Minerais et Metaux. NA 2.13.71 (MvOL) 413; Algemeen Rijksarchief Belgie, Min. Just., Police des Etrangers, Dossiers Individuels, Vreemdelingenpolitie, Individuele Dossiers (hereafter ARB police) 1210717; ST 4045, Verslag.

36. Van Schaardenburgh was an executive with the Eliott-Fisher Organization. NA 2.13.71 (MvOL) 413; ST 4045, Verslag; WA BR van Schaardenburgh; Nederlandsche Vereeniging, Terruwe, Belgium (hereafter NEDVER). I would like to thank the Nederlandsche Vereeniging and particularly Kees Veenstra for facilitating my research.

37. They escaped from wagons 257 and 258 of convoy XVIII. The Van Cleeffs owned a textile shop in The Hague. Mr. and Mrs. van Cleeff and their younger son perished in Auschwitz on January 18, 1943; their daughter died there on April 30, 1943. WA BR van Cleeff; WA WC 30 van Cleeff; Dienst Archief en Documentatie, Directie-generaal Oorlogslachtoffers (hereafter DGO) 275211; Nederlands Rode Kruis, Den Haag (hereafter NRK) 158.055; ST 4045 Verslag. Vleeschdrager was first arrested when a customs agent confiscated his false documents on the Dutch-Belgian border. In October 1942 he escaped from convoy XVI. NRK 78.779; DGO 275211; WA BR Vleeschdrager.

38. The family lost their son when his ship was torpedoed off North Africa. They hosted some twenty Jewish fugitives in their home. Nieulant-Pelkman, an engineer, also found jobs for two Dutchmen at his company to protect them from being sent to work in Germany. WA WC BR Nieulant-Pelkman; NA 2.13.71 (MvOL) 413; Liagre, "De Zwitserse Weg en de Dutch-Paris line."

39. WA BR van Cleeff; WA BR Vleeschdrager.

40. His family owned a textile shop in The Hague. WA BR Wisbrun, WA WC 36 Wisbrun.

41. For example, Philip Israels, who left his two children in hiding in the Netherlands when he and his wife fled to Belgium, worked as a courier for several months until the stress became too much for him. He was captured after leaving the Comité and died on the day he arrived at Auschwitz. WA BR Israels; NRK Brussels Archief box XI; ST 4045 Verslag.

42. WA BR Verloop; WA WC 28 Strengers; WA WC 32 Verloop; NARA Dutch-Paris dossier. For the Kindercomité see Moore, *Survivors*, 296–99; Flim, *Omdat hun hart sprak*; Broeyer, *Het Utrechtse universitaire verzet.*

43. WA BR Bol.

44. Chris ten Kate, Adriaan van Haaften, and Daan van der Most van Spijk, friends and classmates at the University of Utrecht. NA 2.13.71 (MvOL) 413; NA 2.13.71 (MvOL) 2571; NRK 192275; "Einige Gegevens MBT Adriaan Johan van Haaften (1920–1945) Tijdens de Tweede Wereldoorlog," put together from family papers by Adriaan Johan van Haaften, Middelburg, September 4, 2010. I would like to thank Frits Broeyer for sharing this memoir. For Utrecht students see Broeyer, *Het Utrechtse universitaire verzet.*

45. The same can be said for F. H. Iordens and Anne Maclaine Pont, who had an impressive resistance record in the Netherlands before cooperating with Dutch-Paris to take Allied pilots to Spain. WA WC 11 Dutch Resistance in France; WA BR Bol; ST 4045, Verslag; NA 2.13.71 (MvOL) 413; Fritz Broeyer personal communication with the author; Utrechtsch Studenten Corps, *Utrechtsche Studenten Almanak, 1946*; de Graaff, *Stepping Stones*, 130; Moore, *Survivors*, 315. For Hijmans see NA 2.13.71 (MvOL) 413; WA BR Hijmans; Willy Hijmans interview, May 25, 1990, Verzetsmuseum Amsterdam (hereafter VA).

46. Herbert and Walter Rothbarth. Hijmans letter to author, November 17, 2009; Hijmans in discussions with the author, April, June, July 2010; NA

2.09.06 (MvJL) 10642; NA 2.13.71 (MvOL) 2419; NA 2.13.71 (MvOL) 2571; NA 2.13.71 (MvOL) 2621.

47. This must have happened in fall 1943. Willy Hijmans, personal communication with the author, May 16, 2012. Nauta figures on the official Dutch-Paris lists as a courier, but he had such a tangled career in the resistance that he did not identify himself as belonging to Dutch-Paris. WA BR Nauta; WA WC 28 Strengers; WA WC 11 Dutch Resistance in Belgium; NA 2.13.71 (MvOL) 413.

48. For Henry see WA BR Henry; interview of Piet Henry, June 8, 1990, VA; ST4045 Verslag; Henry, "Piet Henry Vertelt." Verloop also recruited Jonkheer W. H. van Swinderen, who brought money, clothing, and people from the Netherlands to Brussels from the turn of 1943 until his capture in February 1944. NA 2.13.71 413; ST4045 Verslag; WA WC 11 Dutch Resistance in Belgium; WA BR van Swinderen; NRK 55817.

49. Henry made the trip to Brussels for Dutch-Paris every week for six months until late February 1944, when he went under for six weeks. Chris Lindemanns betrayed him when he reemerged. Henry, "Piet Henry Vertelt"; interview of Piet Henry, June 8, 1990, VA; NA 2.13.71 (MvOL) 2571; NA 2.13.71 (MvOL) 413; ST4045, Verslag; WA BR Nauta; WA BR Vleeschdrager.

50. Willy Hijmans, personal conversation with the author, May 2009.

51. Receipts for October 1943: 45,000 Belgian francs; expenditures: 60,000 Belgian francs. NA 2.13.71 (MvOL) 413; NA 2.05.49 (GzZw) 853.

52. The equivalent of 100,000 French francs. WA WC 9 Dutch-Paris Finances Visser 't Hooft.

53. WA WC 26 Segers.

54. He was arrested at the home of the Dutch widow Petronella van Gellicum-Kamps in a roundup of Karst Smit's Bravery Line. Van Cleeff may have been in her apartment at the time of the raid by Geheime Feldpolizei 530 to discuss the evasion of aviators with Elise Chabot, who had connections to the Service EVA. See Ministry of Justice, Belgium, Cour Militaire, Affaire Duncker, Karl et Consorts, Geheime Feldpolizei 530, 1950–1951 (hereafter AJB GFP 530); WA WC 30 van Moorleghem; WA WC 26 Segers; Center for Historical Research and Documentation on War and Contemporary Society, Brussels (hereafter CEGES) AA 1742/22; NA 2.13.71 (MvOL) 413; NARA Dutch-Paris dossier.

55. His phone was tapped from November 24, 1943, to January 8, 1944. NA 2.13.71 (MvOL) 413.

56. WA BR Verhagen; WA WC 26 Segers; NA 2.13.71 (MvOL) 413; ST4045 Verslag; Steinberg, Le Comité de défense des Juifs en Belgique, 115; de Lathouwer, "Comité des défense des Juifs."

57. He feared for Van Gellicum because she had sheltered many fugitives and had contacts with England. WA WC 26 Segers.

58. NA 2.05.49 (GzZw) 853.

59. WA WC 26 Segers.

60. The widow at the Café Hulstkamp was Mevrouw Richmond-van Witzenburg. In addition to Dutch-Paris Lejeune also belonged to the Resistance network Orde Dienst. He ferried people and microfilm between Amsterdam and Brussels every two weeks from fall 1943 to spring 1944. WA WC 5 Chait 6; WA WC 26 Segers; WA WC 18 Lejeune; Enquêtecommissie Regeringsbeleid, *Enquêtecommissie Regeringsbeleid*, 4cII:1483–85; Liagre, "De Zwitserse Weg en de Dutch-Paris line"; Cammaert, *Het Verborgen Front*, 1133–39; also see Verkijk, "Weg naar de Vrijheid, Meer dan 1080."

61. WA BR Borst; WA WC 26 Segers; WA BR Wisbrun.

62. For example, Willy Hijmans brought illegal papers from Leiden. WA WC 13 Hijmans.

63. Among other resistance groups, Didier de Thomas de Bossière belonged to Réseau Zéro, as did Nijkerk. CEGES AA 1333; NA 2.13.71 (MvOL) 413; WA BR de Thomaz [*sic*]; WA BR van Cleeff.

Chapter 4

1. WA WC 11 Dutch-Paris members biographical information.
2. For the family correspondence, see Carper, "The Weidners in Wartime."
3. Association de Secours aux Refugiés Hollandais. For Okhuysen see NA 2.13.71 (MvOL) 413; NA 2.13.71 (MvOL) 2571; SHD 16P 523259; SHD 16P 449448; SHDC 220117340; WA WC 11 Dutch Patriotic Association; WA WC 22 Okhuysen; WA WC 7 D'Aquin-Boot.
4. Testimony of C. de Graeff in front of the Commissie Meeuwen, January 1946, WA WC 20 Mouwen. For Okhuysen and Roume's aid to fugitives see SHD 16P 523259; WA WC 25 Senn; WA WC 22 Okhuysen; Oord, *Vervolgd en vergeten*, 37, 48.
5. NAUK KV 4/25.
6. WA WC 22 Okhuysen.
7. WA WC 20 Mohr, WA WC 29 Tourne, NA 2.05.80 (BuZaL) 3559.
8. WA Gazan; Bosch van Rosenthal interview with the Commissie Cleveringa, NA 2.05.48.02 (BZ) 15.
9. Congregation of the Holy Ghost Archives, Gemmet 98D-T in WA Congregation du Saint-Esprit; WA WC 29 Tourné.
10. Particularly the Families Jurius, Kamp, and Huitema in Gazeran, thirty-four miles southwest of Paris near the forest of Rambouillet, and the Family van den Bogaard in Gometz-la-Ville, twenty-five miles southwest of Paris.
11. WA WC 29 Tourné. For Laureijssen see NA 2.13.71 (MvOL) 2521; WA WC 18 Laurryssens [*sic*]; WA WC 29 Tourné; NAUK KV 4/25.
12. WA WC 26 Segers.
13. WA WC 26 Sevenster; WA WC 17 Laatsman; Plantinga, "Principieel pragmatisch," 6.
14. Mme Duchemin at the Prefecture de Police, Mlle Greve at the rationing office in the *mairie* of the XIV arrondissement, and Homme Huitema at Gazeran, seventeen miles southwest of Versailles. WA WC 17 Laatsman 2.

15. NRK 68755, WA WC 11 Dutch Patriotic Association 1, and family papers generously shared with the author by Marcella Langhout.

16. Telegram dated November 30, 1942, Archives nationales, France (hereafter AN), 72AJ CHDGM Ariège. The author thanks David Delfosse for this reference.

17. It was not an Adventist church. WA WC 26 Sevenster 1.

18. For Gabrielle's life in Paris see Carper, "The Weidners in Wartime."

19. WA WC 26 Segers; WA WC 17 Laatsman.

20. WA AS Meyer; WA WC 19 Meyer; WA WC 11 Dutch-Paris Organization; WA WC 17 Kraay 1.

21. The ambulance was driven by the taxi owner Fayolle. NA 2.05.57 998; NIOD 187 46R.

22. WA WC 17 Laatsman.

23. NARA, MIS-X, French, box 406, Weidner; Alain Souloumiac, personal discussion with the author, January 2011.

24. SHDC 21P 516 887. Also see NARA, MIS-X, French, box 406, Weidner; WA WC 10 Dutch-Paris history 2; SHDC 16P 420368; WA WC 17 Laatsman; NRK 37109.

25. NARA Dutch-Paris dossier.

26. The German was Karl-Heinz Gerstner, who made a political career in East Germany after the war. See Gerstner, *Sachlich, kritisch, und optimistisch.*

27. He also belonged to Corps francs Vengeance. SHD 16P 420368.

28. NARA, MIS-X, French, box 406, Weidner.

29. Laatsman considered him a communist and their link to the Front National. WA WC 19 Milleret; WA WC 20 Mincowsky [sic]; WA WC 8 Duchanel; WA WC 17 Laatsman 2.

30. SHD BCRA 286273; SHDC 101408594; WA EC; WA WC 17 Laatsman 2; WA WC 10 Dutch-Paris History 1; WA WC 8 Duchanel.

31. She worked for Colonel Thomas. WA EC.

32. SHD BCRA 40LN1852; SHD 17P 115.

33. This intelligence relay was not incorporated in the Swiss Way, although some of Weidner's colleagues appear to have used it to transport false documents as well as messages between Brussels and Amsterdam. WA WC 17 Laatsman.

34. For Brantsen see NA 2.05.57 (BuZaAmFr) 998; SHD 16P 87903; WA WC 17 Laatsman; WA WC 11 Dutch Resistance in France; WA WC 8 de Wit; de Graaff, *Stepping Stones to Freedom*, 131. With thanks to Frans van Elk for information on the "circusbaron."

35. Jeanine Caubo, Harry Caubo personal email to the author, May 7, 2015.

36. WA WC 17 Laatsman; WA WC Caubo; WA WC 35 Wientjes.

37. WA WC 6 Comiti.

38. Victor Swane; WA WC 28 Swane; SHD 17P 115; NARA DPL dossier.

39. Starink, *Mémoires*; WA WC 28 Starink; WA WC 36 Wyssogota; NA 2.13.71 (MvOL) 2571; NARA, MIS-X French box 373.

40. NA 2.13.71 (MvOL) 2571; SHD 17P 115; WA WC 28 Starink; WA WC 29 Tourne; NARA, MIS-X, French, Neyssel.

41. NARA, MIS-X, French, Neyssel; Alain Souloumiac, personal discussion with the author, January 2011.

42. WA WC 20 Mohr, WA WC 29 Tourne, NA 2.05.80 (BuZaL) 3559.

43. Henri Scharrer; see NA 2.13.71 (MvOL) 2571; WA WC 28 Starink; NAUK KV 4/25; Starink, *Mémoires*.

44. The Belgian Louis Debray and Dutchman Karel van Charante, aka Van der Woude. Debray sent at least two German agents from Paris to England on an unidentified Dutch line (not Dutch-Paris). The British found Laatsman's calling card among Debray's possessions when they arrested him in Brussels in 1944. NAUK KV2/120; NAUK KV4/25.

45. Houry met Calmels, who introduced her to Nahas, who introduced her to Rens. WA EC; WA WC 14 Houry; AN 72 AJ 126.

46. See Eychenne, *Pyrénées de la liberté*, 55, 75–85 ; Eychenne, *Montagnards de la liberté*, 35–40.

47. Marie Combes. For the *filière* see SHD BCRA P252501; WA WC 8 Derrac; WA WC 6 Combes; WA WC 29 Toulouse; WA WC 16 Klatser; WA WC 4 Caparros; WA WC 32 Verdier; WA WC 2 Battault; Archives départementales de la Haute-Garonne (hereafter ADHG) 2546W124 247; NAUK WO0208/5459 ; Eychenne, *Montagnards de la liberté*, 134, 191.

48. NIOD 244 1074. Lykele Faber arrived in Spain via Caparros on October 10, 1943.

49. NARA Nahas; NARA Dutch-Paris; WA WC 26 Segers; WA WC 20 Nahas; WA EC; AN 72AJ 126; SHD 16P 439196; SHD BCRA 40LN1994; NAUK WO208/5453.

50. I would like to thank Scott Goodall and Leentje van der Harst for giving me a private tour of the Musée du Chemin de la Liberté in St Girons.

51. SHD 17P 115; SHD 16P 577323; NARA Dutch-Paris Dossier; WA EC; AN 72AJ 126; personal letter from Jeanette Treillet to Rudy and Berna Zeeman, May 12, 2011, with thanks to Rudy Zeeman.

52. WA WC 5 Chait 4; WA WC 24 Rens; WA WC 18 Marrot; ADHG 44 J 33; Treillet to Zeeman, 2011.

53. For Calmels see WA WC 4 Calmels; WA EC; SHD 16P 101880; NAUK WO208/5459; Balfet, "Testimony," 148. For Moulouguet see WA EC; AN 72 AJ 126; NARA DP Line. For Boucoiran see WA WC 4 Chait 1; NARA MIS-X Dissard; NARA Dutch-Paris Line; AN 72 AJ 126.

54. WA WC 1 Aarts.

55. The answer was yes. WA WC 3 Biographical Information.

56. WA Susy [*sic*] Kraay, 1945. Josette Molland belonged to the French network MLN/MUR. SHD 16P 424863; ADR 3335W19; SHDC 201325774; WA WC 17 Kraay.

57. Jean Weidner to Gabrielle Weidner, May 14, 1943, in Carper, "The Weidners in Wartime."

58. Enquêtecommissie Regeringsbeleid, *Enquêtecommissie Regeringsbeleid*, 4cII:1527. For Christmann's role in the *Engelandspiel* see Giskes, *London Calling North Pole*.

59. Hotel Oria, 65 place Pigalle, IX, Paris. WA WC 17 Kraay. Also see Enquêtecommissie Regeringsbeleid, *Enquêtecommissie Regeringsbeleid* 4cII: 1527; WA WC 5 Christmann; NA 2.09.09 (MvJ, CABR) 83; Archief Ministerie de Justitie, Afdeling Politie-Kabinet, dossier 1779.

60. WA WC 17 Kraay 1.

61. NIOD 187c.

62. The Engelandvaarders were R. Schouten, P. ten Have, F. van Hutten, E. Fetter, Henk de Jonge (aka Albrecht), and Charles Pahud de Mortagnes. SHD 17P 125; SHD 16P 387788; SHDC 100715492; ADHG 44J 33; WA WC 18 Maltrait; NIOD 187c.

63. Arrived with Rens: H. Hymans, Bamberger; at the Panier Fleuri: A. de Vries, Leo Auping, Joop Born, J. Klausner, M. Janssen, Cassé, M. de Zwart, Van Hasselt, Wins, and Henri Valck Lucassen; and in town: Franck, M. Weisglass and Van Zeer; arrived November 19: J. Bakker; L. Goes de Bakker; H. Milborn; H. Perlstein; H. Klein, and L. Heil (names as written in Rens's report), NIOD 187 49R.

64. NA 2.13.71 (MvOL) 2516; NAUK WO 208/5582; Balfet, "Testimony"; personal letter from Jean Raffanel to Herman Grishaver, with thanks to Herman Grishaver.

65. Balfet, "Testimony."

66. NAUK WO208/5582; NIOD 187c; NA 2.13.71 (MvOL) 2571.

67. Dutch investigators concluded that Harry Hymans and Abraham de Vries were deported and killed as Jews. Dutch-Paris, however, spent 7,000 French francs to get Joop Born to Switzerland. NA 2.05.57 (BuZaAmFr) 1267; WA WC 9 Dutch-Paris Finances.

68. NIOD 187c; NA 2.13.71 (MvOL) 2571.

69. Germans arrested M. de Zwart and W. Janssen in the foothills. Thirteen arrived in Spain: L. Auping, H. Bamberger, P. Dourlein, B. van Hasselt, L. van Holk, H. Klein, E. van Leer, H. Perlstein, C. van Rossum, E. Schiff, B. Ubbink, T. Valc Lucassen, and M. Weisglas. WA WC 25 Schiff; NIOD 187 49R Rens.

70. For the German perspective see Giskes, *London Calling North Pole*. For Dourlein and Ubbink's escape see Foot and Langley, *MI-9*, 205.

71. WA WC 4 Chait 2; WA WC 26 Segers.

72. WA WC 25 Schiff; NA 2.13.71 (MvOL) 2524.

73. He died of natural causes in 1945. NA 2.13.71 (MvOL) 2412; NA 2.13.71 (MvOL) 2571; WA WC 26 Segers. His assistant, Jacob van Praag, a "particularly good and courageous young man" who had refused to go to Spain without his parents, also refugees in Toulouse. His friends believed he was shot by the Gestapo in his home. WA WC 26 Sevenster 2.

74. WA WC 26 Segers; WA WC 5 Chait 5; AEG JetP Ef/2 no 5652.

75. WA WC 11 Dutch Patriotic Association 1; NARA, MIS-X, French, box 406, Weidner.

76. Arrested on September 9, 1943, F. H. Kraay was sentenced to death for Feindbegunstigung (aiding and abetting the enemy), deported a year later, and died in Neuengamme in December 1944. NRK EU 22.297; WA WC 17 Kraay. For Rouwendal's betrayal of Kraay and others see WA WC 17 Kraay; WA WC 26 Segers; Enquêtecommissie Regeringsbeleid, *Enquêtecommissie Regeringsbeleid*, 4cII:1527.

77. WA WC 26 Segers.

78. Eychenne, *Montagnards de la liberté*, 80. Because Bazerque did not survive the war to tell his own story, he's been claimed by several *réseaux*. Eychenne, however, argues that he ran his own, independent *filière* (132–33). The research on Dutch-Paris supports that conclusion.

79. NIOD 187 49R Rens; WA WC 26 Segers.

80. Eychenne, *Pyrénées de la liberté*, 148.

81. WA WC 6 Combes; WA WC 8 Derrac.

82. ADHG 16J 347 Comminges.

83. Eychenne, *Montagnards de la liberté*, 190.

84. Eychenne, *Pyrénées de la liberté*, 148.

85. WA WC 20 Nahas 3; WA EC. Wyssogota subsidized Poles with Dutch money. NARA Dutch-Paris dossier and NARA; RG 498, HQ ETO US Army WWII: MIS-Y, French Evasion Organizations and Networks, Reseau Wissogotha-Lorraine and Benedictine, National Archives Identifier 6005930 (hereafter NARA, Wissogotha-Lorraine).

86. Dr. Anselm Polak-Daniels and Ariane Boon-Hartsink; de Vos and Seerp Postma; V. A. Mans, Georges Alexandre, Lannoy, a Belgian named Charles Hoxa; Philip Tuts, Kroone, Greidanus, Lex Gans, Jack Bottenheim, Kobus and Hugo Visser. NA 2.13.71 (MvOL) 2571; NIOD 187 49R; WA WC 26 Segers; Gans, "Engelandvaart, barbaarse reis." Also First Lieutenant Norman Mackie and Captain Jeffrey Morphen, RAF. NAUK WO 208/5582.

87. Engelandvaarders on that convoy: Gans, Bottenheim, Tuts, Kroone, Greidanus, Kobus, H. Visser (WA WC 9 Dutch-Paris finances individual Chait). Wardle's comment: Gans, "Engelandvaart, barbaarse reis," 218.

88. WA WC 6 Combes; WA WC 2 Bartoli; ADHG 44 J 33.

89. The Engelandvaarders who joined Dutch-Paris in France were Bernard van Gich and Cassé. Van Gich died in deportation. The Engelandvaarders looking for lodging after the raid were Kornelis Idema and René de Vries. WA WC 26 Segers; WA WC 9 Dutch Consul; WA WC 28 Starink; NA 2.13.71 (MvOL) 2571.

90. For example, he talked to his German contact, a commandant, about getting the Dutch consuls Testers and Kolkman out of prison, but to no avail. WA WC 8 de Stegge.

91. Family Dupias, Puis Verts 9, Toulouse, WA WC 4 Chait 1. For Aan de Stegge see Naulaerts, *Internationaal Geheime Dienst*; WA WC 8 de Stegge.

92. Kornelis Idema. NA 2.13.71 (MvOL) 2519; NIOD 187 46R; WA WC 26 Segers.

93. Madeleine and Genevieve Billot. Dutch-Paris also used their parents' pharmacy in Carcassone as a postbox. SHDC 200120777; SHD 16P 60526; NIOD 187 49R; NIOD 187 62R; WA WC 5 Chait 6; NARA, MIS-X, French, box 406 Weidner. Also Blanche Mossaz. WA WC 26 Segers; WA WC 11 Dutch-Paris Member Biographical Information.

94. Charles Delrue. NA 2.13.71 2516; NA 2.13.76 2419; WA WC 31 van Wijhe-Duteil; Balfet, "Testimony," 149.

95. See NA 2.13.71 (MvOL) 2419; NA 2.13.71 (MvOL) 2894; WA WC 27 Somer; WA WC 26 Segers, and NA 2.13.71 (MvOL) 2419; NA 2.13.71 (MvOL) 2897; Balfet, "Testimony," 149.

96. He did not, however, rely on other Adventists to create the line. J. H. Weidner, interview with Margaret Rossiter, 1977, Rossiter Papers, ROSSICA-39(1), Special Collections Library, University of Michigan, Ann Arbor.

Chapter 5

1. WA WC 23 Pels. See Bruttmann, "The 'Brunner Aktion.'"

2. WA WC 3 Bouchet; WA WC 23 Pels.

3. WA WC 23 Pels; WA AS Bouchet.

4. The Van der Posts had the complicity of local French gendarmes as well as Police Commissioner Castaign in Lons-le-Saunier and Inspector Berthereau of the Groupements de travailleurs étrangers. WA WC 9 Dutch-Paris Finances; WA WC 4 Chait, WA WC 30 van der Post.

5. Bernard van Gich, WA WC 20 van Gich.

6. WA AS Bouchet.

7. CHRD témoignage Pillot.

8. Joop and Lotte Simon and their sons, Marcel and Reinold. Police Inspector G. ter Horst hid the parents in Deventer while the boys hid in Zeeuws Vlaanderen. Kraay took them over the Belgian-French border using her own crossing point at Blanc-Misseron [sic]. WA WC 26 Simon, WC Susy [sic] Kraay; WA WC 26 Segers.

9. The children of François de Menthon and Marie-Madeleine Fourcade. WA Beaujolin 2; WA WC 3 Beaujolin; WA WC 11 Dutch Resistance in France; WA WC 3 Bouchet; WA WC 24 Rossiter. For Nazi policy on using family as hostages, see Harris, *Tyranny on Trial*, 214. For Vichy's Family Hostage Law see Bennett, *Under the Shadow of the Swastika*, 12, 62, 113–15.

10. SBA 4246 1985/196 31015; WA WC 26 Segers; WA WC 26 Sevenster 2; WA AS MacKimmie; WA WC 18 Lavergnat; WA AS Elisabeth Cartier Jolivet interview with Alberto Sbacchi.

11. The French friend was Louise Baudin. Dolf Klein was arrested and deported with Simon Eliasar. WA WC 12 Eliasar Family; WA WC 21 Netherlands Security Service; Eliasar, "Zwitserlandva(ar)der"; Eliasar family documents, generously shared by Maarten Eliasar.

12. See Andrieu, "Assistance to Jews and to Allied Soldiers and Airmen in France."

13. Under the Nacht und Nebel Erlass, see Laub, *After the Fall*, 158, 169; Wachsmann, *Hitler's Prisons*, 272–73.

14. De Graaff, *Stepping Stones to Freedom*, 143–44. Langley of MI-9 believed that for every airman who returned, one Dutch, Belgian, or French helper died (Ottis, *Silent Heroes*, 45).

15. See Ottis, *Silent Heroes*, 64 and throughout.

16. Zeeman, "Luck through Adversity."

17. They sent some aviators with the Service EVA through the Dutch woman Elise Chabot, her two German-born daughters, and the Belgian policeman Ernst van Moorleghem until they were all arrested with Van Cleeff in November 1943. After that they sent men with the Belgian Comet Line through a Dutch woman living in Brussels, Mae Verspyck. NA 2.13.71 (MvOL), 413; NRK 20169; NARA, RG 498, HQ ETO US Army WWII; Office of the Assistant Chief of Staff G-2 Awards Branch, Belgian Helper Files, National Archives Identifier 5701226 (hereafter NARA, Belgian Helper Files), box IV; WA WC 28 Strengers; WA WC 28 Starink; WA WC 31 Verspyck; NAUK AIR 20/8912.

18. WA WC 25 Schiff.

19. NARA 498 MIS-X, French Evasion Orgs, box 2 "Dutch-Paris."

20. Enquêtecommissie Regeringsbeleid, *Enquêtecommissie Regeringsbeleid*, 6a–b summary, 71.

21. WA BR Knoote.

22. Sayers: NRK Brussels Archief XVII. Von der Möhlen: NRK Brussels Archief XIII.

23. Roselaar: NRK Brussels Archief XVI; NA 2.13.71 (MvOL) 413; WA BR Roselaar; WA WC 15 Jacobstahl. Lifman: WA BR Lifman; ST 4045, Verslag; NARA, Belgian Helper Files, Verspyck.

24. NARA Dutch-Paris dossier; NARA, RG 498, HQ ETO US Army WWII; MIS-X, E&E 674, David, National Archives Identifier (NAI) 5555314 [hereafter NARA, E&E 674]; NARA, RG 498, HQ ETO US Army WWII; MIS-X, E&E 531, Lock, National Archives Identifier (NAI) 5555171 [hereafter NARA, E&E 531].

25. Philip Hartog and Jan Fehmers both stayed at the rue Franklin. Personal emails to the author from Peter Hartog, December 14, 15, 19, and 31, 2016.

26. WA WC 26 Segers; Enquêtecommissie Regeringsbeleid, *Enquêtecommissie Regeringsbeleid*, 4cII:1433–35. See also Van Riet, *Handhaven onder de nieuwe order*, 386, with thanks to Sierk Plantinga for this citation.

27. Hijmans also sponsored his friends Dr. Anselm Polak-Daniels and Ariane Boon-Hartsink, who had a scheme for the repatriation of Dutch war victims from the Third Reich, and three Engelandvaarders proposed to him by a resistance contact who passed him information about a Kriegsmarine shipyard in Noord Holland: Jacobus Hijmans (no relation), Victor Lemmens, and Johan de Veer. WA WC 13 Hijmans; Hijmans personal email to the author, July 4, 2011.

28. Mr. D. Goedhuis Esq., a friend of Hijmans's father: WA WC 30 van Doorn; WA WC 13 Hijmans. Police captain F. J. Klijzing: NA 2.13.71 (MvOL) 2571; NA 2.09.06 (MvJL) 12066. Harry Guyt: NA 2.09.06 (MvJL) 12024; Guyt and Guyt, "Harry en Co Guyt vertellen."

29. Timmers Verhoeven, "Een Reis naar Vrij Gebied."

30. Alternatively she passed aviators to the Groep Vrij in Maastricht. Enquêtecommissie Regeringsbeleid, *Enquêtecommissie Regeringsbeleid*, 4c:1193–95; NAUK WO 208/5454.

31. They also took aviators from Raoul Hereng of the Belgian Mouvement nationale Belge/Belgisch Nationale Beweging in Brussels and the Armée Blanche in Chimay. WA WC 15 Jacobstahl; WA WC 32 Vleeschdrager. Olympe Biernaux-Doby ran the group in Hasselt with her husband, Léon Biernaux, and son Raymond, who died in a concentration camp. CEGES AA 1333; NAUK WO 209/5452; WA BR Haenecour.

32. W. van Ende introduced Jacobstahl to Paul Schoenmaeckers in Rekem and Louis Hermans in Smeermaes. WA WC 15 Jacobstahl; WA BR Haenecour; NAUK WO 209/5452; NARA Dutch-Paris dossier; WA WC 32 Vleeschdrager. According to de Graaff, the Groep Vrij contacted Dutch-Paris through Tonnie Gielens when he needed help on a failed Engelandvaart, *Stepping Stones to Freedom*, 91.

33. Hilde Jacobstahl hid with the Dupuis family in Rivière, who introduced her brother to Arthur Cacheux, a resistance leader in Namur. WA WC 15 Jacobstahl; WA WC 10 Dutch-Paris History 2; NRK 156.524. Also see Goldberg, *Motherland*.

34. Aviators also came from Maastricht to Dutch-Paris via the resisters in the Belastingsgroep and the *passeurs* P. Souren and H. Beckers, Dutchmen who lived in Belgium. NIOD 251a EO 3; WA BR Haenecour; NARA Dutch-Paris dossier; NAUK WO 208/5454; de Graaff, *Stepping Stones to Freedom*, 91.

35. NARA, RG 498, HQ ETO US Army WWII; MIS-X, E&E 641, Elkin, NAI 5555281 (hereafter NARA E&E 641).

36. Courier for Dutch-Paris: Jacobstahl; couriers for Groep Vrij: Tonny Gielens, C. A. M. "Toke" Spierings, and Eugène Smits.

37. Owned by Albert Derckx and his English-speaking wife. NA 2.13.71 (MvOL) 2571; WA BR Derckx; WA BR Haenecour; WA WC 32 Vleeschdrager; WA WC 15 Jacobstahl; WA WC 10 Dutch-Paris History 1; NAUK WO 208/5459; NARA E&E 531.

38. Robert Bosschart. NA 2.13.71 (MvOL) 413; WA BR Bosschart; NARA RG 498/290/55/24/1 Box 9 Bosschart; ST 4045 Verslag. For the questionnaire: NIOD 251a EO3; NARA, RG 498, HQ ETO US Army WWII; Office of the Assistant Chief of Staff G-2 Awards Branch, Case Files of Dutch Citizens Proposed for Awards for Assisting American Airmen, 1945–47, NAI 570392 (hereafter NARA, Dutch Helper Files) box 133, Vrij.

39. Mae Verspyck, whom Van Cleeff probably met through the expatriate resistance banker Jan Strengers. He passed aviators to Comet through Mae Verspyck and Jan Strengers before his arrest.

40. NAUK WO 208/5583; NARA E&E 641.

41. WA WC 32 Vleeschdrager.

42. WA BR Wisbrun.

43. NARA E&E 674; NARA, RG 498, HQ ETO US Army WWII; MIS-X, E&E 532, Mullins, NAI 5555281 (hereafter NARA E&E 532).

44. Guyt and Guyt, "Harry en Co Guyt vertellen," 54.

45. For the complete story of the Sarah Jane's crew see Delfosse, *Liberté à tout Prix.*

46. NARA, RG 498, HQ ETO US Army WWII; MIS-X, E&E 398, Tank, (NAI) 5555039 (hereafter NARA E&E 398); WA BR Vleeschdrager; letter from J. Hussong to R. Zeeman, March 26, 1947, with thanks to R. Zeeman.

47. NAUK WO 208/5583; NARA, RG 498, HQ ETO US Army WWII; MIS-X, E&E 629, Mandell, NAI 5555281 (hereafter NARA E&E 629).

48. WA BR Vleeschdrager. For the crossing at Mouscron see Meyer and Meinen, "La Belgique, pays de transit," 171.

49. Henri Scharrer. A set of these papers used by P. E. van Beek in April 1944 can be found at Oorlogsmuseum Overloon, collectie AJ Bakker, nr 961371, with thanks to Carla van Beers for the citation. Ir van Exter donated a complete set of his son's false SD papers to the Verzetsmuseum in Amsterdam.

50. Zeeman stayed with the painter John Ruys after his escape. Ruys belonged to the Nederlands Vereeniging in Brussels and was a friend of the elder Timmers Verhoevens. Zeeman, "Luck through Adversity": personal emails to the author.

51. NA 2.13.71 (MvOL) 2526.

52. SHD 16P 510261; SHD BCRA 40LN1193; WA Congregation St Esprit Archives; NARA Dutch-Paris dossier.

53. NARA E&E 641.

54. Farmer van den Bogaard, WA WC 29 Tourne.

55. Without a doubt Dutch-Paris paid these men for the food, although they might not have charged Milleret the full black market price. WA WC 19 Milleret.

56. NARA E&E 604. Zeeman had a similar story about an Engelandvaarder's French boots. Email to the author, April 6, 2014.

57. Henri Lesieur, rue des Rigoles, Paris, also sheltered some aviators. WA WC 20 Mincowsky; WA WC 8 Duchanel; NARA, RG 498, HQ ETO US Army WWII; Office of the Assistant Chief of Staff G-2 Awards Branch, French Helper Files, National Archives Identifier 5701226 (hereafter NARA, French Helper Files), Duchanel.

58. Gabriel Piveteau, who had been released from a POW camp due to illness, was arrested for providing shoes to Dutch-Paris and died in the concentration camps. SHD 16P 480720; SHDC 21P 526261; WA WC 30 van Doorn.

59. Marcel Labois belonged to Libération Nord. He did not give the Jewish girl's name. WA WC 19 Milleret.

60. M-4, led by the local grocer, Camille Nicolas. SHD 17P 115; WA WC 30 van Nes; NARA, French Helper Files, Duchanel; NARA; RG 498, HQ ETO US Army WWII: MIS-Y, French Evasion Organizations and Networks, Livry-Gargan; National Archives Identifier 6005917 (hereafter NARA Livry-Gargan); NARA, RG 498, HQ ETO US Army WWII; MIS-X, E&E 604, Arp (NAI) 5555244 (hereafter NARA E&E 604); NARA, RG 498, HQ ETO US Army WWII; MIS-X, E&E 636, Miller (NAI) 5555276 (hereafter NARA E&E 636).

61. Rudy Zeeman, email to author, April 2, 2014.

62. WA WC 13 Hilterman.

63. NARA E&E 629.

64. The train did not always leave on time. WA WC 6 Comiti; NARA, RG 498, HQ ETO US Army WWII; MIS-X, E&E 411, Downe, (NAI) 5555052 (hereafter NARA E&E 411); NARA, RG 498, HQ ETO US Army WWII; MIS-X, E&E 446, Miller (NAI) 5555087 (hereafter NARA E&E 446).

65. NARA, RG 498, HQ ETO US Army WWII; MIS-X, E&E 640, Morgan, NAI 5555289 (hereafter NARA E&E 640).

66. WA WC 14 Houry; WA EC; NIOD 187 49R; SHD 16P 296984.

67. WA WC 26 Segers.

68. Timmers Verhoeven, "Een Reis naar Vrij Gebied."

69. Zeeman, email to author, April 14, 2014. For a German document check at the gare Matabiau see NARA, RG 498, HQ ETO US Army WWII; MIS-X, E&E 646, Krengle, NAI 5555286 (hereafter NARA E&E 646). Germans often missed aviators whom local people saw. Ottis, *Silent Heroes*, 27; NARA escape and evasion reports.

70. WA EC.

71. WA WC 9 Dutch-Paris Finances Individual Chait; NA 2.13.71 (MvOL) 2571.

72. WA EC Soum.

73. Rudy Zeeman, email to author, April 14, 2014; Jean-Claude Rivière, "Palo Treillet (1918–2005) Courserannais, Montagnard, Resistant et Passeur," typescript, n.d., with thanks to Rudy Zeeman.

74. Report of February 1944, NAUK WO 208/5583.

75. "L'Américain de Loures-Barousse," Joseph Barrère, SHDC 21P 14562; ADHG 16J 347; NARA, RG 498, HQ ETO US Army WWII; MIS-X, E&E 631, Bachman, NAI 5555271 (hereafter NARA E&E 631); NARA, RG 498, HQ ETO US Army WWII; MIS-X, E&E 749, Brenden, NAI 5555389 (hereafter NARA E&E 749); Eychenne, *Montagnards de la liberté*, 132.

76. NARA E&E 507; NARA E&E 515; NAUK WO 208/5583.

77. Geneviève Petit, who belonged to CIMADE, with thanks to David Delfosse for identifying her. See also NARA, RG 498, HQ ETO US Army WWII; MIS-X, E&E 507, Tracy, (NAI) 5555148 (hereafter NARA E&E 507);

NARA, RG 498, HQ ETO US Army WWII; MIS-X, E&E 515, Hicks, (NAI) 5555156 (hereafter NARA E&E 515); NARA E&E 398; NARA E&E 446.

78. Zeeman, "Luck through Adversity." The seven aviators and French woman who got lost and transferred themselves to a Polish escape line were meant to be on this convoy.

79. NAUK WO 208/5583; NARA E&E 629.

80. NARA, RG 498, HQ ETO US Army WWII; MIS-X, E&E 642, Snyder, NAI 5555282 (hereafter NARA E&E 642).

81. NARA E&E 641.

82. McLaughlin, RAAF; Watts, Harris, and Brown, RAF; and McDonald, McGlinchy, Snyder, Elkin, Kratz, Mellen, Brigman, Boyce, Mandell, Ferrari, and Roberts, USAAF.

83. The French doctor Yves Evenou treated his leg despite the risk of being caught aiding and abetting the enemy. WA WC 10 Dutch Paris History 1.

84. Jan Langeler had made his own way to Paris in the summer of 1943 and found his way to the Association des secours des refugiés hollandais, where a Dutchman sent him to a farmer named Hooymans outside the city. He made his way to the Pyrenees in July 1943, only to be captured. He and seven French prisoners, however, escaped. After a French worker took him to a hospital to have the bullet wounds in his hand and arm tended, he returned to Hooymans. In February 1944 his host put him in touch with Okhuysen and Starink. NA 2.09.06 (MvJL) 7198.

85. Ferdinand "Ferry" Staverman and Gijsbert den Besten. WA WC 28 Staverman; NA 2.09.06 (MvJ) 7531.

86. Timmers Verhoeven, "Een Reis naar Vrij Gebied."

87. Jacobus Hijmans, Victor Lemmens, and Johan de Veer. WA WC 13 Hijmans; Hijmans personal email to the author July 4, 2011.

88. Langeler, Staverman, Den Besten, Van Oosterzee, Timmers Verhoeven, J. Hijmans, Lemmens, De Veer, Bureau, and the Australian aviator McLaughlin.

89. McLaughlin remembers that they took taxis from Cazères. The group may have split up, or he may mean a taxi from Mane to Arbas. NAUK WO 208/5583.

90. Brown, Harris, and Watts, RAF; Boyce, Brigman, Elkin, Kratz, Mandell, McDonald, McGlinchy, Mellen, Roberts, Snyder, USAAF. Ferrari remained in Paris for medical reasons.

91. NARA E&E 641.

92. NARA E&E 629.

93. The aviator remembered this event as happening in Arbas, but it had to have been in Mane. Arbas was too tiny and remote a village. My thanks to Rudy Zeeman for explaining the lay of the land (email to author, April 21, 2014). NARA, RG 498, HQ ETO US Army WWII; MIS-X, E&E 606, Brigman, (NAI) 5555052 (hereafter NARA E&E 606).

94. Antonius Bartmann, David Blanes, and Johannes Sinnige. They did not survive the war to record their trip.

95. John G McLaughlin, RAAF; Phil Brown, Sergeant Harris, and George Watts, RAF; Harold Boyce, Campbell Brigman, Norman Elkin, Harry Kratz, Nicholas Mandell, William McDonald, Frank McGlinchy, Clyde Mellen, Omar Roberts, Walter Snyder, USAAF; Roger Bureau (Belgium) and Antonius Bartman, Gijsbert den Besten, David Blanes, Jacobus Hijmans, Jan Langeler, Victor Lemmens, Christiaan van Oosterzee, Johannes Sinnige, Ferdinand Staverman, Sam Timmers Verhoeven, Johan de Veer, Engelandvaarders.

96. Gijsbert den Besten remained in St-Girons until after the liberation of the region in August 1944. In April or May 1944 Chait paid the hospital in St. Girons 5,000 French francs, probably for Den Besten's care. NA 2.09.06 (MvJL) 7531; Timmers Verhoeven, "Een Reis naar Vrij Gebied"; Treillet to Zeeman, 2011; WA WC 9 Dutch Paris Finance Individual Chait.

97. Bartmann, Lemmens, de Veer, Hijmans, Langeler, Sinnige, Staverman, and Blanes. Some used the false names on their false documents. SHDC, register of Foix prison 1944, not yet cataloged in 2012.

98. Lemmens and Langeler jumped out of the truck. They arrived in Spain in a big convoy on March 28, 1944. NA 2.09.06 (MvJL) 7198.

99. Bartmann, de Veer, Hijmans, Staverman, and Blanes all died in Mauthausen. Sinnige perished in a labor commando near Landeshut. There is now a granite monument at the site of the "cabane des évadés" near Route national 618 in memory of the ambush of February 6, 1944. Treillet and Timmers Verhoeven inaugurated it in an official ceremony.

100. The enlisted men went to Stalag 17B, the officers to Stalag Luft 1 or Stalag Luft 7. With thanks to David Delfosse.

101. NARA E&E 606.

102. Timmers Verhoeven, "Een Reis naar Vrij Gebied"; NARA E&E 629; NARA E&E 606; Treillet to Zeeman, 2011.

103. Timmers Verhoeven said the station was in Arbas, but Zeeman is certain that it was in Mane because Arbas had only a dirt road leading in from the north and a dirt track leading out to the south. Timmers Verhoeven, "Een Reis naar Vrij Gebied"; Zeeman, email to author, October 5, 2012 and April 21, 2014.

104. WA WC 17 Laatsman.

105. WA WC 14 Janse; NA 2.05.49 (GzZw) 853; WA WC 26 Segers.

106. WA WC 26 Segers.

107. WA WC 26 Segers.

Chapter 6

1. Unless otherwise noted, the story of Kraay's arrest, interrogation, and torture is based on the deposition she gave in 1945. WA Kraay, 1945.

2. See Berlière and Chabrun, *Les Policiers français sous l'Occupation*.

3. For the stories of Kraay's arrest given by the French arresting officers when they were under investigation for collaboration, see Archives de la préfecture de Police (hereafter APP) KB cartons 4, 10, and 13.

4. USAAF: Carl Bachmann, Elwood Arp, Edward Shaffer, William Miller, Howard Sherman, Loral Martin, and Herman D. Morgan. RAF: John Vass and Fred Page. Engelandvaarders: A. L. Regout, L. E. van Holk, Adolf Mantel, Pim de Nerée tot Babberich, C. G. Gips, T. W. Spijker, and Arie van der Heijden. Some of these men were passed to Dutch-Paris through Starink. NARA, RG 498, HQ ETO US Army WWII; MIS-X, E&E 634, Martin, NAI 5555274 (hereafter E&E 634); NARA E&E 640.

5. WA WC 17 Kraay.

6. The brave neighbor was a Mme Haller. This account is based on the reports written by the Caubo children in 1945. WA WC 4 Caubo.

7. WA WC 13 Hiltermann.

8. WA WC 26 Segers; WA WC 17 Laatsman.

9. Abbé Kees van Doorn. NIOD 187 46R; WA WC 18 Laurrijssens [sic]; WA WC 30 van Doorn.

10. WA WC 29 Tourne.

11. WA WC 17 Kraay.

12. A couple weeks later he was arrested and deported. SHDC 21P 515561; WA WC 19 Meriot.

13. WA WC Caubo.

14. WA WC 26 Segers.

15. NAUK WO 344 101 2; NARA E&E 640; WA WC 5 Chanoinat, and WA WC 13 Hilterman.

16. Marguerite and Louis Chanoinat. WA WC 13 Hilterman.

17. WA WC 29 Tourne.

18. The briefcase also contained a receipt for 200,000 French francs that Caubo had loaned Dutch-Paris to cover the January expenses; it was signed by Laatsman in the name of the Dutch government in exile. WA WC 17 Laatsman, WA WC 26 Segers.

19. WA WC 15 Jacobstahl.

20. WA WC 26 Segers; WA WC 13 Hilterman.

21. WA WC 17 Kraay.

22. Weidner made this observation at the postwar purge trial of Bizoire as evidence of his collaboration. WA WC 17 Kraay. For the repression of resisters in France see Wieviorka, *Histoire de la Résistance*, 441–66.

23. Bennett, *Under the Shadow of the Swastika*, 12, 113.

24. WA Kraay 1945, translation by Tony Sluis.

25. F. H. Kraay was a civil servant at the Amsterdam town hall. He died at Neuengamme in December 1944. NRK EU 22.297; WA WC 17 Kraay.

26. WA Kraay, 1945.

27. RAF: Sydney Smith. USAAF: Charlie Mullins, Donald Schuman, William Lock, Clayton David, Buckner, Kenneth Shaver, and Koenig. They knew the unidentified Dutchman as "Jack." He was probably arrested late on February 26, 1944.

28. William Lock, evading with his waist gunner, Charlie Mullins. NARA E&E 531; NARA E&E 532.

29. Koenig, Buckner, and Shaver.
30. Survivors of the ambush at the Col du Portet d'Aspet: Watts (RAF); McLaughlin (RAAF); Mandell, Snyder, Elkin, Kratz, and Brigman (USAAF); Bureau, Van Oosterzee, and Timmers Verhoeven (Engelandvaarders).
31. Men hiding with Gaston and Joan Lejeune: Krengle (USAAF) and Davenport (RCAF).
32. Engelandvaarders who left Paris on February 11: A. L. Regout, L. E. van Holk, Adolf Mantel, Pim de Nerée tot Babberich, C. G. Gips, T. W. Spijker, and Arie van der Heijden. Aviators who left Paris on February 11: Bachmann, Arp, Shaffer, Miller, Sherman, Martin, and Morgan (USAAF); Vass and Page (RAF).
33. NARA E&E 634 and NARA E&E 640.
34. WA EC; NARA Dutch-Paris dossier.
35. WA WC 9 Dutch Paris Finances Individual Chait.
36. NARA E&E 629.
37. WA WC 20 Minkowsky [sic].
38. WA WC 13 Goetschel.
39. Dominee and Mrs. Hokendijk-Laman. Visser 't Hooft paid for their escape and put them on the official Swiss "liste des non-réfoulables." NIOD 187 46R; SBA 6351(F)1 522 1942; Enquêtecommissie Regeringsbeleid, *Enquêtecommissie Regeringsbeleid*, 4cIIa:1485.
40. Starink and D. de Boer went to the home of Eva de Graaff, aka Mme Vassias, at rue de Clichy 26 on February 12, 1944, on an errand involving the Visigoths-Lorraine Resistance network (Starink, "Mémoires").
41. He returned to Paris in late March. Because German police has raided his hotel room earlier in the month and he could not make contact with Dutch-Paris, Starink went into hiding in northern France until the Liberation. WA WC 26 Segers; Starink, "Mémoires."
42. WA WC 5 Chanoinat.
43. WA WC 20 Minkowsky [sic]. Duchanel was able to get police seals put on their apartments in early January 1945 to preserve what was left. WA WC 8 Duchanel.
44. WA WC 17 Laatsman.
45. WA AS, Annette Weidner Hipleh interview with Alberto Sbacchi, August 2, 1994, transcribed by Janet Carper; WA WC 26 Segers; NA 2.13.71 (MvOL) 2419.
46. WA WC 17 Laatsman.
47. KdS agents F. Wilhelm, R. Birk, and F. Paul under the command of Kreft. WA WC 5 Christmann. For German police in France see Laub, *After the Fall*.
48. The café owner was Marcel Labois. After the war Duchanel wrote that Milleret must have been tortured into talking. WA WC 17 Labois, WA WC 9 Duchanel.
49. WA WC 23 Prilliez.

50. WA Congregation St. Esprit.
51. Administrators at the ENS helped the three Prilliez children after their parents' arrest. WA WC 23 Prilliez.
52. WA Congregation St. Esprit.
53. Four men were captured by the Germans and survived the war as POWs; two reached Spain on April 14, 1944, and two arrived in England by sea on March 23, 1944. NARA E&E 531; NARA, RG 498, HQ ETO US Army WWII; MIS-X, E&E 674, David, NAI 5555314 (hereafter NARA E&E 674). NARA E&E 674; NARA, RG 498, HQ ETO US Army WWII; MIS-X, E&E 675, Shaver, NAI 5555315 (hereafter NARA E&E 675).
54. M. Bruat, assistant director of the ENS, died in deportation. The Germans also arrested and deported the ENS chauffeur, M. Pouls. He gave Brother Rufus ration cards for bread but was not part of Dutch-Paris.
55. WA Congregation St. Esprit.
56. WA WC 17 Laatsman.
57. The Mitropa lawyer was named Ten Cate. WA WC 26 Segers; WA WC Laatsman; NRK 22439.
58. Three days later Goetschel was deported to the concentration camps with a few of her Dutch-Paris colleagues. WA EC.
59. WA WC 26 Segers; WA WC 16 Koeleman; AAdv 10CP1 7d.
60. Ellis was liberated from a POW camp in Bavaria in April 1945. NAUK WO 344-101-2; NARA Dutch-Paris dossier.
61. Pastor Oscar Meyer. WA WS, Sbacchi interview with Annette Weidner Hipleh.
62. WA WC 26 Segers.
63. WA Kraay, 1945.

Chapter 7

1. See Bower, *Klaus Barbie*; Morgan, *An Uncertain Hour*.
2. WA WC 23 Pillot; WA WC 17 Kraay; ADR 3335 W 27; ADR 3335 W 8; CHRD Lyon, *Témoignage* Pillot.
3. A Mr. Grun and Benjamin and Hendel Taub with their teenage daughter Sonja, who was born in Rotterdam. SHDC 21P 542964; SHDC 21P 542961; SHD 21P 542960; NA 2.13.71 (MvOL) 2572.
4. WA WC 15 Jacquet; WA WC 9 Dutch Foreign Ministry; WA WC 13 Grand-Clément; NA 2.05.48.02 (BZ) 81; NA 2.05.57 (BuZaAmFr) 956.
5. Weidner's partner in the shop, Gilbert Beaujolin, was active in the Alliance network. A Mr. Bloch and a Mr. and Mrs. Levy were arrested, but a Mr. Siegelman escaped. WA WC 17 Kraay.
6. Aviators captured at the rue Franklin: Robert F. Anderson, Henry Steel, James Settle, Leopold Flores, Paul O'Welch, Cecil Brown, James Newton, Albert Stern, and S. Bauer (USAAF); Mervyn Breed (RNZAF).
7. R. F. Anderson, emails to the author, July 11 and August 26, 2010; NAUK WO 344/39/1.

8. SiPO-Brussel IVE-115H. The Engelandvaarder was Jaap Erwteman. Peter Hartog email to the author, December 14, 2106.

9. WA WC 15 Jacobstahl.

10. NRK 19227.5.

11. WA BR Bol; NRK Brussels Archief box XVII; DGO 295155; ST 4045, Verslag.

12. Philip Hartog, arrested under the name Devries and imprisoned at St. Gilles and Leopoldburg. Peter Hartog, email to the author, December 14, 2016.

13. WA BR Bol.

14. After the war Jacobstahl reported that his British unit detained both Barth and Weber, the Germans who had interrogated him. WA WC 15 Jacobstahl; WA WC 17 Kraay.

15. NRK political prisoner dossier 157.165.

16. WA WC 32 Vleeschdrager.

17. Verloop's official date of death is March 7, 1944, but in 1945 his colleagues thought he had died on March 10. NA 2.13.71 (MvOL) 413 and ST 4045 Verslag. Verloop's mother heard the news of her son's death on April 9, when Bol's father, a longtime family friend, relayed it to her. The Dutch embassy in Bern received official notification of the death of "David Vermaes" later that month. WA WC 31 van Tricht. With thanks to H. S. Koelega for the clarification.

18. Jacobstahl did not know about it until May, when he had a chance to speak with Bol and Vleeschdrager. WA WC 15 Jacobstahl.

19. Adriaan Johan van Haaften, "Enige gegevens m.b.t. Adriaan Johan van Haaften (1920–1945) tijdens de tweede wereldoorlog, 2010," unpublished typescript, with thanks to Frits Broeyer and A. J. Van Haaften for sharing it.

20. NIOD 251a EO 3; WA BR Vleeschdrager.

21. The traitor was Chris Lindemanns, aka King Kong. WA BR Nauta; WA BR Vleeschdrager; Verzetsmuseum, interview with Piet Henry, June 8, 1990; Henry, "Piet Henry Vertelt."

22. WA WC 13 Hijmans and Willy Hijmans, conversation with the author June 4, 2010 and email to the author June 10, 2012.

23. WA WC 26 Segers; WA BR Wisbrun; NRK 169.129. For slave labor see Herbert, *Hitler's Foreign Workers*; Homze, *Foreign Labor in Nazi Germany*, 177–203, 230–63, 264–99.

24. SHD 16P 424863; ADR 3335 W 19.

25. An unidentified man using a false name with the same surname that Kraay used on her false French papers, Jean Melinand, was arrested with Molland at her home that morning. Molland belonged to the French *réseau* Combat. SHD 16P 424863; ADR 3335 W 19; SHDC 201325774; WA Kraay 1945.

26. Roume: SHD 16P 523159. Neyssel: NARA, French Helper Files; WA WC 22 Neyssel.

27. WA WC 26 Segers; SHDC 21P 515930.

28. Paul Lacôte. SHDC 121403340. Alice Charroin: WA WC 5 Charroin; SHDC 221200862; SHD 16P 144379; ADR 3808 W 1503.

29. Anna and Fred Zurcher, conversation with the author, January 31, 2011.

30. NIOD 187 49R.

31. Eliasar Family Documents.

32. Sietze Huitema, WC S. Kraay.

33. SHDC 101408594; SHDC 200100255.

34. Max Weber or Weder and Mme Vve Valentine Stocker. NIOD 187 49R; NA 2.05.57 998.

35. Cobbler: Gabriel Piveteau; painter: John Ruys; houseguest: T. W. Spijker; hotel keeper: Raymond Mériot. WA WC 19 Meriot; SHDC 21P 515561.

36. Victor Swanne, who chose not to join Dutch-Paris, was arrested at the Hotel Montholon, as was Chris Lindemann's wife. The Comité in Brussels had helped at least one of the Engelandvaarders arrested there (Jeanne van der Donck) with false travels papers. WA BR van Cleeff.

37. Abwehrleitstelle Paris, Ref IIIC, Bundesarchiv, Abteilung Militärarchiv (hereafter BAMA) RW/49/73. German and Austrian Jewish resisters also disguised themselves as Dutch workers for the Organisation Todt, the Nazi organization that recruited foreign labor to work in the Third Reich, Lazare, *Rescue as Resistance*, 169–70.

38. WA WC 26 Segers.

39. Gerrit ter Horst, arrested in April 1944 and died in deportation. NRK 10061; WA WC 17 Kraay; NA 2.09.09 (MvJL, CABR) 83.

40. Louis and Marguerite Chanoinat, jewelers. Louis Chanoinat had won the Croix de Guerre in 1916 and been wounded in World War I. SHD 16P 118955; SHD BCRA P286227; WA WC 5 Chanoinat; SHD 16P 470714; SHD 16P 118956.

41. SHD 16P 415431; WA AS Elisabeth Cartier Jolivet interview with Alberto Sbacchi.

42. WA Congrégation du Saint-Esprit.

43. For use of the NN Erlass in France see Laub, *After the Fall*, 158–66, 293.

44. Simone Collomb, at a bookshop called Librairie Clairière at 44 rue Duranton, Paris. WA WC 26 Segers; SHD 16P 138023.

45. SHD 16P 339268; SHDC 200100255; WA WC 18 Larose-Reinaud.

46. Captain J. H. Zeggers. The trainees' names were lost in the crisis of the arrests. WA WC 13 Hijmans; WA BR Wisbrun; WA WC 10 Dutch-Paris lists members 1.

47. WA WC 18 Larose; SHD 16P 339268; SHDC 200100255.

48. NA 2.05.57 (BuZaAmFr) 998; SHD 16P 87903; WA WC 17 Laatsman; WA WC 11 Dutch-Paris Members Biographical Information; de Graaff, *Stepping Stones to Freedom*, 131. The Germans arrested the baron, his wife, Eloise Whiting Brantsen, Nijkerk, and whoever else was in the apartment. The sixty-nine-year-old baroness was released without being deported in August 1944 due to illness. SHD 116P 87902, NARA MIS-X, DP Line.

49. Bosch, Glukman, Van Alphen, and Post (or Roesin) [*sic*], and possibly others. WA WC 10 Dutch-Paris lists members 1.

50. Jeanne Houry and her husband were involved in French resistance networks but not Dutch-Paris. WA WC 14 Houry; WA EC; SHD 16P 296984; SHD 16P 539787.
51. WA WC 6 Comiti; SHD 16P 139515; NIOD 187 46R.
52. She worked for Dutch-Paris as a courier, taking money to the general's brother, Dr. Barend van Tricht, in Monaco, among other tasks, and for the Françoise network as a guide. WA WC 4 Calmels.
53. WA WC 10 Dutch Paris History 2.
54. Willy Hijmans, personal conversation with the author, May 16, 2009.
55. WA WC 26 Simon.
56. WA WC 5 Chait.
57. Alain Souloumiac, conversation with the author, January 2011.
58. NA 2.13.71 (MvOL) 1387; NRK 157754; WA WC 31 Veerman; NIOD 187 62R and KBI 6920, Veerman, P; VA, Paul Veerman, 1995.
59. NIOD 187 62R.
60. NA 2.13.71 (MvOL) 1387; WA WC 31 van Tricht; WA WC 29 Testimonies; WA WC 12 Gazan, H.
61. WA WC 26 Segers.
62. The clerk was Rizet, who was also the chief of the intelligence bureau for the local Armée Secrète. FFI/AS St-Julien; WA WC 31 van Tricht; WA WC 12 Gazan; NIOD 187 62R.
63. WA WC 18 Loans.
64. WA WC 9 Dutch-Paris Finances; WA WC 9 Dutch-Paris Finances Individual Accounts: WA WC 9 Dutch-Paris Finances Individuals; WA WC 9 Dutch-Paris Finances Visser 't Hooft; NIOD 187 46R.
65. Salary of 300 CHF/month or 350 CHF/month for the *chef*, plus a 10 CHF per diem for up to fifteen days per month spent in Switzerland. Wives received 270 CHF/month, plus an optional 80 CHF/month loan to be paid back after the war. WA WC 31 van Tricht; NA 2.05.57 (BuZaAmFr) 961.
66. WA WC 31 van Tricht.

Chapter 8

1. CHRD, Pillot interview and WA WC Marty Trial.
2. See Boulet, *Les Alpes françaises*, 378–409 ; Rickard, *La Savoie dans la Résistance*.
3. NIOD 187 49R.
4. WA WC 26 Segers.
5. WA WC 31 van Tricht.
6. NIOD 187 46R.
7. WA WC 4 Chait; WA WC 30 van der Post; WA BR von der Möhlen; WA BR Sayers; WA WC 28 ten Kate; NRK Brussels Archief XVII; NA 2.13.71 (MvOL) 413.
8. WA BR Roselaar; NRK Brussels Archief XVI; ST 4045, Verslag; NA 2.13.71 (MvOL) 413.

9. WA WC 5 Chait.
10. Boudin, "Ten Kate, Antoon Geertruidus Berendinus."
11. WA BR Polak; WA BR Polak-Pool.
12. Like Regout, he belonged to the Organisation Militaire Belge de Résistance. WA BR van Kempen; ST4045, Verslag.
13. WA BR Oostendorp; ST4045, Verslag.
14. WA BR Ilegems.
15. WA BR van Kempen.
16. D. Lemaitre and Dronsart, WA BR Moussiax.
17. WA BR Pouillon; NA 2.13.71 (MvOL) 413; ST4045, Verslag.
18. Betsy Bloemist: WA BR Bloemist; NRK Brussels Archief I. Gaston and Carolina Ilegems: WA BR Illegems, ST4045, Verslag; NA 2.13.71 (MvOL) 413. Joseph Lalieu and Elisabeth Wagemans: WA BR Lalieu, NA 2.13.71 (MvOL) 413; ST4045, Verslag; Liagre, "De Zwitserse Weg en de Dutch-Paris line." Joanna van Helden-Hus: WA BR van Helden-Hus; NA (2.13.71) 413; ST4045, Verslag.
19. WA BR van Helden-Hus.
20. They were welcome at the Protestantsch Christelijk Ziekenhuis, also known as the Hollandsche Kliniek. Johanna ten Kate-Vandenbroek had been the director of the Hollandsche Kliniek before marrying Pastor ten Kate. Van Helden-Hus recruited a doctor named Allard and a dentist named Gold. WA BR van Helden-Hus.
21. For the Comité's financial report see NA 2.05.43 (GzB) 1181.
22. NA 2.05.49 (GzZw) 853.
23. Belgische Comité tot steun van vervolgde Israelieten (Belgian Committee for the Support of Persecuted Israelites), of which Nijkerk had been the treasurer. NA 2.13.71 (MvOL) 413; NIOD 187 46R; WA WC 4 Chait.
24. Between March and September 1944 the Comité spent 12,553 Belgian francs on medical expenses such as operations and medicines. NA 2.05.43 (GzB) 1181. See also WA BR Van Helden-Hus.
25. WA WC van Kempen.
26. The packages were put together and mailed to the transit camp at Mechelen by Van Coevorden. NA 2.13.71 (MvOL) 413.
27. Jane Milaire-Engels, WA BR Milaire-Engels.
28. In Vichy the money for Dutch refugees was given to a French civil servant named Verdier. NA 2.05.49 (GzZw) 853; WA WC 9 Dutch-Paris Individual Member Accounts Visser 't Hooft. Weidner had also been working with Dr. Barend van Tricht, brother of the general, in Monaco since August 1942.
29. Weidner had also been delivering cash to Mme Kolkman, wife of the former Dutch consul in Toulouse, via Mohr since her release from prison. WA WC 26 Segers.
30. The arrangement ran from March to August 1944. The money went to the Families Clerx, Warrandyn, Rudelsheim, Montesinos, Mendel, Calff, and possibly others. WA WC 8 aan de Stegge.

31. Chait's contact was the president of the Quaker Foundation in Toulouse, the Swede Ellen Hollweg. WA WC 4 Chait 1; SHD 17P 115.

32. WA WC 23 People 1.

33. Enquêtecommissie Regeringsbeleid, *Enquêtecommissie Regeringsbeleid*, 4cII:1483.

34. Au Truffe de Quercy was owned by Charlie Veron. In April the new courier Veerman was told to go to the Billot's pharmacy in Carcassone for messages, to eat at Au Truffe du Quercy, and to get information at the dry cleaner's on the rue de la Trinité or the home of Madeleine Billot. NIOD 187 62R. The Dutch-Paris contact at the flower shop was named Bovis.

35. The convoy that left on March 25, 1944, included Bureau, Conijn, van Gips, Arie van der Heijden, L. E. van Holk, Langeler, Lemmens, Adolf Mantel, Nederlof, Nerée tot Babberich, Regout, Timmers Verhoeven, and Van Weve, as well as Krengle (USAAF) and John Wattlington (RCAF). A different escape line paid for Witt, Leach, Gavany, Walley, and Yeager (USAAF) to join this convoy. For the trek see NARA E&E 646 and NAUK WO 208/5583. Van Houten Dekker, G. C. Bollee, and E. F. Philipp also crossed the Pyrenees under the auspices of Dutch-Paris around this time. WA WC 10 Dutch-Paris Lists Members; NA 2.09.06 (MvJL) 7198; NA 2.09.06 (MvJL) 7238.

36. Men who left with Bazerque on March 16 to arrive in Bosost on March 18: the Engelandvaarder Van Oosterzee; Martin, Morgan, Kratz, Miller, Shaffer, Arp, Sherman, Ferrari, Bachman, Elkin, Snyder, Mandell, and Brigman (USAAF); Page, Watts, and Vass (RAF); Davenport (RCAF); McLaughlin (RAAF); and other aviators who were not sponsored by Dutch-Paris but were helped in Toulouse and the foothills by helpers who also worked with Dutch-Paris. See NARA, RG 498, HQ ETO US Army WWII; MIS-X, E&E 632, Carson, NAI 5555272 (hereafter NARA E&E 632).

37. The Engelandvaarder was Langeler. NAUK WO 208/5583; NARA E&E 607; NARA E&E 606; NARA E&E 631; NARA E&E 642; NARA E&E 641; NARA E&E 629; NAUK WO 208/5583; NARA, RG 498, HQ ETO US Army WWII; MIS-X, E&E 607, Ferrari, NAI 5555247 (hereafter NARA E&E 607).

38. Chait paid Bazerque for the passage of twenty persons on April 10 without, however, noting their names. WA WC 9 Dutch-Paris Finances Individual Chait.

39. For Van Heuven Goedhart's journey see his *De Reis van "Colonel Blake."* For his testimony before the Dutch Parliament, see Enquêtecommissie Regeringsbeleid, *Enquêtecommissie Regeringsbeleid*, 4cI:525-27. In the archives see WA WC 26 Segers; WA WC 31 Veerman 1; WA WC 1 Dutch Resistance in France; WA WC 9 Dutch Paris Expenses Chait; WA WC 4 Chait 2; NIOD 187 62R. Also see *Het Parool*, October 5, 1946; Verkijk's 1967 documentary.

40. Frans Simons, Dr. Jacques van Goor, and Frits van Os. NA 2.09.06 (MvJL) 6698; NIOD 187 62R.

41. NIOD 187 62R Veerman.
42. NIOD 187 46R; NIOD 187 62R; WA WC 9 Dutch-Paris Finances Individual Chait; *Het Parool*, 5 October 5, 1946; Enquêtecommissie Regeringsbeleid, *Enquêtecommissie Regeringsbeleid*, 4cI:525–27.
43. WA WC 9 Dutch-Paris Finances.
44. Except where noted, the story of Weidner's arrest is based on WA WC Marty Trial; WA WC 26 Segers; NIOD 187 62R.
45. Burrin, *France under the Germans*, 439-55; Delperrie de Bayac, *Histoire de la Milice*.
46. NIOD 187 62R.
47. WA WC 9 Dutch-Paris Finances.
48. WA WC Marty Trial.
49. NIOD 187 62R.
50. WA WC Marty Trial; WA WC 26 Segers; NIOD 187 62R.
51. Naulaerts, *Internationaal Geheime Dienst*, 93–98.
52. Nougarède's office near the cathedral was a regional depot for false documents. In January 1944 he had driven other individuals wanted by the Gestapo out of Toulouse. WA WC 20 Nahas; WA EC; ADHG 44 J 33.
53. WA WC 9 Dutch-Paris Finances, WA WC 20 Nahas 3; WA EC; WA WC Marty Trial; ADHG 44 J 33; SHD 16P 447507.
54. NIOD 215a 80.
55. Chait appears to have collected the Americans, Simon Cohen and John Dutka, somewhere in southern France. WA WC 9 Dutch Paris Expenses Chait; WA WC 4 Chait; NARA, RG 498, HQ ETO US Army WWII; MIS-X, E&E 2157, Dutka, NAI 5556787 (hereafter NARA E&E 2157).
56. NAUK AIR 40/2467; NAUK WO 208/5583; NIOD 215a 80.
57. The third man was a local forester, Pierre Sabadie. NARA, MIS-X, French, box 406, Weidner; NIOD 215a 80.
58. NIOD 215a 80.
59. For the Liberation see Brossat, *Libération, fête folle*; Hitchcock, *The Bitter Road to Freedom*, 11–122; Kedward and Woods, *The Liberation of France*; Koreman, *The Expectation of Justice*; Schrijvers, *Liberators*.
60. SBA E4264 1985/196 18544; AEG JetP Ef/2 no 4157.
61. WA WC 32 Visser 't Hooft.
62. AEG JetP Ef 2 4157.
63. SBA E4320B 1990 133 31; SBA E4264 1985/196 18544.
64. NIOD 187 62R.

Chapter 9

1. WA WC 32 Visser 't Hooft; WA EC; WA WC 18 Lap.
2. WA WC 26 Segers; WA WC 24 Rens; WA WC 18 Lap.
3. NIOD 287 62R.
4. Enquêtecommissie Regeringsbeleid, *Enquêtecommissie Regeringsbeleid*, 4cII:1485.
5. See Wachsmann, *Hitler's Prisons*.

6. NIOD 187 62R; NIOD KBI 6920 Veerman; NRK 157754.

7. NRK 59921; SHDC 21P 517319.

8. Zelamire de Guise. NRK 174555; WA WC 17 Kwantes; WA WC 7 de Guise.

9. WA WC 9 Dutch-Paris Finances Individual Chait.

10. Released from the camp at Noé: Janse, Ten Brink, and Van den Helde. They were unable to ransom a fourth Dutchman who was in the penal section of the camp under German control. WA WC 4 Chait; WA WC 9 Dutch Paris Finances Individual Chait; WA WC 26 Segers.

11. A gendarme from Soest named Dick Kaspers; Dick Uiting, who shot two Dutch SD agents on February 14, 1944; a certain "Edouard" who may have been Alfred Beuckers; and the Belgian Robert Godfrin. WA WC 4 Chait; WA WC 9 Dutch Paris Finances Individual Chait; H. S. Koelega, email to the author, December 10, 2016.

12. WA WC 4 Chait WA WC 9 Dutch Paris Finances Individual Chait.

13. WA WC 4 Chait.

14. Alexander Leopold Hertz.

15. Weidner met with the ambassador and military attaché on August 23, 1944. WA WC 32 Visser 't Hooft.

16. The order for Weidner's internment was issued on September 22, 1944. SBA E4320B 1990 133 31; AEG JetP 2 no 4157.

17. WA AS Bouchet interview with Sbacchi.

18. Resisters liberated Sevenster from the prison in Evaux-les-Bains on June 8, 1944. He remained there until Paris was liberated in late August. With thanks to Sierk Plantinga for the details.

19. For deportation see Bruttmann et al., *Qu'est-ce qu'un déporté?*

20. Kraay's friend Molland was deported on August 13. The last Dutch civil servant in Vichy, Gustava Mouwen, was deported on August 15. She had cooperated with Dutch-Paris's clandestine welfare distribution.

21. WA WC 17 Kwantes, SHD 16P 449448. Also see Fontaine, *Les oubliés de Romainville*.

22. SHDC 220117340. Brantsen's wife, who had been arrested with him at their home, was also released from Fresnes on August 11.

23. CHRD Lyon, Témoignage Pillot.

24. SHD 16P 480720.

25. SHDC 21P 517319.

26. WA Congregation St. Esprit Archives.

27. DGO 54.124.

28. NRK 59921.

29. WA BR Bosschart; WA BR Jacobsthal.

30. Lydia Ogy. NAUK WO 344/39/1; NARA E&E 1892; DGO 55166.

31. NRK 78.779.

32. WA BR Haenecour.

33. Lifman, Ir L. Bosschart, father of Rob, and Mr. Bol, father of J. P. Bol. WA BR Lifman.

34. CEGES AA 1742/22; WA BR van Gellicum; NA 2.13.71 (MvOL) 2571; AJB GFP 530.
35. WA WC 5 Chait 7.
36. WA BR van Kempen.
37. They also included Elisabeth van Altena, who had worked with Van Gellicum to shelter Engelandvaarders and been arrested in the same raid as Van Cleeff. She did not consider herself a member of any resistance organization, although Dutch-Paris claimed her, possibly to facilitate her official status. AJB, GFP 530; NEDVER.
38. NRK 156.524. Also see Goldberg, *Motherland*.
39. WA BR van Cleeff.
40. WA WC 5 Chait.
41. He paid Van Cleeff, Vleeschdrager, Bosschart, Wisbrun, and others. He also helped resistance colleagues who had not been captured, such as Borst and Van Dorp, out of financial difficulties at the Liberation. WA WC 30 van Cleeff.
42. WA WC 21 Netherlands Security Service.
43. Swiss resisters encountered difficulties after the war because their government considered their resistance actions to have endangered the country's neutrality.
44. For the Return see Wyman, *DPs*, 38–85; Shephard, *The Long Road Home*, 62–96; Taylor, *In the Children's Best Interests*.
45. WA WC 17 Laatsman.
46. The white buses evacuated seven thousand female prisoners from Ravensbrück between April 22 and April 29, 1945, including Brousse, Hiltermann, Kraay, Larose-Reinaud, Mouwen, Neyssel, Pillot, and Julia Prilliez. For Ravensbrück see Dufayel, *Un convoi des femmes*; Morrison, *Ravensbrück*.
47. NRK 75.461.
48. Gabrielle Weidner died on February 15, 1945. AAdv 10CP1 9. Thanks to Janet Carper for helping to identify the dates.
49. WA WC 6 Comiti.
50. WA WC 23 Pillot.
51. Laatsman, April 28; Julia Prilliez, May 1; Neyssel, May 4; Larose-Reinaud, May 14; Milleret, May 22; Houry, May 24; Marguerite Chanoinat, May 26; Comiti, May 30; Brother Rufus, May 31; Brother Robo, June 3; Goetschel, July 2; Hiltermann, July 20; Pillot (date unknown). Kraay's friend Molland returned on May 1.
52. WA WC 19 Meunier.
53. AADV 10CP1 7.
54. Born in 1897, Raymond Mériot was probably an escaped POW of the First World War. SHDC 21P 515 561.
55. Weidner helped her to apply for widows' and orphans' benefits. SHDC 21P 516 887; WA WC 12 FFCI.

56. In 1948 a Dutch deportee confirmed the story of Nijkerk's death in the bombing raid. DGO 54.124; WA WC 22 Nijkerk; NRK 1222.
57. WA WC 4 Caubo; NRK 8502.
58. Information from Jeanine Caubo; Harry Caubo email to the author, May 7, 2015.
59. WA WC 17 Kraay, report written by Weidner at the request of the French investigator, 1948.
60. ADHG 2546 W 124 247.
61. WA WC Marty Trial.
62. "La Résistance Hollandais en France et Belgique," n.d., WA WC 11 Dutch Resistance in France.
63. NA 2.13.71 (MvOL) 413.
64. Weidner, November 17, 1944, WA WC 3 Biographical Information.
65. Hiltermann gave her report to American officers within days of returning to Paris. NARA, MIS-X, French, box 406, Weidner.

Conclusion

1. *Nieuwe Israelische Weekblad*, January 6, 1950.
2. See Fogelman, *Conscience and Courage*; Klempner, *The Heart Has Reasons*; Monroe, *The Hand of Compassion* and *The Heart of Altruism*; Oliner and Oliner, *The Altruistic Personality*.
3. WA BR Haenecour.
4. CHRD, témoignage Pillot.
5. Jean Weidner, November 17, 1944, WA WC 3 Biographical Information; Visser 't Hooft, 142; NA 2.13.71 (MvOL) 413.
6. Semelin, "Introduction," 10.
7. See Varese and Yaish, "The Importance of Being Asked."
8. Jean Weidner, November 17, 1944, WA WC 3 Biographical Information.
9. See Snyder, *On Tyranny*.
10. For the culture of the outlaw see Kedward, *In Search of the Maquis*, 56–57.
11. For the imagined communities of the national and transnational see Kruizinga, "A Trans-National Army?"

BIBLIOGRAPHY

Ahonen, Pertti, Gustavo Corni, Jerzy Kochanowski, Rainer Schulze, Tamás Stark, and Barbara Stelzl-Marx. *People on the Move: Forced Population Movements in Europe in the Second World War and Its Aftermath.* Oxford: Berg, 2008.

Alary, Eric. *La Ligne de démarcation.* Paris: Editions Perrin, 2003.

Andrieu, Claire. "Assistance to Jews and to Allied Soldiers and Airmen in France: A Comparative Approach." In *Resisting Genocide: The Multiple Forms of Rescue*, ed. Jacques Semelin, Claire Andrieu, and Sarah Gensburger. Trans. Emma Bentley and Cynthia Schoch. New York: Columbia University Press, 2011. 51–63.

Andrieu, Claire. "Conclusion: Rescue, a Notion Revisited." In *Resisting Genocide: The Multiple Forms of Rescue*, ed. Jacques Semelin, Claire Andrieu, and Sarah Gensburger. Trans. Emma Bentley and Cynthia Schoch. New York: Columbia University Press, 2011. 495–506.

Balfet, Louise. "Testimony of Louise Balfet: My Resistance at 18." In *Unrecognized Resistance: The Franco-American Experience in World War Two*, ed. François-Georges Dreyfus. Trans. Paul Seaton. New Brunswick, NJ: Transaction, 2004. 145–49.

Belot, Robert, Eric Alary, and Bénédicte Vergez-Chaignon. *Les Résistants: L'Histoire de ceux qui refusèrent.* Paris: Larousse, 2004.

Benet, Claude. *Passeurs, fugitifs et espions: L'Andorre dans la 2e guerre mondiale.* Trans. Marguerite Pascual and Maxime Berrio. Toulouse: Pas d'Oiseau, 2009.

Bennett, Rab. *Under the Shadow of the Swastika: The Moral Dilemmas of Resistance and Collaboration in Hitler's Europe*. New York: New York University Press, 1999.

Berlière, Jean-Marc, and L. Chabrun. *Les Policiers français sous l'Occupation*. Paris: Tallandier, 2010.

Bodson, Herman. *Downed Allied Airmen and Evasion of Capture: The Role of Local Resistance Networks in World War II*. Jefferson, NC: McFarland, 2005.

Boudin, Hugh Robert. "Les lignes d'évasion." In *La Croix et la Banière: Les Protestants et les Anglicans face a l'Occupation en Belgique, 1940–1945*. Brussels: Editions Prodoc, 2012.

Boudin, Hugh R. "Ten Kate, Antoon Gertruidus Berendinus." In *Dictionnaire historique du protestantisme et de l'anglicanisme en Belgique du XVème siècle jusqu'à nos jours*. Brussels: Editions Prodoc, 2014.

Boulet, François. *Les Alpes françaises 1940–1944: Des montagnes-refuges aux montagnes-maquis*. Bordeaux: Les Presses Franciliennes, 2008.

Bower, Tom. *Klaus Barbie: The Butcher of Lyons*. New York: Harper Collins, 1984.

Broeyer, Frits. *Het Utrechtse universitaire verzet 1940–1945. "Heb je Kafka gelezen?"* Utrecht: Uitgeverij Matrijs, 2014.

Brossat, Alain. *Libération, fête folle*. Paris: Autrement, 1994.

Bruttmann, Tal. "The 'Brunner Aktion': A Struggle against Rescue (September 1943–March 1944)." In *Resisting Genocide: The Multiple Forms of Rescue*, ed. Jacques Semelin, Claire Andrieu, and Sarah Gensburger. Trans. Emma Bentley and Cynthia Schoch. New York: Columbia University Press, 2011. 279–91.

Bruttmann, Tal, Laurent Joly, and Annette Wieviorka. *Qu'est-ce qu'un déporté? Histoire et memoires des déportations de la Seconde Guerre mondiale*. Paris: CNRS, 2009.

Burleigh, Michael, and Wolfgang Wippermann. *The Racial State: Germany 1933–1945*. Cambridge, UK: Cambridge University Press, 1991.

Burrin, Philippe. *France under the Germans: Collaboration and Compromise*. Trans. Janet Lloyd. New York: Free Press, 1997.

Caestecker, Frank, and Bob Moore, eds. *Refugees from Nazi Germany and the Liberal European States*. New York: Berghahn Books, 2010.

Cammaert, A. P. M. *Het Verborgen Front: Een geschiedenis van de georganiseerde Illegaliteit in de Provincie Limburg tijdens de Tweede Wereldoorlog*. 2 vols. Leeuwarden: Eisma, 1994.

Cappalletto, Francesca, ed. *Memory and World War II: An Ethnographic Approach*. Oxford: Berg, 2005.

Caron, Vicki. "Unwilling Refuge: France and the Dilemma of Illegal Immigration, 1933–1939." In *Refugees from Nazi Germany and the Liberal*

European States, ed. Frank Caestecker and Bob Moore. New York: Berghahn, 2010. 57–81.

Carper, Janet Holmes, ed. "The Weidners in Wartime: Daily Life and Heroism; Family Correspondence during World War II." Unpublished manuscript in author's possession, 2014.

Carr, Gilly, Paul Sanders, and Louise Willmot. *Protest, Defiance and Resistance in the Channel Islands: German Occupation, 1940–1945*. London: Bloomsbury, 2014.

Conway, Martin, and Peter Romijn, eds. *The War for Legitimacy in Politics and Culture 1936–1946*. Oxford: Berg, 2008.

Courier Savoyard. "Abbé Camille Folliet, heròs Savoyard." March 16, 1990.

Croquet, Jean-Claude. *Chemins de Passage: Les Passages clandestins entre la Haute-Savoie et la Suisse de 1940 a 1944*. St. Julien: La Salevienne, 1996.

Darling, Donald. *Sunday at Large: Assignments of a Secret Agent*. London: William Kimber, 1977.

Davidzon, Marloes. "The Swiss Road and the Espionage Question during and after the Second World War." Doctoral work in National History, Advisor Prof. dr. J. Th. M. Bank, 1994.

de Graaff, Bob. *Stepping Stones to Freedom: Help to Allied Airmen in the Netherlands during World War II*. Trans. Dee Wessels Boer-Stallman. Marceline, MO: Walsworth, 1995.

de Hartog, Jan and Marjorie de Hartog. *De Vlucht*. Baarn: De Prom, 1999.

de Jong, Louis. "Anti-Nazi Resistance in the Netherlands." In *European Resistance Movements, 1940–1945*. Proceedings of the International Conference on the History of the Resistance Movements. 1958. London: Pergamon, 1962. 137–49.

de Jong, Louis. *Het Koninkrijk der Nederlanden in de Tweede Wereldoorlog*. 12 vols. 's-Gravenhage: Martinus Nijhoff, 1969–94.

de Jong, Louis. *The Netherlands and Nazi Germany*. Cambridge, MA: Harvard University Press, 1990.

de Lathouwer, René, ed. "Comité de défense des Juifs: Témoignages et documents recueillis entre 1947 et 1951." Privately collated. After 1968.

Delfosse, David. "Le 'Sarah Jane.'" *Histoire et Généalogie axoniase*. 9 (2nd semester 2010): 42–47.

Delfosse, David. *Liberté à Tout Prix! L'épopée du B-17 Pickle Dropper/Sarah Jane*. Grandvilliers: Eds. Delattre, 2015.

Delpech, François. "La persecution des Juifs et l'Amitié chrétienne." In *Eglises et chrétiens dans la IIeme guerre mondiale, la region Rhône-Alpes*, ed. Xavier de Montclos. Lyon: Fayolle, 1978. 143–79.

Delperrie de Bayac, J. *Histoire de la Milice, 1918–1945*. Paris: Fayard, 1969.

Dessing, Agnes. *Tulpen voor Wilhelmina: De geschiedenis van de Engelandvaarders*. Amsterdam: Bert Bakker, 2005.

Diamond, Hanna. *Fleeing Hitler: France 1940*. Oxford: Oxford University Press, 2007.

Diamond, Hanna. *Women and the Second World War in France, 1939–1948*. Harlow, UK: Longman, 1999.

Douzou, Laurent. "L'entrée en résistance." In *La Résistance, une histoire sociale*, ed. Antoine Prost. Paris: Editions de L'Atelier, 1997. 9–20.

Dreyfus, François-George, ed. *Unrecognized Resistance: The Franco-American Experience in World War Two*. Trans. Paul Seaton. New Brunswick, NJ: Transaction, 2004.

Dufayel, Pierre-Emmanuel. *Un convoi des femmes 1944–1945*. Paris: Vendémiaire, 2012.

Dwork, Deborah, and Robert Jan van Pelt. *Flight from the Reich: Refugee Jews, 1933–1936*. New York: Norton, 2009.

Eliasar, Maarten. "Zwitserlandva(ar)der." Unpublished memoir in author's possession, 2010.

Enquêtecommissie Regeringsbeleid 1940–1945. *Enquêtecommissie Regeringsbeleid 1940–1945: Verslag houdende de uitkomsten van het onderzoek*. 20 dl. 's-Gravenhage: Staatsdrukkerij en Uitgeverijbedrijf, 1949–73.

Erreygers, Guido, and Albert Jolink. "Perturbation, Networks and Business Cycles: Bernard Chait's Pioneering Work in Econometrics." *European Journal of the History of Economic Thought* 14, no. 3 (2007): 543–71.

Eychenne, Émilienne. *Montagnards de la liberté: Les évasions par l'Ariège et la Haute-Garonne 1939–1945*. Toulouse: Editions Milan, 1984.

Eychenne, Émilienne. *Montagnes de la peur et de l'esperance: Le franchissement de la frontière espagnole pendant la seconde guerre mondiale dans le département des Hautes-Pyrénées*. Toulouse: Privat, 1980.

Eychenne, Émilienne. *Pyrénées de la liberté: Les évasions par l'Espagne, 1939–1945*. Toulouse: Privat, 1998.

Fabre, Emile, ed. *God's Underground: Accounts of the Activity of the French Protestant Church during the German Occupation of the Country in World War II*. Collected by Jeanne Merle d'Aubigné and Violette Mouchon. Trans. William and Patricia Nottingham. St. Louis, MO: Bethany, 1970.

Fitzpatrick, Sheila, and Robert Gellately, eds. *Accusatory Practices: Denunciation in Modern European History, 1789–1989*. Chicago: University of Chicago Press, 1997.

Fivaz-Silbermann, Ruth. "The Swiss Reaction to the Nazi Genocide: Active Refusal, Passive Help." In *Resisting Genocide: The Multiple Forms of Rescue*, ed. Jacques Semelin, Claire Andrieu, and Sarah Gensburger.

Trans. Emma Bentley and Cynthia Schoch. New York: Columbia University Press, 2011. 231–43.

Flim, Jan-Bert. *Omdat hun hart sprak*. Utrecht: Kok-Kampen, 1996.

Fogelman, Eva. *Conscience and Courage: Rescuers of Jews during the Holocaust*. New York: Anchor, 1994.

Fogg, Shannon. *The Politics of Everyday Life in Vichy France*. Cambridge, UK: Cambridge University Press, 2009.

Fontaine, Thomas. *Les oubliés de Romainville: Un camp allemande en France, 1940–1944*. Paris: Tallandier, 2005.

Foot, M. R. D., and J. M. Langley, *MI 9: Escape and Evasion, 1939–1945*. Boston: Little Brown, 1979.

Ford, Herbert. *Flee the Captor*. Nashville, TN: Southern Publishing Association, 1966.

Friedman, Philip. *Their Brothers' Keepers*. New York: Crown, 1957.

Gans, Lex. "Engelandvaart, barbaarse reis." In *Den vaderland getrouwe: Een boek over oorlog en verzet*, ed. Peter Mathieu Smedts. Amsterdam: De Arbeiderspers, 1962. 207–21.

Gerstner, Karl-Heinz. *Sachlich, kritisch, und optimistisch: Eine sonntägliche Lebensbetrachtung*. Berlin: Edition Ost, 1999.

Gildea, Robert. *Fighters in the Shadows: A New History of the French Resistance*. London: Faber & Faber, 2015.

Gildea, Robert. *Marianne in Chains: In Search of the German Occupation, 1940–1945*. London: Macmillan, 2002.

Giskes, H. J. *London Calling North Pole*. New York: British Book Center, 1953.

Goldberg, Rita. *Motherland: Growing Up with the Holocaust*. London: Halban, 2014.

Guillon, Jean-Marie. "Talk Which Was Not Idle: Rumours in Wartime France." In *Vichy, Resistance, Liberation: New Perspectives on Wartime France*, ed. Hanna Diamond and Simon Kitson. Oxford: Berg, 2005. 73–85.

Guyt, Harry, and Co Guyt. "Harry en Co Guyt vertellen: 'Ik kon niet alleen maar toekijken.'" In *"Ik kon niet alleen maar toekijken . . . ,"* ed. Rien Breeman, Marloes Davidson, Bart Funnekotter, Jolanda Hendriksen, and Willy Hijmans. Warmond: Stichting Geschiedenis in de Klas, 1999. 1:53–55.

Hallie, Philip P. *Lest Innocent Blood Be Shed: The Story of the Village of Le Chambon and How Goodness Happened There*. New York: Harper & Row, 1979.

Harris, Witney. *Tyranny on Trial: The Evidence at Nuremberg*. 1954. New York: Barnes & Noble Books, 1995.

Hawes, Stephen, and Ralph White, eds. *Resistance in Europe 1939–1945*. London: Allen Lane, 1975.

Henry, Piet. "Piet Henry Vertelt: 'Je moet niet langs elkaar heen leven.'" In *"Ik kon niet alleen maar toekijken . . . ,"* ed. Rien Breeman, Marloes Davidson, Bart Funnekotter, Jolanda Hendriksen, and Willy Hijmans. Warmond: Stichting Geschiedenis in de Klas, 1999. 2:22–26.

Herbert, Ulrich. *Hitler's Foreign Workers: Enforced Foreign Labor in Germany under the Third Reich.* Trans. William Templer. Cambridge, UK: Cambridge University Press, 1997.

Hirschfeld, Gerhard. *Nazi Rule and Dutch Collaboration: The Netherlands under German Occupation, 1940–1943.* Trans. Louise Wilmot. Oxford: Berg, 1988.

Hitchcock, William. *The Bitter Road to Freedom: A New History of the Liberation of Europe.* New York: Free Press, 2008.

Homze, Edward. *Foreign Labor in Nazi Germany.* Princeton, NJ: Princeton University Press, 1967.

International Conference on the History of the Resistance Movements. *European Resistance Movements, 1940–1945.* 1958. London: Pergamon, 1962.

Jackson, Julian. *France: The Dark Years, 1940–1944.* Oxford: Oxford University Press, 2001.

Kasaboski, Tracy, and Kristen den Hartog. *The Occupied Garden: Recovering the Story of a Family in the War-Torn Netherlands.* Toronto: McClelland & Stewart, 2008.

Kedward, H. R. *In Search of the Maquis: Rural Resistance in Southern France, 1942–1944.* Oxford: Clarendon, 1993.

Kedward, H. R. *Resistance in Vichy France.* Oxford: Oxford University Press, 1978.

Kedward, H. R., and Nancy Woods, eds. *The Liberation of France.* Oxford: Berg, 1995.

Kitson, Simon. *The Hunt for Nazi Spies: Fighting Espionage in Vichy France.* Trans. Catherine Tihanyi. Chicago: University of Chicago Press, 2008.

Klarsfeld, Serge. *Vichy-Auschwitz: Le role de Vichy dans la solution finale de la question juive en France.* 2 vols. Paris: Fayard, 1983–85.

Klempner, Mark. *The Heart Has Reasons: Holocaust Rescuers and Their Stories of Courage.* Cleveland, OH: Pilgrim, 2006.

Koreman, Megan. *The Expectation of Justice: France 1944–1946.* Durham, NC: Duke University Press, 1999.

Kosmala, Beate, and Georgi Verbeeck, eds. *Facing the Catastrophe: Jews and Non-Jews in Europe during World War II.* Oxford: Berg, 2011.

Kruizinga, Samuël. "A Trans-National Army? Being Dutch in the International Brigades, 1936–1939." Paper presented at the workshop A Transnational Approach to Resistance, Dublin, March 2017.

Laffitte, Michel. "Was the UGIF an Obstacle to the Rescue of Jews?" In *Resisting Genocide: The Multiple Forms of Rescue*, ed. Jacques Semelin, Claire Andrieu, and Sarah Gensburger. Trans. Emma Bentley and Cynthia Schoch. New York: Columbia University Press, 2011. 395–409.

Lagrou, Pieter. "Belgium." In *Resistance in Western Europe*, ed. Bob Moore. Oxford: Berg, 2000. 27–63.

Lagrou, Pieter. *The Legacy of Nazi Occupation: Patriotic Memory and National Recovery in Western Europe, 1945–1965*. Cambridge, UK: Cambridge University Press, 2000.

Laub, Thomas J. *After the Fall: German Policy in Occupied France, 1940–1944*. Oxford: Oxford University Press, 2010.

Lazare, Lucien. *Le Livre des justes: Histoire du sauvetage des Juifs par des non-Juifs en France, 1940–1944*. Paris: Editions J. C. Lattès, 1993.

Lazare, Lucien. *Rescue as Resistance: How Jewish Organizations Fought the Holocaust in France*. Trans. Jeffrey M. Green. New York: Columbia University Press, 1996.

Liagre, Guy. "De Zwitserse Weg en de Dutch-Paris line—Een toelichting bij de bijdrage van de Brusselse predikant A.G.B. ten Kate aan de internationale ontsnappingsroute 1940–1945." *Eigen Schoon & De Brabander, Geschied- en oudheidkundig genootschap van Vlaams Brabant en Brussel* (2010): 181–204.

Lougarot, Gisèle. *Dans l'ombre des passeurs*. Donostia: Elkar, 2004.

Luijters, Guus. *In memoriam: De gedeporteerde en vermoorde Joodse, Roma en Sinti kinderen, 1942–1945*. Amsterdam: Nieuw Amsterdam Uitgevers, 2012.

Lundi, Regula. "Dwindling Options: Seeking Asylum in Switzerland 1933–1939." In *Refugees from Nazi Germany and the Liberal European States*, ed. Frank Caestecker and Bob Moore. New York: Berghahn, 2010. 82–102.

Marcot, François. "La Résistance dans ses lieux et milieux: Des relations d'interdépendance." In "La Résistance et les Français: Nouvelles approches." *Les Cahiers de l'Institut d'Histoire du Temps Présent*, no. 37 (December 1997): 129–46.

Marcot, François. "Pour une sociologie de la Résistance: Intentionnalité et fonctionnalité." In *La Résistance, une histoire sociale*, ed. Antoine Prost. Paris: Editions de L'Atelier, 1997. 21–41.

Marrus, Michael R., and Robert O. Paxton. *Vichy France and the Jews*. New York: Basic, 1981.

McPhail, Helen. *The Long Silence: Civilian Life under the German Occupation of Northern France, 1914–1918*. London: I. B. Tauris, 1999.

Meinen, Insa. "Face à la traque: Comment les Juifs furent arrêtés en Belgique (1942–1944)." Trans. Jacques Déom. *Les cahiers de la mémoire contemporaine/Bijdragen tot de eigentijdse Herinnering* 6 (2005): 161–203.

Menager, Camille. "Roundups, Rescue and Social Networks in Paris (1940–1944)." In *Resisting Genocide: The Multiple Forms of Rescue*, ed. Jacques Semelin, Claire Andrieu, and Sarah Gensburger. Trans. Emma Bentley and Cynthia Schoch. New York: Columbia University Press, 2011. 411–31.

Meyer, Ahlrich. *L'occupation allemande en France.* Trans. Pascale Hervieux. Toulouse: Editions Privat, 2002.

Meyer, Ahlrich, and Insa Meinen. "La Belgique, pays de transit: Juifs fugitifs en Europe occidentale au temps des déportations de 1942." *Bijdragen tot de eigentijdse geschiedenis (1930/1960)/Cahiers d'histoire du temps present (1930/1960)* 20 (2008): 145–94.

Michalczyk, John J., ed. *Resisters, Rescuers, and Refugees: Historical and Ethical Issues.* Kansas City, MO: Sheed & Ward, 1997.

Monroe, Kristen Renwick. *Ethics in an Age of Terror and Genocide: Identity and Moral Choice.* Princeton, NJ: Princeton University Press, 2012.

Monroe, Kristen Renwick. *The Hand of Compassion: Portraits of Moral Choice during the Holocaust.* Princeton, NJ: Princeton University Press, 2004.

Monroe, Kristen Renwick. *The Heart of Altruism: Perceptions of a Common Humanity.* Princeton, NJ: Princeton University Press, 1996.

Moore, Bob. "'Goed en Fout' or 'Grijs Verleden': Competing Perspectives on the History of the Netherlands under German Occupation." *Dutch Crossing* 27, no 2 (2003): 155–68.

Moore, Bob. "Nazi Masters and Accommodating Dutch Bureaucrats: Working towards the Führer in the Occupied Netherlands, 1940–1945." In *Working towards the Führer*, ed. Anthony McElligott and Tim Kirk. Manchester, UK: Manchester University Press, 2003. 186–204.

Moore, Bob, ed. *Resistance in Western Europe.* Oxford: Berg, 2000.

Moore, Bob. *Survivors: Jewish Self-Help and Rescue in Nazi-Occupied Western Europe.* Oxford: Oxford University Press, 2010.

Moore, Bob. *Victims and Survivors: The Nazi Persecution of the Jews in the Netherlands, 1940–1945.* London: Arnold, 1997.

Morgan, Ted. *An Uncertain Hour: The French, the Germans, the Jews, the Barbie Trial and the City of Lyon, 1940–1945.* New York: Arbor, 1990.

Morrison, Jack G. *Ravensbrück: Everyday Life in a Women's Concentration Camp, 1939–1945.* Princeton, NJ: Wiener, 2000.

Munos-du Peloux, Odile. *Passer en Suisse: Les passages clandestins entre la Haute-Savoie et la Suisse, 1940–1944.* Grenoble: Presses universitaires, 2002.

Naulaerts, J. *Internationaal Geheime Dienst: Belevenissen en Ervaringen van een Priester, 1940–1945.* Westmalle: Sint-Jan Berchmansinstituut, 1948.

Neave, Airey. *The Escape Room.* Garden City, NY: Doubleday, 1970.

Oliner, Samuel, and Pearl Oliner. *The Altruistic Personality: Rescuers of Jews in Nazi Europe.* New York: Free Press, 1988.

Oord, Ad, van den. *Vervolgd en vergeten: Duitse en Nederlandse joden in Oisterwijk 1933–1945.* Oisterwijk: Uitgeverij A. van den Oord, 1998.

Ott, Sandra. *War, Judgment, and Memory in the Basque Borderlands, 1914–1945.* Reno: University of Nevada Press, 2008.

Ottis, Sherri Greene. *Silent Heroes: Downed Airmen and the French Underground.* Lexington: University of Kentucky Press, 2001.

Paxton, Robert O. *Vichy France: Old Guard and New Order, 1940–1944.* New York: Columbia University Press, 1972.

Pierrier, Jean-François. *Chronique des années brunes à la frontière genevoise.* Geneva: Journal "Le Courrier," 1984.

Plantinga, Sierk. "Joseph Willem Kolkman (1896–1944) en de Engelandvaarders: De hulp aan Nederlandse vluchtelingen in Vichy-Frankrijk." In *Oorlogsdocumentatie '40–'45*, ed. G. Aalders. Zutphen: Walburg Pers, 1998. 10–36.

Plantinga, Sierk. "Principieel pragmatisch: De Nederlandse vertegenwoordiging in Parijs, 1940–1944." In *Instrumenten van buitenlandse politiek: Achtergronden en praktijk van de Nederlandse diplomate*, ed. Bob de Graaff and Duco Hellema. Amsterdam: Boom, 2007. 1–28.

Portelli, Alessandro. *The Order Has Been Carried Out: History, Memory and Meaning of a Nazi Massacre in Rome.* New York: Palgrave Macmillan, 2003.

Poznanski, Renée. *Jews in France during World War II.* Trans. Nathan Bracher. Hanover, NH: University Press of New England, 2001.

Presser, Jacques. *Ashes in the Wind: The Destruction of Dutch Jewry.* Trans. Arnold Pomerans. Detroit: Wayne State University Press, 1988.

Prost, Antoine, ed. *La Résistance, une histoire sociale.* Paris: Editions de L'Atelier, 1997.

Richardot, Jean-Pierre. *Héros et salauds pendant l'Occupation.* Paris: Cherche Midi, 2012.

Rickard, Charles. *La Savoie dans la Résistance: Haute-Savoie, Savoie.* Rennes: Ouest France, 1986.

Risser, Nicole Dombrowski. *France under Fire: German Invasion, Civilian Flight, and Family Survival during World War II.* Cambridge, UK: Cambridge University Press, 2012.

Rodogno, Davide. *Fascism's European Empire: Italian Occupation during the Second World War.* Trans. Adrian Belton. Cambridge, UK: Cambridge University Press, 2006.

Rousso, Henry. *Où en est l'histoire de la Résistance?* Paris: Seuil Points, 1985.

Rousso, Henry. *The Vichy Syndrome: History and Memory in France since 1944*. Trans. Arthur Goldhammer. Cambridge, MA: Harvard University Press, 1994.

Sandberg, H. "Interview met Kapitein Weidner: Hoe de Hollanders door Frankrijk werden gesmokkeld." *Vrij Nederland*, February 23, 1946.

Schrijvers, Peter. *Liberators: The Allies and Belgian Society, 1944–1945*. Cambridge, UK: Cambridge University Press, 2009.

Schulten, C. M. *"En Verpletterd Wordt het Juk": Verzet in Nederland, 1940–1945*. Den Haag: Koninginnegracht, 1995.

Schulten, C. M. *"Zeg mij aan wien ik toebehoor": Het Verzetskruis 1940–1945*. Amsterdam: Rijksinstitut voor Oorlogsdocumentatie, 1993.

Semelin, Jacques. "Introduction: From Help to Rescue." In *Resisting Genocide: The Multiple Forms of Rescue*, ed. Jacques Semelin, Claire Andrieu, and Sarah Gensburger. Trans. Emma Bentley and Cynthia Schoch. New York: Columbia University Press, 2011. 1–14.

Semelin, Jacques. *Unarmed against Hitler: Civilian Resistance in Europe, 1939–1943*. Trans. Suzan Husserl-Kapit. Westport, CT: Praeger, 1993.

Semelin, Jacques, Claire Andrieu, and Sarah Gensburger, eds. *Resisting Genocide: The Multiple Forms of Rescue*. Trans. Emma Bentley and Cynthia Schoch. New York: Columbia University Press, 2011.

Shephard, Ben. *The Long Road Home: The Aftermath of the Second World War*. New York: Knopf, 2011.

Shoemaker, Lloyd. *The Escape Factory: The Story of MIS-X*. New York: St. Martin's Press, 1990.

Snyder, Timothy. *On Tyranny: Twenty Lessons from the Twentieth-Century*. New York: Tim Duggan Books, 2017.

Starink, Albert. "Mémoires Albert Starink." Unpublished manuscript, 1995.

Steinberg, Lucien. *Le Comité de défense des Juifs en Belgique, 1942–1944*. Brussels: Editions Université de Bruxelles, 1973.

Steinberg, Maxime. *La Persécution des Juifs en Belgique, 1940–1945*. Bruxelles: Editions Complexe, 2004.

Suleiman, Susan Rubin. *Crises of Memory and the Second World War*. Cambridge, MA: Harvard University Press, 2006.

Sweets, John. *Choices in Vichy France*. Oxford: Oxford University Press, 1994.

Taylor, Lynne. *Between Resistance and Collaboration: Popular Protest in Northern France, 1940– 1945*. Basingstoke, UK: Macmillan and St. Martin's Press, 2000.

Taylor, Lynne. *In the Children's Best Interests: Unaccompanied Children in American-Occupied Germany, 1945–1952*. Toronto: University of Toronto Press, 2017.

Timmers Verhoeven, Sam G. "Een Reis naar Vrij Gebied: In het jaar 1944."
    Unpublished manuscript, 1992.
Touw, H. C. *Het Verzet der Hervormde Kerk*. Vol. 1. 's-Gravenhage:
    Boekencentrum, 1946.
Ugeux, W. "Quelques considerations techniques et morales sur
    l'expeérience de guerre psychologique menée en Belgique occupée entre
    1940 et 1945." In *European Resistance Movements, 1940–1945*.
    Proceedings of the International Conference on the History of the
    Resistance Movements. 1958. London: Pergamon, 1962. 170–81.
U.S. Bureau of Labor Statistics. "Wage Trends and Wage Policies: Various
    Foreign Countries." *Bulletin of the U.S. Bureau of Labor Statistics*, no.
    934 (1948).
Utrechtsch Studenten Corps. *Utrechtsche Studenten Almanak, 1946*.
    Utrecht: Drukkerij P. den Boer, 1946.
Van Borssum Buisman, Jan. *Agent van de Zwitserse Weg*. Zutphen:
    Verzetsmuseum Amsterdam and Walburg Pers, 2000.
Van Galen Last, Dick. "Netherlands." In *Resistance in Western Europe*, ed.
    Bob Moore. Oxford: Berg, 2000. 189–221.
Van der Heijden, Eugène. "Oorlogsherinneringen: Jean Weidner en de
    geboorte van de Dutch-Parislijn." *Escape* 81 (June 1994): 26–30.
Van der Heijden, Eugène. "Oorlogsherinneringen: Smeergeld." *Escape* 80
    (March 1994): 31–34.
Van der Wee, Herman, and Monique Verbreyt. *The General Bank 1922–
    1997: A Continuing Challenge*. Tielt, Belgium: Lannoo, 1997.
Van Heuven Goedhart, Gerrit Jan. *De Reis van "Colonel Blake."* Utrecht:
    Erven J Bijleveld, 1945.
Van Riet, Frank. *Handhaven onder de nieuwe order: De politieke geschiedenis
    van de Rotterdamse politie tijdens de Tweede Wereldoorlog*. Zaltbommel:
    Aprillis, 2008.
Varese, Federico, and Meir Yaish. "The Importance of Being Asked: The
    Rescue of Jews in Nazi Europe." *Rationality and Society* 12, no. 3 (2000):
    307–34.
Verkijk, Dick. "Weg naar de Vrijheid, Meer dan 1080." Episode of
    Geschiedenis 24, a VPRO series, aired in 1967. 44:38. Subtitled in English
    and posted by Maarten Eliasar, March 23, 2012, http://youtube.com/
    watch?v=96V6SiqMlc.
Vinen, Richard. *The Unfree French: Life under the Occupation*. New Haven,
    CT: Yale University Press, 2006.
Visser, Frank. *De Schakel: De geschiedenis van de Engelandvaarders*. Baarn:
    MC Stok, 1976.
Visser 't Hooft, Willem. *Memoirs*. Geneva: World Council of Churches, 1973.

Vromen, Susan. *Hidden Children of the Holocaust: Belgian Nuns and Their Daring Rescue of Young Jews from the Nazis*. Oxford: Oxford University Press, 2008.

Wachsmann, Nikolaus. *Hitler's Prisons: Legal Terror in Nazi Germany*. New Haven, CT: Yale University Press, 2004.

Wagner, Meir. *The Righteous of Switzerland: Heroes of the Holocaust*. Hoboken, NJ: Ktav, 2001.

Warmbrunn, Werner. *The Dutch under German Occupation, 1940–1945*. Stanford, CA: Stanford University Press, 1963.

Warmbrunn, Werner. *The German Occupation of Belgium, 1940–1944*. New York: Peter Lang, 1993.

Weidner, Jean H. "De Weg naar de Vrijheid." In *Onderdrukking en Verzet: Nederland in Oorlogstijd*, ed. J. J. van Bolhuis. Arnhem: van Loghum Slaterus, 1949–54. 3:730–39.

Werkgroep Geschiedenis Heemkundevereniging Schin op Geul. *Oorlogsherrineringen Schin op Geul: Mobilisatie—bezetting—bevrijding 1939–1945*. Schin op Geul, 1994.

Wieviorka, Olivier. "France." In *Resistance in Western Europe*, ed. Bob Moore. Oxford: Berg, 2000. 125–55.

Wieviorka, Olivier. *Histoire de la Résistance 1940–1945*. Paris: Editions Perrin, 2013.

Willemsen, W. J. M. "Enkele reis de Peel-Engeland." *Escape* 54 (September 1987): 30–33.

Wyman, Mark. *DPs: Europe's Displaced Persons, 1945–51*. Ithaca, NY: Cornell University Press, 1998.

Yagil, Limore. *Chrétiens et Juifs sous Vichy (1940–1944): Sauvetage et désobéissance civile*. Paris: Editions du Cerf, 2005.

Yagil, Limore. *La France terre de refuge et de désobéissance civile (1936–1944): Exemple du sauvetage des Juifs*. Vol. 2, *Implication des fonctionnaires—Le sauvetage aux frontiers et dans les villages-refuges*. Paris: Editions du Cerf, 2010.

Yagil, Limore. *La France terre de refuge et de désobéissance civile (1936–1944): Exemple du sauvetage des Juifs*. Vol. 3, *Implication des milieux catholiques et protestants—L'aide des résistants*. Paris: Editions du Cerf, 2011.

Zeeman, Rudy. "Luck through Adversity." Unpublished manuscript, 2013.

Zuccotti, Susan. *Holocaust Odysseys: The Jews of Saint-Martin-Vésubie and Their Flight through France and Italy*. New Haven, CT: Yale University Press, 2007.

PHOTO CREDITS

Introduction

[2] John Henry Weidner Papers, Hoover Institution Library & Archives, Stanford University, box 73.

[4] John Henry Weidner Papers, Hoover Institution Library & Archives, Stanford University, box 74.

Chapter 1

[28] Private collection of Maarten Eliasar.

[30] John Henry Weidner Papers, Hoover Institution Library & Archives, Stanford University, box 73.

[31] Private collection of the Jacquet family.

[36] John Henry Weidner Papers, Hoover Institution Library & Archives, Stanford University, box 74.

[37] John Henry Weidner Papers, Hoover Institution Library & Archives, Stanford University, box 74.

[39] John Henry Weidner Papers, Hoover Institution Library & Archives, Stanford University, box 74.

[41] John Henry Weidner Papers, Hoover Institution Library & Archives, Stanford University, box 15, folder 18.

[42]   *Left*, private collection of the Lehmann family; *right*, private collection of the Zurcher family.

[42]   Private collection of the Zurcher family.

[44]   John Henry Weidner Papers, Hoover Institution Library & Archives, Stanford University, box 73.

[51]   Private collection of the Eliasar family.

Chapter 2

[52]   Private collection of Maarten Eliasar.

[54]   Private collection of the Eliasar family.

[55]   John Henry Weidner Papers, Hoover Institution Library & Archives, Stanford University, box 55.

Chapter 3

[72]   Private collection of Maarten Eliasar.

[74]   John Henry Weidner Papers, Hoover Institution Library & Archives, Stanford University, box 74.

[76]   Still from the documentary *Weg naar de vrijheid: Meer dan 1080*, by Dick Verkijk, 1967, VPRO.

[78]   Private collection of Micheline van Lint Nieuwkerk.

[80]   Archives of the Protestant Church, Brussels.

[86]   Private collection of Gaia Son.

[86]   John Henry Weidner Papers, Hoover Institution Library & Archives, Stanford University, box 74.

[87]   John Henry Weidner Papers, Hoover Institution Library & Archives, Stanford University, box 74.

[87]   Private collection of the Ten Kate family.

[89]   Private collection of Ype Henry.

[90]   Private collection of Willy Hijmans.

[91]   Private collection of Daniel Lebouille and Marie-José Lebouille.

Chapter 4

[98]   Private collection of Maarten Eliasar.

[100]   Private collection of Naomi Weidner.

[102] John Henry Weidner Papers, Hoover Institution Library & Archives, Stanford University, box 74.
[103] John Henry Weidner Papers, Hoover Institution Library & Archives, Stanford University, box 74.
[106] John Henry Weidner Papers, Hoover Institution Library & Archives, Stanford University, box 74.
[108] Private collection of the Caubo family.
[111] Private collection of the Caubo family.
[112] Private collection of the Starink family.
[117] John Henry Weidner Papers, Hoover Institution Library & Archives, Stanford University, box 74.
[117] John Henry Weidner Papers, Hoover Institution Library & Archives, Stanford University, box 74.
[122] Private collection of Sierk Plantinga.
[126] Private collection of Paul Gans.

Chapter 5

[132] Private collection of Maarten Eliasar.
[138] Mélanie Curdy, Denis Peschanski, Benoit Pouvreau, and Thierry Zimmer, *The Graffiti of Drancy Camp: The Names on the Walls* (Gent: Snoeck, 2014).
[145] Courtesy of Rita Goldberg, *Motherland: Growing Up with the Holocaust* (London: Halban, 2014).
[150] Private collection of Rudy Zeeman.
[152] Private collection of the Prilliez family.
[155] Private collection of Rudy Zeeman.
[157] Private collection of Pally van Oosterzee-Worp.
[158] Private collection of Pally van Oosterzee-Worp.
[159] Private collection of Rudy Zeeman.
[165] Private collection of Pally van Oosterzee-Worp.
[167] Private collection of Pally van Oosterzee-Worp.
[169] Private collection of Pally van Oosterzee-Worp.

Chapter 6

[172] Private collection of Maarten Eliasar.

Chapter 7

[196]   Private collection of Maarten Eliasar.

Chapter 8

[216]   John Henry Weidner Papers, Hoover Institution Library & Archives, Stanford University, box 74.
[225]   Private collection of Philip Veerman.

Chapter 9

[238]   Private collection of Maarten Eliasar.
[243]   Nederlands Instituut voor Oorlogsdocumentatie, Amsterdam, 187 62R.
[251]   Courtesy of Rita Goldberg, *Motherland: Growing Up with the Holocaust* (London: Halban, 2014).
[254]   *Above,* © Service historique de la Défense, CHA Caen AC 21 P 560 126; *below,* © Service historique de la Défense, CHA Caen AC 21 P 560 218.
[255]   Private collection of Mariette Bremell.
[257]   © Service historique de la Défense, CHA Caen AC 21 P 527 934.

Conclusion

[262]   John Henry Weidner Papers, Hoover Institution Library & Archives, Stanford University, box 74.
[271]   Private collection of the Eliasar family.
[271]   Private collection of Alain Souloumiac.

INDEX

———⊰⊙⊙⊙⊱———

Page numbers in **bold** indicate illustrations.